Predestination and Preaching

Studies in the History of Church and Theology

Edited by
Andreas J. Beck, Leuven

In cooperation with
Ulrich L. Lehner, Milwaukee
Kenneth P. Minkema, New Haven
Richard A. Muller, Grand Rapids
Peter Opitz, Zurich
Ulrike Treusch, Giessen

VOLUME 1

Pieter Rouwendal

Predestination and Preaching

in Genevan Theology
from Calvin to Pictet

Summum

This publication was made possible in part by financial support from the Van Coeveren Adriani Foundation, the Jurriaanse Foundation, the Gilles Hondius Foundation, and the Zonneweelde Foundation.

Cover design: Brainstorm
Typesetting: Gewoon Geertje

ISSN 2543-0777
ISBN 9789491583995

Copyright (c) Summum Academic Publications, Kampen, The Netherlands.

All rights reserved. No part of this publication may be reproduced, translated, stored in a retrieval system, or transmitted in any form by any means, electronic, mechanical, photocopying, recording or otherwise, without prior written permission from the publisher.

INHOUD

PREFACE		1
1.	**INTRODUCTION**	**3**
	1.1 Status Quaestionis	3
	1.2 Genevan Reformed Theology as an Appropriate Subject of Research	8
	1.3 Method	11
2.	**THE REFORMATION: JOHN CALVIN**	**13**
	2.1 Calvin and the Question of Predestination and Preaching	13
	2.2 Earlier Research	17
	2.3 Outline of this Chapter	20
	2.4 Calvin on Predestination	22
	2.4.1 Definitions	22
	2.4.2 Calvin's use of the word 'reprobation'	25
	2.4.3 Supralapsarianism or Infralapsarianism?	26
	2.4.4 Steps in Election	27
	2.5 Predestination and the Extent of the Atonement	28
	2.6 Predestination and the Covenant	31
	2.7 Predestination and Church	38
	2.8 God's Purpose and the Preacher's Purpose in Preaching	41
	2.9 The Mode of Preaching the Gospel: Conditionally and Unconditionally	44
	2.10 The Particularity and Universality of the Promises	50
	2.11 Predestination and the Response to Preaching	52
	2.12 Predestination, Faith, and Assurance	55
	2.13 Preaching the Doctrine of Predestination	57
	2.14 Summary: Predestination and the External Call	58
	2.15 Commentary and Sermon on 1 Timothy 2:4	62
	2.16 Sermons on Micah	64
	2.16.1 Covenant	65
	2.16.2 Predestination	66
	2.16.3 The Purpose of Preaching	68
	2.17 The Sermons on Genesis	70
	2.18 Summary: Theory and Practice	76

3. EARLY REFORMED ORTHODOXY - THEODORE BEZA 79
3.1 Beza and the Question of Predestination and Preaching 79
3.2 Earlier Research 80
3.3 Beza, Calvin, and Early Reformed Orthodoxy 84
3.4 Between Calvin and Bullinger: Beza's Initial Ideas on Predestination (1551-1555) 86
   3.4.1 Disagreement between Calvin and Bullinger 86
   3.4.2 Beza's Letters of 1551 and 1552 88
   3.4.3 Beza's View of Calvin's De aeterna praedestinatione 93
   3.4.4 Statements for the Classis of Lausanne 94
   3.4.5 The Tabula is Completed 95
   3.4.6 The Tabula Not Sent Immediately to Bullinger 101
3.5 Beza's Tabula: Title, Editions and Intention 103
   3.5.1 Title 103
   3.5.2 Editions 104
   3.5.3 Intention 111
3.6 Beza's Mature Doctrine of Predestination After 1555 114
   3.6.1 The Decree 114
   3.6.2 Supralapsarianism 118
   3.6.3 The Execution of the Decree 120
3.7 Predestination and the Extent of the Atonement 122
3.8 Predestination, The Covenant, and the Church 125
   3.8.1 The Covenant 125
   3.8.2 The Church 129
3.9 God's Purpose and the Preacher's Purpose in Preaching 131
3.10 The Mode of Preaching the Gospel 135
3.11 Predestination and the Response to Preaching 136
3.12 Predestination, Faith, and Assurance 141
3.13 Preaching the Doctrine of Predestination 142
3.14 Summary: Predestination and the External Call 144
3.15 Beza's Sermons on the Resurrection of Christ 148
   3.15.1 Predestination 148
   3.15.2 The Atonement 151
   3.15.3 The Covenant and Church 152
   3.15.4 Conditionality 153
3.16 Summary: Theory and Practice 154

4. GENEVA AND THE SYNOD OF DORT - JOHN DIODATI AND THEODORE TRONCHIN 157
4.1 Diodati, Tronchin, and the question of Predestination and Preaching 157

4.2	Earlier research	159
4.3	The Genevan Remarks on the First Article	160
4.4	The Genevan Remarks on the Second article	164
4.5	Less Bezan than Others? McComish's Thesis Examined	167
4.6	Supralapsarianism or Infralapsarianism? Beeke's Thesis Examined	171
4.7	From Supralapsarianism to Infralapsarianism	173
4.8	The Canons on Predestination	176
4.9	The Canons on the Atonement	179
4.10	Predestination and the External Call in the Canons	181
4.11	Conclusions	182

5. HIGH ORTHODOXY - FRANCIS TURRETIN — 185

- 5.1 Turretin and the Question of Predestination and Preaching — 185
    - 5.1.1 Historical Developments: Saumur — 185
    - 5.1.3 Turretin's Life — 187
    - 5.1.3 Turretin against Saumur — 190
- 5.2 Earlier Research — 192
- 5.3 Predestination — 193
- 5.4 Predestination and the Extent of the Atonement — 200
- 5.5 Predestination and the Covenant — 202
    - 5.5.1 Turretin's View of the Covenant Compared with Calvin's — 206
- 5.6 Predestination and the Church — 208
- 5.7 God's Purpose and the Preacher's Purpose in Preaching — 209
- 5.8 The Mode of Preaching the Gospel — 211
- 5.9 Predestination and the Response to Preaching — 213
- 5.10 Predestination, Faith, and Assurance — 214
- 5.11 Preaching the Doctrine of Predestination — 218
- 5.12 Summary: Predestination and Preaching — 218
- 5.13 Turretin's Sermons — 222
    - 5.13.1 Predestination — 224
        - 5.13.1.1 The Sermon on Making One's Calling and Election Sure — 224
        - 5.13.1.2 The Sermon on the Firm Foundation — 227
        - 5.13.1.3 Other Sermons — 229
        - 5.13.1.4 Conclusions — 230
    - 5.13.2 The Extent of the Atonement — 231
    - 5.13.3 The Covenant — 232
    - 5.13.4 The Congregation — 234
    - 5.13.5 The Assurance of Election — 235

	5.13.6 God's Purpose in Preaching	236
	5.13.7 Conditionality	238
	5.13.8 The External and Internal Calls	240
	5.13.9 The Object and Nature of Faith	243
5.14	Summary: Theory and Practice	243

6. LATE ORTHODOXY - BENEDICT PICTET — 245

- 6.1 Pictet and the Question of Predestination and Preaching — 245
  - 6.1.1 A Changing Theological Climate — 245
  - 6.1.2 Jean-Alphonse Turretin — 246
  - 6.1.3 Pictet's Life and Works — 249
- 6.2 Earlier Research — 254
- 6.3 Predestination — 255
- 6.4 Predestination and the Atonement — 262
- 6.5 Pictet's Ambivalence on Predestination and the Atonement — 263
- 6.6 Predestination and the Covenant — 266
- 6.7 Predestination and the Church — 269
- 6.8 God's Purpose and the Preacher's Purpose in Preaching — 270
- 6.9 The Mode of Preaching the Gospel — 272
- 6.10 Predestination and the Response to Preaching — 273
- 6.11 Predestination, Faith, and Assurance — 274
- 6.12 Preaching the Doctrine of Predestination — 278
- 6.13 Summary: Predestination and the External Call — 280
- 6.14 Pictet's Sermons — 282
  - 6.14.1 The Examination of Religions — 283
  - 6.14.2 The Fourteen Sermons — 288
- 6.15 Summary: Theory and Practice — 295
- 6.16 Appendix: Later Developments in Geneva — 296

7. SYNTHESIS AND CONCLUSIONS — 301

- 7.1 Introduction — 301
- 7.2 Genevan Theologians and Their Involvement in the Question of Predestination and Preaching — 301
- 7.3 The Doctrine of Predestination — 302
- 7.4 Predestination and the Extent of the Atonement — 304
- 7.5 Predestination, the Covenant, and the Church — 305
- 7.6 God's Purpose and the Preacher's Purpose in Preaching — 308
- 7.7 The Mode of Preaching the Gospel: Conditionally and Unconditionally — 309
- 7.8 Predestination and the Response to Preaching — 311
- 7.9 Predestination, Faith, and Assurance — 312

7.10 Preaching the Doctrine of Predestination	313
7.11 Genevan Sermons and Predestination	314
7.12 General Conclusion	318
Bibliography	323
Index	339

Preface

The choice for the subject of this study was a result of two subjects I had researched as a student at Utrecht University. The first was a controversy on the well-meant Gospel offer. I was interested in such controversies that had caused schisms over several centuries, in several churches, and in several countries. The most important question at all times was how God could be serious in offering or promising salvation to the reprobate, i.e., those of whom he had decreed he would not give grace to. Another subject that attracted my attention was Reformed Scholasticism. When I began my theological studies at Utrecht in 1991, this was largely seen as a deviation from Calvin and of pure Calvinism, and the term was used to express dislike for certain theological views. Yet nobody could explain to me what scholasticism actually was. So when I saw a course in scholastic theology announced at the Catholic University of Utrecht, I decided to enroll in that course. We read Thomas Aquinas' tract on grace in his *Summa Contra Gentiles*. That was my first encounter with scholastic theology, and it fascinated me.

It was during that time that I met Willem van Asselt for the first time. He started to teach at Utrecht University in 1993, and we talked during a break in one of his seminars. I told him that I was taking a course in scholastic theology at the Catholic University, not knowing what his thoughts on the subject were. Never before I had seen a Protestant theologian reacting with such enthusiasm to the word "scholasticism." It did not take long before he asked me to become his assistant, and together we compiled a syllabus on Reformed Scholasticism, which eventually grew into a book in 1998, which was translated into English in 2011 as *Introduction to Reformed Scholasticism*.[1] Van Asselt was also the supervisor for my master's thesis on the objections of Dr. C. Steenblok to the well-meant gospel offer.

Having finished my master's thesis, I decided to research how Reformed scholastic theologians in Geneva viewed the relation between predestination and preaching. Willem van Asselt was of course my supervisor. I would like to express my gratitude and appreciation for this fine scholar. From the first time we met to the last, I have appreciated him

---

1 Grand Rapids: RHB, 2011.

both as an individual and because of his knowledge: always cheerful, always friendly, always attentive, often absent-minded. Without him, I would not have known what I know; I would not have written what I have written. This study is inconceivable without him. Even more than two years after his death, it is almost unimaginable that he will not see the result of research that undeniably bears his mark.

Another person without whom this study would have never been completed is my wife Gerdien. Even though she did not understand my fascination with this very subject, she saw that I enjoyed studying and always supported me and encouraged me to continue.

The next person I am especially thankful to is Wim Janse. When I had to search for a new promotor in 2012, he readily took up this task. I appreciate his comments and encouragements. His supervision and critical questions led to many improvements. From the moment he accepted the role of supervisor, he showed great interest in the subject of this study. I will not forget the sessions in which we discussed my chapter on Calvin, both of us contributing information from the sources that led both of us to revise our image of the Genevan Reformer.

I am also very grateful to my co-promotor Arie de Reuver, who was quite interested in the subject of predestination and preaching in Reformed theology. I recall his warm interest in what I had written every time we discussed a part of my dissertation.

It is my hope that this study will contribute to a better understanding of the problem of predestination and preaching and of the way Genevan Reformed theologians dealt with it. Since debates on the well-meant Gospel offer never ceased completely and flared up from time to time, this study might not only further our understanding of the history of the church, but it could also contribute to present and future debates on predestination and preaching.

Kampen, January 2017

1. Introduction

1.1 Status Quaestionis

A great deal of research has been done in recent decades on the period of Reformed orthodoxy[1] that has changed the view of Reformed orthodoxy and Reformed scholasticism. The Reformed theology produced in this period was formerly seen as a departure from the "pure" Calvinism of Calvin himself, a resynthesis of Aristotelian thought with biblical doctrine and as a predestinarian system.[2] For instance, in his study on the origins and development of the doctrine of predestination in Reformed Protestantism, C. Graafland concluded that the development of the doctrine of predestination was a tragic one. Originally nothing more than a subsection in Calvin's 1536 *Institutes*, it eventually became a theme that dominated the complete field of theology and church, culminating in 20th-century schisms on the well-meant Gospel offer. This development started with Calvin, who wrote several chapters on predestination in the last edition of his *Institutes*, was continued in the theology of Beza, who systemized the doctrine, and was intensified by the criticisms of Arminius, resulting in the *Canons of Dort*.[3] Graafland repeated his disappointment in his work on the history of the Reformed doctrine of the covenant, stating that the same tragic development can be seen in this doctrine because it was "absorbed" by the doctrine of election.[4]

---

1 Examples of recent research are Herman J. Selderhuis (ed.), *A Companion to Reformed Orthodoxy* (Leiden: Brill, 2013); Jordan J. Ballor, David S. Sytsma, and Jason Zuidema (eds.), *Church and School in Early Modern Protestantism: Studies in Honor of Richard A. Muller on the Maturation of a Theological Tradition* (Leiden: Brill, 2013); Maarten Wisse, Marcel Sarot, and Willemien Otten (eds.), *Scholasticism Reformed: Essays in Honour of Willem J. van Asselt* (Leiden: Brill, 2010); Willem J. van Asselt and Eef Dekker (eds.), *Reformation and Scholasticism: An Ecumenical Enterprise* (Grand Rapids: Baker Academic, 2001); Carl R. Trueman and R. Scott Clark (eds.), *Protestant Scholasticism: Essays in Reassessment* (Carlisle: Paternoster Press, 1999). Richard A. Muller, *Post-Reformation Reformed Dogmatics*, 4 vols. (Grand Rapids: Baker Book House, 1987-2003) proved to be of great importance for this recent research (hereinafter cited as *PRRD*).
2 For a survey of older and more recent research, see Willem J. van Asselt, "Reformed Orthodoxy: A Short History of Research," in Selderhuis, *Companion*, 11-26.
3 C. Graafland, *Van Calvijn tot Barth: Oorsprong en ontwikkeling van de leer der verkiezing in het Gereformeerd Protestantisme* (Zoetermeer: Boekencentrum 1987), 594-95.
4 C. Graafland, *Van Calvijn tot Comrie: Oorsprong en ontwikkeling van de leer van het verbond in het Gereformeerd Protestantisme*, vol. III, parts 5 & 6 (Zoetermeer: Boekencentrum, 1996), 402.

Recent studies have made clear that the truth is not as simple as previous research presented it. For example, Richard A. Muller has shown that the theologies of the Reformation and Reformed orthodoxy are neither wholly continuous nor discontinuous. He also argued that to describe the theology of this period as "scholastic" is to make a statement about its method, not about its content. Moreover, he proved that the doctrine of predestination was neither a central dogma nor a controlling element of Reformed theology since it was omitted from the prolegomena of Protestant scholastic systems.[5] Muller asserted that, although predestination was an important theme in Reformed theology, it did not function as an all-embracing category in the system. Now that it has been proven that the doctrine of predestination was not a *principium* of theology, the question remains as to how important this doctrine actually was. Muller makes clear that predestination did not affect the *system* and *method* of theology. But did it affect (parts of) the *content* of Reformed theology?

This study deals with one principal subject: The Influence of the Doctrine of Predestination on the Doctrine of the External Call. I chose this subject for three reasons. First, although Reformed theology limits the internal call to salvation by the Holy Spirit to the elect, the external call to salvation by the preached Word is broadened to include the reprobate as well. This raises the question of how God can call those to salvation whom he has rejected and still be just in his judgment of them. This question is so obvious that every theologian who accepts the doctrine of predestination and the notion of a general call to salvation is almost forced to deal with it.

Moreover, the notion of the external call is directly related to preaching, which has always been at the heart of Reformed church services.[6] Sermons were preached every Sunday in Geneva – and even daily for a long time. In the words of Scott Manetsch: "Preaching was by far the most important means of mass communication in the early modern era."[7] So, if the doctrine of predestination affected preaching, it affected the weekly or even daily practice of Reformed Christianity. Therefore, if we want to

---

5 Muller, *PRRD*, 9-100; idem, *Christ and the Decree: Christology and Predestination in Reformed Theology from Calvin to Perkins* (Durham: Labyrinth Press, 1986) 1-13; Trueman and Clark, *Protestant Scholasticism*, xi-xix.
6 The plain and simple liturgy of Reformed churches, focusing on the preached word of God, was one of most obvious differences with the Roman Catholic liturgy, with its focus on the Eucharist and its incense, candles, and processions. Scott M. Manetsch *Calvin's Company of Pastors: Pastoral Care and the Emerging Reformed Church, 1536-1609* (Oxford: OUP, 2013) 19, 26, 33, 36.
7 Manetsch, *Company*, 146.

know if and how much the doctrine of predestination affected Reformed theology and practice, researching the possible influence of predestination on views of how the Gospel should be preached can yield more insight than researching its possible influence on the doctrine of creation or eschatology. In this sense, this study is relevant for research in historical theology.

A second reason for choosing this subject was that it was this very question that caused so much difficulty in the last three centuries, especially with regard to the 'well-meant Gospel offer.' How can God, in all fairness, offer salvation to the reprobate? This question has led to schisms between churches in five countries, on three continents, and over three centuries.[8] In all probability, the first theologian to deny that God offered salvation to the reprobate was the English congregationalist theologian Joseph Hussey (1660-1726), who published his *God's Operations of Grace but No Offers of Grace* in 1707.[9] His views became influential among the English Baptists since John Gill adopted his ideas to some extent in his *The Cause of God and Truth* (1735-1738), for instance.[10] At the end of the century, this so-called High Calvinism or Hyper-Calvinism was opposed by Andrew Fuller in his *The Gospel Worthy of All Acceptation* (1786). The debates on "duty faith" and the "Gospel offer" divided the English and American Reformed Baptists and continue to do so today.[11]

In the meantime, the Marrow Controversy erupted in Scotland in 1720. One of the points in this controversy was the "free offer of the Gospel" and whether this implied universal atonement and whether it was consistent with the Reformed doctrine of predestination. "Marrow theologians" like the brothers Ralph and Ebenezer Erskine and Thomas Boston taught that the free offer was consistent with predestination and did

---

8   For a more extensive survey of controversies on the relation between predestination and the external call, see my *Het aanbod van genade* (Apeldoorn: De Rots, 2002), 15-30.
9   On Hussey, see Peter Toon, *The Emergence of Hyper-Calvinism in English Nonconformity, 1689-1765* (London: The Olive Tree, 1967; reprint: Weston Rhyn: Quinta Press, 2003), chapter IV, *No Offers of Grace (The Theology of Hussey and Skepp)*. Online: http://quintapress.macmate.me/PDF_Books/Hypercalvinism.pdf.
10 On Gill, see Michael A.G. Haykin, *The Life and Thought of John Gill (1697-1771): A Tercentennial Appreciation (Studies in the History of Christian Thought)* (Leiden: Brill, 1997).
11 For a survey of controversies in Britain related to so-called Hyper-Calvinism, see Thomas J. Nettles, *By His Grace and for His Glory: A Historical Theological, and Practical Study of the Doctrines of Grace in Baptist Life* (Grand Rapids: Baker, 1986), 73-130 and 385-91.

not imply universal atonement, but they could not convince their opponents.[12]

Among the Dutch Reformed, the discussion on the Gospel offer in relation to predestination started in the 18th century without causing too much commotion. The discussion was continued by the Dutch seceders in the 19th century, leading to a temporary schism. Although unity was restored in The Netherlands, a new schism occurred among Dutch emigrants to the United States and Canada in 1924. In that year, the synod of the Christian Reformed Churches accepted "three points" wherein the well-meant Gospel offer was mentioned. Herman Hoeksema opposed these three points, and his rejection eventually resulted in the establishment of the Protestant Reformed Churches.[13]

The schism in the Christian Reformed Churches had emerged independently of the discussions on the same theme among the English Baptists. Even more curious is that a schism on the same subject occurred in another denomination in The Netherlands that had seceded, independently of what happened in America in 1924. In 1953, the synod of the Gereformeerde Gemeenten dismissed Dr. Cornelis Steenblok because of his opposition to the doctrine of the general, well-meant and unconditional Gospel offer. This led to the formation of a new denomination in The Netherlands, the Gereformeerde Gemeenten in Nederland.[14]

Again independent of former discussions, there was a schism in Australia in 1961 between the Evangelical Presbyterian Church and the Presbyterian Church of Eastern Australia due to different views of how predestination affected the preaching of the Gospel offer. The former denomination eventually sought contact with the Protestant Reformed Churches, where their pastors are currently trained.[15]

---

12 See William VanDoodewaard, *The Marrow Controversy and Seceder Tradition (Reformed Historical-Theological Studies)* (Grand Rapids: Reformation Heritage Books, 2011).
13 For the discussion among the seceders, see C. Veenhof, *Prediking en uitverkiezing: Kort overzicht van de strijd, gevoerd in de Christelijk Afgescheidene Gereformeerde Kerk tussen 1850 en 1870, over de plaats van de leer der uitverkiezing in de prediking* (Kampen: J.H. Kok 1959). For Hoeksema, see P.J. Baskwell, *Herman Hoeksema: A Theological Biography* (unpublished dissertation, 2006) available online http://dare.ubvu.vu.nl/handle/1871/9781.
14 For Steenblok, see my *Het aanbod van genade* (Apeldoorn: De Rots, 2002).
15 There is no printed literature available on the Evangelical Presbyterian Church of Australia. A survey of its history can be found at its website http://www.epc.org.au//history/index.php.

Overseeing these several "battlefields" concerning predestination and preaching, a striking resemblance is that all schisms on this subject occurred in times when or in a denomination in which academic theology was at a low level at best.[16] This raises the question how the problem of predestination and the external call was solved by academic Reformed theologians during the period of the Reformation and Reformed orthodoxy – and whether the relation between predestination and preaching had actually been a "problem" for them.

To avoid being anachronistic, the main question of my study could not be what the classic academic theologians thought about the Gospel offer, which was not an issue in their time. But since predestination and the external call are both classic Reformed doctrines, it is possible to research what academic theologians of the Reformation and Reformed orthodoxy actually thought about the relation between the two doctrines.

This study can be fruitful for modern reflection on the same question by 21st-century heirs of classic Reformed theology. Although I have little hope that historical research will produce reasons for abandoning positions once taken and maintained for decades or even centuries, such research can at least serve to clarify the problems, the terminology, and the historical developments. In this sense, this study is relevant for contemporary theology.

This study is limited in several ways. It is limited *geographically* to Geneva, and developments outside Geneva are mentioned only insofar as they affected Genevan theology – for instance, the Synod of Dort in 1618-1619 and the theology of Saumur. It is limited *temporally* to the period from ca. 1536 (the first edition of Calvin's *Institutes*) to 1724 (the death of Benedict Pictet, which was followed within one year by the abrogation of the *Canons of Dort* at Geneva). The ideas of medieval or early Reformation theologians, like Lombard, Aquinas, Scotus, Luther, Zwingli or Farel, are not researched here. Of course, the Genevan Reformed theologians were indebted to former theologians. Recent research has shown how concepts which were introduced by medieval theologians were used in Reformed theology.[17] Yet in order to understand what Genevan theologians thought

---

16 Gill, Fuller, Hoeksema, and Steenblok were, however, sharp thinkers at least. Autodidacts Gill and Fuller were granted honorary doctorates for their contributions to theology. Steenblok earned his doctorate by writing a dissertation on Voetius. Hoeksema did not earn any academic degree, but he might have been the most original thinker of them all.

17 See for instance W.J. van Asselt e.a. (eds.), *Reformed Thought on Freedom. The Concept of Free Choice in Early Modern Reformed Theology* (Grand Rapids: Baker Academic, 2010), 15-49.

concerning predestination and the external calling, there is no need to investigate the (medieval) sources of the concepts they used. Later developments up until the early 19th century are described only in a short survey at the end of chapter 6 and limited to Geneva. *Methodologically*, it is limited to the influence of predestination on the notion of the external call. Since predestination and the call of the Gospel are related to each other by the doctrines of the church and the covenant, and since the question whether Christ died for all people or only for the elect is important for seeing how the doctrine of election affected the outward call to salvation, we will look at these doctrines as well. The possible influence of the doctrine of predestination on other doctrines is not a part of this study nor the way the Genevan inhabitants reacted to the doctrine of predestination or to the sermons preached. Nor will we look at the extent to which Genevan preachers used the doctrine of predestination as an identity marker. Such questions, though important and interesting, are outside the limits of this study. The central question is simply how the doctrine of election affected preaching in the theology and sermons of John Calvin, Theodore Beza, Theodore Tronchin, John Diodati, Francis Turretin, and Benedict Pictet.

The central question concerns primarily the *theology* of these theologians and their *sermons* only secondarily. This is first and foremost a study in systematic theology, and not one in homiletics. We will examine how the doctrine of predestination affects the external call by looking at how these theologians related the doctrine of predestination to the covenant, church, and the call and what they thought about the task of a preacher who does not know who is elect or reprobate. Their sermons are looked at to see whether their systematic view of the relation between predestination and preaching corresponds with the practice of their preaching. In other words, their sermons are a test case.

1.2 Genevan Reformed Theology as an Appropriate Subject of Research

Of course, Genevan theology did not develop in a vacuum, but was part of a larger, European movement as well as from an intellectual history of universities that dated back to approx. 1200 and went on to approx. 1800.[18] Geneva attracted professors from other countries – Calvin and Beza were French, for instance – as well as students, and Genevan students spent some time in other countries for study purposes before returning to Geneva to serve as pastor or professor, like Turretin. Yet the choice for

---

18 See A. Vos, "Scholasticism and Reformation" in: W.J. van Asselt and Eef Dekker, *Reformation and Scholasticism*, 99-120.

Geneva has been a conscious one. Genevan theology is a good field to study the relation between predestination and the external call. Geneva's ecclesiastical constitutions included the office of doctor or teacher whose task was to interpret the Scriptures, teach sound doctrine, defend the church against doctrinal errors, and educate future pastors. Most, if not all, doctors were also pastors.[19] This office of doctor became even more important when the Academy of Geneva was founded in 1559. Preaching was highly valued in the Genevan constitutions. The ministers were required to conduct up to 33 worship services each week, and people were required to attend services at least on Sundays and Wednesdays.[20]

From Calvin's time on, Genevan theologians – since they were both doctors and pastors – have dealt explicitly with the question of the call of the reprobate. Thus, following the line of the Genevan theologians seems to be a good way to see not only whether predestination affected the external call but also whether the doctrines of predestination and the external call and the influence of the former on the latter changed when Reformation theology turned into orthodox theology in its several stages until the dawn of Enlightenment theology. Calvin was the first Reformed Genevan theologian to write works of systematic theology as well as sermons; Pictet was the last Reformed orthodox theologian to do so.

The period of late orthodoxy lasted for almost the whole of the 18th century all over Europe, but in Geneva, strict orthodoxy ended with the death of Pictet in 1724. Within one year, the *Canons of Dort* had been abrogated as binding for Genevan theologians and pastors. Insofar as Genevan theology was orthodox after Pictet's death, it was a moderate, enlightened, and rational orthodoxy. That is why I limited this study to the Influence of the Doctrine of Predestination on Preaching in Genevan Theology from Calvin to Pictet.

To study the development of a doctrine and practice in Geneva for the complete period of the Reformation and Reformed orthodoxy is unique. Most, if not all, studies that deal with the development of Reformed doctrine tend to neglect Geneva after Beza or even after Calvin and to focus on, for instance, English Puritanism or Dutch orthodoxy.[21] But Geneva

---

19 Manetsch, *Company,* 28-29.
20 Manetsch, *Company,* 23, 28, 129.
21 Examples (in chronological order) are R.T. Kendall, *Calvin and English Calvinism to 1649* (Oxford: OUP, 1979); C. Graafland, *Van Calvijn tot Barth*; G. Michael Thomas, *The Extent of the Atonement: A Dilemma for Reformed Theology from Calvin to the Consensus* (Carlisle UK: Paternoster, 1997) and Joel R. Beeke, *The Quest for Full Assurance: The Legacy of Calvin and his Successors* (Edinburgh: Banner of Truth, 1999).

was an important city for the Reformed churches throughout Europe. It was influential because of its Academy, but the city was important also because it harbored many publishers and printers, whose influence led to Geneva being called *la Rome protestante*.[22]

There is no study on academic theology in Geneva during the Reformation and Reformed Orthodoxy nor one on predestination or the external call in Genevan theology. Some works do partially include these subjects. A.A. van Schelven wrote a book on Calvinism in Geneva and France in the 16th and 17th centuries.[23] He limited his study almost to the influence of the Genevan Academy on other countries and on Calvinistic ethics in Geneva. Other than Calvin and Beza, he mentions only three theological professors at the time of Beza's death. Later theologians like Theodore Tronchin, John Diodati, Francis Turretin, or Benedict Pictet were not considered in his work. Karin Maag researched the Genevan Academy in the first 60 years of its existence.[24] Her study is limited almost to the period of Calvin and Beza and does not touch on doctrinal subjects. Much the same holds for Scott Manetsch's study on Geneva's company of pastors from 1536 to 1609.[25] Geneva was rather anachronistically treated as part of Switzerland in Christian Mosers chapter on Reformed orthodoxy in Switserland, as well as in a volume edited by W. Fred Graham.[26] This volume contains chapters on Beza and the supervision of marriage, Francis Turretin and the concept of the Covenant of Nature, and on Benedict Pictet as a theologian in a time of transition. The origins and development of the doctrines of predestination and the covenant were investigated by C. Graafland.[27] In his volume on predestination, he moved from Calvin and Beza to Perkins and did not return to Geneva. In his volumes on the covenant, he moved from Calvin to Heidelberg and England, and Beza was the only one of the later Genevan theologians he

---

22 John B. Roney, "Introduction," in John B. Roney and Martin I. Klauber, *The Identity of Geneva: The Christian Commonwealth, 1564-1864* (Westport, Connecticut/London: Greenwood Press, 1998), 5, 6.

23 A.A. van Schelven, *Het Calvinisme gedurende zijn bloeitijd: Genève – Frankrijk* (Amsterdam: Ten Have, 1943).

24 Karin Maag, *Seminary or University? The Genevan Academy and Reformed Higher Education, 1560-1620* (Aldershot: Scolar Press, 1995).

25 Manetsch, *Company*.

26 Christian Moser, "Reformed Orthodoxy in Switzerland," in Selderhuis, *Companion*, 195-226; W. Fred Graham (ed.) *Later Calvinism. International Perspectives: Sixteenth Century Essays & Studies vol. XXII* (Missouri: Missouri State University, 1994).

27 See 1.1 notes 3 and 4.

looked at. In my chapter on predestination in *A Companion to Reformed Orthodoxy* I mentioned Calvin, Beza and Turretin as Genevan theologians in the context of European developments.[28]

1.3 Method

This present volume is comprised of six chapters on different periods and their representative theologians.[29] John Calvin (1509-1564) is representative for the Reformation period (ca. 1520-1560). The period of Early Orthodoxy (ca. 1560-1620) is represented by Theodore Beza (1519-1605). The two theologians who represented the church of Geneva at the Synod of Dort, John Diodati (1576-1649) and Theodore Tronchin (1587-1657), did not leave any systematic works on predestination behind nor any collected volumes of sermons. Yet their contribution to the *judicia* of the Remonstrant theses at Dort is important enough to give them due attention in a separate chapter. High Orthodoxy (ca. 1620-1700) is represented by Francis Turretin (1623-1687), and Benedict Pictet (1655-1724) is an example of Late Orthodoxy.

The chapters on these periods have more or less the same structure. After a short historical survey, the doctrine of predestination of each theologian is presented. Then the influence of this particular view on the doctrines of atonement, covenant, church, and call will be explored. Did the Genevan theologians think that Christ died for all people or only for the elect? Did they divide the congregation into the elect and the reprobate or was the whole congregation regarded as elect? Further, what influence did their views of the congregation have on the way they thought people should be called to salvation? Did they think that the content of the doctrine of predestination should be preached? Should salvation be promised or offered indiscriminately to all? Finally, we will look at some sermons by each theologian to see whether their practice was consistent with their theory.

---

28 Pieter Rouwendal, "The Doctrine of Predestination in Reformed Orthodoxy," in Selderhuis, *Companion*, 553-590.

29 Muller uses certain markers to distinguish between these periods. However, it is historians who make the distinctions, and not history itself. I refer to these periods not as clearly defined eras starting and ending at certain dates but only to make it easier to place the different theologians in their own time. Muller *PRRD 1*, 28-40. See also Van Asselt, *Introduction*, 64, 102-03.

The methodological path I follow is to discuss the positions on predestination and the external call of each theologian by posing the following questions:
1. What was his doctrine of predestination?
2. Did his doctrine of predestination affect his doctrine of the extent of the atonement?
3. Did his doctrine of predestination affect his doctrine of the covenant and/or the church?
4. Did his doctrine of predestination affect his doctrine of faith?
5. Did his doctrine of predestination affect his doctrine of the call?
6. Is the way he addressed his congregation in his sermons in accordance with his theological ideas?
7. What place did the doctrine of predestination have in his sermons?
8. Are historical facts and religious developments of his time important to this part of his theology?
9. Is there continuity or discontinuity in the theology and sermons of the theologians examined regarding the doctrine of predestination during the period researched?

The concluding chapter will compare the conclusions drawn in each chapter and see if there is any development.

The question of continuity or discontinuity needs some clarification. Do all differences mean discontinuity? A development can be a continuous process, with differences at each stage. Ideas that remain identical over the years can be a sign of lack of reflection, of stagnation, or even torpor rather than continuity. I will view it as continuity when ideas remain the same or develop over the years, when the basic idea remains the same, even though a new formulation is used to give better expression to that basic idea. I will regard it as discontinuity when a shift can be seen from one basic idea to another – for instance, when a new formulation is used to express a new idea or when a former idea is abandoned.

For the sake of readability, quotations in the text have been translated into English, and the original Latin or French text is provided in the footnotes. Whenever a Latin or French quotation is given in a footnote without a translation in the text, an English translation is added in the footnote. The translation follows the original in italics.

2. The Reformation - John Calvin

2.1 Calvin and the Question of Predestination and Preaching

The Frenchman John Calvin (1509-1564) did not intend to become either a Reformed theologian or a Genevan theologian. But when he became a Protestant, he was forced to flee France. Having published the first edition of his *Institutes* in Basel in 1536, he decided to go to Strasbourg. While on his way there, he passed through Geneva, a city that had chosen the side of the Reformation only two months before.[1] The Reformer William Farel persuaded Calvin to stay in Geneva where Calvin's influence grew so much that he is now known as the Reformer of Geneva.[2]

Calvin was a Reformer of the second generation; in that respect, he should not be grouped with Martin Luther (1483-1546) and Huldrych Zwingli (1484-1531), but rather with Philip Melanchthon (1497-1560) and Heinrich Bullinger (1504-1575). When Calvin arrived in Geneva in 1536, the Reformation in that city had already begun, and Zwingli had died five years before. Thus, Calvin was not one of the initiators of the Reformation but joined it as a movement that had been going on for two decades. Given this, Calvin should be studied in his own time, context, and development.[3]

---

1 For a survey of the initial developments of the Reformation in Geneva, see Manetsch, *Company,* 11-17
2 On Calvin's life, see, for example, Bernard Cottret, *Calvin. Biographie* (Paris: Lattès, 1995). On Calvin's life around the time of his first arrival in Geneva, see W. van 't Spijker, *"Die Fransman …" Calvijn in 1536* (Kampen: De Groot Goudriaan, 1986) and Frans Pieter van Stam, "Calvin's First Stay in Geneva," in Herman J. Selderhuis (ed.), *The Calvin Handbook* (Grand Rapids: Eerdmans, 2009), 30-38; quoted as *Calvin Handbook*.
3 References to Calvin's works are made in different ways. References to the 1559 edition of Calvin's *Institutes* are made by mentioning the number of the section. For example, *Institutes*, III, xxiii, 1 refers to *Institutes* of 1559, book three, chapter 23, section one. If no year is mentioned, it is the *Institutes* of 1559 that is meant. This does not always imlpy that the text referred to dates from 1559. References to Calvin's commentaries and lectures are made by naming commentary / lecture, the Bible book and verse. For example, Comm. Romans 3:5 refers to Calvin's commentary on Romans 3, verse 5. Referring to the *Institutes* and the commentaries this way makes it easier for anyone to look up the reference in any translation, while being exact enough to find the place referred to in the *Calvini Opera,* the *Calvini Opera Recognita* and the *Opera Selecta.* References to other works of Calvin are references to the *Calvini Opera (CO)* and / or to the *Calvini Opera Recognita (COR),* volume, and page. Unless indicated otherwise, translations of Calvin's *Institutes* are quoted from Battles' translation. (Philadelphia: Westminster Press, 1960). Translations from Calvin's commentaries are quoted from the translations of the Calvin Translation Society (Grand Rapids: Baker, 1999 [reprint]).

Within two years after his arrival in Geneva, Calvin published a catechism in which he, for the first time, explicitly related predestination to the notion of call, including that of the reprobate.

> For the seed of God's Word takes root and bears fruit only in those whom the Lord has by his eternal election predestined as his children and heirs of the kingdom of heaven; for all the rest, who were condemned by this same plan of God before the foundation of the world, the utterly clear preaching of truth can be nothing but the stench of death unto death.[4]

Calvin published a second edition of his *Institutes* (1539) during his exile in Strasbourg. Albert Pighius of Kampen wrote an attack against Calvin's doctrines of human freedom and divine predestination as presented in that second edition.[5] It appeared in 1542 as *Ten Books on Human Free Choice and Divine Grace*,[6] the first six books responding to Calvin's doctrine of free choice, the last four to his doctrine of predestination. Calvin, in turn, tried to publish an answer prior to the Frankfurt Book Fair of 1543 but only succeeded in responding to the first six of Pighius' books, those on free choice.[7] Calvin intended to edit a response to Pighius's last

---

4 *Instruction et Confession de Foy dont on Use en l'Eglise de Genève* (1538), CO XXII, 46-47; COR II/III, 32: "Car le semence de la parolle de Dieu prent racine et fructifie en ceux là seulement lesquelz le Seigneur, par son election eternelle, a predestiné pour ses enfans et heretiers du royaulme celeste. A tous les autres, qui par mesme conseil de Dieu devant la constitution du monde sont reprouvez, la claire et evidente predication de verité ne peult estre aultre chose, sinon odeur de mort en mort." Translation by F.L. Battles in I. John Hesselink, *Calvin's First Catechism: A Commentary*, Columbia Series in Reformed Theology (Louisville: Westminster John Knox Press, 1997), 17.
5 For a short survey of Pighius's life and a summary of his thought on free will and predestination, see A.N.S. Lane, "Introduction" in COR, IV/III, 11-66 or his "Introduction," in *The Bondage and Liberation of the Will: A Defense of the Orthodox Doctrine of Human Choice against Pighius*, ed. A.N.S. Lane, transl. G.I. Davies, Texts and Studies in Reformation and Post-Reformation Thought (Grand Rapids: Baker, 1996); Wilhelm Neuser, "Einleitung," in Calvin, *De aeterna Dei praedestinatione*, COR III/I, xiii-xv; G. Melles, *Albertus Pighius en zijn strijd met Calvijn over het liberum arbitrium* (Kampen: Kok, 1973).
6 Albert Pighius, *De libero hominis arbitrio et divina gratia, Libri decem* (Cologne: Melchior Novesianus, 1542).
7 *Defensio sanae et orthodoxae doctrinae de servitute et liberatione humani arbitrii adversus calumnias Alberti Pighii Campensis* (Geneva: Johannus Gerardus, 1543); CO VI, 225-404; COR IV/III, quoted as *Defensio*. An English translation of this work was edited in 1996 as *The Bondage and Liberation of the Will*.

four books before the 1544 Fair, but Pighius died in the meantime and Calvin decided "not to insult a dead dog."[8]

In Geneva, Calvin edited new editions of his *Institutes*, viz. in 1543, 1550, and 1559.[9] The 1543 edition may have been at the printer's when Calvin replied to Pighius, and the alterations in the edition of 1550 did not deal with the topics of the Pighius controversy either. The controversy on predestination seemed to have ceased. But some influence of the debate with Pighius can be found in the last Latin edition of 1559. The reason that Calvin did not include any parts of the controversy with Pighius in his *Institutes* of 1550 might be the same reason why he did not edit his response to Pighius's last four books.[10] But the controversy on predestination flared up again in Geneva itself between 1550 and 1559: Calvin's doctrine of eternal predestination was attacked and derided by Bolsec in 1551.[11] In the meantime, a Sicilian monk called Georgius[12] also attacked the doctrine. Calvin finished his reply to Pighius now so that he could respond to the attacks by Bolsec and Georgius.[13] After giving a lecture

---

8   Calvin's controversy with Pighius is described in Lane, "Introduction" in *COR*, IV/III, 11-66; Idem, "Introduction" to Calvin's *Bondage and Liberation of the Will*; Neuser, "Einleitung," in Calvin, *De aeterna Dei praedestinatione*, COR III/I, xiii-xv; Melles, *Albertus Pighius en zijn strijd met Calvijn over het liberum arbitrium*.

9   I will only mention the Latin editions here. Since Pighius wrote in Latin and Calvin answered in Latin, there is no reason to mention the French editions of Calvin's response to Pighius.

10 However, in his tract on scandals (*De Scandalis, CO VIII*, 38-40) [1550] Calvin wrote a section on arguments by people against the doctrine of predestination, in which he dealt briefly with predestination and preaching. This is not reviewed separately since these remarks do not offer any new insights.

11 For the Bolsec controversy, see P. Holtrop, *The Bolsec Controversy on Predestination from 1551 to 1555* (Lewiston, N.Y.: Edwin Mellen, 1993). Holtrop is useful since he offers a great deal of detailed information, but his interpretation was criticized by, among others, R.A. Muller in his review of this work in *Calvin Theological Journal* 29 (1994), 581-89. E A. de Boer offered a concise description of the Bolsec controversy in chapter 5 of his *The Genevan School of the Prophets: The Congregations of the Company of Pastors and their Influence in 16th Century Europe* (Geneva: Librairie Droz S.A., 2012), 113-42.

12 His original name was Georgio Riolo Siculo, a Benedictine monk, who in his *Epistola di Georgio Siculo servo fidele di Iesu Christo alli cittad'ni di Riva di Trento contra il mendatio di Francesco Spiera et falsa dottrina de' protestanti* (Bologna 1550) objected to the doctrine of the Italian Protestant Francesco Spiera. Georgio himself was also accused of heresy and sentenced to death. He died on May 23 at Ferrara in 1551. On him, see A. Prosperi, *L'eresia del Libro Grande: Storia di Giorgio Siculo e della sua setta* (Milano: Feltrinelli, 2001) and Wilhelm Neuser's "Einleitung," in Calvin, *De aeterna Dei praedestinatione, COR* III/I, xv-xvii.

13 Calvin to Viret, 15 August 1551, *CO* XIV, 165: "Mitto Georgii Siculi deliria quae fratres Itali a me refutari optassent. Ego autem abstinui, quia nullus esset finis, si singuli

for the pastors of Geneva on December 18, 1551,[14] he published a *Treatise on the Eternal Predestination of God* in 1552,[15] which is essentially an answer to the last four of Pighius' books.[16]

It is remarkable that Calvin did not mention Bolsec's name in this treatise. Instead, he explicitly recalled the attack on his doctrine of predestination by Pighius nine years earlier and the recent attack by Georgius of Sicily. In his dedication, he referred to the Bolsec controversy only by writing about "the subtle introduction by Satan of a widespread error." The person who introduced this error "sought notoriety out of the very flames of the temple of God." To prevent Bolsec from attaining this notoriety, Calvin left his name purposely unmentioned, hoping "that it would remain buried in silence."[17] Calvin's hope was in vain. Although Georgius of Sicily has been almost forgotten, Bolsec is still remembered. But, despite Bolsec and Georgius, Calvin's treatise is primarily a reply to Pighius.[18] His name is mentioned throughout the whole work, while Georgius is mentioned only in the last few pages and Bolsec nowhere. Calvin

---

isti canes propriis libris repellendi essent. Praestat igitur multos responso non dignari. Si quando otium suppetet, potius quod iam ante annos octo pollicitus sum praestabo. Ita Pighio respondens aliorum latratus compescam." *(I send you the ravings of George of Sicily, which the Italian brethren wish me to refute. I have declined, however, as there would be no end to replies if every single dog of that sort were to be silenced by a special treatise. It is better, therefore, that many do not deem it worthy of a reply. If I ever find leisure, I should prefer executing what I undertook years ago. By replying to Pighius, I shall put a stop to the barking of others.)* Transl. Jules Bonnet, *Letters of John Calvin*, Vol. II (Philadelphia: Presbyterian Board of Publication, n.d.), 317.

14 This lecture was published in 1562 as *Congregation faite en l'Eglise de Genève par Jean Calvin, en laquelle la matiere de l'election eternelle de Dieu fut sommairement et clairement deduite et ratifiée d'un commun accord par les freres ministres*. A recent edition is in COR VII/1, 57-132. De Boer suggests that a French synod of that year that discussed Bolsec could have been the occasion for this lecture. De Boer, *Genevan School*, 127.

15 *De aeterna Dei praedestinatione*, [1552] CO VIII, 249-366; COR III/1. There are two English translations available of this treatise. *Concerning the Eternal Predestination of God*, translation by J.K.S. Reid (Cambridge: James Clarke & Co 1961), and *Calvin's Calvinism*, translation by H. Cole (Grand Rapids: RFPA, n.d.). Quotations here are based on the latter (quoted as CC), which is a reprint of a 19th century (1856) edition. Since it is somewhat free, I sometimes altered the translation a bit to make it correspond more closely to the Latin text.

16 According to Neuser, this treatise was also meant as an answer to the theologians of Basel, Bern, and Zurich. Wilhelm Neuser "Einleitung," in Calvin, *De aeterna Dei praedestinatione*, COR III/1, xvii-xviii.

17 *De aeterna Dei praedestinatione*, CO VIII, 253-54, 258; COR III/1, 3 (CC, 19-20, 25-26).

18 *De aeterna Dei praedestinatione*, CO VIII, 255-56; COR III/1, 8 (CC, 23).

responded to Pighius and Georgius because he supposed Bolsec had used them as sources.[19]

2.2 Earlier Research

Calvin is probably one the most researched theologians ever, and many aspects of his theology have been examined. Some of these studies have been written on his doctrine of predestination. Nevertheless, the influence of this doctrine on his ideas concerning the external call has not been examined. Paul Jacobs, in his study to Calvin's view of predestination and responsibility, wrote on the relation between predestination and *vocatio* but did so in relation to the theme of sanctification: those who are called are called to sanctification. The call entails responsibility.[20] Jacobs only dealt with predestination and responsibility in relation to ethics. Although he discussed when and how Calvin dealt with the doctrine of reprobation in his sermons, he did not write about the relation between predestination and the call of the Gospel to salvation.

Another work on Calvin's doctrine of predestination is C. Graafland's volume on the development of the doctrine of predestination in Reformed Protestantism. Graafland started with Calvin's doctrine of predestination, dealing explicitly with Calvin's view of election and the preaching of the Gospel promises.[21] Having stated that Calvin preached "the offer of the promise" to all, both reprobate and elect, he asks what form this preaching took. His answer, based on *Institutes* III, 24, xvii, is that there is no difference between the elect and the reprobate as far as the address of the gospel. Yet there is a difference with respect to faith: this faith is given only to the elect. Hence, Graafland states, the promises are preached and offered to all, but the content of this promise is that God's grace is (only) available to those who ask for it, i.e., the elect. His conclusion is that, although there are great tensions and unclear passages in Calvin's thinking on this topic, Calvin's theology does not include the offer of grace to all because Christ did not die for all. Due to the survey character of Graafland's work, he does not examine Calvin's view of this subject very thoroughly.[22]

---

19 *De aeterna Dei praedestinatione*, CO VIII, 255; COR III/1, 8 (*CC*, 23-24). It seems that Calvin's answer to Pighius was almost ready at the time the Bolsec controversy began and that he, in haste, added his reply to Georgius. See also 2.1 note 13.
20 Paul Jacobs, *Prädestination und Verantwortlichkeit bei Calvin* (Neukirchen: Kreis Moers, 1937), 110-12.
21 Graafland, *Van Calvijn tot Barth*, 41-46.
22 For instance, he does not look at any of Calvin's sermons and restricts himself mainly to his *Institutes*.

Harald Rimbach examines Calvin's doctrine of predestination in relation to the knowledge *(Erkenntnis)* of God and grace.[23] *The Calvin Handbook* offers surveys of actual knowledge and research on Calvin.[24] Mirjam van Veen provides a survey on Calvin and his opponents, including those who opposed his doctrine of predestination.[25] Wilhelm Neuser wrote a chapter on Calvin's doctrine of predestination,[26] stating that the stress Calvin laid on the Fall led him to make use of predestination as an explanation for unbelief. Neuser's thesis is that Calvin's doctrine of predestination underwent many changes. He concludes that Calvin had, in fact, two doctrines of predestination: a pastoral one in the first-person "we" form and a more logical one in the third person. Neuser's conclusion was contradicted by E.A. de Boer who stated that Calvin did not hold two doctrines of predestination but used different modes to present it.[27]

Calvin's sermons have been examined in several studies but not in relation to his doctrine of predestination. For example, T.H.L. Parker's classic study on *Calvin's Preaching* did not discuss the subject of preaching related to predestination at all.[28] Another example is Ronald Wallace's study of *Calvin's Doctrine of the Word and Sacrament*. In this work, he dealt with the "preached Word" and its twofold effect. According to Wallace, Calvin holds that God's words are heard out of the mouth of his servants in preaching when he sovereignly wills this. Wallace denied that the external call can lose its effect by not being received in faith. Instead, it has a power in and of itself, apart from receptive hearing, i.e., a power not only to save believers but also to condemn unbelievers. Thus, preaching has a twofold effect, and a preacher ought to have two voices: one to gather the sheep and one to drive away the wolves and thieves.[29] Although

---

23 Harald Rimbach, *Gnade und Erkenntnis in Calvins Prädestinationslehre: Calvin im Vergleich mit Pighius, Beza und Melanchthon* (Frankfurt am Main: Peter Lang, 1996).
24 Selderhuis (ed.), *Calvin Handbook*.
25 Mirjam G. K. van Veen, "Calvin and His Opponents," in *Calvin Handbook*, 156-64.
26 Wilhelm H. Neuser, "Predestination," in *Calvin Handbook*, 312-23. Cf. idem, "Calvin als Prediger: Seine Erklährung der Prädestination in der Predigt von 1551 und in der Institutio von 1559," in Michael Beintker (ed.), *Gottes freie Gnade: Studien zur Lehre von der Erwählung* (Wuppertal: Foedus, 2004), 69-91. Neuser also wrote an introduction with historical information in the COR edition of *De aeterna Dei praedestinatione*, COR III/1.
27 E.A. de Boer, "John Calvin's 'Disputatio de Praedestinatione': The Relevance of a Manuscript on his Doctrine of Providence and Predestination" in *Dutch Reformed Theological Journal/Nederduitse Gereformeerde Teologiese Tydskrif*, 2009, 580-94. Idem, *Genevan School*, 141-42.
28 T.H.L. Parker, *Calvin's Preaching* (Edinburgh: T&T Clark, 1992).
29 Ronald S. Wallace, *Calvin's Doctrine of the Word and Sacrament* (Edinburgh/London: Oliver and Boyd, 1953), 82-95.

a link with predestination seems obvious here, Wallace does not make it.

In his dissertation on the relationship between God and the hearers of God's Word in Calvin's sermons on Acts 4:1-6:7, Moehn points out that predestination did not make Calvin's preaching any less sure but even supported the idea of preaching to all since Calvin preached God's election "in the first-person plural." Moehn states that Calvin preached the promise "to all, without exception." But God does not fulfill his promises to those who do not believe them. The responsibility of the hearers is to believe God's promises. According to Moehn, Calvin stressed the human being's reaction to the Gospel.[30] Moehn also wrote a chapter on Calvin's sermons in *The Calvin Handbook* but did not mention predestination.[31] Michael Parsons studied Calvin's sermons on Micah but did not elaborate on his use of predestination and covenant in those sermons.[32]

V.A. Shepherd did take up the subject of predestination and preaching somewhat in his study to *The Nature and Function of Faith in the Theology of John Calvin*. Seeing that Calvin did not agree with his own theory of God's grace towards all people, Shepherd states that God, according to Calvin, is not to be taken at his word because God does not make his promise sincerely to all. Calvin failed to acquit God of the accusation of unrighteousness with respect to predestination.[33]

The covenant is what connects predestination and preaching in Calvin's thought. This subject has been researched in depth by Peter Lillback,[34] whose work is important not only for a helpful survey of conflicting interpretations of Calvin's use of the covenant but primarily for his analysis of the conditionality of the covenant and its relation to predestination. As I will argue in this chapter, in Calvin "covenant" and "external call" are used almost synonymously, and conditionality is the means by which Calvin shows that God's election of some is consistent with his honest call of many who are not elect.

---

30 W.H.T. Moehn, *God roept ons tot Zijn dienst: Een homiletisch onderzoek naar de verhouding tussen God en de hoorder in Calvijns preken over Handelingen 4:1-6:7* (Kampen: Kok, 1996), 277-90. English translation: *God Calls us to his Service: The Relationship between God and His Audience in Calvin's Sermons on Acts* (Geneva: Droz, 2001).
31 W.H.T. Moehn, "Sermons" in *Calvin Handbook*, 173-81.
32 Michael Parsons, *Calvin's Preaching on the Prophet Micah: The 1550-1551 Sermons in Geneva* (Lewiston: The Edwin Mellen Press, 2006).
33 V. A. Shepherd, *The Nature and Function of Faith in the Theology of John Calvin* (Macon, Georgia: Mercer University Press, 1983), 78, 87.
34 Peter A. Lillback, *The Binding of God: Calvin's Role in the Development of Covenant Theology* (Grand Rapids: Baker, 2001).

In addition to these works on an aspect of Calvin's theology, there are some studies of certain episodes in his life that are relevant to Calvin's view of predestination and the external call. G. Melles analyzes Calvin's debate with Pighius,[35] and P.N. Holtrop researched the Bolsec controversy.[36] It is in his debates with Pighius and Bolsec that Calvin is clearest in his statements concerning the external call in relation to predestination.

2.3 Outline of this Chapter

Almost all the works mentioned above contain remarks related to the subject of this study, but none discuss this subject completely and comprehensively. The main aim of this chapter is to do precisely that. Moreover, some of the conclusions of earlier research will be tested.

There are different ways to research Calvin's works for a study like this. One could focus on Calvin's *Institutes* of 1559 as a summary of his theology that he was satisfied with. Another way is to read his polemical works on this subject. A third option is to read his commentaries to see how Calvin dealt with texts that are relevant for this subject. Finally, one might read Calvin's sermons to see how he dealt with the subject of predestination while preaching.

Choosing only one of these ways provides too small a basis for conclusions. It is of course necessary to look at Calvin's polemical writings, but polemics tends to lead to one-sidedness. His polemical remarks need to be placed in the context of his theology. This theology could be summarized in Calvin's *Institutes*, but such an approach could leave the question unanswered as to how Calvin bases his theology on Scripture. Hence studying his commentaries is necessary. Researching both the *Institutes* and the commentaries is all the more necessary since Calvin regarded these works as two complementary projects.[37] But seeing how Calvin thought about the relation between predestination and preaching without researching how this worked out in the practice of his preaching would be unsatisfactory. Hence, we need to research Calvin's theological work in all its aspects.

Again, there are different ways to do this. The first is to read his works in chronological order to see how his theological thoughts on this subject

---

35 G. Melles, *Albertus Pighius en zijn strijd met Calvijn over het liberum arbitrium* (Kampen: Kok, 1973).
36 P. Holtrop, *The Bolsec Controversy on Predestination from 1551 to 1555* (Lewiston, N.Y., Edwin Mellen, 1993).
37 See Richard A. Muller, *The Unaccommodated Calvin: Studies in the Foundation of a Theological Tradition* (New York/Oxford: OUP, 2000), 101-17.

developed. The other is to read his works thematically. A combination of these two seems to me the best way to find an answer. Calvin did write some things in, for example, his commentaries related to the subject of this study that could be of interest, but he did not himself make that connection explicitly. To avoid drawing any premature conclusions about such statements, it seems that the best way to start investigating the different aspects of Calvin's answer to the question on predestination and preaching is to examine his polemical writings against Pighius, Bolsec, and Georgius. Once these aspects have been identified, they will be traced chronologically to see whether Calvin developed his view in answer to his opponents or based his answer on aspects of earlier ideas that are contracted into one argument. Calvin's sermons will be referred to throughout the different sections and examined in a separate section to see how his theory worked out in practice.

Given the large number of Calvin's sermons that have survived, we need to make a selection. For this study, I have chosen the sermons on Micah (1550-1551) and some of the sermons on Genesis (1559-1560) because the former series was delivered shortly before the Bolsec controversy (1551) and the latter series some years after – even after the final edition of Calvin's *Institutes*. Any possible development in the way Calvin dealt with predestination in his sermons can be expected to have taken place within this period.

As Calvin wrote, Pighius had stated that he could not believe in particular election because Christ commanded that the Gospel be preached to all men, promiscuously, generally and without distinction. This Gospel is, according to Pighius, preached so that those who hear it might be saved.[38] In his answer to Pighius's criticism, Calvin touched on at least six subjects related to predestination and preaching. These six subjects are very suitable for finding out Calvin's ideas on their relation. Other subjects will be introduced because of their relation to these six. The first subject is God's purpose in the preaching of the Gospel in relation to his decree of predestination (2.8). The second is the task of the preacher, who does not know who are elect and who are not (2.8). The third is the way the Gospel has to be administered (2.9 – 2.10). The fourth is the question whether or not predestination should be preached (2.13). The fifth is the relation between predestination and the response to preaching (2.11). The sixth is the positive reaction to preaching, i.e., faith: its object and nature (2.12). These sections are preceded by surveys of Calvin's doctrine of predestination (2.4), atonement (2.5), covenant (2.6), and church (2.7), the understanding of which is necessary to understand Calvin's view of

---

38 *De aeterna Dei praedestinatione*, CO VIII, 298; COR III/ 1, 106 (*CC*, 93-94).

preaching in relation to predestination. A summary of Calvin's theological ideas on predestination and preaching is given (2.14), which is followed by some sections on the questions whether and how Calvin's theological ideas affected his sermons. First, his commentary (written before the Bolsec controversy) on 1 Timothy 1: 4 is compared with his sermon on the same text (delivered after the Bolsec controversy) (2.15). Then his sermons on the book of Micah (dating before the Bolsec controversy) (2.16) and some of Calvin's sermons on Genesis (dating after this controversy) are examined (2.17), followed by a summary on theory and practice (2.18).

2.4 Calvin on Predestination
2.4.1 Definitions
Calvin wrote on the doctrine of predestination as early as 1536 when he published the first edition of the *Institutes*. The number of pages devoted to this subject expanded over the years. In the first edition, which was primarily a catechetical work, he did not treat predestination separately but as part of the doctrine of the church. In the edition of 1539, which was no longer a catechetical work but a study book for candidates for the ministry, he devoted a separate chapter to predestination and providence. In the edition of 1559, he separated predestination and providence, locating providence in Book I on the knowledge of God the Creator and predestination in Book III on the way in which the grace of Christ is received.[39] He also wrote on predestination in his commentaries and catechism.

In the first edition of the *Institutes* (1536) Calvin states:

> For even if at once from the beginning the human race was, by Adam's sin, corrupted and vitiated, yet from this as it were polluted mass, he sanctifies some vessels unto honor ...[40]

---

39 The possible reasons for and implications of this change in place have been discussed, for instance, in Graafland, *Van Calvijn tot Barth*, in Muller, *The Unaccommodated Calvin*, 101-39, and in Neuser in *Calvin Handbook*, 312-23. Muller argues that the addition of this chapter in 1539 was partly the fruit of Calvin's exegetical work, for at the same time that he was editing the *Institutes* for the second time, he was preparing a commentary on Romans, and partly the result of the change of the genre of the *Institutes*. It would be a kind of *loci communes* instead of a catechism. In giving these *loci* an *ordo recte docendi*, Calvin was very dependent in 1539 on the *Loci communes* of Melanchthon. Neuser correctly remarks that the different place for discussing predestination did not mean a different content, for, in the 1559 edition, Calvin took the complete text of the 1539 edition and expanded it. For my hypothesis on the place of predestination in the 1559 *Institutes* see 2.14.

40 *Institutes* 1536, II, 4. *CO* I, 74: "Nam etsi statim a principio hominum genus, Adae peccato, corruptum ac vitiatum est, ex hac tamen, ceu polluta massa, semper aliqua

The catechism of 1538 does not give any short definition of predestination, yet it does offer a good summary of Calvin's idea of predestination. Here, for the first time, Calvin mentions *praedestinatio gemina*, using the words *élection* and *reprouvez*. Election is why the seed of God's Word takes root and bears fruit, whereas reprobation is not introduced as an explanation of unbelief.[41] The reason behind God's decree is hidden from us, yet we know that it is a righteous decree. Assurance of salvation cannot be gained by penetrating God's decree but only by faith in Christ.[42] The second Latin edition of the *Institutes* (1539) contained this definition, which remained until the final 1559 edition:

> We call predestination God's eternal decree, by which he compacted with himself what he willed to become of each man. For all are not created in equal condition; rather, eternal life is foreordained for some, eternal damnation for others. Therefore, as any man has been created to one or the other of these ends, we speak of him as predestined to life or to death.[43]

In 1552, he defined the same doctrine as follows:

> God, by His eternal pleasure (which depends on no other cause), appointed those whom he pleased unto salvation, rejecting others ...[44]

---

vasa sanctificat in honorem ..." Translation by F.L. Battles (Atlanta: John Knox Press, 1975), 80. Calvin did not explicitly mention reprobation in this first definition.

41 This means that Calvin himself offers no basis for Neuser's conclusion that Calvin's stress on the Fall led him to use predestination as a cause for unbelief, as far as the catechism concerns. Neuser, *Calvin Handbook*, 312-23 See 2.1 note 4 for the quotation from Calvin. See 2.11note 127 for a quote from Calvin where he actually states that reprobation is a cause of unbelief.

42 *Instruction et Confession de Foy dont on Use en Leglise de Genève* (1538), CO XXII, 46-47; COR II/III, 32.

43 *Institutes*, III, xxi, 5. "Praedestinationem vocamus aeternum Dei decretum, quo apud se constitutum habuit, quid de unoquoque homine fieri vellet. Non enim pari conditione creantur omnes; sed aliis vita aeterna, aliis damnatio aeterna praeordinatur. Itaque, prout in alterutrum finem quisque conditus est, ita vel ad vitam vel ad mortem praedestinatum dicimus." (Book, chapter and section refer to the 1559 edition, wherein this definition was incorporated.)

44 *De aeterna Dei praedestinatione*, CO VIII, 261-62; COR III/ I, 20 (CC, 31) [1552]: "Deum aeterno suo beneplacito, cuius aliunde causa non pendet, quos illi visum est, destinasse ad salutem aliis reiectis."

Calvin added a description of predestination to his commentary on Romans in the 1556 edition:

> But the foreknowledge of God, which Paul mentions, is not a bare prescience, as some unwise persons absurdly imagine, but adoption by which he had always separated his children from the reprobate. [45]

Finally, in 1563, at the end of his life, Calvin stated in his lectures on Jeremiah:

> When Paul adduced this similitude, - that we are in the power of God as the clay is in the hand of the potter, he spoke not in so popular a manner: for he did not speak of repentance, but ascended higher and said, that before the world was created, it was in God's power to determine what he pleased respecting every individual, and that we are now formed according to his will, so that he chooses one and rejects the other. Paul then did not refer to faithfulness nor to repentance, but spoke of the hidden purpose of God, by which he has predestinated some to salvation and some to destruction (Romans 9:21).[46]

Despite differences in context and details, these quotes show that the essence of Calvin's doctrine of predestination remained the same: God choose some people to be saved (i.e., sanctified, adopted, appointed to salvation, predestined to life, predestined to salvation) and did not choose others.[47]

The only reason humans can perceive why God elected some and reprobated others is his pleasure. Sin is not the cause of reprobation, nor are faith or good works the causes of election. The just reasons for why God

---

45 Comm. on Romans 8:29 [1556]. "Dei autem praecognitio, cuius hic Paulus meminit non nuda est praescientia, ut stulte fingunt quidam imperiti: sed adoptio, qua filios suos a reprobis semper discrevit."
46 Lect. on Jeremiah 18:7-10 [1563]: "Paulus dum hanc similitudinem affert (Rom. 9, 21), nos esse in Dei potestate non secus atque lutum est in manu figuli, non loquitur ita populariter. Neque enim disputat de poenitentia, sed altius conscendit: nempe antequam creatus esset mundus, fuisse in arbitrio Dei statuere de singulis quid fieri vellet: nunc etiam nos formari pro eius arbitrio, ut alios eligat, alios reprobet. Paulus ergo illic neque fidem, neque poenitentiam attingit, sed concionatur de arcana Dei voluntate, qua alios ad salutem, alios ad interitum praedestinat."
47 This is also the content of article 3 of Calvin's "disputatio de providentia et praedestinatione" *CO* IX, 713-14. *COR* VII/1, 473-474. See De Boer, *Genevan School*, 133-11 for a discussion of these theses and 302-03 for a translation.

reprobated part of humankind are hidden from people. There is an inseparable connection between election and reprobation: one cannot accept the doctrine of election without accepting the doctrine of reprobation since electing some means, without doubt, leaving others behind or their reprobation.[48]

2.4.2 Calvin's use of the word 'reprobation'
Concerning Calvin's use of the word "reprobate" *(reprobus)* one should be cautious. When one compares the translations of Calvin's *Institutes*, for instance, by Beveridge and by Battles concerning the use of the word "reprobate," it will be seen that Battles used the word far more often than Beveridge. For instance, I, 5, viii contains a sentence which is translated by Battles as:

> And hence ground for rejoicing is given to the godly, while as for the wicked and the reprobate, their mouths are stopped.[49]

Beveridge translated the same sentence as follows:

> furnishing ground of joy to the righteous, and at the same time stopping the mouths of the ungodly.[50]

Calvin's Latin has:

> atque hinc piis dari materiam laetitiae, impiis vero et reprobis ora obstrui.

At first, Battles' translation seems to be more accurate since Beveridge did not translate the word *reprobis*. A second glance, however, shows Calvin does not place "elect" over against "reprobate" but "pious" over against "impious and reprobate." Calvin's own French translation has:

> que de là les fideles ont occasion de s'esiouir, & que la bouche est fermee à tous pervers.[51]

---

48 *Institutes*, III, xxiii, 1-5; *De aeterna Dei praedestinatione*, *CO* VIII, 295-296; *COR* III/I, 100 (*CC*, 89).
49 John Calvin, *Institutes of the Christian Religion*, edited by John T. McNeil, translated by Ford Lewis Battles (Philadelphia: Westminster Press, 1960).
50 John Calvin, *Institutes of the Christian Religion*, translated by Henry Beveridge (Edinburgh: T&T Clark, 1863; reprint: Grand Rapids: Eerdmans, 1989 [1995]).
51 Jean Calvin, *Institution de la religion chrestienne, nouvellement mise en quatre livres, et distinguée par chapitres, en ordre et methode bien propre. Augmentée aussi de tel*

Calvin himself did not translate the word *reprobis* separately, but translated the Latin words *impiis et reprobis* with one French equivalent, viz. *pervers*. So, he regarded the two Latin words as synonyms. It should be noted, therefore, that Calvin did not always use the word *reprobatus* and similar words in the doctrinal sense they later acquired but sometimes as meaning "impious" or "ungodly." This can be derived from the late Latin use of the word *reprobus* as referring to something that is to be rejected, like "false coin" (cf. Vulgate Jer. 6:30 *argentum reprobum*), or to persons who can be rejected on the basis of their faith (Vulgate 2 Tim. 3:8 *reprobi circa fidem*).

2.4.3 Supralapsarianism or Infralapsarianism?

In later Reformed theology, there were supralapsarians, who held that the decree of predestination preceded the decrees of creation and fall, and infralapsarians, who held that the decree of predestination followed the other two decrees.[52] Whether Calvin was a supra- or an infralapsarian is a matter of dispute. There are infralapsarian statements in his works, for instance in his lecture on predestination in 1551.[53] Yet when writing that not all people are created in the same condition but as preordained to eternal life or eternal death, he seems to have tended to supralapsarism.[54] When Calvin deals with the charge that according to him, "at [God's] mere pleasure men are, without any desert of their own, predestinated to eternal death,"[55] he did not deny this accusation, which suggests a tendency toward supralapsarism. In section 2 of his chapter on predestination in the *Institutes*, Calvin's first answer is that "the will of God is the supreme rule of righteousness." In section 3, however, he writes that "all whom the Lord predestines to death are naturally liable to the sentence of death," which seems to reflect infralapsarianism. Then, in section 4, he acknowledges that all things, even the Fall, have their cause in God's will, which again seems to tend to supralapsarianism.[56] Or maybe he consciously endorsed supralapsarianism but was reluc-

---

accroissement, qu'on la peut presque estimer un livre nouveau. Par Jean Calvin. (Geneva: Jacques Bourgeois, 1561).

52 For supra- and infralapsarianism, see W.J. van Asselt, "Infra- and Supralapsarianism," in K. Pollmann et al., *The Oxford Guide to the Historical Reception of Augustine from 430 to 2000, Part III* (Oxford: Oxford University Press, 2013) and my "The Doctrine of Predestination" in Selderhuis, *Companion*, 555.

53 COR VII/1, 90.

54 *Institutes*, III, xxi, 5.

55 *Institutes*, III, xxiii, 2: "si nudo eius arbitrio, citra proprium meritum, in aeternam mortem praedestinantur." (Translation Beveridge.)

56 *Institutes*, III, xxiii, 2-4: "summa est iustitiae regula Dei voluntas …" (2). "Quod si iudicio mortis obnoxii sunt omnes naturali conditione, quos ad mortem Dominus praedestinat …" (3). "atque id est quod principio dicebam, redeundum tandem sim-

tant to accept all the consequences, for, in section 8, he distinguishes between a remote (God's decree) and a proximate cause of sin (the Fall) and warns against going beyond the proximate cause. However, one should be aware that the question concerning the order of the decrees was not an actual question in Calvin's time. It seems that he did not made a conscious choice between supra- and infralapsarianism.

2.4.4. Steps in Election

Calvin distinguishes some steps *(gradus)* in election. The first was the election of Abraham and his seed out of all peoples to be his peculiar people. But some of Abraham's seed were reprobate, although they were included among God's people. This separation among Abraham's seed is the second step *(gradus)* of election. Those who are elected in the first way will know God and his covenant. But to those who are elected in the second way God not only offers salvation but assigns it in such a way that the certainty of the result remains neither dubious nor suspended.[57]

Calvin's remarks concerning these *gradus* can be visualized in three concentric circles. The outer circle reflects the reprobate world, the middle circle reflects the election of Abraham's posterity out of this world, and the smallest circle reflects the elect to salvation.

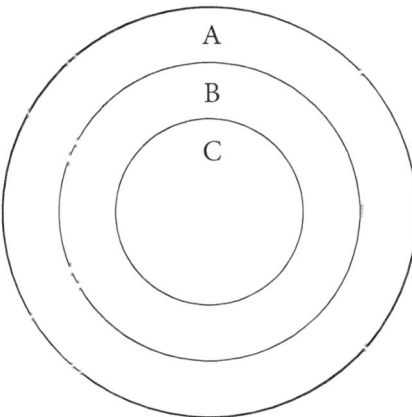

A: The world
B: Abraham's seed (first step of election / general election)
C: The elect to salvation (second step of election / special election)

---

per esse ad solum divinae voluntatis arbitrium, cuius causa sit in ipso abscondita…"
(4). (Translation: Beveridge)
57 *Institutes*, III, xxi, 5-7, xxii, 1; Comm. on Romans 9:6 [1540].

2.5 Predestination and the Extent of the Atonement

In later Reformed theology, the doctrine of the atonement by the death of Christ became closely associated with the doctrine of predestination. There is no consensus on whether Calvin taught general or particular atonement.[58] Since Christ is the main object of faith (as will be shown below, 2.12) his sacrifice is important for the content of the external call.

Earlier research does not agree on what Calvin taught on this subject. Some are persuaded that Calvin taught (hypothetical) universal atonement.[59] Others are just as persuaded that he taught limited atonement.[60] The amusing fact of this discussion is that both parties were very convincing in showing that the incorrectness of the opposite view but not as convincing in proving their own views to be true. In other words, what was proved was that Calvin taught neither limited nor universal atonement. This fact led two other scholars to the conclusion that Calvin did not have a consistent view of the atonement,[61] and that there are tensions in his theology on this point.[62]

In an article on Calvin's use of the classic sufficiency-efficiency formula, I pointed out that Calvin did not take any sides in this discussion on particular or general redemption since this subject was discussed only after his death.[63] The doctrines of limited or universal atonement were

---

58 For a survey of views see Pieter L. Rouwendal "Calvin's Forgotten Position on the Extent of the Atonement," *Westminster Theological Journal,* Vol. LXX, No. 2 (Fall 2008), 317-18 and Richard A. Muller, *Calvin and the Reformed Tradition: On the Work of Christ and the Order of Salvation* (Grand Rapids: Baker Academic, 2012), 70-73.

59 See, for example, R.T. Kendall, *Calvin and English Calvinism to 1649* (Oxford: Oxford University Press, 1979), and Allan C. Clifford, *Calvinus. Authentic Calvinism: A Clarification* (Norwich: Charenton Reformed Publishing, 1996).

60 See, for example, Roger Nicole, "John Calvin's View of the Extent of the Atonement," in *Standing Forth: Collected Writings of Roger Nicole* (Geanies House, Fearn, Ross-shire: Christian Focus Publications, 2002). This article was originally published in *Westminster Theological Journal,* Vol. XLVII, No. 2, Fall 1985. See also Paul Helm, *Calvin and the Calvinists* (Edinburgh: The Banner of Truth Trust, 1982 [1998]). Helm states that Calvin "did not *commit himself* to any version of the doctrine of definite atonement" but was "committed *to* that doctrine." In a somewhat more nuanced article, Helm later explains that he means that Calvin's "thought is consistent with that doctrine." Paul Helm, "Calvin, Indefinite Language, and Definite Atonement," in David Gibson and Jonathan Gibson (eds.), *From Heaven He Came and Sought Her: Definite Atonement in Historical, Biblical, Theological, and Pastoral Perspective* (Wheaton: Crossway, 2013), 97-120.

61 Hans Boersma, "Calvin and the Extent of the Atonement," *Evangelical Quarterly,* 64:4 (1992) 333-55.

62 Thomas, *Extent,* 12-40.

63 Rouwendal "Calvin's Forgotten Position," *Westminster Theological Journal,* Vol. LXX, No. 2 (Fall 2008), 317-35.

developed only after Calvin. The common view in the Middle Ages and during the Reformation was that Christ had died sufficiently for all but efficiently only for the elect alone. The atonement did have a universal import (Christ died sufficiently for all) as well as a particular one (Christ died effectively only for the elect). It was Beza who, in 1588, 24 years after the death of Calvin, was the first to criticize this classic formula. The doctrines of limited atonement, universal atonement, and hypothetical universal atonement were only developed after that time. Hence, it is an anachronism to read Calvin in these terms.

Since the doctrine of the atonement was not attacked or discussed in Calvin's time, there was no need for theological reflection on it. Since it was a *communis opinio* that Christ died sufficiently for all but efficiently only for the elect, it is plausible to say that whenever Calvin says that Christ died for all, he had the sufficient aspect in mind; and when he says that Christ died solely for the elect, it is safe to say that he was thinking about the efficient aspect. When Calvin is read this way, in his own time and context, there are no tensions or inconsistencies. They only arise when we start to question Calvin from a post-Calvinian dogmatic position.[64]

Reading Calvin on the question of atonement in his own time and context is what Richard Muller has done.[65] He argues that Calvin stresses that God's intention with Christ's all-sufficient offer on the cross was to save the elect, while the notion of sufficiency provided the basis for God's promise that whoever believes will be saved. This conclusion relates Calvin's use of the formula immediately to the external call, and hence we need to examine it here.

---

64 The main argument – derived from Voetius – in my "Calvin's Forgotten Position," i.e., that Calvin's position is to be distinguished from particular redemption as well as from universal redemption, has until now been largely neglected. For instance, Paul Helm in his "Calvin, Indefinite Language, and Definite Atonement," and Raymond Blacketer in his "Blaming Beza: The Development of Definite Atonement in the Reformed Tradition" in David Gibson and Jonathan Gibson (eds.), *From Heaven He Came and Sought Her*, 121-41, state again that Calvin was committed to particular atonement, while David L. Allen and David W. Ponter argue that Calvin held a universal view on the atonement, Allen inappropriately even used my article as an argument. See David L. Allen, "The Atonement: Limited or Universal," in David L. Allen and Steve W. Lemke. (eds.), *Whosoever Will: A Biblical-Theological Critique of Five-Point Calvinism* (Nashville: B&H, 2010) and David W. Ponter, "Review Essay: John Calvin on the Death of Christ and The Reformation's Forgotten Doctrine of Universal Vicarious Satisfaction: A Review and Critique of Tom Nettles' Chapter in Whomever He Wills" in *Southwestern Journal of Theology*, Volume 55, Number 1, Fall 2012, 139-159 (Part One), and Number 2, Spring 2013, 253-71 (Part Two).

65 Muller, *Calvin and the Reformed Tradition*, 70-106.

Calvin mentions the classic distinction between sufficiency for all and efficiency for the elect at least three times. In his commentary on 1 John 2:2, he acknowledges the truth of the distinction but denies that it was appropriate for this passage since "world" in this text refers only to believers and future believers who are scattered through various parts of the world and does not include the reprobate.⁶⁶ In his tract on predestination, he again argues that the distinction is true but does not help to untie the knot. For when it comes to the saving power of the Gospel, the question is not whether the Gospel is to be preached to all people but whether the power to believe is conferred on all people.⁶⁷ And the question with respect to Christ as the propitiation for the sins of the whole world is not what the virtue of Christ is in itself but who those who actually enjoy it are, i.e., believers or the elect.⁶⁸ Although acknowledging the truth of the classic formula, Calvin either rejects its applicability to the actual question or denies that it was really helpful. Over against those who used the distinction to argue for a general will in God to save all people unconditionally, Calvin argues for one will in God to save the elect.

In his comments on Bible texts that speak of Christ's death as being "for the whole world" or "for all people," or state that God wills the salvation of all, Calvin never saw these texts as opposed to the notion of God's predestination. We will examine his ideas on texts concerning the will of God in sections 2.8 and 2.15 below.

Calvin's comments on John 3:16 are an example of how he dealt with texts from Scripture that seem to extend salvation by Christ to the whole world. Calvin related the words "whoever" *(quis)* and "world" *(mundus)* in this text to the invitation of the Gospel that comes indiscriminately to all. Yet he immediately added that although life is promised universally to all who believe in Christ, faith is nevertheless not common to all but to the elect alone, whose eyes are opened by God.⁶⁹ Calvin indeed thought

---

66 Comm. on 1 John 2:2.
67 *De aeterna Dei praedestinatione,* CO VIII, 299; COR III/ 1, 107-08 (CC, 94-95).
68 *De aeterna Dei praedestinatione,* CO VIII, 336. COR III/ 1, 197-98 (CC, 165-66).
69 Comm. on John 3:16: "Et universalem notam apposuit, tum ut promiscue omnes ad vitae participationem invitet, tum ut praecidat excusationem incredulis. Eodem etiam pertinet nomen mundi quo prius usus est ... Caeterum meminerimus, ita communiter promitti omnibus vitam in Christo qui crediderint, ut tamen minime communis omnium sit fides. Patet enim omnibus Christus ac expositus est, solis tamen electis oculos Deus aperit, ut fide ipsum quaerant." *(And he has employed the universal term whosoever, both to invite all indiscriminately to partake of life, and to cut off every excuse from unbelievers. Such is also the import of the term World, which he formerly used ... Let us remember, on the other hand, that while life is promised universally to all who believe in Christ, still faith is not common to all. For Christ is made known and held out to the view*

the language expressing the universality of salvation or of Christ's offer were the basis for preaching the Gospel to all people, while at the same time he maintained that salvation was for the elect alone.[70]

2.6 Predestination and the Covenant

Earlier research did not agree on the importance of the covenant in Calvin's theology. Some thought that covenant theology was absent from Calvin's works, while others stated that the beginnings of such theology are to be found in Calvin's ideas. A third group maintained that Calvin developed an extensive if incomplete form of covenant theology.[71] The most recent research agrees that the concept of the covenant was important in Calvin's theology,[72] that this concept is related to his doctrine of predestination,[73] and that conditionality is part of it.[74] Graafland saw a relation between covenant, predestination and the external call.[75] Although Calvin did not devote a separate treatise or even chapter to the covenant anywhere in his complete oeuvre, these conclusions are reason enough to give special attention to Calvin's ideas on the covenant.[76]

---

of all, but the elect alone are they whose eyes God opens, that they may seek him by faith.)
70 In response to Helm's argument that Calvin's thought is consistent with definite atonement, I grant that Calvin's conscious reflections on this subject are indeed consistent with the doctrine of definite atonement that was developed later. But there are too many passages in his works that seem to reflect indefinite atonement to conclude that Calvin "was committed" to this doctrine. The development in his thought on this subject however, points in the direction of definite atonement.
71 See Lillback, *Binding of God*, 13-28, for previous research on Calvin and the covenant. The first group includes Heinrich Heppe and Perry Miller, the second Everett Emerson and Lyle Bierma, and the third group W. van den Bergh and Anthony Hoekema.
72 See, for instance, Graafland, *Van Calvijn tot Comrie*, 71-72 (1992). According to Lillback, "Calvin's hermeneutical application of the covenant is central to his entire system." *Binding of God*, 307. Andrew A. Woolsey states that Calvin's "entire system would be seriously undermined" without the covenant. See Andrew A. Woolsey, *Unity and Continuity in Covenantal Thought: A Study in the Reformed Tradition to the Westminster Assembly* (Grand Rapids: Reformation Heritage Books, 2012), 254.
73 Graafland, *Van Calvijn tot Comrie*, 147-70, 195. According to Graafland, the relation with predestination was "threatening (*bedreigend*) for the covenant" (195). Lillback however, in his *Binding of God*, 210-30, stated that "Calvin's use of the covenant was not hampered because of his belief in the doctrines of sovereign election and reprobation" (229). Woolsey acknowledges the relation without assigning it any value, *Unity and Continuity*, 318-35.
74 Graafland, *Van Calvijn tot Comrie*, 108-06; Lillback, *Binding of God*, 162-75; Woolsey, *Unity and Continuity*, 306-17.
75 Graafland, *Van Calvijn tot Comrie*, 110-17.
76 I largely follow Lillback, *Binding of God*, as an outstanding study of Calvin's concept of the covenant.

Calvin indeed connects election, covenant, and the external call of the Gospel very closely. In the opening sentence of the *Institutes,* book III, chapter XXI, on predestination, he cites election in order to explain why "the covenant of life is not preached equally to all" and why salvation is "offered" to some, while others have no access to it.[77] Other places confirm that Calvin saw a connection between election, the covenant, and the call.[78] The connection between election and covenant is so strong that

---

77 *Institutes,* III, xxi, 1. These sentences date from the edition of 1539: "Iam vero quod non apud omnes peraeque homines *foedus* vitae *praedicatur,* et apud eos quibus *praedicatur,* non eundem locum vel aequaliter vel perpetuo reperit, in ea diversitate mirabilis divini iudicii altitudo se profert. Nec enim dubium, quin aeternae Dei *electionis* arbitrio haec quoque varietas serviat. Quod si palam est Dei nutu fieri, ut aliis ultro *offeratur* salus, alii ab eius aditu arceantur, hic magnae et arduae protinus emergunt quaestiones, quae aliter explicari nequeunt, quam si de *electione ac praedestinatione* constitutum habeant piae mentes quod tenere convenit" (italics mine). *(In actual fact, the* covenant *of life is not* preached *equally among all men, and among those to whom it is* preached, *it does not gain the same acceptance either constantly or in equal degree. In this diversity the wonderful depth of God's judgment is made known. For there is no doubt that this variety also serves the decision of God's eternal election. If it is plain that it comes to pass by God's bidding that salvation is* freely offered *to some while others are barred from access to it, at once great and difficult questions spring up, explicable only when reverent minds regard as settled what they may suitably hold concerning* election and predestination.*)*

78 For example, compare these sentences in *Institutes,* III, xxi, 7: "[G]ratuita eius *electio,* donec ad singulas personas ventum fuerit, quibus Deus non modo salutem *offert,* sed ita assignat, ut suspensa vel dubia non sit effectus certitudo… Scite itaque Paulus ex Malachiae loco, quem nuper citavi, ratiocinatur, ubi Deus, interposito vitae aeternae *pacto,* populum quempiam ad se *invitat, specialem electionis modum* in parte subesse, ut non omnes promiscua gratia efficaciter *eligat…* Quod autem *generalis electio* populi non semper firma et rata sit, in promptu se offert ratio: quia cum quibus *paciscitur* Deus non protinus eos donat spiritu regenerationis, cuius virtute usque in finem in *foedere* perseverent; sed externa mutatio absque interiori gratiae efficacia, quae ad eos retinendos valida esset, *medium quiddam est inter abiectionem humani generis, et electionem exigui piorum numeri.* Haereditas Dei vocatus est totus populus Israel, ex quo tamen multi fuerunt extranei." (Italics mine.) *([His] free* election *has been only half explained until we come to individual persons, to whom God not only offers salvation but so assigns it that the certainty of its effect is not in suspense or doubt… Therefore Paul skillfully argues from the passage of Malachi that I have just cited that where God has made a* covenant *of eternal life and* calls *any people to himself, a* special mode of election *is employed for a part of them, so that he does not with indiscriminate grace effectually* elect *all… It is easy to explain why the* general election of a people *is not always firm and effectual: to those with whom God* makes a covenant, *he does not at once give the spirit of regeneration that would enable them to persevere in the* covenant *to the very end. Rather, the outward change, without the working of inner grace, which might have availed to keep them,* is intermediate between the rejection of mankind and the election of a meager number of the godly. *The whole people of Israel has been called "the inheritance of God", yet many of them were foreigners)* (reverse italics mine).

Calvin sometimes even treats these words as synonyms.[79]

It is hard to find the essence of Calvin's covenant theology. This part of his theology is, to say the least, complex and even called unclear by some.[80] However, at least five elements seem to be of importance. The first element is that the covenant is established with all those who are generally elect. Second, God promises something. Third, God requires something. Fourth, the covenant is in some way breakable and is broken indeed by all reprobates. Fifth, God himself effects the condition of the covenant in the elect. A summary of the first four elements is to be found in Calvin's commentary on Romans 9:6-9. We will quote the entire paragraph, for four of these elements can be found here immediately.

> The statement is, – that *the promise was so given to Abraham and to his seed* (1) that the inheritance did not belong to every seed without distinction; it hence follows that the defection of some does not prove that the covenant does not remain firm and valid. But that it may be more evident *on what condition the Lord adopted the posterity of Abraham as a peculiar people to himself,* (3) two things are to be here considered. The first is, *That the promise of salvation given to Abraham belongs to all who can trace their natural descent to him* (1, 2); for it is offered to all without exception, and for this reason they are rightly called the heirs of the covenant made with Abraham; and in this respect they are his successors, or, as Scripture calls them, the children of the promise. For since it was the Lord's will that his covenant should be sealed, no less in Ishmael and Esau, than in Isaac and Jacob, it appears that they were not wholly alienated from him; except, it may be, you make no account of the circumcision, which was conferred on them by God's command; but it cannot be so regarded without dishonour to God. But this belonged to them, according to what the Apostle had said before, "whose are the covenants," though they were unbelieving; and in Acts 3:25, they are called by Peter, the children of the covenants, because they were the descendants of the Prophets. The second point to be considered is, That the children of the promise are strictly those in whom its power and effect are found. *On this account Paul denies here that all the children of Abraham were the children of God, though a covenant had been made with them by the Lord, for few continued in the faith*

---

79 For example, *Institutes,* III, xxi, 5: "Saepe etiam odiose et probri loco hanc *electionem* prophetae Iudaeis obiiciunt, quoniam ab ea turpiter desciverant... Ad hoc etiam *principium gratuiti foederis* revocantur Israelitae ..." (italics mine). *(Also, the prophets often confront the Jews with this election, to the latter's displeasure and by way of reproach, since they had shamefully fallen away from it... Also, the Israelites are recalled to this principle of a freely given covenant ...)* (italics mine). See also the quotes in 2.6 notes 77 and 78.
80 For a survey of scholars who hold this view, see Lillback, *Binding of God,* 158-61.

of the covenant (3, 4); and yet God himself testifies, in the sixteenth chapter of Ezekiel, that they were all regarded by him as children. In short, when a whole people are called the heritage and the peculiar people of God, what is meant is, that they have been chosen by the Lord, *the promise of salvation having been offered them* (2) and confirmed by the symbol of circumcision; *but as many by their ingratitude reject this adoption, and thus enjoy in no degree its benefits* (4), there arises among them another difference with regard to the fulfillment of the promise. That it might not then appear strange to any one, that this fulfillment of the promise was not evident in many of the Jews, Paul denies that they were included in the true election of God.[81]

The fifth element is to be found in, for example, his commentary on Romans 11: 22:

But as he speaks not of the elect individually, but of the whole body, a *condition* is added, If they continued in his kindness. I indeed allow, that as soon as any one abuses God's goodness, he deserves to be deprived of the offered favor; but it would be improper to say of any one of the godly particularly, that God had mercy on him, when he chose him, provided he would con-

---

81 Comm. on Romans 9: 6-9 [1540]: "Propositio est, sic *datam esse Abrahae promissionem et semini eius*, ut non ad quodlibet semen haec spectet haereditas: unde consequetur, nihil impedire quorundam defectionem quo minus firmum et stabile foedus maneat. Sed quo melius pateat *qua conditione Dominus Abrahae posteritatem sibi in peculiarem populum adoptarit*: duo sunt hic consideranda, *promissionem salutis Abrahae datam ad omnes pertinere, qui ad eum carnis originem referunt*, quia omnibus sine exceptione offeratur: atque hac ratione iure appellari foederis cum Abrahamo percussi haeredes ac successores, sive (ut scriptura loquitur) promissionis filios. Nam quum Dominus voluerit foedus suum non minus in Ismaele et Esau quam in Isaac et Iacob obsignari, apparet non fuisse penitus ab ipso alienos: nisi forte pro nihilo habeas circumcisionem, quae illis Dei mandato communicata fuit: quod sine Dei contumelia dici non potest. Atque id erat quod antea dicebat apostolus, eorum esse pacta, etiamsi infideles forent. Et Act. 3 vocantur a Petro filii pactorum, quod essent prophetarum progenies. Alterum est, filios promissionis proprie nuncupari in quibus ipsius virtus et efficacia exstet. *Ea ratione hic negat Paulus omnes Abrahae filios esse filios Dei, etiamsi pactum cum illis initum esset a Domino: quia pauci in fide testamenti stabant*: quum tamen omnes sibi esse filiorum loco testetur Deus ipse apud Ezechielem capite 16. In summa, ubi totus populus vocatur haereditas et peculium Dei, significatur cooptatum esse a Domino, *oblata salutis promissione* et circumcisionis symbolo confirmata. *Sed quia multi eorum sua ingratitudine adoptionem illam repudiant*, ideoque eius beneficio minime fruuntur, inde emergit inter ipsos altera differentia, dum promissionis impletio respicitur. Eam ergo impletionem in plurimis Iudaeorum non apparere ne cui mirum videatur, Paulus eos esse comprehensos in vera Dei electione negat" (italics and enumereration mine).

tinue in his mercy; *for the perseverance of faith, which completes in us the effect of God's grace, flows from election itself.*[82]

His other works show that these elements are important for the whole of his covenant theology.[83] The conditionality of the covenant is a frequently recurring element in Calvin's theology.[84] Calvin frequently uses *hac lege* to

---

82 Comm. on Rom. 11: 22-24 [1556]: "Quia autem de singulis electis non disputat, sed de toto corpore, additur *conditio*, si in lenitate permanserint. Fateor quidem, simul ac De bonitate quispiam abutitur, dignum esse qui privetur oblata gratia: sed improprie de aliquo piorum hoc specialiter dictum foret, Deum eius misertum esse quum eum elegit, si modo in misericordia permaneat. *Nam fidei perseverantia, quae effectum gratiae Dei in nobis complet, ex electione ipsa manta*" (italics mine).
83 See Lillback, *Binding of God*, 126-41.
84 See, for instance, the following quotations.
Comm. on Romans 3: 3 [1540]. "Proinde, utcunque maior pars Dei foedus fefellerit ac proculcarit, ipsum nihilominus efficaciam suam retinere ac vim suam exercere: si non in omnibus, saltem in ipsa gente. Vis autem est, ut Domini gratia et in aeternam salutem benedictio inter eos vigeat. *Id autem esse non potest nisi ubi fide promissio recipitur, atque ita confirmatur [utrinque mutuum] foedus.*" (Italics mine; the words between [ ] were added in 1556.) *(Though then the greater part had nullified and trodden under foot God's covenant, it yet retained its efficacy and manifested its power, not indeed as to all, but with regard to a few of that nation: and it is then efficacious when the grace or the blessing of the Lord avails to eternal salvation. But this cannot be, except when the promise is received by faith; for it is in this way that a mutual covenant is on both sides confirmed.)*
Comm. on Acts 3:23 [1552]: "Nam sibi Deus *hac lege* adoptaverat Abrahae genus, ut hoc ad summam felicitatem sufficeret, reputari in illo numero ..." (italics mine). *(For God had adopted the stock and kindred of Abraham unto himself, upon this condition, that this might be sufficient for them unto the chiefest felicity to be reckoned in that number ...)*
Comm. on Acts 10:43 [1552]: "Et scimus, *hac lege* nos adoptari a Deo in filios, ut spiritu nos suo gubernet" (italics mine). *(And we know that we are adopted by God to be his children upon this condition, that he may govern us by his Spirit.)*
Comm. on Gen. 17: 1 [1554]: "Nam *hac lege* filios sibi adoptat ut vicissim patris obtineat locum et honorem. Sicut autem ipse non mentitur, ita iure mutuam fidem a suis exigit" (italics mine). *(For on this condition, he adopts children as his own, that he may, in return, obtain the place and the honour of a Father. And as he himself cannot lie, so he rightly demands mutual fidelity from his own children.)*
Sermon on Gal. 1:3-5 [1557]: *CO* L, 159: "Il faut donc que les fideles s'adonnent à toute pureté de vie, et qu'ils cognoissent qu'estans rachetez par nostre Seigneur Iesus Christ, et par le sacrifice de sa mort et passion, c'est à ceste *condition* qu'ils renoncent à eux-mesmes" (italics mine). *(The faithful therefore must give themselves to all pureness of life, and consider that the redeeming of them by our Lord Jesus Christ, and by the sacrifice of his death and passion, is upon condition that they should forsake themselves ...)*; translation by Arthur Golding (Audubon: Old Paths Publications 1996, reprint of a translation of 1574).

indicate the condition. The Latin words for covenant, condition, and law (*foedus, conditio, lex*) were closely related, with *lex* and *foedus* even being treated sometimes as synonyms by, for instance, Calvin's contemporary, the Reformed theologian Wolfgang Musculus.[85] It is the fulfilling of the condition that actually differentiates between the elect and the reprobate in history. One can enter the covenant by true faith, by hypocritical faith, and by being born in a Christian home. The reprobate who do not have true faith do not fulfill the condition and thus break the covenant. The elect fulfill the condition by God's grace and thus keep his covenant.[86]

The covenant is usually made with a community, and not with individuals. Individual partakers of the covenant can break it. Nevertheless, God's covenant will stand, for he will effect the condition in at least some of the covenant community. Not attaining the blessings of the covenant does not mean that the covenant is defective. Rather, it points to a defect in human beings. Those who are cut off from the covenant are cut off by their own defects and guilt, for while they know the condition of faithfully keeping God's covenant, they do not meet that condition.[87]

Adoption into the covenant does not mean an indissoluble bond with Christ. For all those who are joined with Christ will never be cut off from salvation, while the covenant can be broken. Nor does adoption into the covenant mean that the gifts of regeneration and perseverance are given to all members of the covenant.[88] One cannot be sure of one's salvation on the basis of one's inclusion in God's covenant, for that covenant requires perseverance but does not guarantee it. One could fall out of the covenant in the future. One cannot use the covenant as a basis to rejoice in the forgiveness of sins, for being in the covenant does not automatically imply that one is joined with Christ. Knowledge that one is in the covenant cannot be the basis for the assurance of being among the elect, for being

---

Comm. on Is. 41:9 [1559]: "Itaque meminerimus nos hac *conditione* electos a Deo esse, ut permaneamus in eius familia, tametsi possemus merito abdicari" (italics mine). *(Let us therefore remember that we have been elected by God on this condition, that we shall continue in his family, though we might justly have been abandoned.)* Obviously, Calvin talks about common election here, which is to be identified with the covenant.

85 See Lewis and Short, *Latin Dictionary* on "lex," meaning D, "*A contract, agreement, covenant*" and E, "*A condition, stipulation.*" For the use of these words by Musculus, see Jordan J. Ballor, *Covenant, Causality and Law: A Study in the Theology of Wolfgang Musculus* (Göttingen: Vandenhoeck & Ruprecht, 2012).
86 See Lillback, *Binding of God*, 221-25.
87 *Institutes*, III, xxi, 6; Comm. on Rom. 9:3, 11:22; see Lillback, 134-37, 162-75, 214-30.
88 *Institutes*, III, xxi, 7 (quoted in 2.6 note 78); see Lillback, *Binding of God*, 215-17.

elect in the general sense of being a member of the covenant community does not automatically translate into being elect in the special sense of salvation.

Nevertheless, Calvin is very clear in arguing why one should not regard it as vain and unprofitable to be included in God's covenant. God's plan to save sinners applies only to members of the covenant community.[89] In other words, we can summarize Calvin's position by stating that the covenant is God's means to salvation, assurance, perseverance, etc. For Calvin, God's covenant is a means or a way to an end; it is not an end in itself. It occupies a middle position between particular election and reprobation and between salvation and damnation. The importance and weight of the covenant according to Calvin – as well as the possibility that the covenant gives an individual no profit – can be illustrated by his words on Ishmael:

> Lo then Ismael who was circumcised: as much as was on God's behalf, he received the sacrament that might assure him that God accounted him of the number of his children, that he was a member of Jesus Christ, that the curse which he had drawn from Adam, was abolished: yea but this stood him in no stead at all.[90]

The word "might" *(pouvoit)* is important here. Calvin did not say that Ishmael *was* assured as to being included among God's children. He *could have been* assured by the sacrament of the covenant, but Ishmael did not keep God's covenant, he violated the condition and was thus cut off from adoption.[91]

Just like Calvin's view on the *gradus* in election, his view of the covenant can be visualized in three concentric circles. The outer one reflects the reprobate world, the middle one the covenant-community in which the promises are offered conditionally, and the inner circle reflects the elect to whom the accomplishment of the condition is given by free grace.

---

89 *Institutes,* III, xxi, 7; Comm. on Romans 9:7.
90 *Treze sermons de M. I. Calvin tractans de l'election gratuite de Dieu en Iacob, et de la reiectrion en Esau, CO* LVIII, 36: "Voila Ismael qui est circonci: quant est du costé de Dieu, il a receu un sacrement qui le pouvoit asseurer que Dieu le tenoit du nombre de ses enfans, qu'il estoit membre de Iesus Christ, que la malediction qu'il avoit tiree d'Adam estoit abolie. Voire-mais si est-ce que cela ne lui a de rien servi." (English translation by John Field, *Sermons on Election and Reprobation* (Audubon: Old Paths Publications, 1996, reprint of a translation of 1579).
91 *Institutes,* III, xxi, 6.

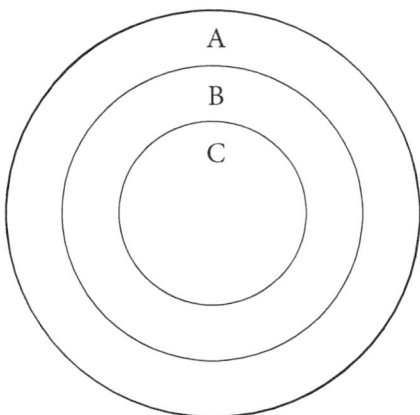

A: The world
B: The covenant, conditionality
C: Election, granting the accomplishment of the condition by free grace.

Considering Calvin's view of the covenant and conditionality, it is remarkable that he did not use this concept of conditionality when he was accused by Joachim Westphal of making the effect of the sacraments dependent on election. In his 1556 answer to Westphal, Calvin denied he did so. It would take us beyond the limits of this study to explore the reasons why Calvin did not use this concept of conditionality in relation to the sacraments in this dispute, but it is worth noting that Calvin, though he clearly cited this concept throughout his life, does not use it in this controversy on the sacraments as he had done in controversies with Pighius and Bolsec on the promises in the external call in 1544 and 1551.[92] A possible reason is that Westphal attacked Calvin with respect to baptized children who cannot, while infants, fulfill the conditions.

2.7 Predestination and Church
In book IV of the *Institutes* of 1559, Calvin deals with the church in a way that was already contained *in nuce* in the first edition.[93] The church consists of all God's elect, both alive and dead. Everyone should join the outward community of believers and believe the one Catholic Church in that

---

92 For Calvin's controversy with Westphal, see Wim Janse, "The Controversy between Westphal and Calvin on Infant Baptism (1555-1556)," in *Perichoresis* 6.1. (2008), 3-43.
93 For a survey of Calvin's ecclesiology, see Georg Plasger, "Ecclesiology," in *Calvin Handbook*, 323-32. Plasger mentioned the relation between predestination and church but not that between covenant and church.

way, that he is himself a member of it. The knowledge of who really belongs to the church must be left to God: He alone knows his people. Humans cannot know the true members of the church and should not try to do so.[94]

Thus, Calvin distinguishes between the "true" or invisible church of the elect and the "outward" or visible church in which not all are elect.[95] This reminds us of Calvin's view of the two steps *(gradus)* of election. The first was the election of Abraham and his seed. God chooses one people out of all others to be his peculiar people. This is an election of a community, in the Old Testament the community of Abraham's seed; in the New Testament that of the (visible) church. The second step was God's election of certain individuals whom God will bring to eternal life. In other words, Calvin's two forms of election (community-individual) correspond with the two forms of the church (visible-invisible).

Calvin did not speak of two churches but of one church, whose members are the elect. But all who confess their faith, walk according to the Gospel, and partake of the sacraments should be judged with charity to be members of the church, for we cannot know who are the elect. Even if we see ungodly people in the church, whom we cannot believe to be true members of the church, we should treat them as brothers and sisters as long as they have a legitimate place among believers. We should judge the individuals of the church with charity, but we should judge the community of the church by certain marks, i.e., the pure preaching of God's Word and the pure administration of the sacraments. The reprobates who join the outward community of believers should be counted as Christ's sheep, not because they really are his sheep but because they are found among the sheep.[96]

Calvin's doctrine of the church is closely related to his doctrine of the covenant and predestination. But it was not the case that the doctrine of predestination influenced his ecclesiology; rather, it was precisely the reverse. The doctrine of election was treated in the context of ecclesiology in the first edition of the *Institutes*. There Calvin wrote about the one catholic church, the elect, who are united with Christ and each other. It is from these remarks on predestination in the first chapter on the church that the chapters on election in the later editions evolved.

That Calvin's ecclesiology influenced his doctrine of predestination is also clear from the first sentences of Calvin's chapter on election in the

---

94 *Institutes* IV, i, 1-4, 7.
95 For instance, *Institutes,* IV, i, 5.
96 *Institutes,* III, xxiv, 9; IV, i, 9-10.

1559 edition of the *Institutes*.[97] Here, Calvin first shows the reader some empirical facts, i.e., that the Gospel is not preached everywhere and that not everyone who hears it accepts it. This experience is explained by predestination. From statements like this and, moreover, from the development of the doctrine of predestination from a chapter on the church, we can conclude that Calvin's doctrine of predestination did not influence his doctrine of the church. Rather, his (ecclesiastical) experience influenced both his doctrines of predestination and of the church.

Calvin's view of the relation of predestination to the church is bound up with his view of the preaching of the Gospel in two ways. First, the fact that the Gospel is preached in some places and not in others is in accordance with God's predestinating will. Second, the fact that, of those who hear the preaching of the Gospel, some believe and some do not is also in line with God's predestination. These two relations between church and predestination again reflect the two steps of predestination.

Calvin's view of the church can again be visualized in three concentric circles. The outer circle reflects the world, the middle the visible church, and the inner circle the invisible church of true believers.

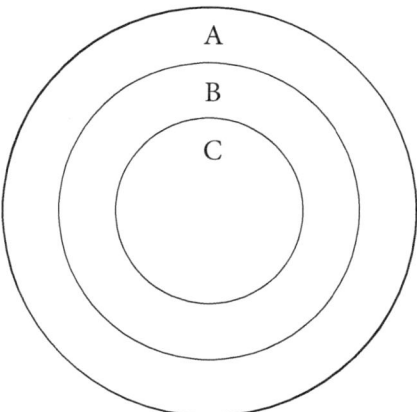

A: The world
B: The visible church of believers and hypocrites
C: The invisible church of true believers

We can now integrate the circles we discussed above in relation to predestination and covenant with these here. In all cases, each circle reflects the

---

97 See 2.6 note 77 for the quotation.

same group of people. The outer circle is the world of all people. Most of them are left in sin and ignorance (reprobation). God established his covenant with some people – the middle circle. The Gospel is preached to them, and they receive the sacraments. They are elect in a general sense, and salvation is promised to them if they continue in the covenant and accomplish the conditions of faith and repentance. To some of these people in the middle circle, who are elect to salvation, God unconditionally bestows the power to accomplish the conditions. They receive faith and act on faith, whereby they will be saved and God preserves them in his covenant.[98]

This scheme, of course, falls short since it presents Calvin's idea in a static way, which it is not. Although the number of the elect in God's council is indeed static, its number in history is not. In history, the line between the world and Abraham's seed/covenant/visible church is continuously crossed by those who break the covenant or by those who join the church. The border of the inner circle is also continuously crossed – but only in one direction: God continues to add people to the number of true believers. In other words, the two steps of election establish the historical circles of the covenant and of the true believers by continuously changing them.

The boundaries of the circles are, of course, not real boundaries since the inner and middle circles are part of the middle and the outer circle respectively. The elect, the true believers or the members of the invisible church, all belong to the middle circle of the covenant or the visible outer circle of all people.

2.8 God's Purpose and the Preacher's Purpose in Preaching

Calvin denies Pighius's idea that God's purpose in preaching is that all who hear the Gospel might believe and be saved. If this is what God wanted, he would give faith to all humans. But since God does not give faith to all who hear the Gospel, it is clear that his purpose in having the Gospel preached to all is not that all will believe and thus be saved. God's purpose in preaching the Gospel to both the elect and the reprobate differ from each other. With respect to the elect, it is that they might believe and

---

98 The three circles can also be applied to the classes of people Calvin mentions with respect to justification, for, although he mentions four classes, he combines the second and the third. The first class are those in the outer circle, i.e., those who do not know God. The people in the second class are included in the covenant but in name only since they deny God by the vileness of their life. Those in the third class are hypocrites. The second and third classes are included in the middle circle. The fourth class are those who are truly regenerated. *Institutes*, III, xiv, 1, 7, 9.

be saved, and preaching is a means to this end. God's purpose in having the Gospel preached to the reprobate is not to save them. God does not give them the inward teaching of the Spirit. They only hear a human being; they do not learn from God. God withholds this internal teaching from them, so that they might be hardened.[99]

Calvin answered Pighius' charge that he was teaching two opposite wills in God by pointing to the conditional structure of the promise of salvation (see 2.9 and 2.10). The fact that God tells us in his Word that he wants all people to be saved and that he decreed in his council that some people will not be saved does not mean that God has two wills. The claims "that God does not want the death of a sinner" and "that he wants the sinner to turn from his ways" should be read in connection with each other. Since, as a Lawgiver, God has pleasure in the repentance of all, he can be said to have pleasure in the eternal life of all. But this does not conflict with his secret counsel to bestow repentance only on the elect.[100]

The question of the alleged two wills in God was also answered by Calvin in his *Institutes* and in a sermon on 1 Timothy 2:3, 4 (1554/1555). The sections 15-17 of III, 24 in the *Institutes* of 1559 were new or rewritten and show much similarity with Calvin's tract on predestination (1552). Calvin proceeded with his reply to Pighius in his *Institutes* after his controversy with Bolsec and Georgius.[101] It seems this controversy was the reason why he added or rewrote some sections. Given this similarity, we will pass over these sections. Calvin's sermon on 1 Timothy 2:3, 4 will be examined at the end of this chapter (2.15).

Calvin's writings dating from before the controversy with Pighius did not treat this subject as clearly as his anti-Pighian writings did. Yet the basic elements are to be found in his commentary on Romans 10:16

---

99 *Institutes*, III, xxii, 10; xxiv, 12-14; *Defensio* [1543], *CO* VI, 252-54, 344-46, 381-82, 396; *COR* IV/ III, 99-102, 238-41, 295-96, 316; *De aeterna Dei praedestinatione* [1552], *CO* VIII, 261-62, 298-99, 325-26, 329-31, 336-37, 340-41, 344; *COR* III/I, 21, 107-08, 170-72, 179-85, 197-200, 206-08, 215-16 (*CC*, 31, 94-95, 144-46, 152-57, 166, 173-74, 181); *De Scandalis* [1550], *CO* VIII, 38-40.

100 *De aeterna Dei praedestinatione, CO,* VIII, 301; *COR* III/I, 113 (*CC*, 100): "Caeterum id cum arcano ipsius consilio non pugnat ... tamquam legislator omnes externa vitae doctrina illuminet, ad vitam omnes priore modo vocet: hoc autem altero quos vult adducat, tanquam pater regenerans spiritu filios duntaxat suos." *(Now all this does not conflict with His counsel ... because as a Lawgiver, He enlightens all men with the external doctrine of life. In this primary manner He calls all men unto life. But, in the latter manner, He brings unto life those whom He willed, as a Father, regenerating by His Spirit His own children only.)*

101 Compare for instance *Institutes*, III, xxiv, 15-16 with *De aeterna Dei praedestinatione*, *CO* VIII, 300-01; *COR* III/I, 110-13 (*CC*, 98-100).

(1540).¹⁰² Calvin's controversy with Pighius seems to have been the occasion for deeper reflection on and refinement of his thought on the issue of God's purpose in preaching.

The preacher does not and cannot know who is elect and who is reprobate, but he has to preach to both. Without being urged by Pighius or anyone else, Calvin introduces the question what a preacher should do when he realizes that there might be elect and reprobate among his hearers but is ignorant of who these elect and reprobate are. The occasion was a quote from Augustine on the use of preaching the doctrine of predestination. According to Calvin, one should not neglect Augustine's words to the effect that the preacher ought to desire that all be saved since he does not know who is predestined and who is not. The preacher should desire to make whoever crosses his path a partaker of God's peace.¹⁰³ It is God's command that the Gospel be preached to all and that all people be exhorted to repent and believe.¹⁰⁴

---

102 Comm. on Romans 10:16 [1540]. *CO* IL, 206: "Rationem tamen postea notat quum addit: Brachium Domini cui revelatum est? Significa: enim non aliter exstare verbi profectum, nisi dum spiritus sui luce Deus affulget, atque ita ab externa hominis voce distinguitur interior vocatio, quae sola efficax est et solis electis propria. Unde facile liquet quam stulte quidam ratiocinentur, promiscue electos esse omnes, quia universalis est salutis doctrina, et promiscue omnes ad se Deus invitat. Neque enim promissionum generalitas sola et per se communem omnibus salutem facit: quin potius eam ad electos restringit peculiaris ista revelatio, cuius meminit propheta." *(He however does afterwards point out the reason, by saying, "To whom has the arm of the Lord been revealed?" by which he intimates that there is no benefit from the word, except when God shines in us by the light of his Spirit; and thus the inward calling, which alone is efficacious and peculiar to the elect, is distinguished from the outward voice of men. It is hence evident, how foolishly some maintain, that all are indiscriminately the elect, because the doctrine of salvation is universal, and because God invites all indiscriminately to himself. But the generality of the promises does not alone and by itself make salvation common to all: on the contrary, the peculiar revelation, mentioned by the Prophet, confines it to the elect.)*

103 Calvin quotes from Augustine's *De correptione et gratia*, chapter 15. *De aeterna Dei praedestinatione, CO,* VIII, 328; *COR* III/1, 176 (*CC*, 150): "Quia nescimus quis ad praedestinatorum numerum pertineat, vel non pertineat, sic nos affici decere, ut omnes velimus salvos fieri. Ita fiet, ut quisquis nobis occurret, eum studeamus facere pacis consortem." *(Since we know not (says he) who belongeth to the number of the predestinated, and who doth not, we ought to feel as to wish all to be saved. From this it will come to pass that whosoever shall come in our way, we shall desire to make him a partaker of the peace which we ourselves enjoy.)*

104 *De aeterna Dei praedestinatione, CO,* VIII, 344; *COR* III/1, 215 (*CC*, 180): "[E]t tamen, quousque revelationis dies advenerit, agendum quod Dominus mandat, ut sine exceptione ad poenitentiam et fidem omnes hortemur. Communis enim omnibus est doctrina: et hac lege apud nos deposita est, donec qui reprobi sunt deplorata

Not only should a preacher wish all to be saved, but all members of the church should even be treated as partakers of God's covenant.[105] This does not mean that Calvin regards them all as true believers. The congregation consists of people who enter the covenant community by true faith, by hypocritical faith, or by being born in the covenant community. All must be exhorted to repentance and faith without distinction; but not all should be exhorted without distinction to regard themselves as true believers. The community is treated as partaking of God's covenant. The covenant community holds a middle position between the rejection of the human race and the election of a small number. Calvin addresses the community as a whole in his sermons, rather than individuals. This is rooted in his view of the covenant. How this notion takes shape is the application in preaching of the conditionality of the covenant.

2.9 The Mode of Preaching the Gospel: Conditionally and Unconditionally

Among other arguments against Calvin's doctrine of predestination, Calvin named an objection of Pighius that Christ commanded to preach the Gospel to all men, indiscriminately, generally, and without distinction. According to Pighius, this Gospel is preached so that those who hear it might be saved. He could not believe that the same God who commanded this Gospel to be preached to all elected some and reprobated others.[106]

Calvin agreed that the nature of the preaching of the Gospel provided the best basis for judging the universality of the grace of Christ. By its very nature, this Gospel is able to save all. Nevertheless, not all are saved, and this is according to God's eternal counsel. Therefore, we have to understand the principle on which the doctrine of the Gospel offers salvation to all, according to Calvin. The promise of salvation is preached to all who are in the covenant or to all who are elect in a general sense. Christ is presented to all, as the only One who can reconcile sinners to God, and all are called to repentance and faith. But the Gospel is a power

---

    obstinatione viam nobis obstruant." *(For until the day of the revelation of the issues shall come, our duty is to do what God commandeth: to exhort all men, without exception, to repentance and faith. For the doctrine and preaching of the gospel belong to all men, and are for the benefit of all men; and for those ends are they committed unto us, to be openly declared by us, even until the reprobate shall, by their deplorable obstinacy, block up our way and shut the door.)*

105 See sections 2.6 and 2.7.
106 *De aeterna Dei praedestinatione, CO,* VIII, 298; *COR* III/1, 106 (*CC*, 93-94). Pighius's objection is quoted via Calvin, since it is not Pighius's actual objection but Calvin's response that is important for this study.

unto salvation only to everyone who believes. Although mercy is offered to believers and non-believers, only the believers obtain mercy.[107] The others are simply rendered inexcusable; they are not saved. Thus, salvation is offered on the condition of faith.

Calvin himself called faith a condition in his comments on Ezekiel 18: 23 in *De aeterna Dei praedestinatione*.[108] In this text, according to Calvin, God did not state that he wanted all sinners or all people to be saved. When God says that he does not will the death of a sinner but that the sinner should return and live, God is speaking in a conditional sense. Just as God's threats did not turn into real punishments when sinners repented, so it is with respect to the promises that invite all people to be saved. These promises "do not positively prove that which God has decreed in his secret counsel, but declare only what God is ready to do to all those who are brought to faith and repentance."[109] God requires conversion from all people. He takes pleasure in repentant sinners and promises salvation to all who repent. In this way, he enlightens people with the doctrine of life and invites all men to eternal life. The promise of salvation is in this (conditional) way preached to all, but salvation is not promised

---

107 *De aeterna Dei praedestinatione, CO*, VIII, 298-99; *COR* III/1, 106-07 (*CC*, 94-95): "Quare in eo sita est nodi solutio, si tenemus quomodo salutem omnibus offerat evangelii doctrina. Equidem omnibus sua natura salvificam esse non nego. Tantum hoc quaeritur: an Dominus aeterno suo consilio communem illic omnibus salutem destinaverit. Vocari omnes indifferenter ad poenitentiam et fidem: proponi omnibus eundem mediatorem, qui patri ipsos reconciliet, satis notum est: sed aeque notum est, nihil nisi fide percipi: ut illud Pauli impleatur: Evangelium esse Dei potentiam in salutem omni credenti (Rom. 1: 16)." *(If we see and acknowledge, therefore, the principle on which the doctrine of Gospel offers salvation to all, the whole sacred matter is settled at once. That the Gospel is, in its nature, able to save all I by no means deny. But the great question lies here: Did the Lord by His eternal counsel ordain salvation for all men? It is quite manifest that all men, without difference or distinction, are called to repentance and faith. It is equally evident that the same Mediator is set forth before all, as He who alone can reconcile them to the Father. But it is as fully well known that none of these things can be understood or perceived but by faith, in fulfillment of the apostle Paul's declaration that "the Gospel is the power of God unto salvation to every one that believeth".)*
108 In his lectures on Ezekiel 18:23 [1565], Calvin did address this question briefly in the same way. *CO*, XL, 445-46.
109 *De aeterna Dei praedestinatione, CO*, VIII, 300-01; *COR* III/1, 112-13; (*CC*, 98-99): "Sed tales loquendi formas conditionales esse … Ita rursum promissiones, quae omnes ad salutem invitant, non simpliciter nec praecise quid in arcano suo consilio statuerit Deus, sed quid omnibus ad fidem et poenitentiam adductis facere paratus sit, demonstrant."

unconditionally to all. Hence this promise is not made to all men generally and indiscriminately.[110]

This way of preaching (the promises of) salvation to all is consistent with the decree of predestination by which God decreed to save none but the elect. Although he requires faith and repentance from all men, he bestows faith and salvation only on his elect.[111] This reflects Calvin's concept of the conditional covenant. The conditional promise is preached to all. It explains why Calvin could make the covenant and the external invitation of the Gospel into virtual synonyms.[112] The conditional structure of the promise or offer of the Gospel is to be found in several of Calvin's works.[113] This proves again that conditionality is an important issue in

---

110 *De aeterna Dei praedestinatione, CO*, VIII, 301; *COR* III/1, 113 (*CC*, 100).
111 *De aeterna Dei praedestinatione, CO*, VIII, 298-91, 301; *COR* III/1, 106-07,113 (*CC*, 94-95, 99-101). The argument by V.A. Shepherd against Calvin's ideas on the relation between predestination and preaching is virtually the same as that of Pighius. He also argues that God, according to Calvin, is not to be taken at his word. Shepherd tries to convince his readers that Calvin taught only one will in God – the will of mercy – but fails to see that the (non-meritorious) conditionality of the promises is essential for Calvin's thought on this issue. In fact, Shepherd's critique of Calvin is a result of his not accepting Calvin's conditional language. Cf. Shepherd, 39-90.
112 See section 2.6.
113 Comm. on Romans 3:3 [1540]: "Proinde, utcunque maior pars Dei foedus fefellerit ac proculcarit, ipsum nihilominus efficaciam suam retinere ac vim suam exercere: si non in omnibus, saltem in ipsa gente. Vis autem est, ut Domini gratia et in aeternam salutem benediction inter eos vigeat. *Id autem esse non potest nisi ubi fide promissio recipitur, atque ita confirmatur utrinque mutuum foedus*" (italics mine). *(Though then the greater part had nullified and trodden under foot God's covenant, it yet retained its efficacy and manifested its power, not indeed as to all, but with regard to a few of that nation: and it is then efficacious when the grace or the blessing of the Lord avails to eternal salvation.* But this cannot be, except when the promise is received by faith; for it is in this way that a mutual covenant is on both sides confirmed.)
Comm. on Romans 4:14 [1556]: "Ita evanesceret promissionum effectus, quia nihil prosunt *nisi fide acceptae*" (italics mine). *(Thus the effect of the promises would vanish, because they are of no avail except when received by faith.)*
Institutes, III, 24, xv: "Teneamus ergo prophetae consilium, non placere Deo mortem peccatoris: ut confidant pii, *simulac poenitentia tacti fuerint*, sibi paratam esse apud Deum veniam; impii vero sentient duplicari crimen suum, quod tantae Dei clementiae et facilitati non respondent" (italics mine). *(Let us therefore regard the prophet's [Ezekiel 33:11] instruction that the death of the sinner is not pleasing to God as designed to assure believers that God is ready to pardon them* as soon as they are touched by repentance *but to make the wicked feel that their transgression is doubled because they do not respond to God's great kindness and goodness.)* These sentences date back to 1539.
Institutes, III, 24, xvi: "Aliae sententiae non declarant quid de omnibus occulto suo iudicio Dominus statuerit, sed paratam denuntiant omnibus peccatoribus veniam,

Calvin's covenant theology. Since the conditional structure is already found in his commentary on Romans (1540), this was already an integrated part of his thought before the controversy with Pighius (1542).[114]

Unlike his stress on conditionality in some passages, Calvin insists elsewhere in his *Institutes* on the unconditionality of the promises:

> faith properly begins with the promise, rests in it, and ends in it. For in God faith seeks life: a life that is not found in commandments or declarations of penalties, but in the promise of mercy, and *only in a freely given promise. For a conditional promise that sends us back to our own works does not promise life unless we discern its presence in ourselves.*[115]

These words seem to contradict Calvin's own remarks on the conditionality of promises. Still, there are two reasons that make it unnecessary to conclude that Calvin is inconsistent here.[116] First, we need to realize that there is a difference in context. Conditionality is a mark of Calvin's doctrine of the covenant, just as the exclusion of works as a condition is a mark of his doctrine of justification. In the last passage quoted, it is clear from the context that a conditional promise means a promise that sends us back to our own works. "Conditional" here means "with a condition of works." Calvin is here opposing the conditions or works of the law as a ground for justification. He is not talking about faith as a condition of the covenant here but about faith as excluding works. Second, there is a distinction between meritorious conditions and the condition of faith. Faith

---

qui modo se ad eam requirendam convertunt" (italics mine). *(The other statements do not declare what God has determined in his secret judgment regarding all men, but they proclaim that there is ready pardon for all sinners, provided they turn back to seek it.)* These sentences date back to 1539.

Sermon on Galatians 4: 15-20 [1557]. CO L, 628: "Or cependant nous avons aussi à noter quand il dit, que Iesus Christ sera derechef formé en eux, *voire s'ils se reduisent à son obeissance*" (italics mine). *(But by the way we have to mark, that whereas he saith that Jesus Christ shall be fashioned in them new again it is meant* conditionally that they return under his obeisance.)

114 See 2.6 note 84.
115 *Institutes*, III, ii, 29: "[P]roprie tamen a promissione incipit, in ipsa constat, in ipsam desinit. Vitam enim in Deo quaerit, quae non in mandatis, aut poenarum edictis, sed misericordiae *promissione* reperitur, eaque nonnisi *gratuita*; *quoniam conditionalis, qua ad opera nostra remittimur, non aliter vitam promittit, quam si perspiciamus esse in nobis sitam*" (italics mine).
116 Although Calvin did not address this paradox in his works and hence did not make the following distinctions himself in this context, the content of the distinctions can be derived from his theology.

is the way wherein justification is attained. Faith excludes all works of the law, and, to be justified, one must stop trying to appease God with works of the law, even in the smallest way. To be justified one needs to stop trying to pay God on one's own, and this can itself be called a condition. And this is why Calvin sometimes used conditional phrases in relation to faith and justification. Sometimes, he even seems to see the conviction or confession itself "that in us lives no good" as a condition.[117]

---

117 For example, in his sermon on Galatians 2:15-16, [1557] CO L, 422: "Voilà Dieu qui est appaisé *moyennant* que nous ne cherchions autre payement, sinon le sacrifice qui luy a esté offert par son Fils unique, nostre Seigneur Iesus Christ" (italics mine). *(God is appeased towards us, conditionally that we seek not to pay him with any other thing, than with the sacrifice that was offered up to him by his only son our Lord Jesus Christ.)* (Translation by Arthur Golding (Audubon: Old Paths Publications 1996, reprint of a translation of 1574), 184-85.
See also his sermon on Galatians 2:20-21. CO L, 454: "Voulons nous donc posseder nostre Seigneur Iesus Christ? Il faut que nous sçachions pourquoy nous venons à luy: c'est d'autant que nous sommes desia damnez par la Loy, que nous sommes maudits de Dieu: que nous sommes retranchez de l'esperance de vie, que nous n'avons que corruption en nous: qu'il faut que Dieu nous purge par son sainct Esprit: et d'autant qu'il y a beaucoup d'infirmitez en nous, il nous faut tousiours venir à ceste fontaine, pour puiser en luy ce qui nous deffaut. Or si nous sommes contraints par nécessité de venir à nostre Seigneur Iesus Christ, confessans qu'il n'y a en nous que toute malediction et misere, il faut que nous venions à ceste conclusion de sainct Paul, qu'il seroit mort en vain s'il faloit obtenir iustice par la Loy, voire du tout ou en partie. Il faut que nous confessions cela. Et ceux qui sont les plus idiots le peuvent bien appercevoir: tellement que si nous ne recevons Iesus Christ à telle *condition*, il est certain que sa venue ne nous profitera de rien. Il n'y aura sinon un vent pour nous confier, en sorte que nous ne serons plus capables de la misericorde de Dieu qui nous est presentée en nostre Seigneur Iesus Christ" (italics mine). *(Will we then possess our Lord Jesus Christ? It behooveth us to know wherefore we come unto him: namely because that by the Law we are already condemned, cursed of God, cut off from hope of life, and full of all corruption, so as God must be pleased to cleanse us by his holy spirit, and forasmuch as there are many infirmities in us, we must always come [to this fountain to achieve from him what we miss. And if we by necessity are constrained to come] to our Lord Jesus Christ, and to confess that there is nothing in us but all cursedness and misery: we must needs come to this conclusion of Saint Paul, that Christ had died in vain, if it behooved us to obtain righteousness by the law, whither it were wholly or partly. We must needs confess that, and the veriest idiots are able to perceive it, insomuch that if we receive not Jesus Christ with that condition, it is certain that his coming shall profit us nothing at all. It will be but as a wind to blow us away together, so as we shall be no more able to take hold of God's mercy that is offered us in Jesus Christ* (italics mine). Golding left out the words between the square brackets, which I have inserted.
NB. These quotations are taken from Calvin's sermons on Galatians, the epistle in which Paul excluded all meritorious conditions.

Calvin's view can be summarized as follows: a person can approach God in Christ on condition that he rejects all (meritorious) conditions to satisfy God by his works. This element was already present in Calvin's theology in 1539, when he wrote his answer to Sadolet[118] and prepared the edition of his commentary on Romans.[119]

---

118 Letter to Sadolet, *CO* V, 397: "Primum, iubemus hominem a sui recognitione incipere, et illa quidem non levi nec defunctoria, sed ut conscientiam coram Dei tribunali suam sistat: et quum suae iniquitatis satis convictus fuerit, simul iudicii illius severitatem reputet, quod in omnes peccatores edicitur: ita miseria sua confusus ac perculsus, coram Deo prosternatur, et humilietur: abiecta omni sui fiducia tanquam ultimo exitio perditus ingemiscat. Tum unicum salutis portum esse ostendimus in Dei misericordia, quae nobis in Christo exhibetur: quia omnes salutis nostrae partos in eo sunt adimpletae. Quum ergo universi mortales perditi sunt coram Deo peccatores, dicimus Christum unicam esse iustitiam: quandoquidem obedientia sua transgressiones nostras abolevit, sacrificio iram Dei placavit, sanguine maculas abstersit, cruce maledictionem nostram sustinuit, morte pro nobis satisfecit. In hunc ergo modum dicimus hominem Deo patri in Christo reconciliari, nullo suo merito, nulla operum dignatione, sed gratuita clementia. Quum autem fide amplectamur Christum, et veluti in eius communionem veniamus, hanc, secundum scripturae morem, vocamus fidei iustitiam." *(First, We bid a man to begin by examining himself, and this not in a superficial and perfunctory manner, but to sist his conscience before the tribunal of God, and when sufficiently convinced of his iniquity, to reflect on the strictness of the sentence pronounced upon all sinners. Thus confounded and amazed at his misery, he is prostrated and humbled before God; and, casting away all self-confidence, groans as if given up to final perdition. Then we show that the only haven of safety is in the mercy of God, as manifested in Christ, in whom every part of our salvation is complete. As all mankind are, in the sight of God, lost sinners, we hold that Christ is their only righteousness, since, by his obedience, he has wiped off our transgressions; by his sacrifice, appeased the divine anger; by his blood, washed away our stains; by his cross, borne our curse; and by his death, made satisfaction for us. We maintain that in this way man is reconciled in Christ to God the Father, by no merit of his own, by no value of works, but by gratuitous mercy. When we embrace Christ by faith, and come, as it were, into communion with him, this we term, after the manner of Scripture, the righteousness of faith.)* (Translation taken from *Selected Works of John Calvin – Tracts and Letters* Edited by Henry Beveridge and Jules Bonnet (Grand Rapids: Baker, 1983 [reprint]), 105. These remarks might reflect Calvin's own experience in conversion.
119 Comm. on Romans, "Argumentum," [1540] *CO* IL, 1 : "Verum, quia homines suis vitiis indormiunt et blandiuntur, et falsa iustitiae opinione se deludunt, ut se indigere fidei iustitia non putent, nisi iam omni confidentia deiecti: rursum libidinum dulcedine inebriati, atque in alta securitate demersi sunt, ut non facile excitentur ad quaerendam iustitiam, nisi divini iudicii terrore perculsi: utrumque exsequitur, ut suae iniquitatis eos convincat, et torporem convictis excutiat." *(But as men are asleep in their sins, and flatter and delude themselves with a false notion about righteousness, so that they think not that they need the righteousness of faith, except they be cast down from all self-confidence, – and further, as they are inebriated with the sweetness of lusts, and sunk in deep self-security, so that they are not easily roused to seek righteousness,*

Calvin himself never makes clear how his conditional language and his statements on the unconditionality of grace should be reconciled. It does not seem to have been a problem for him, anyway. But those paradoxical statements are not proof of intended tensions in Calvin's theology, for they are consistent with each other when read in their own context. Moreover, whenever Calvin points to a seeming inconsistency, he never calls it a tension or something similar but argues that those statements were in harmony.[120]

2.10 The Particularity and Universality of the Promises

In his commentary on Romans (1540), Calvin states that God hates everyone outside of Christ; in his *Tract on Predestination* (1552), he denies that some promises were given to all and that Christ's benefits anyone other than the elect. In his *Institutes* (1559), he denies that the covenant and its promises are saving for all.[121] He writes something quite different elsewhere in his *Institutes*. In section III, ii, 32 (dating from 1539), Calvin first asserts that the promises are intended even for the reprobate. Second, he wrote that any promise, even when made to the reprobate, is a testimony of God's love. Third, it follows that this love, even for the reprobate, is not separate from Christ.[122]

---

except they are struck down by the terror of divine judgment, – the Apostle proceeds to do two things – to convince men of iniquity, and to shake off the torpor of those whom he proves guilty.)

120 For instance, *De aeterna Dei praedestinatione*, CO, VIII 301; COR III/I, 113; (CC, 100).
121 Comm. on Romans 5:10; *De aeterna Dei praedestinatione*, CO, VIII 301, 336-37; COR III/I, 113, 197-200 (CC, 100, 165-66); *Institutes*, III, 21, vii.
122 *Institutes*, III, ii, 32: "Rursum non sine causa in Christo promissiones omnes concludimus, quando et eius agnitione totum evangelium apostolus (Rom. 1, 17) concludit, et alibi docet, quotquot sunt Dei promissiones, in ipso esse etiam et amen (2 Cor. 1, 20). Cuius rei in promptu est ratio. *Si quid enim pollicetur Deus, eo benevolentiam suam testatur, ut nulla sit eius promissio, quae non sit dilectionis testimonium.* Nec refert quod ingentibus atque assiduis divinae largitatis beneficiis dum impii cumulantur, eo graviori iudicio éese induunt. Quum enim ea sibi e Domini manu provenire nec cogitent, nec agnoscant, aut si quando agnoscant, eius tamen bonitatem nequaquam apud se reputent, non possunt inde magis de eius misericordia edoceri quam brutae pecudes, quae pro conditionis suae modo, eundem liberalitatis fructum recipiunt, neque tamen prospiciunt. Nihilo magis obstat quod destinatas plerumque sibi promissiones respuendo ultionem hac occasione maiorem sibi accersunt. Quanquam enim tum se demum profert promissionum efficacia ubi fidem apud nos invenerunt, vis tamen ac proprietas earum nostra infidelitate aut ingratitudine nunquam exstinguitur. Ergo quum Dominus suis *promissionibus*, non ad percipiendos modo suae benignitatis fructus sed etiam cogitandos, hominem *invitet*, suam illi dilectio-

At first sight, Calvin seems to contradict himself and to have changed his mind between 1539 and 1559. But if this were true, it is strange that he did not remove that section from 1539 (III, ii, 32) from the edition of 1559. It seems that Calvin himself saw no contradiction here, so we could attempt to resolve the seeming contradictions between these passages. Again, reading these passages in their own context makes things clear. In *Institutes* III, ii, 32, Calvin is not talking about individuals but about the covenant community. The promises are intended for this community, although some people in it are reprobate and reject the promise (see the quotation on Ishmael in 2.6). Although the promises are intended or addressed to the covenant community, they are effectual only for the elect, for only they accept them in faith, which the Spirit works in them. This is the essence of *Institutes* III, xxi, 7.

With respect to the passages on whether God's love in Christ is for the elect alone or also includes the reprobate, we also have to take into account Calvin's view of the covenant community. God loves the individual believers in Christ, and hence he loves the community of believers in Christ. Although many hypocrites and natural descendants of believers are mingled in with this outward covenant community, Calvin regards it in the first place as a covenant community to whom the promises are made. That he had this community in mind is clear from the words in III,

> nem simul declarat. Unde huc redeundum est, promissionem quamlibet esse divinae erga nos dilectionis testificationem. Atqui extra controversiam est, neminem a Deo extra Christum diligi" (italics mine). *(Again, it is not without cause that we include all the promises in Christ, since the apostle includes the whole gospel under the knowledge of him, and elsewhere teaches that "however many are the promises of God, in him they find their yea and amen." The reason for this fact is at hand; for if God promises anything, by it he witnesses his benevolence, so that there is no promise of his which is not a testimony of his love. Nor does it make any difference that, while the wicked are plied with the huge and repeated benefits of God's bounty, they bring upon themselves a heavier judgment. For they neither think nor recognize that these benefits come to them from the Lord's hand; or if they do recognize it, they do not within themselves ponder his goodness. Hence, they cannot be apprised of his mercy any more than brute animals can, which, according to their condition, receive the same fruit of God's liberality, yet perceive it not. Nothing prevents them, in habitually rejecting the promises intended for them, from thereby bringing upon themselves a greater vengeance. For although the effectiveness of the promises only appears when they have aroused faith in us, yet the force and peculiar nature of the promises are never extinguished by our unfaithfulness and ingratitude. Therefore, since the Lord, by his promises, invites man not only to receive the fruits of his kindness but also to think about them, he at the same time declares his love to man. Hence we must return to the point: that any promise whatsoever is a testimony of God's love toward us. But it is indisputable that no one is loved by God apart from Christ.)*

ii, 32 in which he states that by his promises the Lord *invites* people, not that he *assures* them.

When addressing Calvin's ideas on particular and general promises, we have to look at the conditional structure of the promises of the covenant. The condition relates to the promise only in the context of the covenant community, not when the promise is given to the individual true believer. A key passage here is Calvin's comment on Romans 11:22.

> But as he speaks not of the elect individually, but of the whole body, a condition is added, If they continued in his kindness. I indeed allow, that as soon as any one abuses God's goodness, he deserves to be deprived of the offered favor; but it would be improper to say of any one of the godly particularly, that God had mercy on him, when he chose him, provided he would continue in his mercy; for the perseverance of faith, which completes in us the effect of God's grace, flows from election itself. Paul then teaches us, that the Gentiles were admitted into the hope of eternal life on the condition, that they by their gratitude retained possession of it.[123]

So, when God gives his promises to individuals, they are unconditional but particular. When God gives his promises to the covenant community, they are universal for all partakers of the covenant but conditional.

2.11 Predestination and the Response to Preaching

As we have seen, for Calvin, predestination is the reason why some who hear the Gospel believe, while others do not. In this section, we will discuss Calvin's ideas on the relation between predestination and the response to preaching.

By nature, all people will reject the Gospel; by nature, human beings are blind and opposed to God. The wickedness or original corruption of humankind is the cause of all sin, even of unbelief. Yet there is a deeper reason why those who do not believe do not so, i.e., the secret counsel of God. God decreed that the reprobate would be left in their corruption. In line with his judgment, he does not reveal himself to the reprobate. The

---

123 Comm. on Rom. 11: 22 [1556]: "Quia autem de singulis electis non disputat, sed de toto corpore, additur conditio, si in lenitate permanserint. Fateor quidem, simul ac Dei bonitate quispiam abutitur, dignum esse qui privetur oblata gratia: sed improprie de aliquo piorum hoc specialiter dictum foret, Deum eius misertum esse, quum eum elegit, si modo in misericordia permaneat. Nam fidei perseverantia, quae effectum gratiae Dei in nobis complet, ex electione ipsa manat: gentes ergo Paulus ascitas hac lege esse docet in spem vitae aeternae, ut eius possessionem sua gratitudine retineant."

Gospel is preached to them so that they, "seeing, may see and not perceive." For the Gospel tells them that God gives freely to those who ask him, but by their own will the reprobate do not seek a remedy for their need. Hence, the Gospel leaves them inexcusable, and it becomes a savor of death unto death to them.[124]

That there is a relation between unbelief and reprobation is clear in Calvin's writings on the subject. He denies that God is the author of sin and hence of unbelief.[125] He does not deny that God is the cause of sin or unbelief, although he usually does not state that either. Yet he seems to imply it throughout his tract on predestination.[126] There is at least one place in Calvin's writings where he states it explicitly. Commenting on John 10:26, Calvin remarks:

> He [Jesus] assigns a higher reason why they do not believe either in his miracles or in his doctrine. It is, because they are reprobate.

Yet Calvin acquits God of all blame for causing unbelief.

---

124 See for example *De aeterna Dei praedestinatione*, CO VIII, 271-72, 275, 279, 288-92, 298-300, 310; COR III/1, 43-44, 52, 62-63, 82-83, 85-92, 107-17, 134 (CC, 47, 53, 61, 76, 79-84, 95-96, 98, 117); Comm. on Romans 1:16, 17, 2:4, 7:14, 8:30, 11:2.

125 For instance, already in his *Institutes* of 1536, CO I, 60, and in *De aeterna Dei praedestinatione*, CO VIII, 363; COR III/1, 260 (CC, 251). An ambiguous passage in *Institutes* III, xxiii, 3 [1559], seems to state that God is the author of sin. "Unde apparet quam perversa sit obstrependi affectatio, quod data opera supprimunt quam in se agnoscere coguntur damnationis causam, ut Dei praetextus eos liberet. Atqui, ut centies Deum esse autorem confitear, quod verissimum est, non protinus tamen crimen eluunt quod eorum conscientiis insculptum subinde eorum oculis recurrit." *(How perverse is their disposition to protest is apparent from the fact that they deliberately suppress the cause of condemnation, which they are compelled to recognize in themselves, in order to free themselves by blaming God. But though I should confess a hundred times that God is the author of it—which is very true—yet they do not promptly cleanse away the guilt that, engraved upon their consciences, repeatedly meets their eyes.)* God as author seems to refer to "damnationis causam", which is sin, for the perverse have to recognise it in themselves. Given Calvin's denial of God being the author of sin (see 2.11 note 128) it seems he means that God is the author of damnation and not the author of the cause of damnation.

126 For instance, when he writes about unbelief: "[A]ltius tamen conscendit. Spectandum enim est eius consilium" (CO VIII, 291; COR III/1, 90) *(we should ascend higher. His council has to be observed.)* Cole's translation is too bold here: "[Y]et the cause of their not believing must be traced back to a far higher source. The secret and eternal purpose and counsel of God must be viewed as the original cause of their blindness and unbelief" (CC, 81). Cole here makes explicit what is only implicit at this point in Calvin's writings.

> If any one murmur at this, arguing that the cause of unbelief dwells in God, because he alone has power to make sheep; I reply, He is free from all blame, for it is only by their voluntary malice that men reject his grace.[127]

Since Calvin wrote this in 1553, after the Bolsec controversy and after Bullinger's accusation that, in tracing unbelief back to God's decree, Calvin seems to make him the author of sin, it is unlikely that they represent a "slip of the pen." Calvin likely consciously used the word *causa* to denote the relation between reprobation and unbelief. Calvin does not explain why God could be a *causa* of sin without being the author of sin any further than to point to the distinction between proximate and remote causes.[128]

The response of the elect to the preached Gospel is faith. Those who believe do so not by their own will but because they are given by the Father to Christ. They are called with a special, effectual call, a call according to God's purpose. Calvin distinguishes this call from the outward call or invitation to repentance and faith. This effectual call is the inward teaching of the Holy Spirit in the elect, whereby he delivers them into the hands and possession of Christ. At the same time, God gives them the power and the will to do as they are taught. Preaching is a means to produce faith.[129]

According to Pighius, preaching would be pointless if God had predetermined the eternal destination of each human being. Calvin's response is to quote from Augustine in which the latter pointed to Paul, whose teaching was replete with this doctrine of predestination. Nevertheless,

---

127 Comm. on John 10:26: "Altiorem causam adducit cur neque miraculis, neque doctrinae fidem habeant, nempe quia sint reprobi… Si quis obmurmuret, causam incredulitatis residere in Deo, quia penes eum solum sit oves facere: respondeo, ipsum omni culpa liberari, quando homines nonnisi voluntaria malitia gratiam reiiciunt."

128 *De aeterna Dei praedestinatione*, CO VIII, 363; COR III/I, 260 (CC, 251): "Ergo quum iusta de causa, licet nobis ignota, a Domino procedant, quae scelerate ab hominibus maleficia perpetrantur, etiamsi rerum omnium prima causa sit eius voluntas, peccati tamen eum esse authorem nego. Nec vero oblivione tegenda est illa, quam posui, causarum diversitas, quod alia est propinqua, alia autem remota causa …" (*Wherefore, when the wickedness of men proceeds thus from the Lord, and from a just cause, but from a cause unknown to us, although the first cause of all things be His will, that He is therefore the author of sin I most solemnly deny. Nevertheless, that difference of causes on which I have before dwelt, is by no means to be forgotten – that one cause is proximate, another remote.*)

129 *Defensio*, CO VI, 252-54, 344-46, 381-82; COR IV/III, 99-102, 238-41, 295-96 *De aeterna Dei praedestinatione*, CO VIII, 261-62, 267, 271-75, 292, 298-300, 324-25, 331, 341, 344; COR III/I, 20, 34-35, 43-52, 92-93, 107-17, 170-72, 183-85, 206-08, 215-16 (CC, 31, 40, 47-53, 84, 95-98, 144-46, 156-57, 174, 181; Comm. on Romans 10:16, 11:2.

Paul never ceased to exhort people to will and to work. Moreover, Jesus himself taught that no one could come to him unless the Father draws him; but he nevertheless called on them to believe in him. The preaching of duty should not be withheld by reason of the doctrine of predestination, and the preaching of predestination not withheld by reason of the preaching of duty. Preaching the Gospel is by no means pointless, for God works through instruments.[130]

The development of these ideas in Calvin was not caused by Pighius's criticism, but they were already present in his commentary on Romans (1540). His answer to Pighius brings together various elements which were already present in his theology.

2.12 Predestination, Faith, and Assurance
Calvin is very clear in teaching what predestination is and why it should be preached, but he is as eager to assure his readers repeatedly not to seek their knowledge of salvation in God's counsel, but in Christ.

> For whosoever walketh not in the plain way of faith, to him the election of God can be nothing but a labyrinth of destruction… We must by no means make our beginning with the investigation of what God decreed concerning us before the world began. Our contemplation must be what God, of His fatherly love, has revealed to us in Christ, and what Christ Himself daily preaches to us through His Gospel. We must seek nothing higher than to become the sons of God. But the mirror of free adoption, in which alone we can behold so high and unspeakable a blessing, is the Son.[131]

Although salvation will be given to all the elect, it is inseparably connected with their faith. And the object of saving faith is not the doctrine of predestination or the secret counsel of God, but Christ revealed in the Gospel and its promises. Nobody has to be afraid of being rejected when

---

130 *De aeterna Dei praedestinatione,* CO VIII, 324-28; COR III/1, 144-75 (CC, 144-49); Comm. on Romans 1:16, 10:17.
131 *De aeterna Dei praedestinatione,* CO VIII, 307; COR III/1, 127 (CC, 111): "Nam, quisquis plana fidei via non ingreditur, illi Dei electio nihil quam exitialis erit labyrinthus. Itaque, ut certa sit nobis peccatorum remissio, ut in vitae aeternae fiducia conscientiae nostrae acquiescant, ut Deum intrepide patrem invocemus, hinc minime faciendum est exordium, quid de nobis ante mundum conditum Deus statuerit, sed quid de paterno eius amore nobis in Christo sit patefactum, et quotidie per evangelium Christus ipse praedicet. Nihil altius nobis quaerendum, quam ut filii Dei simus. Atqui gratuitae, qua hoc tantum bonum consequimur, adoptionis speculum, arra et pignus est filius …"
These ideas were already present in Calvin's *Catechism* of 1538.

he comes to Christ, for he himself has promised not to cast out those who come to him.[132]

Christ is the main and first object of faith, and knowledge of salvation should be sought through faith in him. Nevertheless, faith should not stop at Christ but should lead the faithful further. After fixing the eye of faith on Christ, faith can then look up to the source of life in God's eternal decree. Election is not the object of faith, but it supports the confidence of the faithful.[133] Because Christ, revealed in the Gospel and its promises, is the object of faith, he should also be the main content of preaching. The Gospel is called the doctrine of salvation, for Christ and his righteousness are offered in it.[134] Election, let alone reprobation, is not the object of faith.

According to Calvin, faith is

> a firm and certain knowledge of God's benevolence toward us, founded upon the truth of the freely given promise in Christ, both revealed to our minds and sealed upon our hearts through the Holy Spirit.[135]

This definition of faith raises an important question. For Calvin repeatedly writes that all men in preaching are called to have faith and to repent in order to be saved. And if this faith to which all are called is knowledge of God's benevolence towards us, how can all be called to have this faith unless God is actually benevolent to all? But Calvin taught that God's

---

132 *De aeterna Dei praedestinatione*, CO VIII, 253, 275, 292, 307; COR III/I, 3, 53, 84, 127 (CC, 21, 53, 83-84, 111-12, 132-33); *Institutes*, III, 2, vi-vii, xvi, xxix; Comm. on Romans, "Argumentum," 5:11.

133 *De aeterna Dei praedestinatione*, CO VIII, 260; COR III/I, 19 (CC, 29-30): "Sic enim vitam in Christo manifestatam fide apprehendimus, ut eadem fide duce procul intueri liceat, ex quo fonte vita prodierit. In Christo fundata est salutis fiducia, et in evangelii promissiones recumbit. Sed haec non parum valida fultura est, quum nunc, ut in Christum credamus, audimus nobis divinitus esse datum, quia ante mundi originem tam ad fidem ordinati, quam ad vitae coelestis haereditatem electi eramus." (*Thus, when we lay hold of life in Christ, made manifest to our faith, the same faith being still our leader and guide, our sight is permitted to penetrate much farther, and to see from what source that life proceeded. Our confidence of salvation is rooted in Christ, and rests on the promises of the gospel. But it is no weak prop to our confidence, when we are brought to believe in Christ, to hear that all was originally given to us of God, and that we were as much ordained to faith in Christ before the foundation of the world, as we were chosen to the inheritance of eternal life in Christ.*)

134 Comm. on Romans, "Argumentum," 1:2, 1:16.

135 *Institutes*, III, ii, 7: "Nunc iusta fidei definitio nobis constabit, si dicamus esse divinae erga nos benevolentiae firmam certamque cognitionem, quae gratuitae in Christo promissionis veritate fundata, per spiritum sancttum et revelatur mentibus nostris et cordibus obsignatur." Cf. Comm. on Romans 1:7, 4:14.

saving benevolence is only for his elect. This again seems to be an inconsistency in Calvin's thought. The questions this inconsistency does raise are of both pastoral and doctrinal importance. It is even stranger that Calvin, both pastor and systematic theologian, does not really engage with these problems in order to solve them. It is true that Calvin adds some pastoral remarks for those faithful who wanted this sure knowledge. He writes that the least drop of faith is real faith, and enough to have this sure rest in God.[136] But this does not answer the question how people who are unbelievers at this moment (and perhaps will be such all their lives since they are reprobate, i.e., people for whom there is no divine favor,) can be called upon to believe that there is divine favor toward them. That Calvin himself did not answer this question is remarkable. Obviously, he did not consider it a problem.

The answer is again probably to be found in Calvin's thinking on the covenant. Calvin's definition of faith is not only that it is "a firm and certain knowledge of God's benevolence toward us" but also that it is "founded upon the truth of the freely given promise in Christ." This promise is given in the preaching of the Gospel, and this Gospel is preached to the covenant community. The members of the congregation should not start with regarding themselves as favored by God in themselves but should start with the promise to the covenant community. Calvin could call all his hearers to this faith because all were in the community of the covenant. The divine favor is promised to this covenant community on the condition of faith.[137] Those who join the covenant community can rely on these promises, but only the elect actually do so with real faith. The reprobate reject God and his Gospel and thus bring a heavier judgment on themselves.

An answer can also be sought in relation to Calvin's position on the atonement. According the formula accepted by all parties in his time, Christ died sufficiently for all men. This could mean that, in some way, God does look favorably on all.[138]

However, neither argument is altogether persuasive. First, Calvin does not make them clear anywhere in his works. Second, there is a great difference between Christ dying sufficiently for all and effectively for the elect only. The question remains: Can everyone trust God's saving favor

---

136 For a study of Calvin's doctrine on the nature and assurance of faith, see Beeke, *Quest*, 37-72.
137 The conditionality of the promises might also be the reason why Calvin called faith "obedience" to the Gospel. Comm. on Rom. 1:5.
138 It was especially this consequence that later occasioned Beza's critique. See my "Calvin's Forgotten Position on the Extent of the Atonement."

toward him personally since Christ died sufficiently for all? So, there seems to be a real tension or contradiction in Calvin's thought here, even if it is not plausible that Calvin intended it as such.

2.13 Preaching the Doctrine of Predestination

In his tract on predestination, Calvin approvingly quoted Augustine to the effect that there seem to be good reasons not to preach the doctrine of election. There might be some people who, hearing this doctrine, give themselves up to indolence and unconcern and follow their own lusts.

Some may be rendered worse after hearing the truth of election proclaimed. On the other hand, it is necessary to preach this truth.[139]

Calvin presents several reasons why election should be publicly preached. This is the only doctrine that teaches that salvation flows from the free mercy of God. If election is not preached, people will be inclined to think that there is something in themselves that leads to God's acceptance of them; so not preaching this doctrine impairs true humility. Election is the foundation of salvation and offers a sure ground of confidence.[140] Therefore, preaching about election is not "a mere thorny and noisy disputation, nor a speculation which wearies the minds of men without any profit; but a solid discussion eminently adapted to the service of the godly."[141]

It is therefore the task of preachers to preach the doctrine of election, so that those who have ears might hear. But they should try to do this without giving offence. Preachers should not say to those who hear them that the reason they do not believe is because God has predestined them to eternal destruction. Much less should they say that their hearers will never believe because they are reprobate. Preachers who preach thus should be expelled from the church. Instead, a preacher should help his hearers advance in the right way. He must take care not to go beyond the limits of what is revealed in Scripture.[142]

---

139 *De aeterna Dei praedestinatione, CO,* VIII, 326-27; *COR* III/1, 170-74 (*CC*, 147-48).
140 *Institutes,* III, xxi, 1; cf. *De aeterna Dei praedestinatione, CO,* VIII, 260-61; *COR* III/1, 18-21 (*CC*, 29-31).
141 *De aeterna Dei praedestinatione, CO,* VIII, 260; *COR* III/1, 18 (*CC*, 29). "Non esse, ut quibusdam falso videtur, argutam hanc vel spinosam speculationem, quae absque fructu ingenia fatiget: sed disputationem solidam, et ad pietatis usum maxime accommodam."
142 *Institutes,* III, xxi, 3-4; *De aeterna Dei praedestinatione, CO,* VIII, 327; *COR* III/1, 174-75 (*CC*, 148-49).

Calvin (or actually Augustine, quoted with approval by Calvin) almost consistently used the word "election" when affirming the necessity of preaching it; rarely does he use "predestination" and never "reprobation." Instead, when Augustine warned against a bad way of preaching this doctrine, he used examples of where the audience was said to be reprobate. Calvin approved what Augustine said. Hence, it seems that it was not the doctrine of the *praedestinatio gemina* that Calvin wanted preached but the doctrine of God's gracious election.

2.14 Summary: Predestination and the External Call

It is remarkable that Calvin did not write a separate chapter on the external call but only devoted a section to this subject in relation to predestination, in combination with the justice of the condemnation of the reprobate.[143] It seems that Calvin's remarks on the call are nothing more than an appendix to his chapters on election. But the opposite hypothesis is also plausible: the chapters on predestination can be read as an introduction to his thoughts on the call. Book III of the *Institutes* deals, after all, with the way in which grace is received. Predestination is not actually a way in which grace is received, but the call is. Hence, Calvin might have put the chapters on predestination in Book III in his 1559 edition for the sake of the call rather than for the sake of election itself.

As we have seen in the sections on predestination, the covenant, and the church, Calvin's thinking on these three subjects can be visualized in three concentric circles (2.4, 2.6, 2.7). Calvin's doctrine of a twofold call is closely related to these circles. The external call is heard primarily within the walls of the visible church. Those outside the visible church who hear the external call are invited to join the church. Those who break the covenant and turn to the world reject the external call of the Gospel. It is the external call, according to God's general election, that establishes the circle of the covenant and the visible church.

---

143 *Institutes*, III, xxiv, Electionem sanciri Dei vocatione: reprobos autem sibi accersere iustum, cui destinati sunt, interitum.

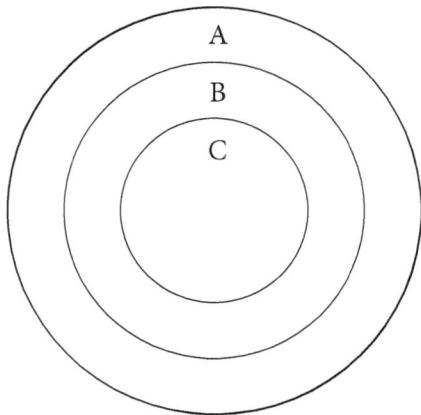

Circle	Transition to next circle by	Based on
A: The world	External call	General election
B: The covenant/visible church		
C: True believers/invisible church	Internal call	Special election

God's Spirit working in the hearts of his elect so that they obey the call of the Gospel in faith and repentance is the internal call. Only through this call do people become true believers. It is the internal call, according to God's special election, that establishes the circle of the elect, i.e., true believers or the invisible church.

The above table summarizes the relation between Calvin's doctrines of predestination, the covenant, the church, and the call. As we concluded in 2.7, it was Calvin's ecclesiastical experience that affected his view on predestination, rather than the other way around. Since his view of the covenant is closely linked to his ecclesiology, we could conclude the same of the relation between predestination and the covenant or perhaps that his ecclesiology affected his views of both the covenant and predestination.

The same holds true for the most part for the relation between the external call and predestination. As in Calvin's theology, the external call is closely related to covenant and church, and the internal call to the elect and the true believers, the relation between the call and predestination is given with the relation between predestination and covenant and church. We cannot conclude that predestination unilaterally influenced Calvin's views of the covenant, the church, and the call, even though the three are inextricably connected.

At one point, Calvin's doctrine of predestination might have influenced his view of the call. When Pighius argued on the basis of general promises and invitations of the Gospel that election and reprobation could not be true, Calvin was forced to answer the question concerning the call of the reprobate and whether God could be viewed as sincere in inviting them to eternal life. However, Calvin's answer did not really contain anything new but was an elaboration of elements already present in his thinking on the covenant and in his commentary on Romans. Since the covenant and the external call, which affect both the elect and reprobate, are conditional, God can truly say that he does not desire the death of a sinner, even a reprobate sinner, but wants him or her to live. For God invites people to eternal life by urging them to faith and repentance, and he promises life only to those who actually repent and believe. God unconditionally bestows faith and repentance on his elect, passing over the reprobate, and yet he is sincere in his general but conditional invitations (2.9, 2.10).

According to Calvin's theology, a congregation should not be divided into the elect and the reprobate. All people should hear the same word that is addressed not to individual people as being predestinated but to a covenant community. Wallace's conclusion that a preacher ought to have two voices, one to gather the sheep and one to drive away the wolves and thieves is not supported by Calvin's view of preaching. (2.7).[144]

There are two areas on which predestination clearly did not have any influence. The first is the atonement by Christ. Calvin used, though somewhat reluctantly, the classic formula that Christ died sufficiently for all but efficiently only for the elect (2.5). The second is faith. In terms of systematic theology, there is indeed a tension or contradiction in Calvin's theology in that he called on all people to acknowledge that God is benevolent to them, while at the same time teaching that God was benevolent only to his elect (2.12).

Historical facts and events have not been of major influence on this part of Calvin's theology. There is a consistent line from his first Reformed publications to the end of his life. *Praedestinatio gemina* and the concept of conditionality have been elements of his theology throughout. Events like the attacks of Pighius and Bolsec forced him to elaborate what was already present *in nuce* in his theology.

---

144 Wallace, *Calvin's Doctrine of the Word and the Sacrament*, 82-95.

Graafland's conclusion, mentioned in 2.2, that there are great tensions and unclear passages in Calvin's thinking on predestination and the external call[145] is true only with respect to the tensions regarding predestination and the general exhortation to believe that God is benevolent to people. When read in the context of Calvin's coherent view on predestination, the covenant, and the church, the other supposed contradictions are solved, either by Calvin himself or by applying several elements of his theology. When Graafland states that Calvin's theology does not include an offer of Christ to all since Christ did not die for all, he was obviously wrong (2.5). First, Calvin does not deny that Christ died for all. Second, Calvin presents Christ to all and argues that God does so as well. The conditional structure of the covenant and the external call enabled Calvin to maintain both God's eternal *praedestinatio gemina* and the sincere offer of Christ (2.9, 2.10).

Graafland's criticism of Calvin is quite similar to that of Shepherd who posits that God, according to Calvin, is not to be taken at his word, because God does not make his promise sincerely to all. Shepherd writes that Calvin fails to acquit God of the accusation of unrighteousness with respect to predestination.[146] These critical remarks can be answered by pointing to the concept of conditionality as applied by Calvin to the covenant, the promises, and the external call (2.9, 2.10).

2.15 Commentary and Sermon on 1 Timothy 2:4

Having researched the doctrinal answers Calvin provided to the questions of our study, it is important to see how those answers functioned in his sermons. In this and the next sections, we will examine some of his sermons. Here we will compare Calvin's exegesis of 1 Timothy 2:4 in his commentary and his sermon to see whether Calvin treated the text in different ways. The following sections will look at Calvin's sermons on Micah and a selection of his sermons on Genesis.

In 1548 Calvin edited his commentaries on the Epistles to Timothy[147] and he preached a series of sermons on 1 Timothy during the period 1554-1555.[148] The question is whether Calvin's explanation of the words of 1 Tim. 2:4, "Who will have all men to be saved," changed in the years

---

145 Graafland, *Van Calvijn tot Barth*, 41-46.
146 Shepherd, *The Nature and Function of Faith*, 78, 87.
147 *Ioannis Calvini commentarii, in utranque Pauli Epistolam ad Timotheum*, CO LII, 241-396.
148 *Sermons sur la Premiere Epistre a Timothée*, CO LIII. Translation by L.T. *Sermons of M. John Calvin on the Epistles of S. Paule to Timothie and Titus* (London: G. Bishop and T. Woodcoke, 1579; facsimile Edinburgh 1983).

between commentary and the sermon, for it was in that intervening period that the Bolsec controversy took place.[149]

In his commentary, Calvin remarks that all those to whom the Gospel is addressed are invited to the hope of eternal life. Those who are partakers of the Gospel are saved, for the call is a proof of secret election. However, Paul is not speaking here about all individuals but about classes of people. There is no nation or class that is excluded from salvation because God wishes the Gospel to be preached to all. He does not want to debate with those who use these words of Paul to reject (individual) predestination because Paul is not speaking of individuals here.[150]

In his commentary, Calvin makes the remark that Paul is not speaking about individuals but about classes of people at the end of his comment on the text. In his sermon, however, he leads off with this remark and stresses it strongly. He did not want to discuss the question of those who misused Paul's words in his commentary but did so thoroughly in his sermon. He uses two arguments to prove that election, and not free will, is the source of salvation. First, human nature is depraved and at enmity with God, so no one can partake of God's salvation unless God himself draws him. But since we see that God does not draw all people to him, we conclude that there is a secret election by God. Second, if God really wills all individual people to be saved, why did he choose a special people in the Old Testament, and why did he not suffer Paul to preach in Bithynia and Phrygia? Although Paul does not point to God's hidden eternal decree in 1 Tim. 2:4, he does point to his will as far as we are able to know it.

In addition, Calvin explains to his congregation that there are not two wills in God. The Scripture speaks of God's one will in two forms for several reasons. The first reason is that election is a counsel from which we are excluded. That there is such a counsel is revealed in order to humble believers and to remove all doubt that it is Christ who saves them. Second, there is a will of God that is revealed to people. This is the will whereby God calls and exhorts people to repentance. It is a general doctrine that God will treat with mercy sinners who come to him and ask forgiveness in Christ's name. In this respect, God wills that all people be saved. These two seemingly contradictory wills meet each other in the doctrine that God himself works in his elect so that they come to him and ask forgiveness in Christ's name. The Gospel is offered to all, but it does not benefit all. People are rebellious by nature against God and their corrupt nature becomes even worse, as long as the Spirit does not work

---

149 1 Tim 2:4 is explained in a sermon on 1 Tim. 2:3-5, *CO* LIII, 147-60.
150 Comm. on 1 Tim 2:4.

together with the preaching of the Gospel. So, God must go further to bring people to salvation, i.e., he must bring the Gospel into their hearts and draw them to himself.

To apply this doctrine to the congregation, Calvin first explains what the text means when it says that God wills that all people be saved when he commands the Gospel to be preached. If God exhorts us to repentance, he is ready to receive us when we come to him. God reaches out his hand. Second, it is not enough to receive the preaching: God must speak inwardly to us to bring us to the knowledge of the truth. Third, people themselves are at fault if they do not receive the word that is offered. Fourth, we must not separate salvation from knowledge of the truth. Fifth, do we want God to receive us? If so, then we must receive the doctrine in these words. Sixth, we have to desire the salvation of all.[151]

Calvin's commentary on 1 Timothy 2:4 takes up approximately one column in the *Calvini Opera*, while his sermon on the same text takes twelve. In his sermon, he adds an excursus on the two wills of God and makes the doctrine more practical. There is no difference from the content of Calvin's exegesis of the text. That Calvin makes the text practical is obviously due to the homiletical genre of the sermon. But the addition of an excursus on the two wills and Calvin's starting with and stressing his remark that Paul does not speak of individual election here could be a result of the Bolsec controversy. In his reply to Bolsec (i.e., Pighius) in his *Treatise on Predestination*, Calvin argues against the same views that he does in his sermon, views that he barely comments on in his commentary.[152]

2.16 Sermons on Micah

Calvin's sermons on Micah are a thorough reading, explication, and application of each verse of Micah.[153] Starting with Micah 1:1-2 on November 12, 1550, and finishing with Micah 7: 10-12 on January 10, 1551, he preached through the whole book on all days except Sundays, every other week.[154] Since the aim of this study is to research the influence of the doctrine of predestination on preaching, we will only look at those

---

151 *Sermons sur la Premiere Epistre a Timothée*, CO LIII, 147-60 (sermon 13).
152 This can also be due to the genre of Calvin's commentaries. See Muller, *The Unaccommodated Calvin*.
153 Jean Calvin, *Sermons sur le Livre de Michée*, publiés par Jean Daniel Benoit, Vol. V of the *Supplementa Calviniana* (Neukirchen-Vluyn: Neukirchener Verlag 1964). Quoted as *Michée*.
154 B.W. Farley, "Introduction" in John Calvin, *Sermons on the Book of Micah* (Phillipsburg, New Jersey: P&R Publishing, 2003), vii. For a chronological chart of Calvin's sermons see T.H.L. Parker, *Calvin's Preaching* (Edinburgh: T&T Clark, 1992), 150-52.

aspects that concern our subject. Calvin's sermons on Micah have been studied in detail by Michael Parsons, but Parsons does not pay much attention to questions related to predestination in these sermons.[155]

The doctrines of predestination and the covenant as such are not treated overtly but by implication in Calvin's sermons on Micah. He nowhere explains these doctrines but presupposes them. References are made to the doctrine of predestination or the doctrine of the covenant in almost all of his sermons on Micah. The content of what Calvin says about these subjects in his sermons is consistent with what he writes in his more doctrinal works, although the form and genre differs.

2.16.1 Covenant
Calvin viewed the congregation as a covenant community. As described above in 2.6, this did not mean that Calvin thought all members were elect or saved, and this is exactly what produces tensions or paradoxes in Calvin's sermons. On the one hand, he regarded all members of the congregation as members of Christ's flock and thus argues that God unites "us" increasingly to himself *(nous y soyons conjoinctz quant et quant)* when he teaches "us." On the other hand, "we" run away from him, and hence God governs us in a different manner, i.e., he withdraws from us, punishes us, and saves only a remnant.[156] Calvin uses the first-person plural in both a positive and in a negative sense: both to tell the people he is preaching to that God governs them, unites himself to them, and will keep them, as well as to tell them that God withdraws from them and punishes them. The word *nous* indicates that Calvin the preacher is identifying himself with his congregation and not that he viewed all his hearers as elect believers.[157]

Although Calvin often seems to regard his entire congregation as elect believers, such as when he opposes unbelievers and the reprobate *(infidels et reprouves)* over against "us," i.e., the congregation,[158] at other times he

---

155 Michael Parsons, *Calvin's Preaching on the Prophet Micah: The 1550-1551 Sermons in Geneva* (Lewiston: The Edwin Mellen Press, 2006). In the indexes, it appears that predestination is mentioned on four pages; election on three, reprobation nowhere, and covenant on eleven pages.
156 *Michée*, [9], 72-74; [19], 155. Numbers in square brackets refer to the sermon, and other numbers to the pages.; Translation: John Calvin, *Sermons on the Book of Micah*, transl. Benjamin W. Farley (Phillipsburg, New Jersey: P&R Publishing, 2003), 130-31, 274. Quoted as *Micah*.)
157 Manetsch, *Compary*, 162.
158 *Michée*, [6] 47; [19] 157 (*Micah*, 83, 278). Perhaps Calvin meant the first step of election and reprobation.

makes it clear that not all those attending his services were believers. He calls the church a threshing floor where the chaff and grain are mixed[159] or states that many are still blind and untouched by God's goodness, as a result of which the Devil has more control than ever.[160] All this is consistent with his doctrinal statements about the covenant.

It is possible to place idle trust in the covenant, for being included in the covenant does not save one from evil.[161] How does Calvin clarify to his congregation the difference between idle trust and saving trust? In exegeting Micah 3:11-12, Calvin tried to answer the question how God can punish people, even though they trust in God. The answer is that those people are hypocrites. They glory in God but at the same time offend and mock God's Word and do not think too much about him. Hypocrites just accept one side of the promise that God is in their midst. But there is another side as well: they have to be cleansed of worldly filth. It is impossible to keep God's promises halfheartedly. Rather, the members of the covenant must acknowledge what God commands and requires of them: they need to serve God in faith and repentance.[162]

Calvin's description of those who place idle trust in the covenant already sheds light on what it means to put saving trust in that covenant. But there is a slight difference in how Calvin talks about these matters. With respect to idle trust, he states very clearly that persons who act in a certain way put an idle trust in the covenant. But when it comes to saving trust, Calvin usually does not state clearly that there are people who do something, but he exhorts his hearers to do something. This element will be discussed in more detail below in connection with Calvin's preaching about the conditions and promises.

2.16.2 Predestination

Although Calvin does not treat predestination as a doctrine in his sermons, he presupposes the knowledge of predestination. Despite his view that the congregation is to be treated as a covenant community, Calvin sometimes indicated that some members of the congregation were unbe-

---

159 *Michée*, [17] 144-45 (*Micah*, 255).
160 *Michée*, [12] 99 (*Micah*, 177). "[L]e diable y regnera plus que jamais; ... touresfoys il y en a qui sont aveuglez, qu'ilz ne congoissent point le bien qu'il leur a apporté, et ne sont point touchez de la bonté de Dieu." *([T]he Devil reigns here today more than ever before. ... [M]any are still blind and fail to recognize the good that has been brought to them, or still remain untouched by God's goodness.)*
161 *Michée*, [4] 34-35 (*Micah*, 61).
162 *Michée*, [12] 102-03; cf. [8] 65-66 (*Micah*, 181-82, cf. 117).

lievers.[163] For example, in sermon 19 he expresses doubt that only one out of twenty people was confident that God was speaking in Geneva by the preaching of the Gospel.[164] In the next sermon, he even stops addressing the covenant community as a whole.[165]

> Thus, he is not speaking here of all those who were known as the people of God, but only of those who were privileged to be the remnant. That being the case, we have to think carefully about ourselves, for bearing the name of a Christian and the mark of Baptism is not enough. God did not extent his loving-kindness to all those who were known as God's people. Thus, Micah is not speaking of everyone in general, but only of a remnant. For that reason, as I have already warned, each must look carefully to himself. True, we are all called to be God's people. But since many mock God's grace and provoke his wrath, they have to be pared away, resulting in God's reduction of the number whom he has chosen. Hence, instead of there being a large multitude to whom God addressed himself, the number being diminished, Micah says that God will preserve only a remnant, or small seed …[166]

---

163 Farley gives the impression that Calvin even called some members of the Genevan church "reprobate" when he translated "That is how the reprobate want to make adultery honorable" (*Micah*, sermon 19, 287). But the French word translated as "reprobate" by Farley is "malheureux" (*Michée*, [19], 163) which is better translated as "wretches," as Farley did on page 335, for instance. Here Calvin is addressing Genevan citizens who were responsible for public order and pretended to be Christians, i.e., members of the Genevan church, and yet thought it legal to sing filthy songs. Indeed, he thought they were subject to reproof but did not call them reprobate.
164 *Michée*, [19] 163 (*Micah*, 287).
165 The exegetical occasion for these words was Micah 5:7 on the remnant of Israel. The practical occasion for speaking this way was perhaps that on the day he delivered this sermon, Thursday, December 25, 1551, Calvin saw many more people in the church than he did on other weekdays. They expected a Christmas sermon. Calvin reproved them severely at the end of his sermon, since in Geneva, December 25 was an ordinary workday, and Christmas was observed on the Sunday following.
166 *Michée*, [20] 165 (*Micah*, 291-92): "Il n'est point donc icy parlé de tous ceulx qui portoient le nom du peuple de Dieu, mais de quelque semence qui a esté gardée par un privilege singulier. Voyans donc cela, nous avons bien à penser à nous, car ce n'est pas le tout que nous portions le nom de chrestien, que nous en ayons la marcque qui est le Baptesme; nous voyons que Dieu n'estend point sa misericorde sur tous ceulx qui ont eu le tiltre d'estre son people. Il n'est donc point parlé de tous en general, mais d'un residu. Et pourtant, comme j'ay desja touché, qu'un chacun regarde bien à soy. Nous sommes tous appelez pour estre peuple de Dieu, voire, mais d'autant qu'il y en a beaucoup qui abusent de sa grace, qui provocquent son ire, il faut qu'ilz soyent retranchez, et qu'il diminue le nombre de ceulx qu'il avoit choisiz. Au lieu donc qu'il y avoit une grande multitude de ceulx ausquelz Dieu s'estoit presenté, ce nombre là estant diminué, il est dict maintenant que Dieu gardera un residu, ou quelque petite semence …"

Elsewhere, Calvin states that there are "a few wretches among us whom the Devil possesses." These people think they render God a service by not eating meat on Friday or Saturday. But God has rejected them as not even worthy of being called dogs.[167]

These examples might suffice to show that, although Calvin treats his congregation as a covenant community, he neither believed nor preached that all were converted believers on their way to heaven. When Moehn states that Calvin's doctrine of predestination supports preaching to all since Calvin preached God's election "in the first-person plural,"[168] he does not mention that Calvin's speaking in the first-person plural was rooted in his doctrine of the covenant or general election and that, by using the word "us," Calvin does not (always) mean the specially elect or true believers. A very clear passage in this respect is found in sermon 10 in which Calvin states that God does not always give "us" the grace to call upon him since it is a special gift for the elect.[169] Calvin's use of the first-person plural is not rooted in the doctrine of predestination but in his view of the covenant. Hence, it is clear that, for Calvin, the congregation and the elect do not precisely coincide. The difference between the two will also be made clear below when we deal with conditionality and promises and with the response to preaching in Calvin's sermons.

2.16.3 The Purpose of Preaching

The question of the purpose of preaching can be divided into two. First, what is God's purpose in preaching? And, what was Calvin's purpose in preaching? As we have seen in 2.8, Calvin denies that God's purpose is that all who hear the Gospel will be saved. Rather, God's purpose is twofold: the salvation of the elect and the hardening of the reprobate. Nevertheless, it was argued that Calvin and all preachers were to desire that all people be saved. Unlike his polemical writings, Calvin's sermons on Micah do not contain any passage in which he explicitly states that it is not God's purpose to save all. But there are many passages where he states it implicitly. God will save only a remnant of the covenant community; there are wretches in the congregation whom God has already rejected;

---

167 *Michée*, [22] 190 (*Micah*, 335): "Et mesmes il y a encores de ces malheureux entre nous que le diable a en sa possesion ... desja Dieu les rejecte et pronoce icy qu'ilz ne sont pas dignes d'estre appelez chiens et d'estre mis au rang des bestes brutes ..."
168 W.H.T. Moehn, *God roept ons tot Zijn dienst*, 277-90.
169 *Michée*, [10] 83 (*Micah*, 147): "En quoy nous avons à noter que Dieu ne nous faict point tousjours la grace de l'invocation ... C'est donc un don special que Dieu faict à ses eleuz ..."

the Lord will save "a few" that are "his own."[170] Such words teach implicitly but clearly that it is not God's purpose to save all.

Nonetheless, there are also at least three passages where Calvin seems to tell his congregation that God does indeed want to save all of them. In sermon 10 he says that some people are so obstinate that, even though God works in them through his Holy Spirit, he cannot achieve his purpose. In sermon 21 he tells his congregation that preaching is like saying "The only thing God wants is for us to be at peace with him." And in sermon 25 he remarks that God's purpose in preaching the Gospel is that humankind might be saved, but human malice frustrates God's intention.[171] These paradoxes should not be made into inconsistencies. The genre and audience of a sermon are quite different from that of a systematic work. In his sermons, Calvin is addressing a distinct audience, to wit, his Genevan congregation. In his polemics against Pighius and others, he is reflecting on preaching and God's will. Calvin distinguishes between a hidden and a revealed will of God. He does not mention God's hidden purpose in his sermons but restricts himself to speaking about God's revealed will. God has not revealed that he will actually save all people or all members of the covenant community, but he has revealed that he will save all who believe, and he urges all people to believe the Gospel. The covenant is conditional, and hence preaching is conditional. Calvin does not always mention the conditions. But we should not conclude that Calvin held that God wants to save all hearers unconditionally, even though he does not mention the conditions explicitly in his sermons. In the examples mentioned above, it is obvious from the resistance of human beings that Calvin is talking about the resistible and conditional administration of the covenant.

Calvin's own intention with his sermons is not often apparent. In most sermons, he is silent about himself and just explains and applies the words of Micah. But, sometimes, when explaining and applying, he reveals his own desires and maybe even permits his congregation a glimpse into his heart. The clearest example is to be found in sermon 25 on Micah 7:1, where Micah complains about the absence of fruit of his labors. Calvin argues that in such cases preachers should not be too disappointed but must continue to perform their office because God approves the preaching of the Gospel. His own disappointment is almost palpable when he applies it especially to his own situation and that of his fellow preachers in Geneva by saying that "especially today, we must be armed against this

---

170 *Michée,* [19] 155; [20] 165-66; [22] 190; [25] 209 (*Micah,* 274, 292; 335; 369).
171 *Michée,* [10] 83; [21] 178; [25] 209-10 (*Micah,* 147, 314, 371).

temptation."[172] They need to be "motivated by the desire to see the entire world brought to God" and seeing that the world chooses to oppose God, they are "right to feel dejected and sad … because to see souls created in the image of God move toward their own damnation is hardly a light matter, especially souls that were redeemed at such a cost by the blood of God's Son." Shortly after, he talked about disappointed hopes and a desire that was not matched by the outcome and concluded that preachers must strive with all their might to procure the salvation of the world and not abandon the desire to bring salvation to the world.[173]

Although Calvin taught that, as long as we are looking at human beings, we should desire the salvation of all, it is different when we lift up our eyes to see God's kingdom. Then we can "forget humankind" and even rejoice in the damnation of the wicked as well as of the devil. But Calvin warns against two things here: desiring the damnation of certain individuals we hate and judging anyone too hastily. Even though we may judge someone to be wicked, we have to desire his salvation, for we do not know whether God will save him in the end.[174]

2.17 The Sermons on Genesis

Calvin's sermons on Genesis were given in 1559 and 1560. He was 50 years old and his health was suffering. Nevertheless, he had just finished a new edition of his *Institutes* and had seen a wish fulfilled: the Academy of Geneva opened in June 1559. The last years of the Reformer were marked by fewer conflicts than before.[175]

Many characteristics of Calvin's sermons on Micah are also characteristic for his sermons on Genesis. Therefore, I will only address matters that provide new information. I also made a selection of some series of Calvin's sermons on Genesis. The series on Melchizedek was chosen, since this priest and king was called a type of Christ by the author of Hebrews. I choose the series on Abraham's justification since justification was not only a central theme for Calvin, but was also related to election.

---

172 See Parson's study for the historical context of Calvin's sermons on Micah.
173 *Michée*, [25] 208-11 (*Micah*, 368-73). In lamenting the little fruit he saw, Calvin did not mention reprobation but always ascribed it to the hardness and sinfulness of human beings.
174 *Michée*, [28] 231-33 (*Micah*, 410-13).
175 For the context of Calvin's sermons of Genesis, see Max Engammare, "Introduction" in Jean Calvin, *Sermons sur la Genèse,* Supplementa Calviniana Vol XI/1, vii-lviii. Neukirchen-Vluyn: Neukirchener Verlag, 2000

The series on Jacob and Esau were selected because Paul brought this story by as a proof of election in his letter to the Romans.[176]

One of the most striking differences between the sermons on Micah and those on Genesis, is that there are many sermons on Genesis in which no reference at all is made to the doctrine of predestination or to the doctrine of the covenant. This is remarkable, given that the sermons on Genesis were delivered after the Bolsec controversy. A possible reason for this fact is that Micah's prophecy was addressed to a covenant community, while the book of Genesis contains the history of persons.

In his sermons on the history of Abraham and Melchizedek, Calvin seldom makes any reference to the covenant or to predestination. The conclusion about the sermons on Micah, i.e., that Calvin's sermons were less Christocentric than one would suppose from his remarks on preaching and the object of faith, also holds for most of the sermons on Genesis. But one sermon, i.e., the second, has a definite Christocentric character.[177]

Calvin speaks consistently about "us" and "we." In contrast to his sermons on Micah, Calvin does this only in a positive sense here.[178] In his sermons on Melchizedek, Calvin usually does not clearly address the doctrine of predestination. He does not even talk about the fact that people are predestined, either to life or to death but made a more practical distinction between the wicked *(meschans)* and believers *(fideles)*.[179]

Although the sermons on Abraham's justification by faith follow those on Melchizedek immediately, they are very different regarding the covenant and predestination. While there are hardly any references to these subjects in the series on Melchizedek, there are plenty in the series on justification. It is possible that this is because the series begins with a sermon on God's declaration that Ishmael will not be Abraham's heir. The references to predestination and covenant do not differ from those in Calvin's sermons on Micah. In these sermons, he repeated the content of what he said in his *Institutes* concerning Abraham's posterity. Not all

---

176 The first two series are included in *CO* XXIII and in Jean Calvin, *Sermons sur la Genèse,* Supplementa Calviniana Vol XI/II (quoted as *Genèse* Vol. II. The last series was just rediscovered before the edition of *CO* was finished and was included in *CO* LVIII. It is not in the *Supplementa Calviniana* Vol XI. Translations of the Genesis sermons are taken from *Sermons on Genesis Chapters 11-20* (Edinburgh: The Banner of Truth, 2012), translation by Rob Roy McGregor.
177 Calvin, *Trois Sermons sur l'histoire de Melchisedec, CO* XXIII, 654-68; *Genèse,* Vol. II, 708-19 (these are sermons 63-65 in the McGregor translation)
178 *Melchisedec, CO* XXIII, [2] 655, [3] 682; *Genèse,* Vol. II, 708, 730 (Sermon 64, 251-69).
179 *Melchisedec, CO* XXIII, [2] 659; *Genèse,* Vol. II,711.

descendants of Abraham are really his seed. And although Jacob's seed was adopted, the majority of them became estranged from God.

> [W]e must think higher and distinguish between Abraham's children who remain in their order and their status, and are, in this way, God's recognized and avowed children, as opposed to the children who are rejected, although they descended from him. As we see later, Isaac begat Esau and Jacob. Even though Esau was the firstborn, he is nonetheless rejected, though of the same birth.[180]

The actual seed of Abraham is Jesus Christ. If we want to be real children of Abraham, we should be joined to Christ.

> Therefore, that seed must have a head or we will not have the truth of that promise. It is true that they spoke not only of Jesus Christ, as some have understood him too inadequately, but we must hold to this course: that Jesus Christ is set forth before us, and we are gathered into him, and that union will cause us to be esteemed and reckoned as Abraham's children. Consequently, there would be no seed of the kind spoken of here, if Jesus Christ did not hold the sovereign position and we had not been united in him as members of his body to be gathered into God's house, and consequently, into Abraham's.[181]

In this series of sermons, we can find more detailed information about Calvin's view of the order of salvation. In dealing with how we can please God by faith, Calvin speaks of the order in which one comes to faith. This is illustrative of how he deals with questions of faith, assurance, and the need to acknowledge one's sinfulness, and it agrees with what he wrote to Sadolet years before.

---

180 *Quatre sermons sur la iustification*, CO XXIII, [1] 684-85; *Genèse*, Vol. II, 742 (Sermon 67, 311): "[C]'est de savoir discerner entre les enfans d'Abram qui demeurent en leur ordre et en leur estat, et par ce moyen sont aussi recognus et avouëz enfans de Dieu, et les enfans qui s'abastardissent, combien qu'ils soyent descendus de sa race. Comme depuis quand Isaac a engendré Esau et Iacob: combien qu'Esau soit le premier né, toutesfois il ne laisse pas d'estre reietté de la maison: et si est-il d'une mesme ventrée."

181 *Iustification*, CO XXIII, [1] 685; *Genèse*, Vol. II, 742 (Sermon 67, 311-12): "Il faut donc qu'il y ait un chef de ceste semence, ou nous n'aurons point la verité de ceste promesse. Vray est qu'ils n'ont point seulement parlé de Iesus Christ, comme aucuns l'ont prins trop cruement: mais il nous faut tenir cest ordre, c'est que Iesus Christ nous soit là mis en avant, et que nous soyons recueillis en luy: et ceste union-la fera que nous serons tenus et reputez enfans d'Abram. Il n'y auroit point donc de semence telle qu'il est ici question, si Iesus Christ n'obtenoit le degré souverain, et que nous ne fussions unis en luy estans membres de son corps, afin d'estre recueillis en la maison de Dieu, et par consequent en la maison d'Abram."

The first requirement is that we need to see our condition: that we are accursed, damned, and lost. We should be deeply affected by this conviction, to the extent that we become empty, like poor starving people. We must be mortally wounded and brought into utter despair. This is not because God takes delight in humbling us but because he knows it is necessary. Unless we see our misery, we will be lulled into sleep in our hypocrisy. It is humility that leads us to our Lord Jesus Christ. And these two things cannot be separated. In order to humble us, God uses his holy law.[182] Next, we should realize that justification does not mean that we are made righteous but that God accepts us, even though we are miserable sinners, and forgives us our sins. Now we see our need of Christ. It is he who has made satisfaction for us, and discharged us of all our debts by the merit of his death, and shed his precious blood to wash us. Calvin does not mention predestination at all but consistently talks about "we" and "us."[183]

Nevertheless, it seems that Calvin makes a restriction. At this point, he very explicitly refers to his earlier remarks about the necessity of seeing one's misery:

> [W]e cannot receive forgiveness of our sins – although God offers it to us – until we are completely confounded within ourselves, until we are awakened, until there is no hypocrisy or pretence to cause us to believe one thing or another, until there is no dissembling, until we are not double-minded or asleep in our indifference; but, to receive that forgiveness, we must be like poor condemned, lost people, whom the judgment of God persues until we do not know what to do and are already viewing death as present, so to speak, as if beholding God's hand armed to carry out the sentence of curse which he pronounces against us.[184]

---

182 *Iustification*, CO XXIII, [2] 697-703; *Genèse*, Vol II, 753-758 (Sermon 68, 331-32, 335).
183 *Iustification*, CO XXIII, [2] 703-06; *Genèse*, Vol. II, 758-760 (Sermon 68, 338). Calvin consistently told his congregation that "we" are justified.
184 *Iustification*, CO XXIII, [2] 708; *Genèse*, Vol. II, 762 (Sermon 68, 343): "[N]ous ne pouvons recevoir la remission de nos pechez, combien qu'elle nous soit offerte alors de Dieu, iusqu'à ce que nous soyons du tout confus en nous mesmes, que nous soyons bien resveillez, qu'il n'y ait point d'hypocrisie ne de fiction qui nous face à croire ceci ou cela et qu'il n'y ait nul desguisement, que nous ne soyons point doubles, ni endormis en nostre non-chalance: mais que nous soyons comme povres gens damnez et perdus, que le iugement de Dieu persecute, tellement que nous ne sachions que faire, et que nous soyons là comme si desia nous voyons la mort presente, comme si nous voyons la main de Dieu armée pour executer la sentence de malediction qu'il prononce à l'encontre de nous."

And a little later:

> Therefore, so that we may remember these things, it will be enough for us to know the way we must become sharers in the eternal salvation which has been brought to us by the Son of God. We must realize how wretched our condition is – not to confess it with our mouths and have some uncertain concept of it – so that we will be broken with such sadness that we will be confounded before God to the point of hating and despising ourselves. When we are thus our own judges, then we have been absolved by God. When we are thus dead within ourselves, then we will find our lives within Jesus Christ. It is not enough that we know we are pitiable sick people, poor and indigent, but we must be completely dead so that we may be made alive by nothing but the grace of our Lord Jesus Christ.[185]

These two quotes suggest that Calvin's view was not only that knowledge of one's misery was necessary but also that some degree of misery was necessary. And hence we can conclude that, although Calvin does not make a restriction in these sermons via the doctrine of predestination, he does make a restriction via the notion of humility. The humility of sinners even seems to become a condition for appropriating the promise of salvation. This seems to be inconsistent with his remarks about the universality and unconditionality of the promises, but Calvin does not address this inconsistency in his sermons. Again, it does not seem to have been a problem for Calvin himself. Strictly spoken, the condition is not required before justification is offered or ought to be accepted, but before it will be accepted. (See 2.9 for other possible solutions to these conflicting statements).

---

185 *Iustification, CO* XXIII, [2] 710; *Genèse*, Vol. II, 763-764 (Sermon 68, 346): "Il suffira donc à fin que les choses soyent bien retenues, d'avoir cognu quelle ouverture il nous faut avoir pour estre participans du salut eternel qui nous a esté apporté par le Fils de Dieu, c'est que nous sachions combien nostre condition est miserable, et que ce ne soit point pour le confesser de bouche, et pour en avoir quelque imagination volage; mais que nous soyons navrez d'une telle tristesse que nous soyons confus devant Dieu iusques à nous hair et nous despiter contre nous mesmes. Quand nous serons ainsi nos iuges, voila comme nous serons absouts de Dieu. Quand nous serons ainsi morts en nousmesmes, voila comme nous trouverons nostre vie en Iesus Christ. Car il ne suffit point que nous cognoissions que nous sommes povres malades, et que nous sommes povres et indigens: mais il faut que nous soyons morts du tout, à fin que nous soyons vivifiez par la seule grace de nostre Seigneur Iesus Christ."

The sermons on Jacob and Esau are of special interest since this story is a classic *locus* for the doctrine of predestination.[186] Not all 13 sermons in the series deal with Jacob and Esau. Sermons 6 to 9 are about Isaac. Those sermons do not contain anything of interest additional to what already has been said. The remaining nine sermons are examples of Calvin's way of addressing questions regarding the covenant and predestination in his preaching. The first sermon is on Isaac and Ishmael. The latter was cut off from the church; he was reprobated and left the country of Canaan. But he was circumcised "as if he was an heir of God."[187] Calvin does not address the tension between these two facts in the first sermon but deals with it at length when preaching on Jacob and Esau.

Calvin paid special attention to Rebecca's fear with respect to the struggle that seemed to rage in her womb. God used the struggling twins in her to make clear that not all who proceeded from her and Isaac after the flesh would be included among the believers. Isaac would father some who would be cut off from the church by God. This was a cause of sorrow for Isaac and Rebecca.

Calvin takes the time to explain something more about the covenant and predestination for his audience. He explains the covenant with Abraham as an offer of grace, leaving God free to elect whoever he wills and passing over all others. This was true with respect to Isaac and Ishmael and Jacob and Esau. But it was also true regarding Jacob's posterity, for most of them were rejected by God. Nevertheless, Calvin sees God's distinguishing among Jacob's seed not negatively but positively. There are two kinds of grace among Abraham's posterity. The first is that they are blessed above others by receiving the sacrament of the covenant; the second is that God "holds fast" those whom he wills. Calvin was convinced that, without this latter grace, all of Jacob's seed would have fallen away. Ishmael himself left Canaan, and Esau despised the right of the firstborn. Hence, the election within the covenant community is not a negative act of cutting off those who would otherwise be saved but of saving those who would otherwise cut themselves off.

These things led Calvin to some practical remarks. The first is that we should not take pride in the fact that we are members of the church; rather, we have to make our election sure by the inward testimony of the

---

186 *Treze sermons de M. I. Calvin tractans de l'election gratuite de Dieu en Iacob, et de la reiectrion en Esau.* CO LVIII (Quoted as *Iacob et Esau*) (English translation by John Field, *Sermons on Election and Reprobation* [Audubon: Old Paths Publications 1996, reprint of a translation of 1579]).
187 *Iacob et Esau*, CO LVIII, [1] 18-30.

Holy Spirit. The second is that we should accept what God does – even in reprobating some of our children – with adoration and without protest. The third is that we not use the doctrine of predestination to excuse our behavior. There are "dogs" who bark against the doctrine, and there are "swine" who say: "If I'm elect, I will be saved, whatever I do, and if I'm reprobate, I will be damned, whatever I do." The fourth is that we should turn to the Scriptures with all our questions.

A striking omission in Calvin's practical remarks concerns Christ. Although Calvin instructs his hearers that their election is "in Christ," he does not address the question of the object of faith nor does he point in these sermons to Christ as the "mirror of election." Christ is not given the prominent place in these sermons as we would expect in Calvin, given what we know about his views.

Another striking fact is that, in his third sermon, Calvin repeats some parts of his arguments against Pighius, although Calvin does not mention Pighius or Bolsec by name. Bolsec's arguments were probably still known and sometimes discussed in Geneva.[188]

The eternal decree of God's predestination is hidden but reveals itself in history.[189] Election is revealed in Jacob's life, and reprobation in Esau's. The latter can be seen when Esau sells his birthright for some of Jacob's red soup. Jacob shows his faith in God's promise that Esau will serve him; Esau despises God's promise for the firstborn.[190] A second step in Esau's despising of God's promise was his marrying two Hittite women. Calvin regards this as a second proof of his reprobation: he was not led by God's Spirit; he was not "held fast."[191] In explaining this history at length, Calvin shows that his doctrine of predestination does not abolish human responsibility. Although Jacob's faith is given him by God through election, Esau acted on his own, without any compulsion. This accords with Calvin's frequently speaking of God "holding fast" the elect and "letting loose" the reprobate. This "letting loose" eventually results in "cutting off" the reprobate from the covenant.

2.18 Summary: Theory and Practice

The sermons of Calvin that we have examined here are consistent with his systematic-theological remarks concerning predestination and preaching. He preached one message to the entire congregation. Although it

---

188 *Iacob et Esau, CO* LVIII, [2,3] 31-60.
189 *Iacob et Esau, CO* LVIII, [4] 59.
190 *Iacob et Esau, CO* LVIII, [5] 73-88.
191 *Iacob et Esau, CO* LVIII, [10] 154.

sometimes becomes clear that he regarded his congregation as consisting of both the elect and the reprobate, he usually addressed them as elect believers. He viewed them as a covenant community that had to be addressed as a community of believers in line with charitable judgment.

The one message for the whole congregation was an explanation of the text, applied to the people of Geneva. Calvin usually restricted himself entirely to the text for his sermon, be it a promise or a threat. That means that doctrinal subjects like predestination almost only occur in his sermons when the text gave occasion for them.[192] Whenever this happened – for instance, in the sermons on Jacob and Esau – Calvin did not hesitate to address election and reprobation. The occasions when, and how, he dealt with predestination in his sermons is in line with what he taught elsewhere.

In one respect, Calvin's sermons are not consistent with his more theoretical remarks. Despite his observations on the place of Christ in preaching, in these sermons Calvin seldom points to Christ as the mirror of election and the object of faith. These sermons are less Christocentric than one might expect from his remarks in his more doctrinal and polemical works. For Calvin, preaching Christ did actually depend on the occasion the text gave for it, just like the theme of predestination, despite his view that the Scriptures should be read with the aim of finding Christ in them.[193]

A second inconsistency is that, in contrast to his systematic remarks on preaching predestination, in his sermons on Ishmael, Jacob, and Esau Calvin also mentions reprobation. The text gave him occasion to do so and it seems that the imperative found in the biblical text to speak about reprobation was stronger than his own reluctance to talk about it from the pulpit.

I cannot agree with Neuser's view that Calvin had two doctrines of predestination – a pastoral one and a logical one.[194] Calvin's doctrine of predestination is the same, both in his sermons and in his polemical or systematic books. A different genre and a different audience led him to deal with this doctrine in different ways. That Calvin hardly ever mentions reprobation in his sermons is the practical consequence of his systematic thoughts on predestination and, more importantly, of his limiting himself to the text he was

---

192 An example of an exception to this rule is his sermon on 1 Timothy 2:4. At first sight, the text does not seem to give occasion for talking about predestination. But since Calvin's opponents referred to texts like these to reject predestination, Calvin felt obliged to declare that this text did not argue against it and to explain how they should be read in accordance with predestination.
193 Comm. on John 5:39 [1553], dating from the period between his sermons on Micah and on Genesis.
194 Wilhelm H. Neuser, "Predestination," in *Calvin Handbook*, 312-23.

preaching on. That he addresses the congregation as an elect congregation in the first-person plural is a practical consequence of his systematic ideas on the covenant, church, and predestination.

In summarizing this chapter with respect to the central question whether predestination influenced the theory and practice of the call of the Gospel in preaching, a nuanced answer should be given. Predestination and the external call are closely related in Calvin's theology. In effect, the call is the execution in time of God's eternal decree. The external call is a means to execute general election; the special or internal call is a means to execute special election. And yet, despite this close connection between the two, the external call by a preacher is by no means dominated by predestination, neither in its address nor in its content. The external call to eternal life is addressed to all who hear it, and its content is the complete message of Scripture, of which predestination is only a part.

3. Early Reformed Orthodoxy - Theodore Beza

3.1 Beza and the Question of Predestination and Preaching

Like Calvin, Theodore Beza (1519-1605) was not a native citizen of Geneva but was French by birth.[1] He was born in Vezelay in 1519 and studied in Paris, Orléans, and Bourges. He had the same teacher as Calvin in the latter two cities: Melchior Wolmar.[2] By reading a book by Bullinger and under the influence of Wolmar's teaching, in the end Beza adopted Reformed thought. He left France and went to Geneva, arriving there in 1548. The next year, he went to Germany to meet Wolmar again, visiting Lausanne on the way. Viret was successful in getting him to remain there as a professor and pastor. Beza published a few works while in Lausanne and kept in contact with Calvin. When the council of Geneva founded an Academy, they called Beza as professor. He accepted the call and stayed in Geneva from 1558 until his death in 1605.

The Bolsec affair in Geneva in 1551 had Beza's interest, though he was still in Lausanne at the time. In November, the church in Geneva wrote a letter to Basel, Zurich, and Bern on this matter. Calvin visited Beza in Lausanne that same month, and it is very likely they discussed the situation in Geneva and Bolsec's teachings concerning predestination. The times were difficult for the church in Geneva, for none of the churches mentioned joined its radical refutation of Bolsec. Calvin was especially

---

1 There are several biographies of Beza. The most recent is Alain Dufour, *Théodore de Bèze: Poète et théologien* (Geneva: Droz, 2006). See also Paul F. Geisendorf, *Théodore de Bèze* (Geneva: Alexandre Jullien, 1949; reprint 1967). The only complete biography in English is Henry Martyn Baird, *Theodore Beza, the Counselor of the French Reformation 1519-1605* (New York: G.P. Putnam's Sons, 1899). A Dutch biography is: C. van Sliedrecht, *Calvijns opvolger Theodorus Beza: Zijn verkiezingsleer en zijn belijdenis van de drieënige God* (Leiden: J.J. Groen en Zoon, 1996). Surveys of Beza's life have appeared in, for example, Jill Raitt, *Shapers of Religious Traditions in Germany, Switzerland, and Poland, 1560-1600* (New Haven: Yale University Press, 1981) and David Steinmetz, *Reformers in the Wings* (Philadelphia: Fortress Press, 1971), 162-71. There are two contemporary biographies, one hostile by his opponent Bolsec (1584) and one appreciative by his colleague De la Faye (1607). In the 19th century Beza received much attention in Germany, which resulted in three biographies: Schlosser (1809), Baum (1843-1851) and Heppe (1861).

2 Melchior Wolmar, a humanist with Lutheran sympathies, still needs extensive research. On him, see D.J. de Groot, "Melchior Wolmar: Ses relations avec les réformateurs français et suisses," *Bulletin de l'Histoire du Protestantisme français*, 83 (1934), 416-439.

disappointed by the answers from the church in Zurich, and from Zurich's pastor Bullinger. Beza wrote at least two letters to Bullinger defending Calvin's teachings.[3]

On January 1, 1552, Calvin published his *De aeterna Dei praedestinatione*. Beza responded twenty days later in a letter to Calvin, criticizing Calvin's method and structure to some extent. According to Beza, Calvin was led too much by his wish to answer his opponents Pighius and Bolsec and therefore followed their lead.[4] This is an indication that Beza wanted a more methodical approach for dealing with the questions of eternal predestination and its consequences or effects in time. Beza was then professor at Lausanne, so it is likely that didactical considerations compelled Beza to summarize this part of theology more schematically in order to provide some structure for his students in this complex subject. This resulted in Beza's *Summa totius christianismi* (1555) with its explanation.[5] Some other reasons for writing this book will be discussed in 3.5.3.

Since Beza wrote about the way predestination was effected, the call was one of the subjects he touched on. Indeed, in his very first sentence, Beza quotes Augustine who states that "they that were against him as adversaries in this question [i.e., of perseverance] did allege that this doctrine of predestination hindered the preaching of God's word and rendered it useless."[6]

In 1558, Beza again took part in a conflict on predestination. Once more, the origin of the conflict was an attack on Calvin's doctrine. This

---

3 Beza to Bullinger, October 29, 1551, in Théodore de Bèze, *Correspondance de Théodore de Bèze*, vol. I (1539-1555) (Geneva: Librarie Droz, 1960) 61. (Quoted as *Correspondance*), 71-73; Beza to Bullinger, January 12, 1552, in *Correspondance* 1, 76-79.
4 Beza to Bullinger, January 21, 1552, in *Correspondance* 1, 81-83. See also Van Sliedrecht, *Calvijns opvolger*, 102; Richard A. Muller, "The Use and Abuse of a Document: Beza's *Tabula Praedestinationis*, The Bolsec Controversy, and the Origins of Reformed Orthodoxy," in Carl R. Trueman and R. Scott Clark (eds.) *Protestant Scholasticism: Essays in Reassessment* (Carlisle, UK: Paternoster Press, 1999), 38-39.
5 Beza, *Summa Totius Christianismi, sive descriptio et distributio causarum salutis electorum, & exitij reproborum, ex sacris literis collecta cum Brevis explicatio praecedentis Tabvlae*, in *Tractationum Theologicarum, in quibus pleraque Christianae Religionis dogmata aduersus haereses nostris temporibus renouatas solidè ex Verbo Dei defenduntur Volumen [primum]* (Geneva: Io. Cripspinum, 1570), 170-205. A reprint in 1582 was typeset anew, but the page numbers remained the same. (The *Summa* with the *Brevis Explicatio* are quoted as *Tabula* caput, aphorism, page; the *Tractationum Theologicarum* are quoted as *TT*.)
6 *Tabula*, 1, *TT* I, 171. Calvin had quoted the same sentences by Augustine in his *De aeterna Dei praedestinatione*, *CO* VIII, 325-27; *COR* III/1, 170-74.

time, the attack came from Sebastian Castellio,[7] and Beza decided to defend his colleague.[8] Castellio used some of the same arguments Pighius had used, among those the biblical statements in Ezek. 33:11 and 2 Pet. 3:9 that God does not will the death of a sinner and that God does not want any to perish but all to come to knowledge of the truth. After more than two decades Beza wrote on the doctrine of predestination again: in 1582, he published his *De praedestinationis doctrina et vero usu tractatio absolutissima*,[9] a result of his lectures on the Epistle of Paul to the Romans.[10]

In 1586, Beza and his colleague Anthony Fayus[11] edited their theological theses.[12] This work is more a *summa totius christianismi* than Beza's

---

7 For him, see Hans Rudolf Guggisberg and Bruce Gordon, *Sebastian Castellio, 1515-1563: Humanist and Defender of Religious Toleration in a Confessional Age* (Aldershot: Ashgate, 2003); F.E. Buisson and M. Engammare, *Sebastien Castellion: Sa vie, son oeuvre: 1515-1563* (Geneva: Droz, 2010); M.K. van Veen, *De kunst van het twijfelen: Sebastian Castellio (1515-1563). Humanist, calvinist, vrijdenker* (Zoetermeer: Meinema, 2012).

8 *Ad sycophantarum quorandam calumnias quib vnicum salutis nostræ fundamentum, id est aeternam Dei praedestinationem evertere nituntur, responsio Theodori Bezae Vezelii* (Geneva: Conrad Badius, 1558). In the *TT* this work is called *Ad Sebastiani Castellionis calumnias* [...], *TT*, I, 337-424. (Quoted as *Ad calumnias*.)

9 *De praedestinationis doctrina et vero usu tractatio absolutissima, editio secunda* (n.p. [Geneva]: Eustathius Vignon, 1582; reprint 1583) (quoted as *De praedestinationis doctrina*) (*TT*, III). This treatise on predestination was edited by Raphael Egli or Eglinus, the same student who defended the theses on predestination published in the *Theses theologicae*. For the remarkable life of the theologian and alchemist Egli, see Bruce T. Moran, "Alchemy, Prophecy, and the Rosicrucians: Raphael Eglinus and Mystical Currents of the Early Seventeenth Century," in *Alchemy and Chemistry in the 16th and 17th Centuries*, ed. Piyo Rattansi and Antonio Clericuzio (Dordrecht: Kluwer, 1994), 103-19, and Howard Hotson, *Johann Heinrich Alsted 1588-1638: Between Renaissance, Reformation and Universal Reform* (Oxford: OUP, 2000), 59-65. The scope of this treatise was not polemical or systematic but exegetical. See Raymond A. Blacketer, "The Man in the Black Hat: Theodore Beza and the Reorientation of Early Reformed Historiography," in Jordan J. Ballor, David Sytsma, and Jason Zuidema (eds.) *Church and School in Early Modern Protestantism: Studies in Honor of Richard A. Muller on the Maturation of a Theological Tradition* (Leiden: Brill, 2013), 225-41.

10 Beza's lectures were not published by himself but are available to some extent by means of notes from a student: Théodore de Bèze, *Cours sur les épîtres aux Romains et aux Hébreux 1564–66 d'après les notes de Marcus Widler: Thèses disputées à l'Académie de Genève, 1564–67*, edited by Pierre Fraenkel and Luc Perrotet (*Travaux d'Humanisme et Renaissance*, CCXXVI) (Geneva: Librairie Droz, 1988). (Quoted as *Cours*.)

11 For Fayus, see: Martin Sallmann, "La Faye, Antoine" in Hans Dieter Betz, Don S. Browning, Bernd Janowski, and Eberhard Jüngel (eds.), *Religion Past and Present*. (Leiden: Brill Online, 2012). http://referenceworks.brillonline.com/entries/religion-past-and-present/la-faye-antoine-SIM_12543.

12 *Theses theologicae in schola Genevensi ab aliquot sacrarum literarum studiosus sub DD*,

Tabula, which contained these words in its title. In the theses, the doctrine of predestination was set in a more theological framework, after the discussion of the doctrine of God and his attributes, and providence.

Finally, the doctrine of predestination was debated at the Colloquy of Montbéliard in 1586, where Beza's opponent was Jacob Andreae. Beza was reluctant to discuss predestination there but was forced to by his Lutheran opponent. He was also pressed to present his ideas on the relation between predestination and the atonement, which led him to criticize the formula that Christ died sufficiently for the whole world.[13]

The various works in which Beza dealt with predestination and the external call of the Gospel offer enough material to research his systematic-theological ideas on this matter. The fact that he published some volumes of sermons[14] make it possible to see whether or not his theological convictions affected the way he preached the Gospel.

After looking at Beza's relation to Calvin and early Reformed orthodoxy (3.3), we will examine Beza's *Summa totius christianismi* and its origins as his first extensive work dealing with predestination (3.4, 3.5). Then we will see whether his doctrine of predestination changed or developed in later years (3.6). We will subsequently examine Beza's views regarding the atonement (3.7), the covenant and church (3.8), God's purpose in preaching (3.9), predestination and the call (3.10, 3.11), predestination and faith (3.12), and the way predestination should be preached (3.13). Finally, some of Beza's sermons will be examined to see what role predestination plays in them (3.15) and whether his practice is in line with his theory (3.16).

3.2 Earlier Research

Compared to Calvin, Beza has received little attention, and in the studies devoted to him he is usually compared with Calvin. After two contemporary

---

Theod. Beza & Anthonio Fayo S.S. Theologiae professoribus propositae & disputatae: In quibus methodica locorum communium S.S. Theologiae epitome continetur (Geneva: Eustathius Vignon, 1586). (Quoted as *Theses*). An English translation was published within five years: *Propositions and principles of divinitie ...,* anonymous translator (Edinburgh: Robert Waldegrave, 1591). Translations from the theses are taken from this edition, unless stated otherwise.

13 T. Beza, *Ad Acta Colloquii Montisbelgardensis Tubingae edita Theodori Bezae responsionis* (Geneva: Joannes Le Preux, 1588), 217-218. See Thomas, *Extent*, 56-58, and Jill Rait, *The Colloquy of Montbéliard: Religion and Politics in the Sixteenth Century* (Oxford: Oxford University Press 1993).

14 *Sermons sur les trois premier chapitres du Cantique des Cantiques de Salomo* (Geneva: Iean le Prevx, 1586); *Sermons sur l'histoire de la passion et sepulture de nostre Seigneur Iesus Christ* (Geneva: Iean le Prevx, 1592), and *Sermons sur l'histoire de la resurrection de nostre Signeur Iesus Christ* (Geneva: Iean le Prevx, 1593).

biographies, it took two centuries before a new biography on him was published. After the 19th century, it took almost five decades before a new biography was written, and the next one was not published until the 21st century.[15] Interest in Beza increased in the second half of the 20th century. A number of studies on aspects of his theology appeared. Shawn D. Wright has given a good and extended survey of earlier research on Beza.[16] I refer to his study for an almost complete survey up to 2004. Here, I only mention the works related to the subject of this study and give an overview of literature published since 2004.

In the 19th century, the doctrine of predestination was seen as the central dogma of Reformed theology in general and of Beza in particular.[17] In the 20th century, this axiom was reason enough for some to set Beza (and later Reformed theologians) over against Calvin.[18] This axiom was questioned later, and one of the first to do so was John S. Bray, who concluded that "the location of predestination in Beza's major theological works does not support the claim that the doctrine was a central organizing principle in his theology."[19] He argued that Beza's teaching concerning predestination was basically the same as Calvin's but set in a more systematic and scholastic framework. In 1978, Tadataka Maruyama published his dissertation on "The Ecclesiology of Theodore Beza," in which he studied the relation between Beza's concepts of predestination and the church. Maruyama concluded that Beza related the doctrine of predestination to the reality of the church only in the last part of his life.[20] P.N. Holtrop's voluminous work on the Bolsec controversy threw light upon Beza's involvement in this controversy: he viewed Beza as nothing more than Calvin's shieldbearer.[21] In 1996, C. van Sliedrecht published his

---

15 See 3.1 note 1 for Beza's biographies.
16 Shawn D. Wright, *Our Sovereign Refuge: The Pastoral Theology of Theodore Beza* (Bletchley, Milton Keynes: Paternoster, 2004), 36-85.
17 See Willem J. van Asselt, "Reformed Orthodoxy: A Short History of Research," in Selderhuis, *Companion*, 11-26.
18 For instance, Basil Hall, "Calvin Against the Calvinists," in *John Calvin*, ed. Gervase Duffield (Grand Rapids: Eerdmans, 1966); cf. Brian Armstrong, *Calvinism and the Amyraut Heresy: Protestant Scholasticism and Humanism in Seventeenth Century France* (Madison: University of Wisconsin Press, 1969); R.T. Kendall, "The Puritan Modification of Calvin's Theology," in *John Calvin: His Influence in the Western World*, ed. W. Stanford Reid (Grand Rapids: Zondervan, 1982).
19 John S. Bray, *Theodore Beza's Doctrine of Predestination* (Nieuwkoop: B. de Graaf, 1975), 81.
20 Tadataka Maruyama, *The Ecclesiology of Theodore Beza: The Reform of the True Church* (Geneva: Librairie Droz, 1978), 141.
21 P.N. Holtrop, *The Bolsec Controversy on Predestination, from 1551 to 1555: The Statements of Jerome Bolsec, and the Responses of John Calvin, Theodore Beza and Other Reformed Theologians* (Lewiston: The Edwin Mellen Press, 1993).

dissertation on the doctrine of predestination and the confession of the Triune God by "Calvin's successor, Theodore Beza."[22] Van Sliedrecht regarded Calvin's theology as normative and saw Beza as Calvin's successor, which sometimes resulted in anachronisms.[23] Contra Bray, Van Sliedrecht concluded that the doctrine of predestination was of great importance for the whole of Beza's theology, albeit often in the background, and stressed the differences between Calvin and Beza. The second edition of David Steinmetz's *Reformers in the Wings* was published in 2001, in which he devoted one chapter to Beza. He adequately summarized the results of earlier researchers who saw great differences between Beza and Calvin. According to them, predestination was the nerve center of Beza's theology. Beza took a step backward by bringing predestination back into the context of providence, from which Calvin had removed it. Predestination became thereby a logical and necessary consequence of the doctrine of God, and election and reprobation became of equal worth.[24]

R.A. Muller contributed to the Beza research via several articles, writing a chapter on Beza in his *Christ and the Decree,* an article on the interpretation of the *Tabula,* and a chapter on the "practical syllogism" in Calvin, Beza, and the later Reformed tradition.[25] Muller argued that Beza's *Tabula* was not intended to be a complete theological system but should be read in the context of its origin: the Bolsec controversy. In Wright's own work, *Our Sovereign Refuge: The Pastoral Theology of Theodore Beza*, he criticizes the conclusions or premises of a great part of earlier research, i.e., that Beza's theology was entirely scholastic or predestinarian. His arguments are convincing, but he himself falls more or less in a similar trap since he also views Beza's works from just one point of view. All Beza's ideas are brought into a pastoral framework by Wright, and thus he does not pay enough attention to the different genres Beza used and the different motivations he had. The pastoral motive is evident here and there, but this motive is not the only foundation of his works and ideas. There are also others in Beza, such as an educational motive, an elenctic motive, and a biblical motive.

---

22 Van Sliedrecht, *Calvijns opvolger*.
23 For instance, although Van Sliedrecht was aware that Beza published his *Tabula Praedestinationis* in 1555, he nevertheless compared it (as well as other works of Beza he used) to the 1559 edition of Calvin's *Institutes*.
24 David C. Steinmetz, *Reformers in the Wings: From Geiler von Kayserberg to Theodore Beza*, 2nd ed. (Oxford: OUP, 2001), 118-19.
25 Muller, *Christ and the Decree,* 77-96; idem, "Use and Abuse"; idem, *Calvin and the Reformed Tradition*, 244-76.

Since Wright's survey, there have been various books and articles devoted to Beza. The following are related to the subject of this study. Jeffrey Mallinson's work on faith, reason, and revelation in Beza's theology corrected Walter Kickel's view of the same subject.[26] The Genevan Colloquy of 2005 was devoted to Beza. The publication of its *Actes* contains several contributions important for this study.[27]

Donald Sinnema paid attention to Beza in his dissertation on reprobation. According to Sinnema, Beza's position on reprobation remained consistent during his life. The distinction between purpose and execution was distinctive for Beza. Reprobation is not the cause of unbelief in Beza's theology. Beza saw a strict parallelism between election and reprobation.[28] His article on "Beza's View of Predestination in Historical Perspective" offers insight into features of Beza's doctrine of predestination that were common to the Reformed, as well as those which are distinctive to Beza. Among the common Reformed features are *praedestinatio gemina*, predestination as a free act of God's will from eternity, and reprobation as a result of God's will but damnation because of one's own sin. The four distinctive features are the following. *First*, there is Beza's framework of the distinction between decree and execution: "election" can refer to the decree as well as to a stage in the execution of the decree. *Second*, according to Sinnema, Beza was the first supralapsarian. *Third*, Beza had a specific view of Christ in respect to predestination: as God, he was the origin of the decree, but, as Mediator, he was a means for executing the decree. *Fourth*, Beza's view of how one could gain assurance of salvation was different from Calvin's. The main features, including the distinctive ones, are already evident in Beza's early writings, which were written in Lausanne.[29]

---

26 Jeffrey Mallinson, *Faith, Reason, and Revelation in Theodore Beza (1519-1605)* (Oxford: OUP, 2003). Cf. Walter Kickel, *Vernunft un Offenbarung bei Theodor Beza: Zum Problem des Verhältnisses von Theologie, Philosophie und Staat* (Neukirchen-Vluyn: Neukirchener Verlag, 1957).

27 Irena Backus (ed.), *Théodore de Bèze, 1519-1605: Actes du colloque de Genève, septembre 2005* (Geneva: Droz, 2007). Important contributions are: Emidio Campi on Beza's correspondence with Bullinger (republished in English in Campi, *Shifting Patterns*, 169-83), by Olivier Fatio on Beza's little book of questions, by Donald Sinnema on Beza's doctrine of predestination in historical perspective, by Tadataka Maruyama on ecclesiology, and by Peter Opitz on Beza's "ratio docendi."

28 Donald Sinnema, *The Issue of Reprobation at the Synod of Dort (1618-19) in Light of the History of this Doctrine* (Toronto, PhD thesis, 1985), 66-73.

29 Donald Sinnema, "Beza's View of Predestination in Historical Perspective," in Backus (ed.), *Théodore de Bèze*, 219-39.

Sinnema also published an article on Beza's distinction between God's eternal decree and its execution in time.[30]

In 2012 Andrew Woolsey addressed Beza's ideas on the covenant. Over against the view that the notion of the covenant was virtually absent from Beza's theology, he argued that the doctrine of the covenant was integrated into almost all of Beza's theological works.[31] In 2013, Scott Manetsch published his study of the Genevan company of pastors in which Beza played an important role.[32]

3.3 Beza, Calvin, and Early Reformed Orthodoxy

Given that Beza was only ten years younger than Calvin and hence a contemporary of the Reformer, we need to address the question why Beza is regarded as a representative of early Reformed orthodoxy and not, like Calvin, of the Reformation. This question involves another one: What was the relation between Calvin and Beza and between their theologies.

Some older research regarded Beza primarily as Calvin's successor who altered Calvin's theology of the Reformation into a more scholastic form of theology.[33] But Steinmetz holds the opposite view, i.e., that, although Beza was a third-generation Reformer, he should be regarded as Calvin's co-worker and contemporary rather than as his successor.[34]

On the one hand, it is true that Beza succeeded Calvin as moderator of the company of pastors and as professor in theology. On the other hand, the difference in age was so minor that Beza and Calvin belonged to the same generation. Beza was already developing his theology before he succeeded Calvin as moderator, even before he arrived at Geneva. Moreover, as rector of the Genevan academy, Beza was Calvin's superior. But, despite the minor difference in age, Beza himself regarded Calvin as his teacher and father.[35] When they met for the first time as students of Wolmar, Calvin was 19 years old and Beza only 9. When they met again

---

30 Donald Sinnema, "God's Eternal Decree and its Temporal Execution: The Role of this Distinction in Theodore Beza's Theology," in Mark P. Holt, *Adaptations of Calvinism in Reformation Europe: Essays in Honour of Brian G. Armstrong* (Aldershot: Ashgate, 2007), 55-78.
31 Andrew A. Woolsey, *Unity and Continuity in Covenantal Thought: A Study in the Reformed Tradition to the Westminster Assembly* (Grand Rapids: Reformation Heritage Books, 2012), 344-95.
32 Manetsch, *Company*.
33 For instance, Van Sliedrecht, *Calvijns opvolger*, and Basil Hall in his "Calvin against the Calvinists." See also 3.2 note 18.
34 Steinmetz, *Reformers in the Wings*, 114.
35 For instance, in the earliest known letter from Beza to Calvin (April 19, 1550), he called Calvin *pater* and himself *filius*. *Correspondance* 61.

after Beza fled to Geneva shortly after his conversion to Reformed thought, Calvin had been active as a Reformed theologian for more than 12 years. It is plausible that both the first encounter of Calvin and Beza in 1528, when the latter was a child and the former almost an adult, and with Calvin having more experience in Reformed theology, made Beza view his contemporary Calvin not only as a friend but also as a spiritual father.

Beza's views concerning predestination were expressed in response to the attacks of Bolsec and Castellio on Calvin. Thus, in order of succession, Calvin's ideas were indeed first and those of Beza followed. In conclusion, we can say that Beza can be regarded as Calvin's successor, but that we have to be aware that Beza did not start theologizing when Calvin stopped. It would be anachronistic to compare all Beza's works, even those published before 1559, with the final edition of Calvin's *Institutes*, as if this was a source or touchstone for Beza's works, including his earlier ones.[36]

We also need to address the question whether Beza is a proper representative of the era of early Reformed orthodoxy. There is no exact point in time when this era began,[37] but given a series of important events within a period of five years, most church historians date its origin between ca. 1559 and 1564. For Genevan theology, the year 1559 was important. Calvin had then edited the final Latin edition of the *Institutes* and the Academy of Geneva was founded in the same year. In the following years, some of the most important Reformers of the second generation died: Melanchthon in 1561, Vermigli in 1562, Musculus in 1563, and Calvin in 1564. Several confessions were published in that same period: the *Confessio Gallicana* (1559), the *Confessio Belgica* (1561), and the *Heidelberg Catechism* (1563), among others. Although it is not possible to draw a sharp line between the Reformation and early orthodoxy, it is commonly acknowledged that the Reformed churches entered upon a new phase that started in these years.[38] The period of early Reformed Orthodoxy is marked not only by confessionalization but also by an accent on academic education. The Reformed academic *Gymnasium* of Strasbourg was founded already in 1538 and was for a long time the only

---

36 As is done by Hall, Steinmetz, and Van Sliedrecht.
37 For a survey of early Reformed orthodoxy see Willem J. van Asselt, *Introduction to Reformed Scholasticism* (Grand Rapids: Reformation Heritage Books, 2011), 103-31.
38 Not only the Reformed churches, but the Lutheran and Roman Catholic churches also underwent a similar process of confessionalization.

one of this kind. The Genevan Academy was one of the first of a series of Reformed academies to be erected within a relatively short period.[39]

Beza's lifetime spanned both the period of the Reformation and the period of early Reformed orthodoxy. The Reformation had already begun some years before his birth, and the period of early Reformed orthodoxy lasted until some ten years after his death. Beza's theological production started in 1549 and lasted until his death in 1605, so the larger part of it occurred during the period of early Reformed orthodoxy. That he was involved in the draft of the *French Confession* of 1559 and wrote a confession himself is characteristic for this era. Also, his being the first rector of the Genevan Academy is an argument for regarding him as an early Reformed orthodox theologian. Nevertheless, one should be aware that he lived half of his life in the period of the Reformation. Marking out historical periods does not correspond to the lives of historical individuals. A theologian like Beza can be neither divided nor pressed into one of the periods later church historians distinguish in history.

3.4 Between Calvin and Bullinger: Beza's Initial Ideas on Predestination (1551-1555)

3.4.1 Disagreement between Calvin and Bullinger

Beza's first publication on predestination was his *Summa totius christianismi* in 1555. In the years preceding this publication, Beza was engaged in correspondence with Calvin and Bullinger concerning the Bolsec affair, and in these letters, he expressed his early ideas on predestination and some related themes.[40] Beza's letters from 1551-1555 are examined in connection with the *Tabula* since these were the years in which the *Tabula* was written.[41]

Whereas Calvin tried to condemn Bolsec as a heretic (see 2.1), Reformed cities like Zurich and Bern did not join Calvin in this condemnation.

---

39 After Geneva, for instance, the academy of Heidelberg became a Reformed institute in 1563. In Herborn and Bremen, Reformed *gymnasia* were established in 1584 (Bremen was a *paedagogium* in 1584 and became a *gymnasium* in 1610). In France, Reformed academies were established at Montpelier, Orange, Sedan, Montauban, and Saumur. In The Netherlands, such institutions were erected in Leiden (1575), Franeker (1585), and Groningen (1614).

40 On the correspondence between Beza and Bullinger, see Emidio Campi, "Theodore Beza and Heinrich Bullinger in Light of Their Correspondence," in idem, *Shifting Patterns of Reformed Tradition* (Göttingen: Vandenhoeck & Ruprecht, 2014), 169-83; previously published in German as "Beza und Bullinger im Lichte Ihrer Korrespondenz" in Backus (ed.), *Théodore de Bèze*, 131-44.

41 See Muller, "Use and Abuse," 35-41.

Bullinger even defended Bolsec somewhat and warned Calvin against suggesting that God was the author of sin.[42] Calvin's views on these matters have been expounded in the preceding chapter, but to understand Beza's position and its development, some information on Bullinger's position should be given. Peter Stephens has given a survey of Bullinger's ideas on predestination during several periods of his life.[43] Throughout his life, Bullinger warned against abuse of the doctrine and stressed God's gracious purpose. Election means that some will be brought to life by Christ; reprobation means that others will be condemned for rejecting Christ. People perish by their own fault, for God is not the author of evil. Bullinger insisted that humans were created good by God and that Adam's will was not constrained by necessity. God's foreknowledge of the Fall does not mean that he predestined the Fall.

There is no difference between Bullinger, Calvin, and Beza on the question whether faith was a gift of God to the elect. But whereas Calvin stressed the eternity of God's decrees as the fountain of all things that happen in time, Bullinger was reluctant to penetrate into the decree and stressed rather its execution in time. He proposed this distinction "as a barrier to speculation concerning the inner life of God."[44] What annoyed Bullinger in Calvin's approach was that the latter seemed to have crossed over this barrier. He took offence at Calvin's attitude and views in the Bolsec controversy, stressing that people do not perish because they are compelled by necessity but because they reject the grace of God. As long as Bolsec attributed everything to God's grace, Calvin should seek reconciliation. In some letters, Bullinger warned Calvin not to say that God predestined the Fall and created some men for eternal destruction and blinds them. Such expressions would lead to the idea that God is the author of sin and unbelief.

---

42 For a detailed, although not unbiased, study to this controversy, see Holtrop, *Bolsec Controversy*.
43 W. Peter Stephens, "Predestination or Election in Zwingli and Bullinger," in Emidio Campi and Peter Opitz (eds.) *Heinrich Bullinger: Life-Thought-Influence. Zurich, Aug. 25-29, 2004. International Congress Heinrich Bullinger (1504-1575)*, vol. 1 (Zurich: TVZ, 2007) 313-34. For a more extended study of Bullingers's thoughts on predestination, see Cornelis P. Venema, *Heinrich Bullinger and the Doctrine of Predestination: Author of "the Other Reformed Tradition"?* (Grand Rapids: Baker, 2002).
44 Muller, *Christ and the Decree*, 43. Hence Sinnema's assumption that this distinction is unique to Beza's doctrine of predestination (Sinnema, see 3.2) is not true; rather, Beza used a concept of Bullinger.

3.4.2 Beza's Letters of 1551 and 1552

Beza's letters show his concern about the discord between Calvin and Bullinger. In the letters of 1551 and 1552, he takes Calvin's side and tries to convince Bullinger that Calvin was right both in his doctrine and in the way he dealt with Bolsec. Yet in both letters Beza asks about his "father" Bullinger's view of predestination and whether Bullinger thought something had been left out or if he thought that something was difficult or expressed ambiguously by Beza. If so, he would appreciate it if Bullinger would tell him what he should add, delete, or leave as it is.[45] It seems that such words are not meant to flatter Bullinger while Beza holds firm to his own view. Beza had converted to the Reformed faith just a few years before and had been teaching at Lausanne for only two years. It is obvious that he had high regard for Bullinger, who had been laboring on behalf of the Reformation for almost thirty years by that time and whose work had been a means for Beza's conversion.[46]

The letters show great appreciation for both Calvin and Bullinger, both of whom were addressed as Beza's "father." The discord between them could be a threat to the unity of the Reformed. At various times in his life, Beza tried to promote unity among the Reformed and also between the Reformed and Lutherans. It is likely that he tried to promote unity between Bullinger's Zurich and Calvin's Geneva as well.[47] If this is indeed the case, he had little success in those first years, for Bullinger was not convinced by Beza. He rather seems to have been displeased by Beza's views on predestination, especially with respect to reprobation.

In his first letter to Bullinger regarding Bolsec, Beza summarizes the case and at the same time expresses his own view.[48] He starts with questions

---

45 Beza to Bullinger, October 29, 1551, in *Correspondance* 1, 71-73; Beza to Bullinger, January 12, 1552, in *Correspondance* 1, 76-79.
46 At that very time, Beza was translating Bullinger's *Perfectio christianorum* into French.
47 The importance of a good relationship between Geneva and Zurich is summarized by Campi as follows. 1. Theological harmony between Geneva and Zurich would contribute to concluding the conflict with Bern; 2. With the defeat of the Schmalkaldic League, it seemed that the survival of the Reformation lay in the Swiss Confederation; 3. Theological harmony within the Swiss Confederation would help French Protestants because of the alliance of the confederation with France. Campi, *Shifting Patterns*, 149. See also *Consensus Tigurinus: Die Einigung zwischen Heinrich Bullinger und Johannes Calvin über das Abendmahl*, eds. Emidio Campi and Rüdi Reich (Zurich: Theologischer Verlag, 2009), 9-41.
48 According to Thomas, *Extent*, 43, this letter "reveals a developed, deliberate and logical supralapsarianism, and Aristotelian preoccupation with causality, that would be put forward frequently through the rest of Beza's life." But Beza did not mention any order within the decree in this letter, so it does not entail supralapsarianism, let alone

concerning reprobation. Is someone reprobate and hence turned by God into a vessel of wrath? Are the reprobate reprobate because they do not believe? Or do they not believe because they are reprobate but damned because they are unbelievers? According to Beza, what obtains for the elect should also obtain for the reprobate.[49] But Bolsec thought that this makes God the author of sin and held that God reprobates people because he knew beforehand *(praescivit)* that they would reject the grace offered to them. That would mean, so Beza, that God elected others because he saw before *(praevidet)* their faith. Now we know that we are elect not because we believe, but unto belief.[50]

Beza then summarizes his own position in a few short sentences. If someone takes away reprobation, he cannot hold to election either. We should distinguish between causes. Nothing should be assigned to the

---

a developed, deliberate, and logical supralapsarianism. Beza's ideas on the cause of unbelief later changed, (see 3.11) so this was not argued during the rest of his life. And while "Aristotelian" is used here for "logical" or "rational," Thomas does not take into account that Beza insisted on not assigning anything to the judgment of reason.

49 Beza to Bullinger, October 29, 1551, in *Correspondance* 1, 72: "Sitne quisquam ab aeterno reprobatus, et ideo conditus a Deo ut esset vas irae? Sintne reprobi ideo reprobi quia increduli, an contra, ideo increduli quia reprobi, ideo autem damnati quia increduli? Inde nasci vides quaestionem de arbitrii humani viribus. Nam idem de electis quod de reprobis constituendum erit. Damnari fatemur incredulos propter incredulitatem, et culpam omnem condemnationis in hominem rejicimus. In reprobatione autem solam spectamus Dei voluntatem, quae sola est justitiae regula ..." *(Is someone reprobated from eternity, and hence made by God to a vessel of wrath? Have the reprobate been reprobate because they would be unbelievers, or are they unbelievers because they are reprobate, but damned because they are unbelievers? You see this raises the question concerning the power of men's choice. For regarding the elect the same should be stated as regarding the reprobate. We acknowledge that the unbelievers are damned because of their unbelief, and we throw back the responsibility of condemnation in man. But in reprobation we only behold God's will, which is the only rule of justice.)*

50 Idem: "Ille vero clamat Deum hoc pacto a nobis constitui authorem peccati, et veluti Tyrannum, cui sufficiat pro ratione voluntas. Si quem enim, inquit, Deus reprobat, hoc facit quia simul praescivit fore ut gratiam illi oblatam, quam potuit amplecti rejiciat. Atqui, si Dominus idcirco reprobat, quia praescit incredulitatem, idcirco etiam eligit, quia praevidet fidem, quum tamen constet nos non eligi propter fidem, sed ideo credere quia electi simus, alioqui ex nobis penderet electio, non ex gratia." *(But he [Bolsec] claims that this way God is made the author of sin by us, and as a tyrant, to whom his will is reason enough. For when God, he says, reprobates one, he does so because he at once knew before that he would reject the grace offered to him, which he could have embraced. Now when God reprobates because he knew before unbelief, he likewise elects because he foresees faith, yet it is sure that we are not elect because of faith, but that we believe because we are elected, otherwise election would depend on us, not on grace.)*

judgment of our reason. Although the guilt of sin is to be ascribed to humans, this guilt depends on reprobation, decreed by God for his own honor in punishing the evil ones. With respect to the reprobate, three steps should be considered: reprobation, unbelief or ignorance of God, and eternal death. In the elect these steps correspond to election, faith, and eternal life.[51]

There are noteworthy points in this letter to Bullinger. First, Beza here seems to regard election and reprobation in a similar way, for he states that whatever holds for the reprobate should also hold for the elect. In this letter, Beza's concern is election, but he addresses reprobation extensively because of his view that, if reprobation is based on foreseen unbelief, election should be based on foreseen faith. If faith is the fruit of election, then unbelief is the fruit of reprobation. Beza states that unbelief depends on *(pendet a)* reprobation. He does not use the word *causa* to describe the relation between reprobation and unbelief here, but when he states a little further on that we should distinguish between causes, he seems to be referring to the immediately following distinction between damnation as the result of unbelief and unbelief as the result of reprobation. The fact that Calvin used the term *causa* to denote the relation between reprobation and unbelief[52] makes it the more plausible that Beza indeed expresses the same view in this letter. Despite their view of God as the *causa* of sin and unbelief, both Calvin and Beza deny that God was the author of sin. Yet Bullinger ascribes this error to them, obviously because of statements like these. For Bullinger, God could not be the *causa* of sin without bearing *culpa* for sin, whereas Calvin and Beza affirm that he could.

---

51 Idem: "Dicimus ergo eum qui reprobationem tollat, nullam electionem statuere posse; dicimus inter causas distinguendum. Dicimus hic nihil tribuendum esse nostrae rationis judicio. Dicimus peccati varios fines consyderandos, nam ut est peccatum, ejus culpam omnem in hominum improbitatem esse conferendam, ut autem pendet a reprobatione decerni a Deo ad gloriam ipsius amplificandam malorum suppliciis. Dicimus denique in reprobis tres esse gradus hoc ordine considerandos, Reprobationem, Incredulitatem vel Ignorantiam Dei, Mortem aeternam, quibus totidem respondeant in electis, nempe gratuita Electio, Fides, Vita aeterna." *(We say that he who takes away reprobation, can not state election. We say that we have to distinguish between causes. We say that here nothing should be assigned to the judgement of our reason. We say that we should consider the various ends of sin, for as it is sin, all responsibility of its wickedness should be gathered in man, but it depends on reprobation, decreed by God to magnify his glory in punishing the sinners. We say finally that we should consider three steps concerning the reprobate, in this order: Reprobation, Unbelief, or Ignorance of God, and Eternal Death. To these as steps do respond in the elect: Election, Faith, Eternal Life.)*

52 See 2.11.

It is remarkable that Beza does not want to assign anything to reason in this case, yet he seems to use reason himself in drawing a strict parallel between election and reprobation and deducing properties of the one from the other. The "unreasonable" part of his idea is that the guilt of unbelief is found completely in the human, although this unbelief depends on God's decree of reprobation. In any case, Beza's expressed reluctance to assign something to reason is an argument against those who see Beza as a rationalist theologian, at least in this period of his life.[53]

If Bullinger wrote an answer to Beza, it has not been preserved. Within three months, Beza wrote another letter to Bullinger on Bolsec and the events in Geneva.[54] On the basis of this second, preserved letter concerning Bolsec, it seems that Bullinger had answered him and that he was not pleased with Beza's views on Bolsec and predestination.[55] No wonder, for Beza started with reprobation - precisely the part of predestination Bullinger was reluctant to speak about. Moreover, Beza's letter offered the idea that God was the cause of sin, which should have made Bullinger frown because of his efforts to abstain from expressions that might suggest God is the author of sin.

Beza attempts to set forth his views again. He summarizes Bolsec's idea that grace is offered by God to all people and that God calls them all to salvation in the same way; it is in one's own power to accept or to reject this gift; those whom God knows will accept the offer of salvation are the elect; those whom God knows will reject it are the reprobate; faith should be seen as a cause of election and not the reverse, otherwise, in similar fashion, unbelief would be the fruit of reprobation. Over against this opinion of Bolsec, Beza elaborated on his own view. Bolsec is making some quite subtle arguments,[56] but Jesus said: "[Y]ou did not choose me,

---

53 For instance, Kickel, *Vernunft*.
54 Beza to Bullinger, January 12, 1552, in *Correspondance* 1, 76-79.
55 It is possible Beza wrote more letters concerning this affair or on predestination that have not been preserved, just as Bullinger's answer to Beza has not been preserved. It is also possible that Bullinger did not write a letter to Beza, but that Beza knew Bullinger's answer to the letter from Geneva to Basel, Zurich, and Bern dated November 14, 1551.
56 Beza to Bullinger, January 12, 1552, in *Correspondance* 1, 77: "Fides causa erit electionis, non effectus. Alioqui enim, quum ad alteram partem ventum est, dicendum etiam esset incredulitatem non esse caussam reprobationis sed effectum, ex quo sequeretur Deum esse peccati authorem, Deum velle iniquitatem, in Deo esse contradictorias voluntates. O bellas argutias et subtiles syllogismos." *(Faith should be a cause of election, not and effect. Otherwise when we come to the other side, we should also say that unbelief is not a cause of reprobation but an effect, and then would follow that God is the author of sin, that God wills iniquity and that there are two contradicting wills in God. O, what good argument and subtle reasoning!)*

but I have chosen you," and faith is a gift of God. We need to be drawn, regenerated, and taught. Since this happens only to a very few *(paucissimus)*, we cannot deny that a special grace exists for certain people, the elect *(electi)*. They have been elect before the world began. Now when some are elect from eternity, it follows that others are reprobate *(reprobati)* from eternity.[57]

Bolsec argued that if faith follows election, then unbelief follows reprobation. But Beza could not find this in Scripture, which tells us that God has mercy on whomever he wills, and hardens whomever he wills and thus shows that God's will is supreme *(supremus gradus)*.[58] This will is neither tyrannical nor unjust, and all guilt should be ascribed to men, whatever human reason can introduce against this view. So, with respect to salvation, Beza ascribes everything to God, while with respect to reprobation he acknowledges not only prescience but counsel and an eternal decree, although he assigns all fault to humans.[59] The cause of God's decree is unknown to us. As for Beza, this decree does not cause desperation. God has called him outwardly and inwardly by his word *(Vocavit me Deus externo atque etiam interno suo verbo)* as the Spirit testifies in him, and there are several other signs *(argumenta)* of his election. The sobriety required concerning election is not to abhor it but to treat it within the borders set forth in Scripture.

A difference from the first letter is that Beza does not start with reprobation but with election, and Bullinger could agree with that, in a way. Moreover, in his letter of October 29, 1551, Beza seems to have argued along the very same lines as Bolsec, yet where Bolsec concluded that faith should precede election because otherwise one would have to admit that unbelief follows reprobation, Beza concludes that reprobation should precede unbelief, otherwise faith should precede election. Both Bolsec and Beza saw a strict parallel between election and reprobation. Now, in his letter of January 12, Beza called this a "subtle reasoning" *(subtiles*

---

57 Idem: "Jam vero si ab aeterno illi sunt electi, aliquos esse ab aeterno reprobatos, nemo, opinor, praeter Hieronymum affirmabit." *(Now when those are from eternity elected, others are from eternity reprobated, will nobody affirm more than Hieronymus [Bolsec], I guess.)*

58 Idem, 78: "Si fides electionem sequitur, incredulitas quoque post reprobationem collocanda. At ego in sacris scripturis hoc non invenio. Dicit scriptura, cujus vult miseretur, quem vult indurate."

59 Idem: "Ergo quod ad salutem attinet, omnia Deo tribuo, quoad reprobationem, Dei non tantum praescientiam, sed consilium et decretum aeternum in hac etiam parte agnosco (nec enim electio sine reprobatione potest constitui); et tamen culpam omnem in hominem conjicio."

syllogismos) of Bolsec. It is difficult to understand what Beza means exactly with this passage since his following words at least suggest that he himself also saw unbelief as following reprobation. Yet what he writes no longer indicates a causal relation between unbelief and reprobation. He ascribes all that belongs to salvation only to God and ascribes all guilt only to humans, although there is an eternal decree of reprobation. The suggestion that unbelief is caused by reprobation is absent from this letter, though present in the first. But the formulation is not very clear. It is now very obvious to Beza that faith is a fruit of election, but he seems to have struggled with the relation between reprobation and unbelief and with finding the right words to avoid Bolsec's accusation of making God the author of sin and at the same time maintaining God's decree over all things.[60]

3.4.3 Beza's View of Calvin's De aeterna praedestinatione

It is likely that Beza, when he wrote to Bullinger in January 1552, was already in possession of Calvin's *De aeterna praedestinatione*, which was published on January 1. Beza wrote Calvin a letter about this treatise twenty days later.[61] He approved of the content but had some criticism of Calvin's method and structure.[62] He preferred to start from the beginning.[63] Beza mentioned that he understood from Bullinger's letter that Calvin's publication did not satisfy all.[64] Moreover, Pighius was already dead. In this controversy, Beza prepared certain headings (*certa mihi capita*) that were likely the origin of his *Summa totius christianismi*. Beza also mentioned opposition to Calvin's doctrine of predestination in Lausanne. Election unto faith was accepted, but there was resistance to the notion of reprobation without any cause in humans. Distinctions between reprobation and damnation, between proximate and remote causes, between

---

60 For the development of Beza's answer on this question see 3.11
61 Beza to Calvin, January 21, 1552, in *Correspondance* 1, 81-83. Transl. by Holtrop in his *Bolsec Controversy*, I, 732-35. See also Van Sliedrecht, *Calvijns opvolger*, 102; Muller, "Use and Abuse," 38-39.
62 See 3.1. Neuser's statement that Beza's proposal to explain the doctrine "more methodically" meant "by logical syllogism" is not plausible since Beza hardly used syllogisms in his *Tabula*. Wilhelm Neuser, "Einleitung," in Calvin, *De aeterna Dei praedestinatione, COR* III/1, xx.
63 Beza to Calvin, January 21, 1552, in *Correspondance* 1, 81-83: "mallem tamen ut eam a capite esses exorsus."
64 Idem: "Primum enim satis potuisti ex D. Bullingeri literis intelligere prius illud tuum scriptum non omnibus satisfacere." (The letter from Bullinger that is mentioned has been lost.)

efficient causes and privative causes, and between what is first in order and what precedes in time did not help.⁶⁵

An important point is that, in this letter, Beza mentions his *capita*, obviously the origins of his *Tabula*, in connection with Zurich's dissatisfaction with Calvin's work against Pighius. It seems he hoped or even intended that, unlike Calvin's *De aeterna praedestinatione*, his approach would satisfy the ministers in Zurich. New elements in Beza's treatment of predestination are the distinctions between causes that we mentioned above, but Beza makes no mention of them in his letters to Bullinger. Unfortunately, we do not know exactly how Beza applied them to predestination at that time, for the next sentences of his letter are not completely legible.⁶⁶ It is remarkable that, although Beza used the word *causa* in this letter to Calvin, he did not do so in his second letter on Bolsec to Bullinger.

3.4.4 Statements for the Classis of Lausanne

In this period, Beza tried to convince the other pastors in the Classis of Lausanne to subscribe to three doctrinal statements concerning predestination but was unsuccessful.

I. God has from eternity not only known but even decreed, not only in an indefinite sense, that those who would believe would be saved but also in a definite sense that certain individuals would be born, whom he would save by faith in Christ and who would never fall from faith.

II. In the same way, God has from eternity decreed in a definite way that certain people would be born to destruction, to whom he would never give the Spirit of regeneration and assurance of faith.

III. The fault of damnation should be sought in humans alone, and yet we say that God's decree precedes, whereas it is eternal yet without fault, because although the causes of the eternal decrees are unknown to us, they are nevertheless just, since God's will should be the sure and only rule of justice.⁶⁷

---

65 Idem: "Nihil profuit distinctio inter reprobationem et damnationem, inter caussam proximam et remotam, inter caussam vere efficientem et privativam inter i[llud] quod prius est ordine et quod tempore praecedit."

66 Some legible words give an indication of his thoughts: "the grace that is universally offered" and "original sin." Beza later used the distinction between causes to explain that one should not apply the doctrine of predestination directly but indirectly, via faith or unbelief, for instance.

67 Haller to Bullinger, Bern, December 14, 1552. *CO* 14:439-40 (no. 1688):
"1. Deus ab aeterno non tantum praecognovit sed etiam decrevit, non tantum indefinite, ut quicunque crederent servarentur, sed *definite* ut certi homines nascerentur, quos servaret per fidem in Christum quique nunquam desciscerent a fide.

We only know these statements from a letter by Haller. We do not know whether Haller literally quoted Beza or paraphrased him. Nonetheless, it is likely that they have been adequately reproduced, for they reflect Beza's ideas as presented in his letter of January 12, 1552 to Bullinger. It starts with election, which is – contra Bolsec – not an election of believers but one for the purpose of belief. It is not just an election for salvation, but to salvation by faith in Christ. The means to salvation are included in the decree. The reprobate are described as born to destruction; not, however, in an absolute sense but because the Spirit of regeneration would not be given to them. It is obvious that this is what Beza meant by the privative cause in his letter to Calvin. But the word *causa* is not used to describe the relation between decree and damnation: the decree precedes damnation because it is eternal, yet, as is explicitly stated, the fault of a person's damnation lies in himself.

3.4.5 The Tabula is Completed

Beza hardly mentions Bolsec or predestination in whatever letters survive from the years following. In November 1554, Beza gave an indication that he was still or again preoccupied with Bolsec and that he thought the situation was urgent.[68] In October of that year, the Genevans had written letters to Bern where Bolsec had fled. In the end, the Bernese Senate approved of Calvin's teachings but encouraged the clergy of their jurisdiction (to which Lausanne belonged) not to attempt to penetrate into the deep secrets of God. Yet in this very period Beza was working on his *Tabula*, as a letter from Haller to Bullinger indicates. Haller refers to Sampaulier, who had seen a diagram made by Beza "which demonstrates that all things, even evil, hang down from God himself as the first cause of all."[69] We do not exactly know whether the diagram Sampaulier had seen

---

2. Eadem ratione Deus ab aeterno etiam decrevit *definite* ut certi homines nascerentur ad interitum, quos nunquam donaret spiritu regenerationis et fidei πληροφορίᾳ.
3. Damnationis culpa in solo homine quaerenda est et tamen dicimus Dei decretum praecedere, cum sit aeternum, sine culpa tamen, quia etsi causa decreti aeterni nobis est incognita, justa tamen est, quum Dei voluntas sit certa et sola justitiae regula."
68 Beza to Calvin, November 29, 1554, in *Correspondance* 1, 149: "Praesertim de Hieronymo etiam atque etiam urgendum et modis omnibus instandum censeo."
69 Haller to Bullinger, November 17, 1554 in CO XV, 316: "*Sampaulinus* dicit mihi *Bezam* edidisse figuram quandam orbicularem, qua demonstret omnia etiam mala ab ipso Deo tanquam prima omnium causa propendere. Eam non vidi. Si nactus fuero mittam at te." (*Sampaulinus told me Beza has produced a figure or circular, which demonstrates that all things, even evil, hang down from God himself as the first cause of all. I did not see it myself. When it will be published I will send it to you.*)

is the same as the one found in the *Tabula* as we know it. The quotation is his interpretation and does not reveal what Beza intended by it.

In March 1555, Beza received a letter from Peter Martyr Vermigli that indicates that he had seen the Table and approved of it. But he urged Beza to add some explanation and texts from Scripture.[70] Since Vermigli wrote about "tables" he could have seen another version or even other versions than the one that was actually printed later that year. It is not clear whether Beza had already given some explanation of it since in 1552 he referred in a letter to Calvin to *certa mihi capita*, which might have been an early version of the *Tabula*. What is certain is that Beza's ideas on predestination started to develop with the Bolsec controversy in 1551 and that he finished his *Summa totius christianismi* in the period when this controversy came to an end, in 1555.

Some months later, Beza wrote to Calvin regarding his diagram on predestination.[71] His *Tabula* seems to have been in an almost completed state then, but there seem to have been several unpublished versions circulating.[72] How Beza refers to his tables seems to indicate that he had earlier corresponded with Calvin about them.[73] In this same letter Beza asks Calvin about a question he found difficult, a knot *(nodus)*. It was not the same question that occupied him some years before, i.e., on the relation between the decree and sin. This time, Beza wrestles with the phrase

---

70 Vermigli to Beza, March 1555, in *Correspondance* 1, 153-55: "Quod vero tu, quo rem non minus utilem quam oppugnatam ita producere in medium statueris, ut etiam tabulis quibusdam pictis eam ob oculos ponas, patefacias ac enodate dilucides, et laudo et vehementer probo... In illis enim etsi video methodicam partitionem, et διδακτικήν rationem diligenter observari, non tamen quae tota sit doctrina, dum non additur aliqua explicatio et loca ex divinis literis non adscribuntur, possunt perfecte comprehendere, nihilominus ut de leone queo ex unguibus conjicere, totum id prudenter excogitatum et accurate abs te comprehensum non dubito, quare ut quod delineasti perficias ... moneo et oro." *(That in the mean time you are determined, to bring forth a case as useful as assaulted, in such a way that you even put it before the eyes in drawn tables, lay it open clearly and lucidly, I both praise and ardently approve... In it I see a methodical distribution and didactic ratio diligently observed, but not as if this would be the complete doctrine, if some explanation is not added and no places from the sacred writings are written in addition. They can be comprehended completely, but just as a lion can be recognized by his claws. I do not doubt that it is very skillfully thought out and accurately perceived by you, and hence I advise and ask you to complete what you have sketched.)*
71 Beza to Calvin, July 29, 1555, in *Correspondance* 1, 169-72.
72 Idem, 169: "tabellae nostrae excudantur ... appendicem misero cum reliquis duabus tabellis, in quibus sum conatus adversariorum opinionem repraesentare." It is also possible that Beza referred in the plural to his *Tabula* because of the two sides of predestination presented along two lines.
73 Idem, 169 and 170: "tabellae nostrae excudantur... Sed ecce ad tabellas redeo."

"elected in Christ" (Eph. 1:4). Does it refer to the decree of election or to the execution, which in God's mind is also eternal?[74] And how are we elected in Christ? Is Christ prior to the decree, and did God view us in Christ when he elected us? Or did he first decree to save us and then subordinate Christ to be the one through whom he would execute his decree?[75]

According to Beza, it is not possible to read Paul's words as referring to the decree *(propositum)*. If Christ is placed prior to the decree, then sin should be placed prior to Christ, who is the remedy for sin. And then creation should also be placed prior to the decree. In that case, one might regard the Fall and corruption as causes of reprobation. But if this were true, Beza could not see how he could explain the passage in Romans 9 with its objection to Paul's exposition of predestination *Why does he still find fault? For who can resist his will?* Paul's answer to this objection is: *Who are you, o man, to answer back to God?* In addition, Paul refers to the potter who can make both a vessel of honorable use and one of dishonorable use from the same lump of clay. If corruption is the cause of reprobation, Beza thinks, the objection *why does he still find fault?* would be of no use, for the fault would be in their corruption. Hence, the lump *(massa)* of clay should not be explained as referring to the human race as corrupt in Adam but as not yet created nor fallen.[76]

---

74 Idem, 170: "Hic primum quaero, quomodo sit accipienda electio, an scilicet pro aeterno illo Dei proposito quo nos destinavit adoptioni, an vero potius pro hujus propositi executione quae quidem (si non in nobis, qui certo momento nascimur et vocamur, sed in Deo consideretur) non minus est aeterna quam primum illud propositum, quamvis, ordinis habita ratione, illa isti substernatur." *(The first thing I ask is in which way we should take election here, viz. for God's eternal purpose by which he destined us to adoption, or rather to the execution of the purpose, which is (not considered in us, who are of course born and called at a certain moment, but in God) as well eternal as the first purpose, but subordinated to it in regard of order.)*

75 Idem, 170: "Deinde hoc etiam rogo, quomodo in Christo dicamur electi, an quod Deus in Christum respiceret quum nos praedestinaret, an vero quod, quum nos jam in sese constituisset servare, postea (si caussarum ordinem spectemus) Christum subordinarit per quem suum propositum exequeretur in nobis? Caussa vero haec est cur ista petam." *(Then I ask in which way we are elected in Christ. Does God look upon us in Christ when he predestinates us, or did he, when he had already determined in himself to save us, afterwards (regarding the order of causes) subordinate Christ by whom he would execute his purpose?)*

76 Idem, 170: "Apud eum enim queruntur reprobi, non quod potius quam illi praeteriti sint quum sint omnes ejusdem conditionis, sed quod Dei voluntate adstricti sint cui non possint reluctari. Ergo, ut paucis absolvam, massae puto comparari a Paulo genus humanum nondum conditum …" *(With him [Paul] the reprobate do not complain that they are passed by rather than others when they all were in the same condition, but that they are bound by God's will, which they can not resist. Hence, to untie the knot, I think the lump is compared by Paul to the human race not yet formed.)*

The purpose to elect and to reprobate thus preceded creation, fall, election, and reprobation.

In terms of causality, the *causa finalis* of the purpose of election and reprobation is the glory of God's immense power. The *causa materialis* is God's will alone.[77] Adam and Christ are not among the final or material causes. They are counted among the secondary causes, ordained to the execution of the eternal council, for we are elected in Christ unto salvation, while others are reprobate because of their corruption and iniquity.[78]

---

77 Idem, 171: "Itaque si quaeratur cur Deus alios ab aeterno constituent eligere, alios reprobare, si quidem de fine quaeratur, respondendum puto, ut melius Dei immensa potestas declaretur; sin vero de caussa hujus aeterni decreti materiali quam vocant, non habeo aliud quod afferam, nisi voluntatem Dei, cui saltem idem licet quod figulo, nimirum aliud vas in honorem, aliud in contumeliam fingere. Rursus si quaeratur, cur hos potius quam illos vel saluti vel exitio destinant, iterum afferam Dei voluntatem, in cujus potestate situm est, non modo alia vasa in honorem, alia in contumeliam fingere ex eadem massa, sed etiam in hoc discrimine suum unius judicium sequi." *(And so, when it is asked why God from eternity decided to elect some and to reprobate others, when this is asked concerning the end, I think the answer should be that God's immense power should be the better declared; but when it is asked concerning what is called the material cause of the eternal decree, I can allege nothing but God's will, who anyhow, just like a potter, can make one vessel to honour and another one to insult. When it is asked again why the one rather than the other is destined to salvation or to insult, I allege again God's will, in whose power it is anyway, not only to make one vessel to honour and another one to insult from the same lump, but also in this discrimination to follow his own single judgement.)*

78 Idem, 171: "Itaque in neutra hac quaestione deveniam ad caussas secundas, inter quas Christum et Adamum numero, sed in iis potius quae sequuntur. Nempe si quaeratur, non de decreto eligendi aut reprobandi, sed de executione illius. Sunt enim caussae secundae ordinatae ad consilii aeterni executionem. Afferri potest igitur ratio cur et quomodo electi simus, nimirum quia Deus pro sua immensa charitate nos respiciens in Christo suo, cui nos dare constituit ante tempora aeterna, non potuit nos non amare, ut qui in illo justi et sancti essemus. Contra vero, si quaeratur cur aliquos reprobarit, respondebo caussam in ipsis esse quaerendam. Haerere enim ipsos in corruptione et iniquitate, quae justum Dei odium meretur, itaque merito ejusmodi homines a Deo rejici ac repudiari." *(And so I arrive in neither one of these questions to secondary causes, among which I count Christ and Adam, but [I come to them] rather in those which follow. Certainly, when it is asked, not concerning the decree to elect and to reprobate, but concerning its execution. For they are secondary causes, ordained for the execution of the eternal counsel. Hence the reason can be given why and how we have been elected, truly because God, for the sake of his immense goodness regarding us in his Christ, whom he has disposed before the times of ages, can not fail to love us, since we were in him righteous and holy. And at the other hand, when it is asked why he has reprobated others, I will answer that the cause is to be sought in themselves. For they themselves hold fast to corruption and iniquity, which merit the righteous hate of God.)*

Beza was aware that he was saying something new. He was aware that he was deviating from Augustine because he did not quote any theologian with the same idea he had himself concerning the lump. This might be why he eagerly asked Calvin to comment on and to improve his table and ideas.[79] In this letter we find a supralapsarian order of the decrees concerning predestination, creation, and the Fall. We also find a distinction between the decree to elect and to reprobate *(propositum tum eligendi tum reprobandi)* and election in Christ or reprobation because of corruption as the execution of this purpose. Another important idea is that the execution of the decree can be regarded as relating either to God or people. If the execution is related to God, then he decreed the execution, and, as such, the execution is as eternal as the purpose and is like a decree itself. If the decree is related to people, the execution happens in time.

3.4.6 The Tabula Not Sent Immediately to Bullinger

Given Beza's efforts in 1551 and 1552 to win Bullinger over to the Genevan position and the clues that suggest that he thought or hoped that his presentation of predestination would be acceptable to Bullinger, it is striking that there is no clue that he corresponded with Bullinger on the *Tabula* in 1554 and 1555.[80] He sent some *capita* to Calvin already in 1552, but there is no indication that he sent them to Bullinger at the same time. He sent Vermigli and Calvin the *Tabula* in 1555 and asked for their comments, just

---

79 We do not know what Calvin's answer to Beza's questions was. Arguments that Calvin approved of Beza's views are, first, that Beza did not alter his ideas in his *Tabula* and *Explicatio*, which he likely would have done if Calvin had had objections, and, second, Calvin later recommended "a little book" by Beza, most likely the *Tabula* with its *Explicatio*, to Castellio in the debate with him on predestination. Arguments that Calvin rejected Beza's ideas are, first, that he does not discuss Beza's exegetical remarks in his comments on Romans 9:19-21 in his revised commentary on Romans. Second, in his commentary on Jeremiah, Calvin assented to the view that God's purpose preceded faith and repentance but did not state that it preceded the Fall.

80 According to Ian McPhee, "Conserver or Transformer of Calvin's Theology? A Study of the Origins and Development of Theodore Beza's Thought (1550-1570)," (PhD, Cambridge, 1979), 81, Van Sliedrecht, *Calvijns opvolger*, 104, and Muller, "Use and Abuse," 37, Bullinger read the *Tabula* approvingly in 1554. These writers draw this conclusion from a letter by Bullinger to Calvin in which he mentions a "table from the hand of Theodore" *(tabulam manu Theodori)*. (Bullinger to Calvin, October 25, 1554, in *CO* XV, 296). According to McPhee, Van Sliedrecht, and Muller, this refers to Beza's *Tabula*. But this conclusion is based on an inaccurate reading of this letter. Bullinger is referring to a *Tabula* made by a Theodore that was related to the *Consensus Tigurinus*. The editors of the *CO* identified this Theodore as Bibliander.

as he had asked Bullinger for his comments on his ideas in 1551 and 1552. Beza did send the *Tabula* to Lismanin in Poland in January 1556 and to Farel in Neuchâtel in March 1556,[81] but Bullinger had to wait until June 1557 before the work was sent to him.[82] Despite asking Bullinger for his view, he did not ask Bullinger this time to correct or to advise him as he had asked Vermigli and Calvin.[83]

There are a few facts that might account for Beza waiting so long to send his *Tabula* to Bullinger. Bullinger's reaction to Beza's views as communicated in his letters of 1551 and 1552 might have given Beza little reason to think Bullinger would embrace his *Tabula*. Another reason might have been that Geneva needed the extension of a pact with Bern and that Beza used his political talents to make Zurich and other cities mediate between the two. Beza could have regarded it dangerous to send his *Tabula* in this period, for objections to it could hurt his efforts for unity, especially since Zurich was already irritated by a confession Beza wrote on the Lord's Supper.[84] When a new pact was made in 1557, Beza could then feel free to send his *Tabula* to Bullinger later that year. Finally, Peter Martyr Vermigli, who had already approved of Beza's *Tabula* and had become pastor in Zurich shortly before, became engaged in a conflict with another Zurich pastor, Theodore Bibliander, who attacked Vermigli's views on predestination the very month, June 1557, that Beza sent his *Tabula* to Zurich.[85] Sending it to Zurich's *antistes* Bullinger in that situation could be regarded as supporting Vermigli's view of predestination. At the same time, Vermigli's presence in Zurich meant support among Bullinger's colleagues for Beza's teaching on predestination.[86]

---

81 Beza, *Correspondance* 2, 18, 35
82 Beza to Bullinger, June 5, 1557. *Correspondance 2*, 68: "Tabellam nostram praedestinationis ad te mitto, de qua mihi pergratum feceris si judicium tuum ad me libere perscripseris." *(I send you our Table of predestination, concerning which you would do me a great favor if you would freely write out your judgement to me.)*
83 Bullinger's answer has not been preserved. The correspondence concerning the *Tabula* shows that many letters have been lost. We know Vermigli's answer, but not Beza's letter to Vermigli; we know Beza's letters to Calvin, Bullinger, Lismanin, and Farel, but we do not know their answers.
84 See the biographies of Beza for this episode in his life.
85 Frank A. James III, "The Bullinger/Vermigli Axis: Collaborators in Toleration and Reformation," in Campi and Opitz (eds.), *Heinrich Bullinger*, 170. See for Vermigli's time in Zurich, Michael Baumann, *Petrus Martyr Vermigli in Zürich (1556-1562). Dieser Kylchen in der heiligen gschrifft professor und laeser* (Göttingen: Vandenhoeck&Ruprecht, 2016), although Baumann does not review Vermigli's conflict with Bibliander.
86 For Vermigli's thought on predestination, see Frank A. James III, *Peter Martyr Vermigli and Predestination. The Augustinian Inheritance of and Italian Reformer* (Oxford:

When Beza became involved in the disagreement between Calvin and Bullinger on Bolsec's view of predestination, it was clear that he tried to persuade Bullinger of Calvin's orthodoxy. A closer examination of his *Tabula* with the *Explicatio* is necessary to see whether these writings can be regarded as attempts to bring Calvin and Bullinger into line with each other, and the extent to which he agreed with and differed from the two theologians he both regarded as "father."

3.5 Beza's *Tabula:* Title, Editions and Intention
3.5.1 Title
Beza called his *Tabula* a *Summa Totius Christianismi, sive descriptio et distributio causarum salutis electorum, & exitij reproborum, ex sacris literis collecta cum brevis explicatio praecedentis Tabulae* (The Sum of all Christianity, or description and division of the causes of the salvation of the elect, and of the destruction of the reprobate, collected from the Sacred Writings, with a Short explanation of the preceding Tabula). This title has attracted a great deal of attention in previous studies with contradictory conclusions. The composition of the title gives the impression that the *Tabula* is the most important part, and the explication only an addition. Beza seems to be saying that the *Tabula* itself is the sum of all Christianity, a description and distribution of causes of salvation and destruction, and is collected from the Holy Scriptures. Actually, the description of causes is found in the aphorisms of the explanation, which are accompanied by many proof texts from Scripture. The French *Table* of 1560 does not mention a single text, and the Latin *Tabula* of 1570 only refers to Romans 11:36. The title does not sufficiently represent what the work is. This is important in estimating the different conclusions concerning the first part of the title.[87]

The words *Summa totius christianismi* have been interpreted very differently. Some saw it as a proof that Reformed theology had developed into a predestinarian system.[88] Bray denies this and suggests that it could

---

Clarendon Press, 1998).

87 Dr. Leo van Santen, author of *Das Dorf als literarischer Kosmos. Aegidius Henning (um 1630-1686) - Leben, Werk und Literaturprogramm* (Aachen: Shaker, 2005) and *Bremen als Brennpunkt reformierter Irenik: eine sozialgeschichtliche Darstellung anhand der Biografie des Theologen Ludwig Crocius (1586-1655)* (Leiden: Brill, 2014), suggested to me that this title might have been given by the publisher or printer rather than by Beza himself. Publishers sometimes used superlative language in a title to increase sales.

88 For proponents of this theory see Bray, *Beza's Doctrine*, 71-72. Muller, *Christ and the Decree*, 1-7, and idem, "Use and Abuse," 33-35.

be understood as "the sum total of the Christian life."[89] Muller argued that the *Tabula* is not a full systematic work and should not be interpreted as a *Summa theologiae*. Its focus is not to summarize the entire faith but only the order of causes of salvation and damnation.[90]

Bray's suggestion is implausible since half of the *Tabula* discusses the reprobate, rather than the Christian life. The title of the French edition of 1560 shows that it was understood in its own time as a work that contained the principal points of Christian religion *(contenant les principaus poincts de la religion Chrestienne)*. An English translation from as early as 1556 translated the title in a similar way: *Briefe Declaration of the Chiefe Points of Christian Religion*.[91]

Muller is right in arguing that the *Tabula* does not discuss all doctrines and hence does not summarize the entire faith, but he does not offer any reason as to why this title was nevertheless chosen. It is true that Beza's *Summa totius christianismi* is not a Reformed equivalent of Thomas Aquinas's *Summa totius theologiae*. It is not a complete sum of all Christian theology, yet the title suggests that Beza regarded the doctrines treated in it as principal doctrines. It is indeed less than a *Summa theologiae*, but it is more than simply a description of the order of salvation.[92] Another work by Beza that has the word *summa* in its title might throw light on Beza's intention with this word. In 1561, he published his *Summa doctrina de re sacramentaria*, a small work of only five pages.[93] A work of this size cannot be thought to be intended as a complete work but only as a short compendium. It seems that the word *summa* in the title of the *Tabula* should be interpreted in a similar way.

3.5.2 Editions

The *Tabula* as published in Beza's tracts in 1570 is the edition that is the most known, and it is often assumed that this is the original table of 1555.

---

89 Bray, *Beza's Doctrine*, 72.
90 Muller, "Use and Abuse," 34-35.
91 This translation is mentioned in Joseph Ames, *Typographical Antiquities ...*, Vol. III (London, 1790), 1595.
92 Although there is no evidence, as Muller correctly states, that his contemporaries and successors interpreted the *Tabula* as a system of doctrine in outline form, it is nevertheless true that Beza's order in the *Tabula* (God – His decrees – Creation – Fall – Christ – Calling – Faith – Justification – Eschatology) became widely used in later Reformed theology. Further research into the relation between Beza's *Tabula* and Reformed systematic theology concerning the order of the *loci* is necessary but would go beyond the limits of this study.
93 This work is included in *TT* I, 206-10.

But since no copy of the first edition survives, this remains a matter of speculation. There is, however, a French translation that dates back to 1560 and contains a table that shows some differences with that of 1570.[94] It is plausible that this French table is closest to the original table of 1555.

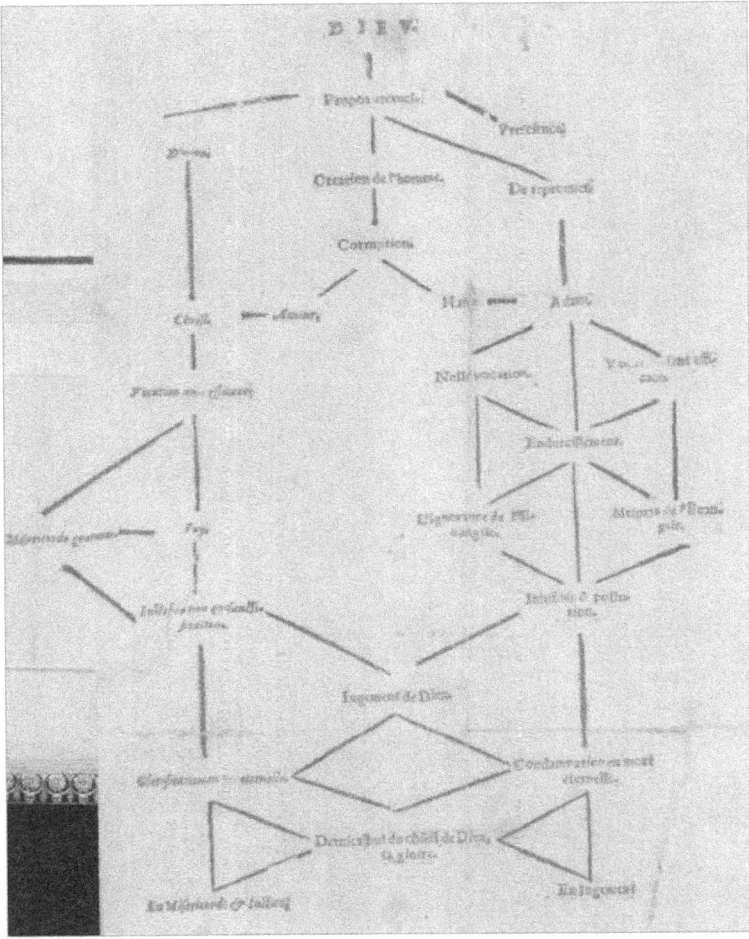

The French Table of 1560.

---

94 Theodore de Besze, *Brefve exposition de la table ou figure contenant les principaus poincts de la religion Chrestienne* (n.p.[Geneva]: Jean Rivery, 1560).

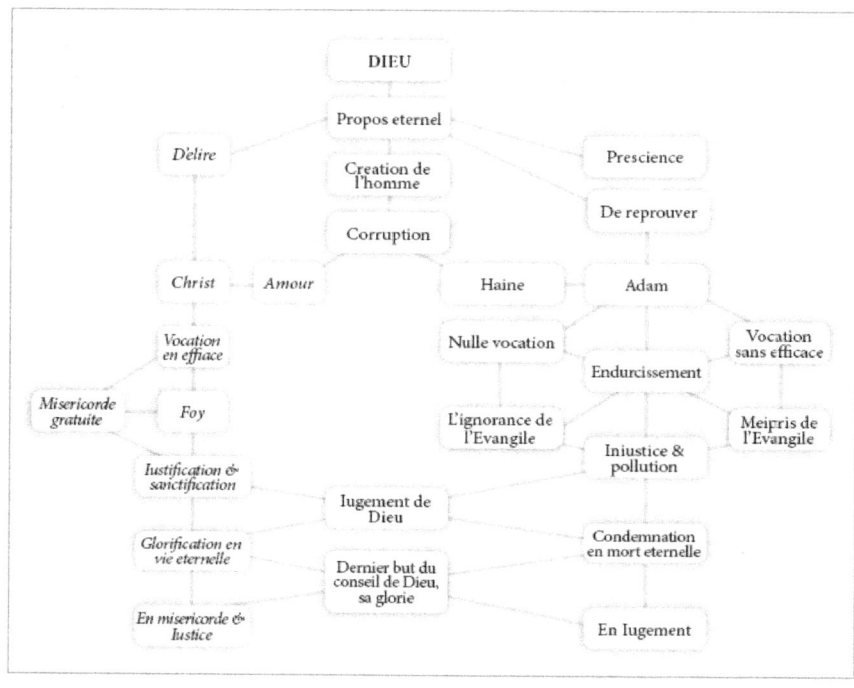
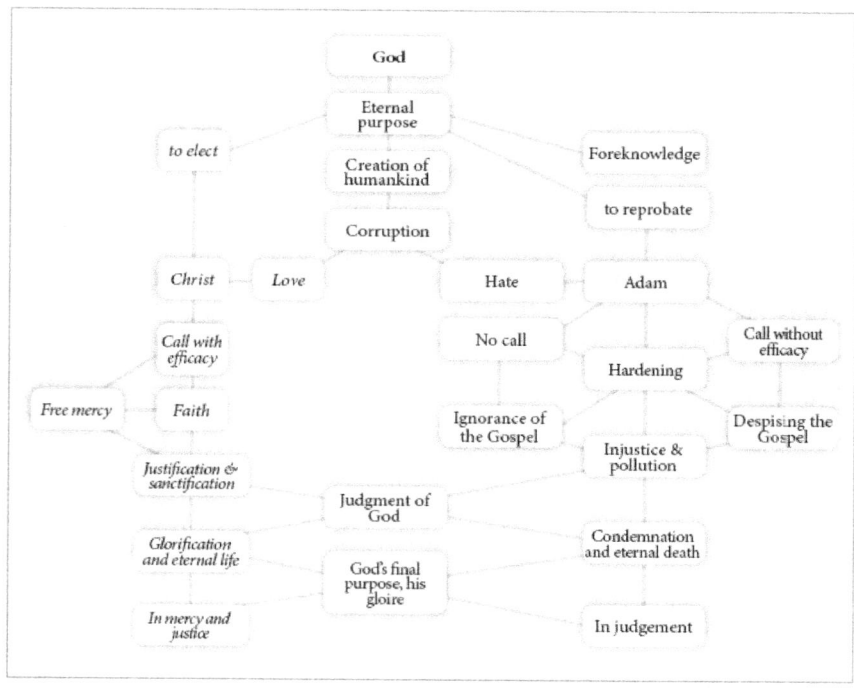

There are some differences between the *Tabula* in Beza's *Tractationes* of 1570 and the French version of 1560.⁹⁵ In the latter, Beza places *Prescience* (foreknowledge) on the side of reprobation, below God's purpose but above reprobation, while prescience is omitted in 1570, as well as "free mercy" as the source of the call, faith, justification, and sanctification which appears besides the left column of 1560. What is more striking is that, in 1560, election and reprobation are not placed on the same level: reprobation is placed below election and even below creation, although not below corruption. In the 1570 edition, they are placed on the same level, above creation. It is also conspicuous that the lines between election and love in Christ in the 1560 edition, as well as those between reprobation and hate because of Adam, are omitted in the 1570 edition. This edition adds "conversion" between "effective call" and "faith." The words from Romans 11:36 are also added in the 1570 edition. Other words are used for concepts, or words are added. The single word "God" at the head of the table in 1560 is expanded in the 1570 edition to "God, whose ways are unsearchable."

The 1582 reprint of Beza's tracts contains another version of the table.⁹⁶ Two Bible verses are added at the top, left and right. "Conversion" has been moved from its position between call and faith to the same level as faith – although if the table is read from left to right, it still precedes faith. The lines between election and love in Christ, as well as those between reprobation and hate because of Adam seem to reappear, but it is not clear if this is intended, since there also seems to be a direct line between corruption and judgment in the 1582 edition. These lines could have been placed there by the designer of the 1582 edition, who used his creativity more extensively than those of the 1560 and 1570 versions did. Justification and sanctification are placed together.

It is tempting to draft hypotheses or even conclusions about these differences. Yet we need to be cautious, for, even with all these changes in the *Tabula*, there are no changes in the content of the explanations in these

---

95 Beza, *Summa Totius Christianismi, sive descriptio et distributio causarum salutis electorum, & exitij reproborum, ex sacris literis collecta cum Brevis explicatio praecedentis Tabvlae*, in *Tractationum Theologicarum, in quibus pleraque Christianae Religionis dogmata aduersus hæreses nostris temporibus renouatas solidè ex Verbo Dei defenduntur Volumen [primum]* (Geneva: Io. Cripspinum 1570), 170-205.

96 Beza, *Summa Totius Christianismi, sive descriptio et distributio causarum salutis electorum, & exitij reproborum, ex sacris literis collecta cum Brevis explicatio praecedentis Tabvlae*, in *Tractationum Theologicarum, in quibus pleraque Christianae Religionis dogmata aduersus hæreses nostris temporibus renouatas solidè ex Verbo Dei defenduntur Volumen primum* (Geneva: Eustathius Vignon, 1582), 170-205.

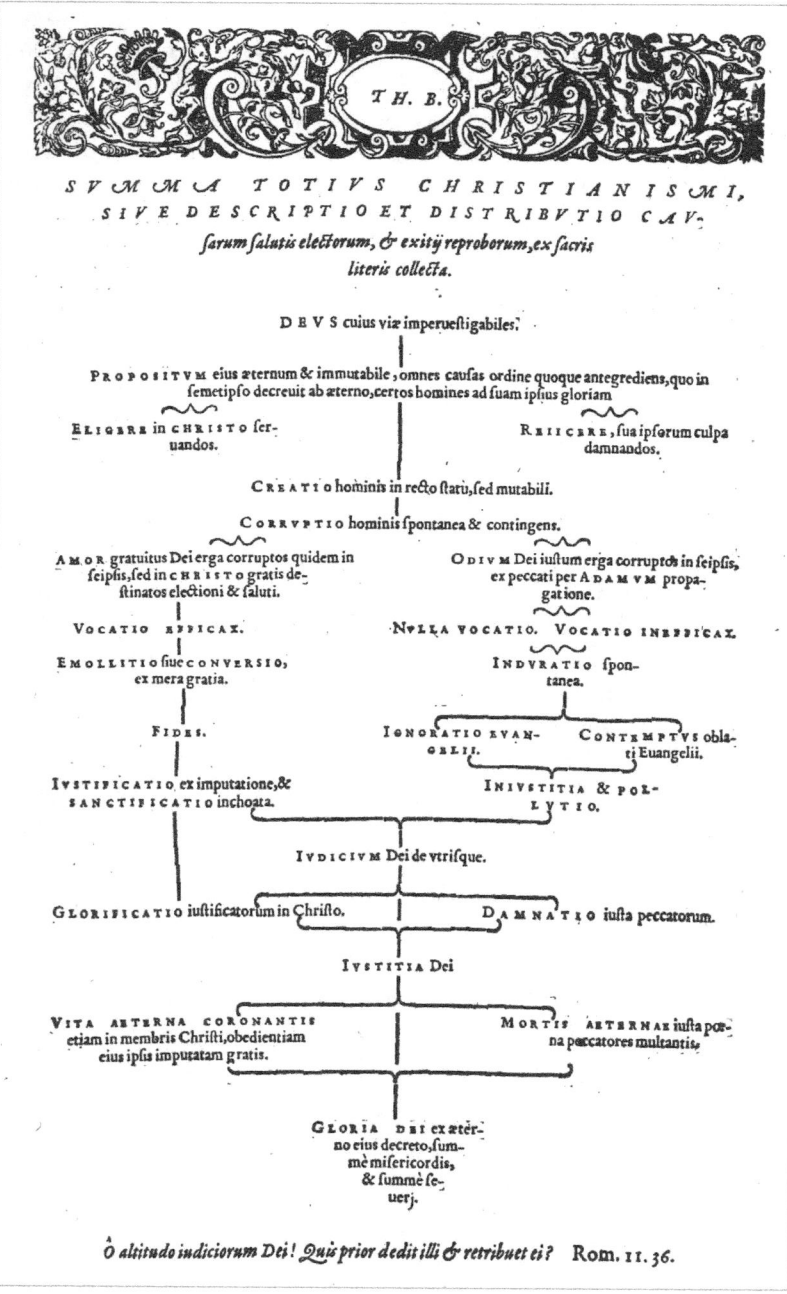

The Tabula of 1570.

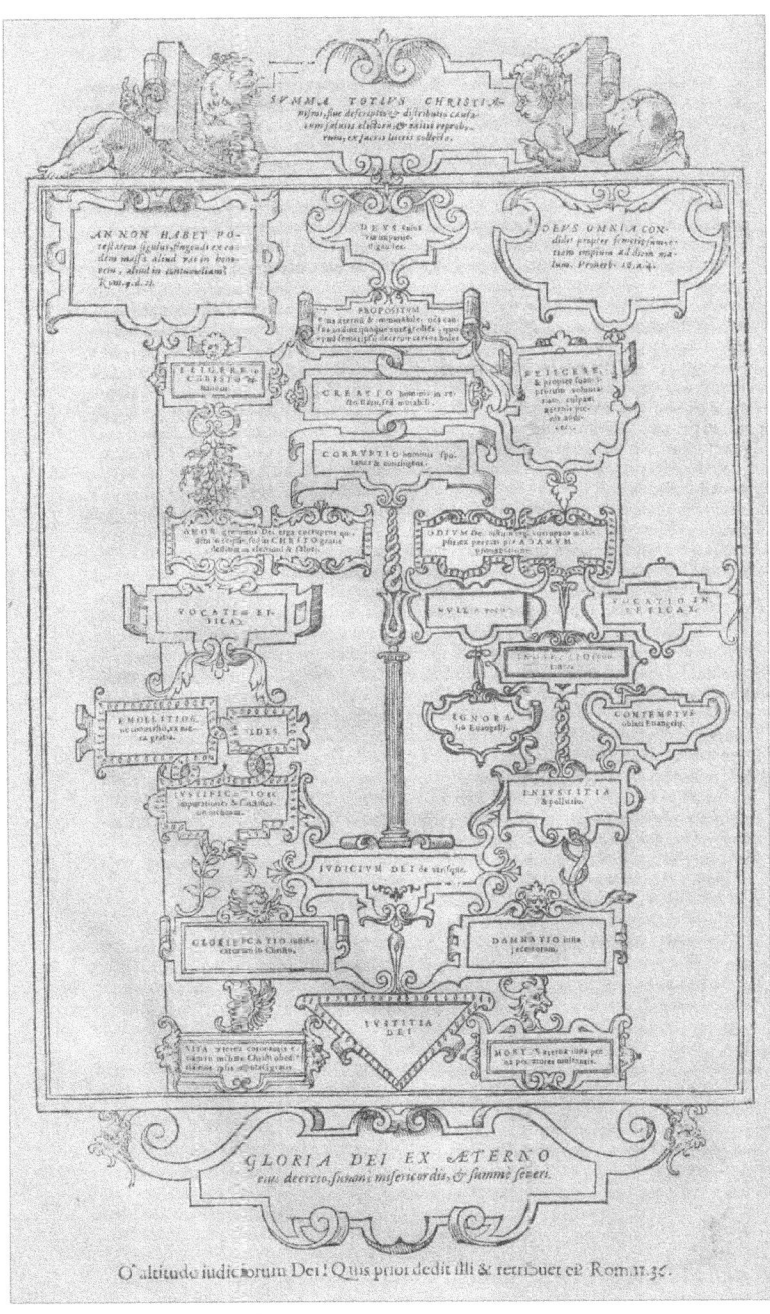

The Tabula of 1582.

different editions.⁹⁷ Hence, we cannot conclude that the differences in these tables reflect a change in Beza's views. It seems that the changes in the design of the *Tabula* over the years are intended to simply give a better impression of Beza's ideas or are due to different graphic designers.

Another version of the *Tabula* appears in Beza's *De praedestinationis doctrina*, which was first published in 1582.⁹⁸ This is a simplified version of the one in the *Summa totius christianismi*, although it seems to have been intended for a more academic readership, in view of the fact that Beza used some Greek here. Notable differences are that the (ineffective) call on the side of reprobation is missing, as well as justification, sanctification, and glorification and God's judgment. There is no reason to conclude that these subjects were also absent from Beza's theology in that period.

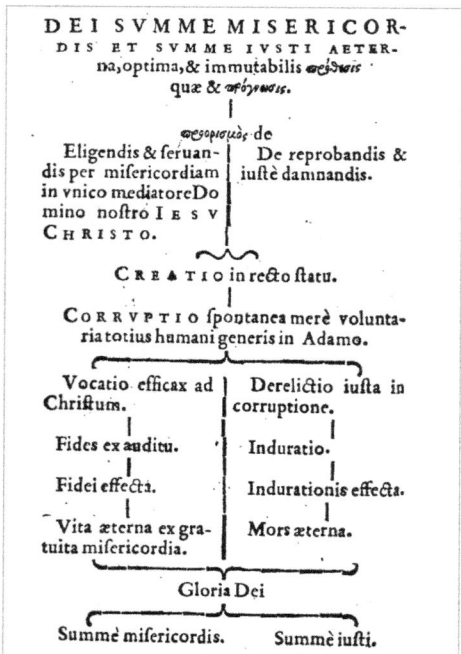

The other Tabula in De praedestinationis doctrina *from 1582.*

---

97 The *Explicatio* as published in 1570 and 1582 do not differ from the *Brefve exposition* from 1560. References will be made to the editions of 1570 and 1582. The edition of Beza's works of 1582 was reset but the pages in the edition are almost a complete match for the pages in the 1570 edition.

98 *De praedestinationis doctrina et vero usu tractatio absolutissima, editio secunda* (n.p. [Geneva]: Eustathius Vignon, 1583), 8.

3.5.3 Intention

There is no evidence that clearly indicates what Beza's intention was in drafting his *Tabula*. Nevertheless, Beza's letters and the time and context of its origin offer at least some suggestions. The first is that Beza was not content with Calvin's method of refuting Bolsec in his *De aeterna praedestinatione*. He preferred a more systematic approach to the subject over a page-by-page refutation of Pighius. This preference might have been prompted by Beza's teaching job in Lausanne. Muller has argued with some plausibility that Beza's *Tabula* might have been intended as a refutation of Bolsec's views.[99]

In addition to these educational and elenctic motives, there may yet be another and, for Beza, even more important reason. As remarked in 3.4, Beza was diligent in promoting unity among Protestants. Animosity between Calvin and Bullinger could be a threat to the unity of the Reformed theology and churches and hence to the cause of the Reformation. Moreover, he regarded and addressed both theologians as his spiritual father. This was reason enough to try to get Calvin and Bullinger on the same page concerning predestination. Beza's first German biographer, Schlosser, remarked correctly that, for Calvin, Beza was "a friend who would correct him, who would diminish his heat which could spoil everything, who could calm down minds, and who would win the Swiss by a right representation of the doctrine."[100] Beza's letters of 1551 and 1552 show his fruitless efforts to convince Bullinger. It is not clear whether or not Bullinger was convinced by the *Summa totius christianismi*.

The hypothesis of an appeasing motive for Beza's *Tabula* finds support in the content of the *Explicatio*. As stated above, the differences between Calvin and Bullinger can be summarized as consisting mainly in these two points: First, Calvin stressed the eternity of God's decrees, while Bullinger was reluctant to speculate God's eternal decrees. Second, Calvin stressed that all things, even unbelief, happen because of God's eternal decree. Bullinger was afraid to make God the author of sin or unbelief and obviously thought that seeing God as the cause of unbelief would also make him the author of unbelief.[101] It seems that Beza tries to bridge these differences. He accepts, uses, and stresses Bullinger's distinction

---

99 Muller, "Use and Abuse."
100 Friedrich Christoph Schlosser, *Leben des Theodor de Beza und des Peter Martyr Vermigli: Ein Beytrag zur Geschichte der Zeiten der Kirchen-Reformation* (Heidelberg: Wohr und Zimmer, 1809), 43. This characterization of Beza is more positive than that of later times, when Beza was seen as someone who hardened Calvin's doctrine of predestination.
101 For studies on Bullinger's thoughts on predestination, see 3.4.1 note 43.

between the eternal decree and its execution in time. Although God's decree was behind all things that happen in time, the greater part of the *Tabula* is about what happens in time and not about the eternal decree. Although the execution was also a part of God's eternal decree, this execution develops in time and hence can be known, unlike the purpose behind it, which remains hidden in God. The reasons and causes of the purpose to elect and to reprobate are God's will alone and cannot be known, while the reasons for salvation and damnation can be seen in human beings. Moreover, the distinction between purpose and execution includes a distinction between the purpose to elect and to reprobate on the one hand and election and reprobation themselves on the other. This enables Beza to write about the eternal purpose similar to remarks made by Calvin concerning eternal predestination, before creation. At the same time, he can write about election and reprobation themselves, similar to Bullinger's thinking as following creation and the Fall. Beza's construction contains elements of both Calvin's and Bullinger's ideas concerning predestination.

In dealing with the execution of the decree in his *Explicatio* of the *Tabula*, Beza starts with creation and the Fall, remarking that it was necessary *(necesse fuit)* that God should include both the elect and the reprobate under disobedience and sin. The Fall, according to Beza, was necessary both for election – for faith is a gift of God (in other words, the Fall was necessary to exclude human merit from salvation) – and reprobation – to provide God with a just cause to condemn the reprobate.[102]

This was something Bullinger had disapproved of in Calvin's thought, for, according to him, teaching the necessity of the Fall would take responsibility away from Adam and make God the cause of the Fall. Bullinger interpreted necessity as the necessity of compulsion.[103] Calvin argued that the Fall occurred according the foreknowledge and will of

---

102 *Tabula*, cap. III, aph. 1, *TT* I, 177: "Dominus vt aeternum illud consilium ad gloriam suam exequeretur, viam quondam sibi muniit pro sua infinita sapientia, vtrisque tum eligendis, tum reprobandis communem... necesse fuit vt vtroque sub contumacia & peccato includeret, vt omnium credentium, id est, electorum (est enim fides donum Dei electis peculiare) misereatur: & e contrario vt iusta damnationis argumentum in iis inueniat, quibus neque credere, neque mysteria Dei nosse datum est." *(To have the eternal counsel executed to his own glory, the Lord has, through his infinite wisdom, prepared a way common to both the elect and the reprobate... it was necessary to include both under disobedience and sin in order to have mercy on all believers, that is, the elect (for faith is the special gift of God to the elect) and, in contrast, to find a reason to condemn those to whom it is not given to believe or to know the mysteries of God.)* (My translation.) See also *De praedestinationis doctrina*, 9-10.
103 See 3.4.1.

God[104] but not that it was necessary.[105] However, this conclusion by Beza follows from Calvin's thinking on the will of God and foreknowledge, and it seems that Bullinger had also drawn this conclusion. Nevertheless, it is remarkable that Beza explicitly uses the word "necessity."

Perhaps because of his attempts to convince Bullinger, Beza includes an excursus on necessity. God had included all people under disobedience in such a wise way that the whole fault of the reprobate's damnation lies in themselves and all the glory of the elect's salvation to God's mercy. For God neither created humans as sinners, nor did he force them to sin – which would have made God indeed the author of sin. Human beings sinned freely *(sponte & libere)*, without constraint *(a nemine prorsus coactus)* and without necessity of concupiscence *(concupiscentiae necessitate impulsus)*, and yet not by chance or without God's will *(neque fortuito evenisse, neque sine eius voluntate)*.[106] Here we see the temporary result of Beza's wrestling with the relation between sin, unbelief, and the decree in the years prior to his formulation of the *Tabula*.

Although it may seem paradoxical at first, the fact that Beza wrote so extensively on the decree of reprobation and its execution can also be interpreted as an attempt to convince Bullinger. It might be that Beza's reason for writing so much about the "dark side" of the decree was not to make reprobation as important for Christian doctrine as election[107] but to convince Bullinger that Calvin's doctrine of *praedestinatio gemina* did not make God the author of sin. Thomas is probably right in asserting that the structure of the *Tabula* is intended to uphold both the sovereignty of God and human responsibility.[108]

On the other hand, Beza was also targeting Bullinger. He remarks that we should not avoid taking up a doctrine revealed in the Scripture, provided we do not cross the boundaries of Scripture, and quotes Augustine on this point. Augustine's authority was so great among the Reformers that Bullinger could hardly oppose it. This quotation can be interpreted as an effort to correct Bullinger's reluctance to talk about predestination.

Looking at these three elements against the background of Beza's zeal

---

104 For example, *De Aeterna Praedestinatione* CO VIII, 297, where Calvin stated that the Fall was ordained *(praeordinatus)*.
105 Using the Boolean search option in the digital *Calvini Opera Database* (laps* w/10 neces*) I could not locate a single place in Calvin's works where he states that the Fall was necessary.
106 *Tabula*, cap. III, aph. 2, 3, 5,6, *TT* I, 178-79. A similar view is found in *De praedestinationis doctrina*, 9-10, and also in *Quaestionem*, 104-05. See also *Cours*, 168.
107 Contra Steinmetz, *Reformers in the Wings*, 119, and Graafland, *Van Calvijn tot Barth*, 53.
108 Thomas, *Extent*, 47.

for unity among the Reformed, the *Tabula* might be regarded as an enterprise to reconcile his spiritual fathers Bullinger and Calvin. His *Tabula* was likely intended as a table where both could confer – a *tabula conferentionis*.

3.6 Beza's Mature Doctrine of Predestination After 1555
3.6.1 The Decree

Beza wrote several works on the doctrine of predestination. The first was his *Brief Declaration of the Tabula Praedestinationis* (1555), in which he defined predestination as follows:

> From eternity, God ... has proposed and determined in himself, to create ... human beings: whom he has made in two very different kinds. He thought it good to make the one kind to be (according to his secret will) partakers of his glory through his mercy. These we call, following the word of God, the vessels of honor, the elect, the children of the promise, and predestined to salvation. He thought it good to show his wrath and power in others, which it pleased him to raise up for this use, to be glorified in them as well. These we call the vessels of dishonor and wrath, reprobate from all good works.[109]

In the eleventh chapter of the *Theses* (1586), Beza and Fayus define predestination in a very similar way,[110] and a similar definition can also be

---

109 *Tabula*, Cap. II, aph., 2, *TT* I, 173: "Deus ab aeterno proposuit & decreuit in semetipso ... creare, ac nominatim quidem homines, idque duobus modis penitus diuersis ita nempe, vt alios quos sibi visum fuerit pro arcane sua voluntate faciat per misericordiam gloriae suae participes, quos vasa honoris, electos, filios promissionis, & praedestinatos ad salutem ex Dei verbo appellamus: in alteris vero, quos item placuerit in eum vsum suscitare, iram ac potentiam suam ostendat, vt in ipsis quoque glorificetur, quos vasa contumeliae & irae, & ad omne bonum opus reprobos vocamus" (my translation).

110 *Theses*, XI, 1: "Praedestinationis vocamus primùm in genere decretum illud Dei aeternum & immotum, quo, provt ipsi opt. maximóque libuit, cuncta, tum vniversaliter, tum singulariter decreuit, & per causas similiter ab ipso, provt libuit, creatas & directas ad gloriam suam patefaciendam, exequitur. 2. Deinde specialiter hoc decretum ad humanum genus applicantes, Praedestinationem vocamus aeternum illud, quod & quale diximus, decretum, quo immutabiliter & ab aeterno constituit, in aliis quidem summa misericordia seruandis, in aliis verò iustissima sua seueritate damnandis, sese, qualis reuera est, ab effectis, summè videlicet misericordem & summè iustum, demonstrare." *(1. First in general, Praedestination is that aeternal and immouable decree of God, whereby, as it pleased his Majestie, he hath decreed all things both vniuersalie and particularlie; and also doth effect them by the causes created in like sort, & appointed by him, as he thoght good to the laying open of his owne glory. 2. Secondly, applying this decree vnto mankind. Wee call Praedestination, that aeternal decree (such as we haue already spoken of:) whereby he hath immutably purposed from*

found in Beza's *Quaestiones* (1570).[111] In his *De praedestinationis doctrina* (1582) he defines predestination, election, and reprobation as follows:

> Since predestination is surely nothing else than the determination of his will to a certain end, either salvation or damnation, it cannot be reasonably denied that predestination pertains both to the twofold ultimate purpose and to the means subordinated to both.
> These two ends are opposed to each other in themselves, but we state, based on God's Word, that they, viz. election and reprobation, come together in this ultimate purpose, when considered in that eternal divine proposition. We correctly define the first thereof, viz. Election, as the eternal decree, proceeding from his pure gracious love, concerning those in whom he delights, to be elected, in whose eternal salvation he declares his greatest goodness and compassion. [We define] Reprobation in the same way, not as it is executed but as he has decreed it from eternity, as God's eternal decree concerning the others, in whose most just and at the same time most severe condemnation, he declares his greatest hatred against all sin and his highest praise.[112]

---

all aeternity, by sauing some in his great mercie, and by damning others in his most just seueritie, to manifest himselfe, what he is indeed by his effects; namely that he is most mercifull and most just.) (Transl. Robert Waldegrave 1591.)

111 *Quaestionum & Responsionum christianarum libellvs. In qvo praecipva christianae Religionis capita κατ' ἐπιτομην proponuntur,* (n.p. [Geneva: I. Crispinus, 1570), 116. Also in *TT* I, 669 (1570) / 654 (1582) (cited as *Quaestionum*): "Praedestinatio ... dicamus esse aeternum & immutabile decretum, ordine antegrediens omnes salutis & damnationis causas, quo Deus constituit in aliis quidem in Christo ex mera gratia seruandis, in aliis verò in Adamo & semetipsis iusto suo iudicio damnandis, glorificari." (*Predestination ... is the eternal and immutable decree of God, going in order before all the causes of salvation and damnation, whereby God has determined to be glorified in some by saving them in Christ by mere grace, but in others by damning them by His rightful judgement in Adam and in themselves.*) Transl. by Kirk M. Summers, *A Little Book of Christian Questions and Responses* (Allison Park: Pickwick Publications, 1985), answer 195, p. 84.

112 *De praedestinationis doctrina* 5, 6. "... praedestinatio vero nihil aliud sit quam eius voluntatis ad certum finem sive salutis sive exitii destinatio, negari iusta ratione non potest, Praedestinationem & ad ultimum illum duplicem finem & ad utrinque subordinate media pertinere...
Duos igitur fines inter se quidem oppositos sed in ultimo illo sine concurrentes statuimus ex Dei verbo, Electionem videlicet & Reprobationem, in aeterno ipso Dei Proposito consideratas: quarum priorem, nempe Electionem, recte definierimus, esse aeternum Dei decretum ex mere gratuito ipsius amore profectum, de certis quos ipsi libuit, hominibus eligendis, in quorum aeterna salute, summam suam bonitatem ac misseridodiam declararet: Reprobationem vero itidem, non quatenus illam exequatur, sed quatenus illam ab aeterno decrevit, aeternum Dei decretum de reliquis hominibus, in quorum iustissima simul & severissima condemnatione, summum illud suum adversus omne peccatum odium summa cum sua laude declararet." (My translation)

This definition is more extensive than the other definitions Beza gives, although the content remains the same. Beza's definitions are also very similar to the definition Calvin gives in his *Institutes*.[113]

There are other similarities with Calvin. First, predestination consists in both election and reprobation *(praedestinatio gemina)*; second, God's will is the only basis for election and reprobation – sin and faith or good works are not causes. Third, God's purpose in reprobation is just, even though people might not perceive that. In his *Brevis Explicatio*, Beza uses the same distinction Calvin used between remote and proximate causes: the remote cause of damnation is God's purpose, but the proximate cause of it is sin. Beza stresses this distinction.[114] In later years, Beza denied that God is the cause of sin, as we will see below in 3.11.

However, Beza differs from Calvin in distinguishing between a purpose to elect *(propositum eligendi)* and to reprobate *(reprobandi propositum)* on the one hand and actual election *(electio ipsa)* and reprobation *(reprobatio ipsa)* on the other.[115] He makes a similar distinction in the *Theses* between "choosing out of bondage," according to "the eternal decree of election."[116] Beza wrote about the *eligendi* and *reprobandi* in *De praedestinationis doctrina* as well.[117]

As stated above, both the purpose and execution are decrees of God, but the execution unfolds in time. Actual election and reprobation are

---

113 Calvin, *Institutes,* xiv (viii), 5 (1539-1554); III, xxi, 5 (1559).
114 *Tabula,* Cap. II, aph, 4-5, *TT* I, 175-76.
115 *Tabula* cap. II, aph. 6, *TT* I, 176: "Debemus enim inter reprobandi propositum & reprobationem ipsam distinguere." *(We have to distinguish between the decree to reprobate and reprobation itself.) Tabula,* cap. II, aph. 7, *TT* I, 177: "Sic quum de causis salutis in gradus & certa serie describendis agitur, in electorum salute propositum eligendi, quod Deus in semetipso decreuit, ab electione ipsa distinguimus, quae est in Christo consituta, ita vt illud ista & caetera omnia quae consequuntur, in causarum serie antegrediatur". *(Likewise, when we describe the causes of salvation in their steps and certain order concerning the elect, we distinguish the proposition to elect, which God has decreed by himself, from election itself, which is constituted in Christ, in that way that the one precedes the other and all things which follow, in order of causes.)* See also cap. VI aph. 7. Cf. Calvin, *De aeterna Dei praedestinatione* CO VIII, 296.
116 *Theses,* XI, 13. "Ex hac servitude Deus nemini debito, secundum aeternam suam in Christo preadestinatam electionem, quos ipsi libuit, ex mera sua misericordia seligere, eadem sua misericordia, quando ipsi visum est, vocat, illuminate, fide donatos & regeneratos gratis in eodem Christo iustificat ..." *(From this bondage, God, who is indebted to no one, chooses according to his eternal predestined election those whom he himself willed out of pure mercy, and, on the basis of that same mercy, when he shows it, he calls, enlightens them and, having given them faith and regeneration, he freely justifies them in Christ)* (my translation).
117 *De praedestinationis doctrina,* 6-7.

therefore both eternal decrees, and acts in time. In the *Theses* of 1591, Beza and Fayus explained this further, stating that the names of election and reprobation are applied to the eternal decree in a metonymic way:

> The differences of predestination are two, of which the one is called election and the other reprobation, in a metonymical way. For election and reprobation taken in the proper sense refer to the human race which is already conditioned by God and corrupted by its own fault, and have no other meaning than either the temporal election of man out of the world (John 15:19) or the abdication from the participation of eternal salvation. But here we take election and reprobation in Scriptural use (Eph. 1:4) metonymical for the decree to elect or to reprobate.[118]

The distinction between the eternal purpose and actual reprobation made it possible for him to call sin and unbelief the causes of reprobation.[119] This must be understood from *reprobatio ipsa*, for Beza denied that sin and unbelief were causes of the eternal purpose to reprobate.[120] This distinction is not apparent in Calvin's works on predestination.[121]

Some church historians have argued that Beza took a step backward by moving predestination back into the context of providence from which Calvin had removed it in his 1559 *Institutes*.[122] What these scholars do not take into account here is that when Beza wrote his *Tabula* in 1555, Calvin had not yet separated predestination and providence, which he did in 1559. Moreover, it was not predestination that was moved in the 1559 *Institutes* but providence. This latter doctrine was placed in the larger doctrine of

---

118 *Theses* (1591), "Theses alia extra ordinem disputata XII, De Praedestinatione," thesis 19, pp. 22-23: "Porro differentiae Praedestinationis duae sunt quarum una Electio, altera Reprobatio, per Metonymiam effecti, nominatur. Nam Electio & Reprobatio propriè acceptae referuntur ad genus humanum iam à Deo conditum & proprio suo vitio corruptum, nihilq. aliud significant, quàm temporalem hominum vel electionem ex hoc mundo (Ioh. 15.19), vel abdicationem à participatione salutis aeternae. Sed hîc Electionem & Reprobationem ex usu Scripturae (Eph. 1.4) Metonymicôs accipimus pro ipso eligendi aut reprobandi decreto."
119 *Tabula*, Cap. II, ap., 4-5, *TT* I, 175-76. Here Beza left his initial idea of strict parallelism between election and reprobation, which Sinnema thought to be Beza's position during his life, for faith is. neither in the decree, nor in the execution, a cause of election.
120 This way of expressing his ideas was closer to Bullinger than to Calvin, which is another argument for my hypothesis concerning Beza's intention with the *Tabula*.
121 See Sinnema, "Beza's View of Predestination" for further information on this, for Beza, important distinction.
122 For instance, Steinmetz, *Reformers in the Wings*, 119; Van Sliedrecht, *Calvijns opvolger*, 53-54.

God the Creator rather than predestination being moved to another place. The subject of Book I of the *Institutes* is the knowledge of God the Creator, and the doctrine of providence properly belongs here. But predestination does not. So, given the structure of the 1559 *Institutes*, it would be illogical to move predestination along with providence to Book I. Beza did not use Calvin's method of ordering the theological *loci* in four books with different themes in his *Tabula* of 1555 nor in his *Theses theologicae* of 1586. Rather, he used a synthetic method to order the *loci* in both works.[123]

The place of predestination in Beza's theology is not unambiguous. It changed places across various publications. It was the main theme in his *Summa totius christianismi*, which led to the unwarranted conclusion that predestination was so prominent in Beza's theology that all other doctrines were subordinated to it. But in several other works, like Beza's confessions and catechism, predestination was not prominent at all but hardly mentioned. It had an important place in the *Quaestiones*, which largely followed the same structure as Calvin's *Institutes*, but only at the end of the work. In Beza's most complete systematic work, the *Theses* that he edited with Fayus, predestination was located after theses on God and his attributes and on providence. Taking all these works into account, it is clear, on the one hand, that predestination was important to Beza, but, on the other, it is evident that conclusions such as those Kickel made do not hold.

3.6.2 Supralapsarianism

Most scholars hold that Beza was a supralapsarian and use the *Tabula* to support this argument.[124] In itself, this is not convincing since in the *Tabula* Beza placed the divine purpose to elect and to reprobate above the Fall, but actual election and reprobation below the Fall. The issue for Beza in 1555 was the relation between the decree and the Fall. Was the Fall willed by God (Calvin) or simply foreseen (Bullinger)? Here Beza took the side of Calvin.

---

123 For the different methods for arranging *loci* in Protestant theology see W.J. van Asselt and Pieter Rouwendal, "Distinguishing and Teaching: Constructing a Theological Argument in Reformed Scholasticism," in Van Asselt, *Introduction to Reformed Scholasticism*, 86-102.

124 For instance, Sinnema, "Beza's View of Predestination"; Joel R. Beeke, "Theodore Beza's Supralapsarian Predestination," in *Reformation and Revival Journal*, vol. 12 nr. 2, 2003, 69-84; see also his, "The Order of the Divine Decrees at the Genevan Academy: From Bezan Supralapsarianism to Turretinian Infralapsarianism," in Roney and Klauber, *The Identity of Geneva, 57-75*.

According to Beeke, Beza did not develop a fully-fledged supralapsarianism in 1555 but did anticipate the supra position by then. In 1582 he "appears to have moved in a more supralapsarian direction."[125] Sinnema, however, argued that Beza presented a supralapsarian position already in a letter from 1555, although he does not explicitly present a supralapsarian formulation in the *Summa*.[126] Yet when Beza writes in the *Brevis explicatio* on reprobation as concealed in God's purpose, he notes in connection with the proof texts Rom. 9:13 and Mal. 1:2 that these words *(Before the children were born, it was said: ... Esau I have hated)* exclude all sin, even original sin, from the causes of God's hate, and the objection by the reprobate that they are, given God's decree, damned without reason, is not to be answered by pointing to their sins but by pointing to God's will, as Paul did in Rom. 9:20.[127] If this is not explicit supralapsarianism, it comes very close. A similar position is formulated in his *De praedestinationis doctrina* of 1582,[128] in which Beza even rejected a kind of infralapsarian position:

> Certain people have advanced something that seems to be reasonable. They say that God, when he himself made the decision from eternity to elect some and to reprobate others, had seen the human race as corrupt and accordingly as worthy of the curse, out of which he had freely decreed by his mercy to elect some and destined others because of their foreseen corruption to destruction. But this view presupposes something that cannot be in God, viz. that he sought counsel with himself concerning the end of human beings, at a time when he considered them to be already corrupt since they say that in God's mind foreseen corruption precedes the decree in the order of causes.[129]

---

125 Beeke, "Supralapsarian Predestination," 73-76; "Order," 50-63.
126 Sinnema, "Beza's View of Predestination," 226.
127 *Tabula*, Cap. II, aph. 6, note on Rom. 9:13, *TT* I, 176: "Quibus verbis originale quoque peccatum & quicquid in persona Esau ab ipsa genitura reputari potest, ab odij causa excludit... [Immeritò eos damnari."
128 *De praedestinationis doctrina*, 68-70.
129 *De praedestinationis doctrina*, 74: "Proferunt tamen quiddam quod speciem aliquam habet rationis. Volunt enim Deum apud se ab aeterno capientem aliquos eligendi & aliquos reprobandi consilium; sibi proposuisse genus humanum ut corruptum, ac proinde ut maledictione dignum, ex qua nonnullos gratis per misericordiam eximere decreverit, caeteris propter illam praevisam corruptionem exitio destinatis. Sed ex hac opinione praesupponitur, quod in Deum cadere non potest, ipsum videlicet tum demum cepisse de hominum fine & exitu consilium, quum illos ut iam corruptos consideraret; quandoquidem corruptionis praevisionem volunt in mente Dei causarum ordine decretum illud antegredi" (my translation).

Concerning the cause of God's hatred, Beza later changed the view he presented in 1555. In his book with questions and answers (1570), although he maintained that the "lump" in Romans 9 means humankind as not yet created nor fallen, he denied that God hated without reason, just because it pleased him.[130]

> For it is certain that no one is despised by God except for sin, for otherwise he would be hating his own work. But it is one thing to hate, and another to predestine to just hatred.[131]

In his *Cours* (1564-1566), he explained that between the decree and destruction is the middle cause of induration and that God's hate is against evil.[132]

It can be confusing that Beza seems to have tended towards infralapsarianism elsewhere. When he writes on what he called *electio ipsa* and *reprobatio ipsa*, he presupposes the Fall. In other words, he then uses infralapsarian language. Yet this "actual" election and reprobation is not the decree of election and reprobation but its execution.

3.6.3 The Execution of the Decree

Like the definition, the execution of the decree is discussed in the *Theses* in a way similar to his discussion in the *Tabula*. Beza and Fayus stress the voluntary Fall. They explain the relation of God's decree to the Fall further by remarking that God's decree imposes no other necessity than what he wills as secondary causes (understanding and will) to be moved according their own nature.[133] They expressly retain the scholastic distinctions between necessity and compulsion, natural and voluntary necessity, absolute and conditional necessity, and the necessity of the consequence and of the consequent as true and profitable.[134] Here Beza and Fayus make

---

130 *Quaestionem*, 129. In the *Theses* on predestination, Beza did not mention God's hatred.
131 *Quaestionem*, 127: "Certum enim est Deo neminem nisi ob peccatum esse exosum, quoniam alioqui opus suum odisset. Verum aliud est odisse, aliud iusto odio destinare."
132 *Cours*, 156-57: "inter dectretum eternum et exitium causa media est induratio ... cum non perdat nisi induratos ... Odium eius adversus iniquitatem."
133 *Theses*, XI, 8: "Nam aeternam Dei decretum, sic eventui a se determinato necessitatem imponit, ut causes medias secundum ipsarum naturam moveri velit." *(For the aeternal purpose of God, doth impose no other necessity vpon the events which he hath determined, then such as hee will haue second causes, to be mooued according vnto their owne nature.)*
134 *Theses*, XI, 10: "Itaque Scholasticas distinctiones necessitatis & coactionis necessitates naturalis & voluntariae, absolutae & ex hypothesi, consequentis & consequen-

use of scholastic distinctions in their doctrine of predestination to retain both God's absolute and immutable decree and voluntary human acts.[135]

Likewise, in his *De praedestinationis doctrina*, Beza explains that the Fall happened according to God's decree and hence necessary: it was impossible for it not to happen. Yet it happened by human free will and hence was contingent.[136] Beza's ideas on the relation between the decree and sin developed since the publication of the *Tabula*. Since this is important for the relation between sin and unbelief, we will discuss this in the section on predestination and the response to preaching.

Calvin spoke of two steps *(gradus)* in election, the first of which was God's choosing of Abraham and his seed out of the world. The second was election to salvation (see 2.4). In Beza's explanation of his *Tabula*, he makes the Fall the first step in the execution of God's predestination and the second step the appointment of a Mediator, Jesus Christ.[137] This might be because Beza wrote his *Tabula* in response to Calvin's *De aeterna praedestinatione* and not to his chapters on predestination in the *Institutes,* in which Calvin developed the idea of *gradus* in election. But in his *De praedestinationis doctrina*, Beza lays down a structure similar to what Calvin wrote in the *Institutes*:

> The human race is regarded in three ways in that eternal decree of God. For those who are born outside the church and always stay outside, viz. those whom God does not deem worthy to call in any way, which is necessary to salvation – that means: no undeserved revelation of his covenant … Others, however, of whom Ishmael is a mirror, are born within the church and provided with all

---

tiae, ut veras & perutiles retinemus." *(Therefore, we do retaine these Scholastical distinctions of necessity and compulsion, of naturall and voluntarie, of absolute and conditionall, of enforced and ensuing necessity as true and profitable.* (The last distinction can be translated as *necessity of the consequent* and *of the consequence.*)

135 So, their use of scholastic material did not result in a predestinarian system in which predestination becomes the Reformed equivalent of fate but was used to avoid a system of that very kind.

136 *De Praedestionationis*, 10: "Nempe ut mutatione ex bono in malum ad excutionem aeterni illius Dei Propositi *necessaria* … sed tamen non aliurde quàm ex intrinseco, spontaneo, & libero voluntatis humanae motu oriretur: ut hanc ratione tum misericordiae tum iusto Dei iudicio aditus, hanc *contingente* hominis mutatione patefieret. "(Italics mine.) *(Certainly, although the change from good to bad was necessary for the execution of God's decree … and yet only originating from the inner, spontaneous and free moving will of men, in this way, by this contingent change of men, the door would be lawfully opened for both God's compassion and his justice)* (my translation). See also page 77 of the same tract.

137 *Tabula*, cap. III, aph. 1; cap. IV, aph.1-3 *TT* I, 177, 180-81.

marks of Christianity, yet they are not of the true sheep in the sight of God, who is indebted to nobody ... Still others, finally, are – only because of God's highest compassionate *eudokia* – efficaciously called to salvation out from among the other people ... [138]

There is great conceptual similarity with Calvin here, but also a difference: Beza did not use the concept of "steps" in election. Other differences concerning the doctrine of predestination are that Beza related it – unlike or more clearly than Calvin – to the Fall and to the work of Jesus Christ. The relation with the former is discussed above. The relation with the latter will be discussed in the next section.

3.7 Predestination and the Extent of the Atonement

It is well known that Beza rejected the classic formula of Christ having died sufficiently *(sufficienter)* for the whole world and efficiently *(efficienter)* for the elect alone at the Mömpelgarten or Montbéliard Colloquy in 1586. According to Beza, Christ died for the elect alone. But what about his earlier works? Is there a development in his ideas on the atonement? Earlier traces that Beza tended to restrict the extent of the atonement to the elect can be found in chapter four of his *Suma totius christianismi* (1555), which discusses the execution of election, and in his *De praedestinationis doctrina* (1582). In the *Tabula* itself, as well as in the table of predestination in *De praedestinationis doctrina*, Christ is mentioned on the side of election. Had Beza used the classic *sufficient-efficient* schema of the atonement, then Christ's birth, suffering, and death could or should have been placed in the middle of the table, under creation and corruption, as applying to all people with respect to its sufficiency or be mentioned at the side of reprobation in the same way as the calling: inefficient though sufficient. But in Beza's tables, the appointment of Christ as Mediator belongs strictly to the execution of the decree of election. Hence, Beza wrote that Christ was appointed as Mediator by "God ... the most merciful Father of the elect," and that Christ "with only one offering and

---

138 *De praedestinationis doctrina*, 58-59: "[T]riplicem esse humani generi rationem in aeterno illo Dei decreto considerati. Nam alli quidem extra Ecclesiam sunt nati, & tales permanent, quos videlicet Deus nulla vocatione ad salutem necessaria, id est, nulla gratuit sui Foederis patefactione dignatur ... Alii verò quorum speculum est Ismael, in Ecclesia nascuntur & Christianismi notis omnibus externis ornantur, nec tamen ex veris ouibus sunt apud Deum nemini debitorem: ... Alii denique ex mera Dei summè misericordia εὐδοκίᾳ à reliquis hominibus ad salutem efficaciter vocantur ..." (my translation).

sacrifice of himself should sanctify all the elect."[139] Although this is not a clear statement that Christ died for the elect *alone*, it can be seen as a sign of Beza's tendency to hold that view. Here Beza differs from both Calvin and especially Bullinger. The latter spoke of Christ as the Savior of all men and brought election in only as an explanation for the faith of those who believe in Christ.

With respect to these remarks made by Beza in 1555 and 1582, it is strange that Beza and Fayus in the chapter on Christ's office in their *Theses* of 1586 did not mention his coming and dying for the elect. There they spoke imprecisely of men *(homines)* to be delivered from misery, and about Christ, the Mediator who "preserved the person of all men, to pay all their debts, and to suffer punishment for them."[140] It seems that Beza and Fayus in the *Theses* used the classic view of Christ as having suffered sufficiently for all people without restriction. At that time Beza did not reject this formula.

This rejection came in 1586 at Montbéliard, or maybe not until 1588, when Beza published his remarks on Andreae's publication on the Colloquy. At the Colloquy, Andreae had maintained that Christ "had satisfied sufficiently for the sins of all individuals." Calvin had been uneasy with this formula, for to him it was not a final anwswer to some questions. But Calvin had neither rejected nor criticized the content of the formula itself.[141] Beza accepted the formula as true, but only in the sense that even if there were many worlds and God would have decided to save all people, Christ's sacrifice would have been sufficient. He regarded it as "ambiguous as well as barbarous" to say that Christ actually died for the whole word. Since the preposition *pro* declared a plan, and God's plan was only to save the elect, the statement "Christ died for …" can only be completed by "the elect." Of course, Christ's death would be sufficient for all individuals, but only if God willed to have mercy on all.[142]

---

139 *Tabula*, cap. IV, aph. 2, 5: "Deus igitur, clementissimus electorum pater … Denique vt vna sui ipsius oblatione eligendos omnes santificaret …" Cf. *De praedestinationis doctrina*, 8, 11. Similar phrases are to be found in *Quaestionem*, 13.

140 *Theses*, XXI, 2, 4: ' huius fuit officium quum personam omnium hominum sustineret, illorum etiam debita omnia soluere, & poenas pro illis luere."

141 See 2.5.

142 Beza, *Ad Acta Colloquii Montisbelgardensis* … (Geneva, 1588), 217-18. The passage was "ambiguè non minus barbarè dicitur … quamvis negandum non sit tanti esse hanc oblationem ut potuerit etiam pro infinitis mundis satisfacere, si plures essent mundi, & mundane omnes fide in Christum donarentur, nedum pro singulis unius mundi, nullo excepto, hominibus, si Deus eorum omnium vellet misereri." (… *although it should not be denied that this offer is so great, that it could make satisfaction even for an infinite number of worlds, if there were more worlds, and if faith was*

In 1591, Beza and Fayus published a second edition of their *Theses*. All theses of the first edition remained unchanged, even the theses on Christ's satisfaction mentioned above. But some sets of theses were added as extra disputations to the existing texts. One set of theses concerns "The Dignity and Efficacy of Christ's Sacrifice, in opposition to the corrupting harm of those who try to hold up a defense of the reprobate."[143] In these theses, Beza states that the two parts of Christ's sacrifice, his intercession and the offering of his body, are intended for the elect alone.[144] Beza argued for the truth of this doctrine in 43 theses.[145] Concerning the commonly accepted phrase that Christ died for all sufficiently but not efficiently, Beza remarks that this phrasing was incorrect, for neither in God's counsel nor in the effects of the atonement did Christ die for the impious.[146]

Given Beza's and Fayus's quite universal words concerning the extent of the atonement in the *Theses* of 1586 and the strict, limiting terms of the theses added in the 1591 edition and given what happened at the Montbéliard Colloquy, we can conclude that this Colloquy was decisive for Beza's development toward a doctrine of particular redemption. This development started already with Beza's first publications on predestination and can be regarded as a consequence of his *Tabula* which placed Christ only on the side of the elect.

---

given to all citizens of the world, much less [should it be denied that it could make satisfaction] for each individual of the world, if God would have mercy on them all.) See also Thomas, *Extent*, 57; Rouwendal, "Calvin's Forgotten Classical Position."

143 *Theses theologicae in schola Genevensi ab aliquot sacrarum literarum studiosus sub DD, Theod. Beza & Anthonio Fayo S.S. Theologiae professoribus propositae & disputatae. In quibus methodica locorum communium S.S. Theologiae epitome continetur. Altera editio emendatior & auctior priore* (Geneva: Eustathius Vignon, 1591) 121-29 (Quoted as *Theses²*) "Theses aliae extra ordinem disputatae de dignitate et efficacia Sacrificij Iesu Christi: oppositae corruptelis eorum dilutis, qui patrocinium reproborum suscipere conantur."

144 *Theses²* LII, 3: "Utramque partem, atque adeò totum sacrificium pro solis electis, in remissionem peccatorum, & iutstitiae imputationem praestitum esse." *(We assert that both parts, and hence the total sacrifice, were intended for the elect alone, for the remission of sins and the imputation of righteousness)* (my translation).

145 The theses can be divided into an introduction (1-3), arguments from Scripture (4-24), arguments from the faith of the catholic church (25-28), an answer to an objection (29), the rejection of absurdities following from the opposite position (30-38), and some additions (1-5).

146 *Theses²* LII, added thesis 3: "In illa phrasi: Christus mortuus est pro omnibus Sufficienter non Efficienter (ut Scholastici loquuntur) ἀκυρολογία esse videtur. Sive enim consilium Dei, sive passionis effectum, sive utrumque spectaveris, pro impiis nullo modo est mortuus."

Thomas argues that Beza went further than Calvin, not only with respect to his rejection of the efficient-sufficient formula but also with respect to the actual effect of the atonement. Calvin had stated that the atonement was actually accomplished, and yet that the benefit of it could be lost without faith. Beza, however, stated that the accomplishment is certain for all those for whom Christ died. According to Thomas, this is a "departure" from Calvin.[147] But, despite the obvious difference in formulation, it is doubtful whether this is actually the case. Calvin was more ambiguous than Beza concerning the extent of the atonement, which was a subject on which he never elaborated, as Beza had done at Montbéliard. Nonetheless, Calvin was clear in arguing that the salvation of the elect by Christ's atonement was certain. Beza in turn was clear in arguing that faith in Christ was necessary. The differences in formulation might be attributed to different contexts rather than different doctrines, and Beza's position might be regarded as a consequence of ideas already existing in Calvin's theology, rather than as a departure from it. Beza went in a direction already implied but not fully present in Calvin.

3.8 Predestination, The Covenant, and the Church
3.8.1 The Covenant
Like Calvin, Beza did not devote a separate chapter or section in his works to the covenant. This might be why his ideas on the covenant were neglected for a long time. It was only in 2012 that a systematic investigation of these ideas was published.[148] Andrew A. Woolsey concluded that he found in Beza's works "what amounts to a fairly substantial theology of the covenant," that "the doctrine of the covenant was integrated into the content of nearly all his theological works," and that "he followed basically the same lines as ... Calvin."[149] We will see whether these conclusions concerning the covenant and predestination and the covenant and the call are justified.

Beza thought intensively about the meaning of the word *diatheke* and how to translate it: as *pactum*, as *testamentum*, or as *foedus*. He vacillated in the several editions of his Latin translation of the New Testament between these terms, even with respect to the title.[150] Perhaps parallel to

---
147 Thomas, *Extent*, 57.
148 Andrew A. Woolsey, *Unity and Continuity in Covenantal Thought: A Study in the Reformed Tradition to the Westminster Assembly* (Grand Rapids: Reformation Heritage Books, 2012), 344-95.
149 Woolsey, *Unity and Continuity*, 394.
150 Brian J. Lee, *Johannes Cocceius and the Exegetical Roots of Federal Theology: Reformation Developments in the Interpretation of Hebrews 7-10* (Göttingen: Vandenhoeck & Ruprecht, 2009), 44-49.

or under the influence of his exegetical work on the word *diatheke*, there seems to be a development in Beza's view of the relation between covenant and predestination in which he moved from Calvin's view of the covenant of grace made with more than the elect to the view that it was established only with the elect.

In 1555 Beza referred to the doctrine of the covenant in his *Summa totius christianismi*:

> Since he includes in his free covenant, of which Christ is the mediator, not only believers but also their posterity, up to a thousand generations, explicitly calling them "holy," there is no doubt that he has given the children of the saints that pertain to election (whom he alone knows) to his Son, who will not cast them out.[151]

Beza states here that the children of believers are included in the covenant of which Christ is the mediator. The question is how to interpret the words "that pertain to election" *(qui ad electionem pertinent)*. Does Beza mean that *all* children of the saints appertain to election, or did he mean the children of the saints, *insofar as* they appertain to election? From the addition "whom he alone knows," it seems that not all children of the saints are elect. Otherwise, people could also know them. At Montbéliard (1587), Beza expressly states that there were thousands of baptized children who were still damned (an idea if not explicit then implicit in Beza's theology), thus answering the first question: not all children of the saints pertain to election.[152] Baptism is not a sure sign of being a child of God but only a probable.[153]

A second question is: Who are the members of the covenant – only the elect children or all children of believers? Beza did not answer this question explicitly in his *Summa,* but since he did not use an adjective like "elect" or "believing" in relation to "posterity," it seems that he meant the posterity of believers in general, both elect and reprobate. This also seems to be his position in his 1558 defense of Calvin against Castellio, which contains some marginal references to the doctrine of the covenant. For instance, in his refutation of Castellio's argument that God does not will

---

151 *Tabula* IV,13, *TT* I, 190: "Quum enim in gratituito suo foedere, cuius Mediator est Christus, non ipsos modo fideles, sed etiam eorum posteritatem in mille generationes comprehendat, adeo vt diserte sanctam esse pronuntiet, minime dubium est quin sanctorum liberos, qui ad electionem pertinent (quos ipse solus nouit) Filio dederit, qui ne hos quidem foras eiiciet" (my translation).
152 Rait, *Colloquy,* 145.
153 Rait, *Colloquy,* 142.

the death of a sinner, Beza remarks that these words are addressed to God's covenant people, among whom he had many elect. This implies that the covenant includes more than simply the elect.[154]

The most explicit statements on the covenant in relation to predestination are to be found in Beza's *De praedestinationis doctrina* of 1582. In this tract he exegetes Romans 9, where the names of Ishmael and Isaac, Esau and Jacob allow Beza to reflect on the covenant. In section 2.6, on Calvin's theology of the covenant, five aspects of Calvin's thinking regarding the covenant are given: 1. the covenant is established with all those who are generally elect; 2. God promises something; 3. God requires something; 4. the covenant can be broken in some way and is indeed broken by all reprobates; 5. God himself effects the condition of the covenant in the elect. These elements of Calvin's thinking are either hardly mentioned or explicitly contradicted by Beza in his *De praedestinationis doctrina*.

As to the first element, Beza denied that the covenant was established with all of Abraham's posterity; this was something Calvin had taught, and even Beza himself earlier. According to Beza, Ishmael was never included in the covenant.[155] Instead, the covenant is established with the elect alone.[156] The second element is not mentioned explicitly, but since

---

154 *Ad calumnias, TT*, I, 354: "Postremò, animadvertere debueras quibus destinetur haec Ezechielis concio, populo certè scelerato, & praefracto, sed tamen populo Dei, in quo quum plurimos haberet electos, minimè mirum est Dominum hoc sermone apud eos uti, quos in suo foedere comprehensos ad se volebat revocare." *(Finally, you [Castellio] should have noted to whom this discourse of Ezekiel is addressed: a people surely wicked and harsh but still God's people, among whom he had many elect. Hence, it is not at all surprising that the Lord used this sermon with those whom he wanted to call back to him, being included in his covenant)* (my translation).

155 *De praedestinationis doctrina*, 58: "Primum igitur in hac hypothesi utrumque, nempe tum Ismaëlem, tum Isaacum videmus in Abrahami familia, id est, in Ecclesia, natos, communia inter se externa omnia habere, nec tamen utruque in eo foedere, quod verae Ecclesiae proprium est, censeri, sed alterum tantùm, & quidem natu minorem." *(First, we see in this hypothesis that both, viz. either Ishmael and Isaac being born in Abraham's family, that means, in the church, had external communion between them, but yet they are not judged to be both in that covenant which is proper to the true church only, but only the latter, who was born later.)*

156 *De praedestinationis doctrina*, 51, 52, 54, 55, 57, 53, 62, 70, 83. Some quotations:
51: "[D]uplex sit Israel, unus videlicet in foedere comprehensus: alter verò non item." *([T]here are two Israels, viz. one comprehended in the covenant, but the other not.)*
52: "Probato non omnes ex Abrahamo prognatos esse semen illud, quicum aeternae vitae foedus erat sancitum." *(Surely, not all who are born out of Abraham are that seed that was sanctified to the covenant of eternal life.)*
83: "[S]alvo manente Dei foedere, non omnes tamen Iudaeos in eo comprehendi …" *(God's covenant was still saving, but not all Jews were comprehended in it.)*

Beza repeatedly called the covenant a covenant of eternal life *(foedus vitae aeternae)* we can conclude that the covenant contains the promise of eternal life.[157] The third, fourth, and fifth elements of Calvin's views on the covenant are all related to its conditionality. This, again, is an element that is missing in Beza's remarks on the covenant. Although he called faith a condition with respect to the offer of Christ,[158] he did not relate this to the covenant. Beza stated explicitly that the covenant cannot be broken, which means that it is in some way unconditional, for a conditional covenant can be broken.[159]

In the 1586 *Theses,* Beza and Fayus write that the principal end of holy ministry was the same in all dispensations: showing God's goodness concerning the salvation of human beings "by means of the free covenant made in Christ."[160] The notion of predestination is absent here. They also mention the covenant in their theses on the church. The Gentiles were separated from the seed of Abraham for a long time and were hence strangers to the covenant of grace.[161] But whether the covenant includes all members of the church or only the elect remains unclear here.[162]

Calvin held that the covenant with the believers and their natural seed was conditional, and Beza seems to have held the same earlier. In his later years, however, Beza seems to have taught an unconditional (at least unbreakable) covenant with the elect only. It is difficult, if not impossible, to answer the question as to what extent Beza was conscious of this

---

157 *De pradestinationis doctrina,* 47, 52, 63, 65. Elsewhere, Beza states, for instance, that faith is given to the elect, but he did not relate this to a promise or to the covenant.
158 *De praedestinationis doctrina,* 14: "Euangelium nonnisi sub unius fidei conditione Christum amplectendum offerat … nec ullos alios quàm electos hac fide donari." *(The Gospel only offers Christ to be embraced under the condition of the one faith … while this faith is not given to any other save the elect.)*
159 *De praedestinationis doctrina,* 51: "…[F]oedus illud Dei excidere non possit." *(That covenant of God cannot fail.)*
160 *Theses,* LXXI, 5, p. 179: "[P]atefactio bonitatis diuinae in seruandis hominibus per gratuitum foedus in vno Christo …"
161 *Theses,* L, 8, p. 115. "[A]lienas à foederis gratiae …"
162 According to Rait, *Colloquy,* 139, 142, in 1586 Beza argued again that children of believers were included in the covenant, and that this is why they should be baptized. I could not find this view expressed in Beza's *Ad Acta.* There, in the context mentioned by Rait, Beza gives another reason to baptize children, viz. that pastors should administer baptism to every child born in the church, since those infants should be indefinitely presumed to be elect ("singulis infantibus in Ecclesia natis iuberi Pastores baptismum administrare qui etiam omnes infantes indefinite sint electi praesumendi") (*Ad Acta,* 101). This indicates rather that at that time Beza held that only the elect are included in God's covenant.

change.¹⁶³ Calvin had never written a separate treatise on the covenant; thus, his thinking on the covenant can only be reconstructed from various passages. We do not know how well Beza knew Calvin's views of the relation between predestination and the covenant. Moreover, Beza himself did not write a separate treatise on the covenant either, and even fewer passages and works exist than in Calvin's works that give us insights into his view. Hence, we should be cautious in concluding that Beza's view of the covenant was the result of a great deal of reflection or that he consciously deviated from Calvin here. The statements on the covenant scattered throughout his works do not give the impression that, in the end, Beza (unlike Calvin) had a coherent and consistent view of the covenant throughout his life. Yet his remarks on the covenant in *De praedestinationis doctrina* do show consistency and coherence. It is this very work that is hardly mentioned in Woolsey's chapter on Beza.¹⁶⁴ His conclusion concerning continuity in the ideas of Calvin and Beza concerning the covenant are correct to a large extent, like their views of the unity of old and new covenants, but there is a development, which Woolsey does not see, in Beza's ideas on the relation between the covenant and predestination that deviates from Calvin.

3.8.2 The Church

If the covenant theme is not often found in Beza's works, the church caught his attention many times. Maruyama distinguishes three periods in Beza's thinking on the church. In the first two periods (until 1578) he described the church as a congregation of the faithful, without relating it closely to the doctrine of predestination. Calvin's distinction between the visible and invisible church is almost absent from Beza's reflections on ecclesiology in these periods.¹⁶⁵ In a third period (1579-1605), he reflected consciously on the relation between the doctrines of predestination and the church [ecclesiology]. Nevertheless, he still made hardly any use of

---

163 It is also unclear whether this development is connected with Beza's exegesis of *diatheke*. First, he preferred to translate it by either *testamentum* or *foedus,* and later (1588) preferred *pactum*. Some years later still (1594) he preferred *foedus* and finally (1598) *pactum* again as referring to the two dispensations of the covenant, while reserving *foedus* "for the Evangelical covenant considered in itself as a unified, perpetual reality" (Lee, *Johannes Cocceius*, 45-46).
164 Woolsey, *Unity and Continuity*. Woolsey's chapter on Beza is weak in that he used primarily English translations of Beza's works. Beza's Latin works are hardly cited in the footnotes.
165 In the second period, Beza hardly reflected upon the church, but what he wrote was in line with the first period.

Calvin's notions of the visible and invisible church since, according to Beza, the true church of Christ cannot be invisible but must be manifest in the world.[166]

Maruyama may be right that the idea of visible-invisible is less prominent in Beza's theology than in Calvin's, but it is nevertheless present. For instance, in their *Theses*, Beza and Fayus made a distinction with respect to the church. The word "church" expresses the company of those who are raised up from the Fall and consent to the true worship of God. But since there always will be tares among the wheat, the church is generally called the congregation of all those who profess true religion, whether true or hypocritical. In particular, however, it is used for all those whom God has elected and whom he calls. This is the content of the distinction between the visible and the invisible church, although Beza did not use these precise terms.[167]

Calvin explicitly stated that he had to view all members of his congregation as believers, according to the judgment of charity. Beza is somewhat cautious here, not viewing all members as believers but "hoping for the best" for all to whom the Word and sacraments are administered, for they are not certain but only possible signs of election.[168] Ministers do not know who are elect and should not attempt to know God's decree but simply administer Word and sacraments to all, leaving God's secret counsel to him, just as Abraham circumcised and catechized Ishmael no less than Isaac.[169]

---

166 Maruyama, *The Ecclesiology of Theodore Beza*, 22, 46, 141-148.
167 *Theses*, L, 2-7.
168 *De praedestinationis doctrina*, 59: " [I]ubeat nos charitas de omnibus, quibus externum verbum proponitur, & praebentur sacramenta, bene sperare: externa tamen illa non esse simpliciter necessaria, sed tantùm probabilia Praedestinationis ad salutem τεκμήρια ..." (*Love requires from us to hope the best of all to whom the external Word is proposed and the Sacraments are given. These external signs are not simply necessary signs, but yet probable signs of predestination unto salvation.*)
169 *De praedestinationis doctrina*, 60: "Tertio, decreti istius aeternis arcanum non esse Verbi & Sacramentorum ministries inquirendum, sed simpliciter curandum illis esse, vt quibuscuncque Dei verbum annunciare & Sacramenta iubentur praebere, relictis Deo arcanis ipsius consiliis ... sicut Abrahamus Ismaëlem non minus, quam Isaacum ex Dei mandato circumcidit, & viam Domini docuit ..." (*Third, the ministers of Word and Sacraments should not inquire after that eternal hidden decree, but just administer them (viz. Word and Sacraments) to whosoever they are commanded to announce the Word and give the Sacraments, leaving to God his hidden counsel ... just like Abraham circumcised and educated in the way of the Lord Ishmael not less than Isaac, according to God's command.*)

Differences between Calvin and Beza are very minor regarding the way the congregation is seen as related to predestination and preaching. Beza made less use of Calvin's distinction between the visible and the invisible church. He stressed that the church should be visible, but, given his acceptance of the essence of the distinction, it seems this is intended more to state that there can be no invisible church if there is no visible one than as a denial of the idea of an invisible church. Also, the difference between Calvin and Beza concerning the "judgment of charity" seems to be rather a difference in formulation than a difference in doctrine. For the actual administration of Word and Sacraments, these slight differences seem to have had no consequences.

3.9 God's Purpose and the Preacher's Purpose in Preaching

In his *Explicatio*, Beza did not mention the words "election" and "predestination" in his aphorisms on the outward call. He stated in general that men are blind and need to have the law preached to them so that they can take refuge in Christ. With the law being preached, the Gospel is proclaimed with the condition that they believe in Christ.[170] But all this would be in vain unless God joins the inward call by the Holy Spirit in his elect with the outward call by the Word.[171] Nevertheless, the outward call is the ordinary means by which Jesus Christ is communicated, and to some degree even necessary.[172]

Thus, despite the general language Beza uses concerning the outward call, it is not intended to save all who hear it but to bring them to the knowledge of sin by the law and to make them take refuge in Christ. Beza calls believing in Christ a condition, just as it was a condition in Calvin's theology. This conditional concept enabled Calvin to preach the Gospel to all while maintaining his ideas concerning predestination. These aphorisms of Beza seem to reflect and summarize Calvin's ideas.[173]

---

170 *Tabula* IV,7-8, *TT* I, 183-85: (7) "[S]unt homines adeo caeci ... Legis suae praedicationem adiungit ... ut ad ... unum illum Mediatorem Iesum Christum refugiant. (8) Itaque post severam illam Legis praedicationem iisdem proponit gratiam ac benignitatem Euangelicam: addita tamen conditione, si in Christum crediderint ..."
171 *Tabula* IV,9, *TT* I, 185.
172 *Tabula* IV,9, *TT* I, 185: "quod tamen ordinarium & ex hypothesi necessarium est instrumentum, quo Iesus Christus nobiscum communicatur."
173 In *De praedestinationis doctrina*, 14 Beza made similar remarks concerning conditionality: "Euangelium nonnisi sub unius fidei conditione Christum amplectendum offerat ..." (*[T]he Gospel offers Christ as to be embraced in no other way than under the condition of the one faith ...*)

Contra Pighius, Calvin maintains that some "universal" passages in the Scriptures did not refute the doctrine of predestination. We looked at how he deals with 1 Tim. 2:4 and Ezek. 18: 23 and 33:11. Castellio used them as arguments against Calvin's doctrine of predestination, so Beza was compelled to exegete them as well. The arguments from both passages in Ezekiel are summed up in the one sentence "I [God] do not desire the death of a sinner." Beza's first response is to state that this text deals with eternal damnation itself, while the argument between him and Castellio is on the *purpose* of damnation. Hence, the text is not suitable for the dispute.[174] Moreover, according to Beza, Castellio thus omitted the means by which God executes his decree. In his *De aeterna Dei praedestinatione*, Calvin argues on the basis of the conditional structure of Ezekiel's words. Beza mentions this only very briefly[175] but actually explains the words as meaning that God did not delight in the destruction of people as such but only in executing justice.[176]

Castelio's argument from 1 Tim. 2:4 is taken by Beza for an argument from 2 Pet. 3:9, to which he answers that Peter meant that the believers should be patient until God has gathered all his elect.[177] It is probably just a mistake by Beza, but it could be that he deliberately switched the texts, for the argument from 2 Peter seems easier to parry than the argument from 1 Timothy. However, Beza later actually answers Castellio's argument from 1 Timothy in his *Quaestiones*. According to Beza, there are just two possibilities. Either we have to confess that men are damned by an unwilling God, or we have to confess that these words should be explained in another way, not meaning "all individuals" but "all kinds of individuals." Moreover, to be saved is linked with coming to the knowledge of truth. This knowledge is faith, which is bestowed by God only on the elect.[178] There is great similarity between Beza and Calvin on this text. It is as if Beza had Calvin's commentary on his desk when he wrote the answer on this question.[179]

---

174 *Ad calumnias, TT,* I, 354: "Non laboramus de morte sive damnatione aeterna (nam inter nos constat neminem nisi suo merito damnari) sed de iusto damnandi proposito …" *(We do not strive concerning eternal damnation (for we both acknowledge that nobody is damned save for his own merit) but concerning the just decree to damn …)* This remark reflects Beza's distinction between *propositum damnandi* and *damnatio ipsa*.

175 *Ad calumnias, TT,* I, 354: "Ego sicut poenitentes recipio, ita non nisi praefractos & contumacies punio." *(As I receive the penitent, so I only punish the stubborn and rebellious.)*

176 *Ad calumnias, TT,* I, 355.

177 *Ad calumnias, TT,* I, 355-56.

178 *Quaestionum, TT,* I, 699 *(Questions,* 87, q. 198).

179 Beza might have leaned on Calvin here, for Calvin's Commentary on Timothy was published in 1548, ten years before Beza's response to Castellio, and Calvin's Com-

Another of Castellio's argument was based on Christ's weeping over Jerusalem (Luke 13:34). According to Beza, Christ's wish to gather Jerusalem under his wings was not a revelation of the hidden will behind the eternal decree. Christ was speaking here as a minister or prophet. As such, his will differs from the eternal decree but is not opposed to it. Sending his ministers to a country, however, does not mean that God necessarily wills the salvation of all people in that country.

> He sends them then, that they should preach the gospel of salvation to some whole country, but he reserves for himself in his secret counsels, in whom he will have the preaching of the gospel to be effectual, and at what time, and again whom he has decreed to blind and harden by the same preaching.[180]

Here Calvin and Beza are of the same view: God does not intend that the indiscriminate preaching to all kinds of people be to the salvation of all. The purpose of the preaching of the Gospel is to save the elect and to harden the reprobate. Preaching is a means for carrying out both election and reprobation.

Admonitions are not superfluous but useful. They have their use for the godly, to reprove them when they err. They have their use for the elect who are not yet called inwardly, in that it conveys knowledge of their miserable condition so that they may flee to Christ when they hear his invitation to lost sinners. In them, the outward ministry of the Word is joined with the inward ministry of the Holy Spirit. They have their use for the reprobate, to render them without excuse, for reprobation does not take away their will, and the necessity by which they sin does not come from God's decree but from their own corruption. So, the admonitions of the Gospel have several uses, according to Beza. Here he differs from Castellio who thought the only purpose of admonitions, i.e., of the preaching of the Gospel, is the conversion of those who hear it.[181]

Although the Gospel is intended for the salvation of the elect alone, its invitation is nevertheless preached indiscriminately to all. God's call and command to believe is serious, even when he does not give all people the grace to believe. Believers, or those who doubt their election, should not

---

mentary on Peter was published in 1551. This exegesis was not unique to Calvin, however, but rather generally accepted since Augustine.

180 *Ad calumnias, TT,* I, 398: "Mittit eos igitur ut universae alicui praedicent Euangelium salutis, sibi vero in arcanis suis reservat in quibus efficacem esse velit praedicationem Euangelii, & quo momento, & rursus quos constituerit ea ipsa praedicatione excaecare & indurare."

181 *Ad calumnias, TT,* I, 413-14.

seek their assurance in election but via Christ and the Gospel. Whoever fears that he or she is not included in the particular election, may know there is a universal calling.[182] With respect to this universal call, according to Beza, there is no difference between him and those who teach a universal grace that is offered to all without respect to persons. But Beza prefers to teach the doctrine first and then its application, while others merge doctrine and application in their teachings.[183] Here Beza shows that his focus on predestination did not detract from the universal call of the Gospel and even that an indiscriminate call belongs to the execution and use of the doctrine.[184]

Although God's purpose in preaching is different with respect to the elect and the reprobate, Calvin thought that a preacher should wish all his hearers to be saved by means of his preaching. Beza agreed. Ministers do not know God's decree and should administer the Word and Sacraments to all, leaving God's hidden counsel to him.[185] Preachers should be as earnest as God in preaching the Gospel to all: they should "plant and water" as commanded, and since they do not know God's hidden decree, they should desire that all those who hear them will believe and be saved.[186] Moreover, Beza's insistence on preaching and administering the Sacraments to all makes clear that his doctrine of predestination did not stand in the way of preaching the Gospel to all.

---

182 *Ad calumnias, TT,* I, 419: "[U]t quicunque in particularis electionis tentatione versantur, norint indefinitam esse vocationem, id est, quosuis homines & quantumvis magnorum scelerum reos, & quavis aetate à Deo vocari, ne suorum vitiorum conscientia deterriti desperent, aut electionis suae declarationem in summo gradu, id est in Dei proposito, extra Christum & vocem illam Euangelii in Ecclesia personantem, quaerant." *([T]hat whosoever is confused by particular election, has to know that vocation is indefinite, that is, each man, he be guilty of whatever great and how much sins, and at whatever age he is called by God, should not do worse by despairing because of the conscience of his sins, or seek the declaration of his election in the highest degree, that is in God's purpose, outside of Christ and of the voice of that gospel that resounds in the church.)*

183 It seems Beza is referring to Bullinger and those who followed him here. *Ad calumnias, TT* I, 419: "Inter nos igitur & quosdam alios qui universalem esse Dei gratiam docent, id est promiscuè quibusvis offerri absque προσωποληψία, nullum est in reipsa discrimen. Sed nos quidem doctrinam seorsim, deinde illius usum docemus. Illi vero una cum doctrina usum ipsius in docendo coniungunt."

184 Beza's few remarks on this subject in *De praedestinationis doctrina* do not add any new insights. See pp. 129-31.

185 *De praedestinationis doctrina,* 60, see 3.8.2 note 169.

186 *De praedestinationis doctrina,* 78-79. "[E]t Deus mittens, et minister missus serio agunt quod agunt. Nam quod ad ministrum attinet, plantat et rigat bona fide sicuti iussus est, et arcanum Dei consilium ignorans ... omnes quidem auditores credere et saluos fieri cuperet."

3.10 The Mode of Preaching the Gospel

For the elect, the preaching of the law and especially the Gospel is a means to their salvation. The reprobate are either not called at all, which means they cannot know God and Christ and hence cannot be saved, or they are called outwardly but without the secret, internal work of the Spirit. They hear the Gospel, but, because of their depravity, they cannot believe and hence they fail to fulfill the condition of the Gospel.[187] Like Calvin, Beza maintained a twofold call: external and internal. Hence, one cannot conclude that one is elected merely from being called by preaching. It is only the call that is conjoined with the power of the Spirit that is a sign of election. The calling of the reprobate is not intended to save them but to render them inexcusable.[188] The promises of God pertain only to the elect.[189]

We noted a paradox in Calvin's theology on conditionality and unconditionality in preaching the promises of the Gospel. Salvation is offered to all on condition of faith, but there are no meritorious conditions: even faith is not a meritorious condition by any means. Since the rejection of all meritorious conditions is necessary, Calvin could call faith – as excluding all merit – a condition, and hence he even sometimes called the conviction that we cannot merit anything a condition. Beza's ideas are quite similar. The appointed Mediator is given to the elect in this way: First *(primum)* since the elect are born blind and sinful, the Lord uses the external call *(vocatio externa efficax)* to show them the great danger they are in through the preaching of his law *(legis sua praedicationem)* so that they should flee *(refugiant)* to Christ. Therefore, after *(post)* the preaching of the law, Christ is then proclaimed *(proponit)* with the condition that they believe in him *(addita tamen conditione, si in Christum crediderint)*. In the elect, God adds the inward working of the Spirit to open their hearts and understanding so that they first know their misery *(primum ... calamitatis illius suae sensu vere afficiantur)*, and next *(deinde)* to plant faith in them enabling them to meet the condition of the Gospel *(conditionem praedicationi Euangelii)*. Beza pointed out that the preaching of the law was a means to show the elect their need of a Savior, but he did not stress this in the same way as Calvin sometimes did. Although Beza

---

187 *Tabula*, IV, 7-10, and V, 3-7, *TT*, 183-87; 191-94. *De praedestinationis doctrina*, 12-22; 129-32.
188 *De praedestinationis doctrina*, 131-32, 151; *Ad Acta*, 93-94.
189 *Cours*, 378, th. 4: "*Promissiones Dei* non pertinent ad *carnis* [9, 8] propaginem, cum populus *Israeliticus* [9, 4] externus re vera non sit pop[u]lus cui factae sint *promissiones* [9, 4, 8], sed solis electis."

did not place it within the framework of the doctrine of the covenant, we see that his view of the practice of preaching did not differ from Calvin's. True faith applies the universally and indiscrimintately proclaimed Christ to oneself.[190] Like Calvin, Beza called faith a condition added to the universal preaching of the Gospel.[191]

According to Thomas, for Beza, the conditionality of the Gospel meant that it could not be universal, referring here to his *Ad acta*.[192] Yet on the page Thomas refers to, Beza proposes an indiscriminate and indefinite preaching of the Gospel promises. The Gospel is not universal in the sense of being extended to all people or every person, but it is universal in that it is extended to all who hear it, which is to more than the elect or to the believers alone.[193] Beza states the same in his *Summa totius christianismi*, viz. that Christ is preached universally and indiscrimintately.[194]

3.11 Predestination and the Response to Preaching
A positive response by faith and repentance arisess only out of God's renewing grace in the elect. They are not only called externally but also internally, not only by the Word but also by the Spirit. Faith and repentance flow from

---

190 *Tabula*, IV, 7-10, *TT*, 183-87. See also *De praedestinationis doctrina*, 132.
191 *Ad Acta*, 95: "[P]er divini Verbi ministros ... et praedictur Euangelium et administrantur Sacramenta: idcirco semper adiecta quidem gregi conditione (quam solus Deus in solis quidem electis praestat) SI RESIPISCITIS, SI CREDITIS." (Emphasis Beza's). *([B]y the servants of God's word, is both the gospel preached and are the sacraments administered; therefore, there is indeed always added a condition to the flock (which alone God certainly alone bestows on the elect) IF YOU REPENT, IF YOU BELIEVE.)* For more examples of conditionality in Beza's theology, see Woolsey, *Unity and Continuity*, 378-81.
192 Thomas, *Extent*, 54.
193 Beza, *Ad acta*, 204: "Euangelium autem consilium illud Dei per Prophetas promissum, et suo tempore ab ipso Christo exhibitum declarat, quo unico constituit homines, in ipso videlicet Christo per veram fidem apprehenso servare. Et haec quidem utraque voluntas iampridem est patefacta et quotidie patefit, nec tamen universaliter id est sine exeptione singulis populis nedum hominibus sed promiscuè et indefinite his vel illis, prout ipsi licet in umbra mortis positis, ut loquitur Esaias, apparêre." *(Now the Gospel declares that counsel of God, which was promised by the prophets, and in his own time revealed by Christ himself, how alone he constituted to save men, viz. in Christ himself, when seized by true faith. And indeed, each of these wills [viz. in law and gospel] is since long laid open and is every day laid open. However, not universally, that is without exception to each single people nor to each man, but indiscriminately and without precise specification: appearing to this or that man, just as he might be lying in the shadow of death, as Isaiah speaks.)* See also *Quaestionem*, 699.
194 *Tabula*, IV, 10, *TT*, 186: "[U]t Christum universaliter et promiscuè oblatam .. "

God's electing love.[195] The reprobate are only called externally, but whether the relation between reprobation and their unbelief mirrors the relation between election and faith is a question Beza struggled with and changed his answer to over a period of some years.

The young Beza gave the impression in his letters to Bullinger (1551-52) that the relation between reprobation and unbelief was the same as that between election and faith.[196] Calvin had also called reprobation a *causa* of unbelief.[197] In the *Tabula* (1555), Beza is no longer so explicit on the relation between reprobation and unbelief. In his *Ad sycophantarum quorandam calumnias* (1558)[198] he is forced by Castellio to reflect on the relation between the decree, the Fall, and sin. In this work, Beza develops a view that went contrary to the one he held formerly. In the beginning of his reply to Castellio he seems to hold somewhat to the view expressed in his letters to Bullinger. For instance, he states that we cannot exclude God's decree from the causes of sin.[199] Elsewhere, however, he writes that, although the damnation of the reprobate depends on God's predestination, the cause of their perdition is found completely in themselves.[200]

The reason for Beza's wrestling is obvious. Like Bullinger, Castellio argued that stating that God is the cause of sin implies that he is the author of sin.[201] It is this argument that Beza tries to refute. Beza's problem is that he could not deny that God decreed sin and that sin in one way or the other depended on God's decree – to deny this would be to deny

---

195 *Ad Acta*, 95. For the text see 3.10 note 191.
196 See 3.4.
197 See 2.11
198 *Ad sycophantarum quorandam calumnias quibus unicum salutis nostrae fundamentum, id est aeternam Dei praedestinationem evertere nituntur, responsio Theodori Bezae Vezelii.* (Geneva: Conrad Badius, 1558). Quotations are taken from the reprint in Beza's *Tractationes Theologicae*, vol. I, 337-423; there is hardly any difference between the editions of 1570 and 1582 where the words "sycophantarum quorandam" were replaced by "Sebastiani Castellionis." For another difference see 3.11 note 211. Quoted as *Ad calumnias*.
199 *TT* I, 340: "De ipsorum quippe peccatorum fonte quaerimus, nimirum de corruptionis causis, à quibus excludere Dei decretum non magis potes quàm quum de corruptionis fructibus quaeritur ..." (*We search for the fountain of these sins, i.e., the causes of corruption, from which [causes] you cannot exclude God's decree any more than when you search for the fruits of corruption ...*) (my translation).
200 *TT* I, 341: "Deinde sic pendere eorum perditionem ex Dei praedestinatione, ut causa & materia tota perditionis in ipsis reperiatur." (*Hence, their perdition depends in such a way on God's predestination that the whole cause and matter of perdition is found in themselves*) (my translation). See also p. 357, where similar words are quoted from Calvin's *Institutes* (III, 23, viii).
201 *TT* I, 362.

God's omnipotence. For the same reason, he could not deny that God was in some way involved in sinful acts, for nothing can happen without God. If God is the first cause of all things, then he is also the first cause of sin. On the other hand, Beza could not agree that God was the author of sin.

In a word, Beza's problem was how to maintain that God decreed sin to occur and at the same time deny that God was the author of sin.

A careful reading of Beza's answer to Castellio gives the impression that he developed an answer while writing the book. Initially, he stated that it was impossible to solve the problem of how God cannot be held accountable if he ordains the causes of damnation; it would even be impious to attempt to do so.[202] Yet Beza later makes some attempts to do so himself. First, he seems to have become reluctant to call God the cause of sin. He did not state this explicitly in his answer to Castellio but did not explicitly deny it either. In the phrase just mentioned, however, Beza used the more cautious idiom that God "ordains the causes of damnation," including sin.

Next, Beza points out that God and Adam had different purposes in the Fall. God decreed the Fall and Adam fell of his own free will (although his will depended on that decree). God's purpose was his glory, and Adam's sinful fall was a means to this glorious end. God can use a sinful instrument to serve a good end. Denying this would mean either that God is not always just or that he is dependent on secondary causes, does not always control them, and does not have knowledge or will concerning some events.[203] That price was too high for Beza.

Third, Beza pointed out that the Fall occurred out of free will, and he blamed Castellio for omitting the middle causes, jumping from the decree of reprobation, to damnation itself.[204] Although it was indeed impossible for Adam not to have wanted to sin, his will was not compelled but moved spontaneously and assented freely to sin when he was not under the dominion of sin.[205] Middle causes like angels and people are moved

---

202 *TT* I, 340: "Sed illud quoque curiosum, atque adeo impium esse dicimus, quaerere, Qui non sit Deus in culpa, si damnationis causas ordinat. Quam quaestionem tu explicandam suscepisti, nos verò cum Apostolo inexplicabilem esse humanis sensibus arbitramur." (*But we say that it is not only prying but also impious to ask how God can be without fault when he ordains the causes of damnation, which question you have undertaken to explain. But with the apostle we judge it to be inexplicable to human understanding*) (my translation).
203 *TT,* I, 352-53.
204 *TT,* I, 353.
205 *TT,* I, 361. "Non potuerunt resistere Dei voluntati, id est decreto. Fateor, sed sicut non potuerunt, ita etiam noluerunt. Verum non poterant aliter velle. Fateor, quo ad eventum & ενεργείαν sed voluntas tamen Adami coacta non fuit, imo non tantum spontaneo, sed etiam libero motu assense est peccato, quum eius δύναμις nondum

inwardly, and in this respect they are efficient causes rather than instruments. God can use them, even though they are sinful, to a good end. When God uses an evil instrument, the evil done by it proceeds from the evil of the instrument and not from the good God who uses it. Sin emerges from a depraved quality, which exists only in the instrument, not in God.[206] Therefore, sin does not actually have an efficient cause but a deficient one. This deficient cause is in the human person, not in God, although it is in God's power when and how sin breaks out.[207]

In the last part of his answer to Castellio, Beza makes use of a scholastic distinction between the *necessitas consequentis* and the *necessitas consequentiae*, quoting from the *Institutes*, where Calvin rejected the Stoic notion of fate. Although Calvin writes not to make use of "distinctions used in schools," he states that events that are necessary because of God's decree are nevertheless not necessary in their own nature.[208] In other words, what happens is not necessary in itself *(necessitas consequentis)*, though it is necessary because of God's will *(necessitas consequentiae)*. Beza explains this using a very long quote from Peter Martyr Vermigli's exposition of I Samuel, which had not yet been published at that time.[209]

---

esset peccati servituti mancipata." *(They could not resist God's will or decree. I grant, but just as they could not, they also did not want to. But they could not will otherwise. I grant, concerning the event, yet Adam's will was not forced: it moved not only spontaneously, but also gave in liberty assent to sin, when his power was not delivered to the slavery of sin.)*

206 *TT*, I, 371-75, theses 9, 10, 13, 19-26. See also p. 399.

207 *TT*, I, 402: "Non est igitur causa efficiens, sed deficiens potius quaerenda... Nam causa peccati a nobis est & intra nos: quo autem tempore & in quem debeat erumpere, in potestate Dei est." Later, in his *Questions and Answers* (1570), Beza wrote that corruption and unbelief are subordinated to the decree in such a way, that the will of man is the first efficient cause of them, although the deficient cause is in God (*Quaestionem*, 125-126. "Corruptio vero vel incredulitas cum ipsius fructibus sic decreto subordinator, ut tamen voluntas hominis sit illarum prima causa efficiens, et tamen decreto subiiciantur, quoniam etsi non per decretum, tamen non praetor decretum, nec absque decreto illa incident, quorum, ut dixi, causa deficiens, not autem efficiens in Deo statuitur.") He seems to use the word "deficient" in these books in different ways. When he states that God was not a deficient cause, he seems to see it as indicating "fault," and when he states in another work that God was a deficient cause, he uses it in contrast to an efficient cause, and thus seems to have meant that God did not hinder Adam from sinning or unbelievers from not believing but did not effect sin or unbelief.

208 *TT*, I, 410: "Sic evenire necesse est quod statuit Deus, ut tamen neque praecise, neque suapte natura necessarium sit" (quoted from *Institutes* I, 16, ix).

209 It was not published until 1564, but Beza had read it earlier. Vermigli did use other words, viz. simple necessity *(necessitas simplex,* which is equal to *necessitas consequentis,* and hypothetical necessity *(necessitas ex hypothesi),* which is equal to *neces-*

One gets the impression that Beza read Vermigli's remarks while almost finishing his answer to Castellio and that this gave him the material to clearly show how God can guide all things while human beings remain accountable and free.[210] Vermigli did not really add any new insights to what Beza had already written on this subject, yet the clarity of his formulations and terminology are lacking in the previous part of Beza's answer to Castellio. In this work, Beza's answer to the question of God as the cause of all things without being the author of sin moves from "it is an insolvable problem" to a detailed solution to it.[211]

Beza's thinking on this question continued to develop, however. Some years later, in his *Cours* (1564-65) on Romans, he explicitly denied not only that God was the author of sin but also that he was the cause of sin. God's decree is not a cause, but it ordains the causes.[212] This was the next logical step, given how Beza's ideas developed in his answer to Castellio and especially how he approved of Vermigli who had elaborated on this in the passage Beza quotes from him. This step was not only a departure from his own former ideas, but also from those of Calvin, albeit more with respect to formulation than to concept. Nevertheless, this deviation from Calvin might be the most important one concerning predestination It resulted not in a predestinarian system, but prevented calvin's ideas from developing towards such a system.

---

sitas consequentiae. See for this distinction W.J. van Asselt et.al. (eds.), *Reformed Thought on Freedom. The Concept of Free Choice in Early Modern Reformed Theology* (Grand Rapids: Baker Academic, 2010), 30-43. See for Vermigli's use of Medieval scholasticism: Luca Baschera, "Aristotle and Scholasticism" in: Kirkby Torrance et al. (eds.) *A Companion to Peter Martyr Vermigli* (Leiden: Brill, 2009). 133-160.

210 The quote takes two and a half pages in Beza's *Tractationes,* 411-13, and is the longest quote in his *Ad calumnias.*

211 In the second edition of the work, included in his *Tractationes,* Beza added a quote from Augustine's *De genesi ad litteram,* VI, 29/18 concerning necessity, *TT,* I, 352: "Nam, ut recte scribit Augustinus, Deus sic condidit causas inferiores, in quibus est & ipsa hominis voluntas, ut ex illis illud cuius causae sunt esse possit, non necesse sit: altiores autem & remotas ita abscondit ut ex eis esse necesse sit, quod fecit ut ex illis interioribus esse possit." *(For, as Augustine writes correctly, God has conditioned the inferior causes, among which is the human will itself, that by them the events whose causes they are, are possible, but not necessary; the other and remote causes he has hidden in such a way, that from them by necessity happens what is possible by means of the inferior causes.* (I read interioribus as inferioribus.)

212 *Cours,* 163. 1564-65: "Dei decretum non est causa, sed ordinat causas." In his *De praedestinatione doctrina,* 100, Beza made a similar remark, viz. that the decree of righteous hate in order precedes all causes of corruption, thereby denying that the decree itself is a cause: " iusti quorundam odii decretum ordine causarum ipsam corruptionem ... antecessisse."

Beza did not apply his ideas on the relation between reprobation, the Fall, and sin explicitly to unbelief. But, since unbelief is a sin, it seems safe to regard his answer to Castellio and his remarks in the course on Romans as being applicable to that question: God's decree of reprobation is not a cause of unbelief but ordains the causes of unbelief.

3.12 Predestination, Faith, and Assurance

According to Beza and Fayus, faith is the hand by which we apply to ourselves what Christ offers to us, with all those benefits that are necessary for our salvation.[213] Hence, Christ and his benefits are the objects of faith. This faith is given by God and is effected by means of the preached Word.[214] The effects of faith are the remission of sins and the imputation of Christ's righteousness to the sinner.[215]

It is remarkable that Beza did not say that faith consists in the assurance of salvation. Nor is assurance part of his definition of faith in his *Questions and Responses*. Faith is defined there as

> not simply that recognition of the facts … but it is a firm assent of one's mind accompanying that recognition of the facts whereby it happens that one applies particularly to himself the promise of eternal life in Christ Jesus, just as if he already were actually a possessor of it [216]

Although Beza spoke of a "firm assent," it is not, as in Calvin's definition of faith, a firm assent that our sins are forgiven. Rather, it is by this assent that one applies the promises of salvation to oneself. In other words, for Calvin, faith was a sure knowledge of the forgiveness of sins, whereas, for Beza, faith is a means for appropriating the promise of this forgiveness. Hence, the question that arose from Calvin's description of faith, especially as

---

213 *Theses*, XXII, 1: "Fides Christiana est manus illa vnica, qua Christum nobis oblatum cum omnibus suis beneficiis ad salutem necessariis apprehendimus, sive nobis applicamus." Cf. *Quaestionum, TT* I, 678 (*Questions*, 29, q. 81).
214 *Theses*, XXII, 7: "Hanc fidem Deus in electis suis creat…"; XXIII, 2, "Medium ordinarium quo id efficitur … est verbi diuini … praedicatio."
215 *Theses*, XXIII, 12.
216 *Quaestionum, TT* I, 678 (*Questions*, 29, q. 81). "Fidem qua distinguuntur filii lucis a filiis tenebrarum, non simpliciter vocamus illam notitiam ipsis etiam daemonibus communem, qua fit ut quis agnoscat vera esse quacunque in scriptis propheticis & apostolicis continetur: sed praeterea firmam animi assensionem illius notitiae comitem, qua fit ut sibi quispiam peculialiter applicet vitae aeternae in Christo promissionem, perinde acsi [sic] esset illius plene ac reipsa compos."

being joined with the assurance of salvation, does not arise from how Beza speaks of faith.[217]

Another difference from Calvin is how assurance is obtained. While Calvin spoke of looking to Christ as the mirror of election, Beza used the *syllogismus practicus*. Faith, repentance, and sanctification give the believer assurance of his election.

> We have to mount up from the effects of regeneration to justification, from justification to real faith, from real faith to effective calling, and finally from effective calling to God's eternal and immovable decree concerning our salvation.[218]

Nobody can be sure about his or someone else's reprobation, for someone who is an unbeliever today could be a believer tomorrow. The only sure marks of reprobation are unbelief until death and the sin against the Holy Spirit.[219]

3.13 Preaching the Doctrine of Predestination

Both in his explanation of the *Tabula* and his *De praedestinationis doctrina*, Beza dealt with the question of how to preach predestination. There is little development in his thinking on this part of the subject. In his first chapter on the *Tabula* Beza insists that the doctrine of predestination does not stand in the way of preaching. He quotes the same statements from Augustine that Calvin had quoted in his treatise on predestination. The doctrine of predestination should be preached, since the Apostles and ancient Doctors of the Church had done so as well. Predestination teaches believers to rejoice in God and not in themselves.[220] Here, not only does Beza agree with Calvin, he simply copies Calvin's quotations from Augustine. Doing so at the outset of his explanation of the *Tabula* was likely to convince Bullinger (and other objectors to speaking about

---

217 Yet we can not conclude that Beza deliberately used another definition to avoid these questions.
218 *De praedestinationis doctrina*, 128-29, 133, 152. For example, 152 thesis VIII: "[A]b effectis videlicet Regenerationis at Iustificationem: à Iustificatione ad veram Fidem, à vera Fide ad Vocationem efficacem, ab efficaci denique Vocatione ad aeternum & immotum illud Dei de nobis seruandis decretum assurgendo ..." See also *Cours*, 376, th. 1. According to Maruyama, *The Ecclesiology of Theodore Beza*, 146-47, Beza introduced the *syllogismus practicus* into Reformed theology. For a survey of Beza's view of the assurance of faith in comparison with Calvin's, see Beeke, *Quest*, 72-81. See also Donald Sinnema, "Beza's View of Predestination".
219 *De praedestinationis doctrina*, 142 and 154.
220 *Tabula*, I, 1, *TT*, 171.

predestination) by pointing to the greatest authority in the church at that time apart from the Bible: Augustine.[221]

In the seventh chapter, Beza addresses the question of how predestination ought to be "observed in preaching and applying the same to every particular man." First, he warns against exchanging predestination for permission or conceiving of a double counsel in God, etc. Rather, we are to keep to God's pure and simple truth. A second warning is not to use a different way of speaking but only to use words approved by Scripture. A third warning concerns keeping in mind that there are different kinds of hearers. The weak should be led gradually, but the stronger ones should also be taught in an adequate way. The best way to do this, Beza thought, was to follow Paul's example in his Epistle to the Romans. Paul starts with the law, proceeds to the remission of sins, and then gradually arrives at the highest degree, i.e., election.[222] A preacher should not begin at the top of the mystery of election and then come down. And even if he sometimes does this for some major reason, he should take heed not to leap between the extremes of God's decree and salvation or damnation, "leaving the near and evident causes of God's judgment."[223]

A last warning is not to apply it to any particular man. Although the preacher should seek to comfort afflicted consciences with the testimony of election and pierce the wicked with the judgment of God, he should always refrain in the latter case from "that last sentence" i.e., reprobation, "for this right and jurisdiction only appertains to God."[224] Most of these warnings can also be found Calvin's treatise on eternal predestination, but, more than Calvin, Beza stresses that we should not start with predestination.[225] There

---

221 It is remarkable that Beza hardly mentions Augustine in his *De praedestinationis doctrina*.
222 *Tabula*, VII, *TT*, 197; cf. *De praedestinationis doctrina*, 140-48
223 Beza followed this order himself in his *Questions* in dealing with predestination at the very end of the book, followed only by perseverance. In his *De praedestinationis doctrina*, 127-28 Beza expressed the conviction that nothing obscured the treatment of the doctrine of predestination as much as when the doctrine itself and its application are discussed conjointly. The doctrine and its application are different and hence should be treated in a distinct way in the church. "Nihil aequè obscruravit doctrinam de aeterna Dei Praedestinatione, atque confusa & perturbata tractatio, dum simul & coniunctim de ipsa doctrina & de ipsius vsu applicatione disseritur, quum tamen hae duae quaestiones plurimùm inter se different, ac proinde distinctè sint in Ecclesia tradendae …"
224 *Tabula*, VII, *TT* 197-98; cf. *De praedestinationis doctrina*, 141-43.
225 Calvin did not stress this in his systematic or polemical works; nevertheless, he did not usually start with predestination in his sermons.

is great similarity and unity in Calvin and Beza concerning the way predestination should be preached.[226]

3.14 Summary: Predestination and the External Call

Whereas Calvin started to write on theology and was forced, due to controversies, to speak out more explicitly on predestination in the course of his career, Beza's theological labor started with a controversy on predestination. The Bolsec controversy (1551) was the occasion for his first theological tract, the *Summa totius christianismi* (1555). The conclusions of earlier research that this illustrates that Beza's theology, or even Reformed theology as a whole, was moving in the direction of a predestinarian system are unfounded. That predestination was the first subject Beza treated was accidental, not essential. Moreover, the *Tabula* does not present a complete theological system (3.4, 3.5).

Also, the view that the *Tabula* is an example of scholastic theology does not hold. Although the *Tabula* and its *Explicatio* offer some theological concepts, Beza did not use scholastic conceptualizations or techniques. This treatise is nothing more or less than a schematic presentation of some *loci communes* Beza found in Scripture on predestination and related subjects. In this period, Beza was averse to the use of reason in theology. He began to use reason and scholastic instruments during his refutation of Castellio (1558) because of the influence of Peter Martyr Vermigli. It seems that reading Vermigli was decisive in Beza's development toward scholastic theology (3.11). Scholastic theology is more evident in Beza and Fayus' *Theses* (1586).

Beza's doctrine of predestination is, in general, the same as Calvin's. Predestination is to faith and is not based on faith. Predestination entails both election and reprobation. Characteristic of Beza is his use of Bullinger's distinction between the eternal purpose *(propositum)* to elect and to reprobate, and election and reprobation temselves *(electio/reprobatio ipsa)* in time, which is already present in his *Tabula*. The purpose precedes the Fall, also with respect to the order of decrees, but actual election and reprobation presuppose the Fall. Beza was supralapsarian

---

226 In their *Theses* Beza and Fayus made similar remarks concerning the certainty of election, which can only to be known from the gifts in people, like good motions of understanding and will, regeneration, imputed righteousness. These attributes allow people to climb higher in attaining the assurance of being predestined for eternal salvation. People cannot be certain about someone's reprobation, since sometimes even the greatest sinners have their sins forgiven at the end of their life. Those on the way to destruction are to be told their duty, and we should not despair of anyone's salvation. *Theses*, XI, 15-18.

with respect to the decree of predestination, but, when speaking about election and reprobation as the execution of this decree, he wrote like an infralapsarian. (3.4 – 3.6)

It is not true that Beza developed a predestinarian system. He did relate the doctrine of predestination explicitly to just one more *locus* than Calvin did. viz. the atonement (the covenant was not a *locus* in their time). The works in which Beza offered a more or less complete theology, such as in his confession and his *Theses*, were not dominated by predestination. The works devoted to predestination do not offer a complete system. Moreover, those works were instigated by attacks from non-Reformed theologians rather than by a wish to make predestination a central dogma: the *Tabula* by the Bolsec controversy and the friction between Geneva and other cities that arose from it, his *Ad calumnias* by the attacks of Castellio, and his *Ad acta* by the attacks of Andreae. The tract *De praedestinationis doctrina*, though nowadays regarded as a systematic work, was in itself the result of exegetical lectures on Romans. Over against those who argue that Beza laid more stress on predestination, it should be stated that it was Calvin who laid more stress on the eternal, immutable decree than Beza did, whereas the latter stressed human responsibility more in the first sin and in persisting in sin (3.4 – 3.6).

Beza developed his own ideas on the relation between predestination and other doctrines related to it. He combined it with Bullinger's distinction between the eternal decree and its execution in time, probably to integrate Calvin's and Bullinger's different approaches to the doctrine of predestination (3.5). Hence, Holtrop's suggestion that Beza was nothing more than Calvin's standard-bearer is not true. With Calvin, the younger Beza had admitted that God was a cause of sin, even though he cannot be regarded as the author of sin. Beza's ideas started to change while responding to Castellio (1558), a change that culminated in a short comment in his *Cours* (1564-1565) that God's decree is not a cause but ordains causes (3.11). Here he deviated from Calvin. Beza also changed his views concerning the cause of God's hatred. In the *Brevis explicatio* he had stated that God hated freely, without cause. In later works he nuanced this to the statement that God freely, without cause, predestined some people to being the objects of righteous hatred because of sin (3.6).

Another development can be seen in Beza's thinking on the extent of the atonement. Although Calvin had his criticisms of the notion, he never rejected the idea that Christ died sufficiently for all. He did use phrases like these throughout his works, even omitting the word "sufficiently." Beza seems always to have restricted the extent of the atonement to the elect, except in his *Theses* (1586), on which he collaborated with Fayus.

Beza was explicit in his remarks at the Montbéliard Colloquy in 1588, where he denied that Christ died for all in any way whatsoever (3.7).

Beza himself was aware that his view that Christ was subordinate to the decree was new. There are no signs that Calvin disapproved of this idea, but neither did he elaborate on it in his own theology (3.4).

It seems that, over the course of time, Beza also deviated from Calvin on the nature of the relation between election and covenant. But this is difficult to determine since neither Calvin nor Beza wrote a separate treatise or even chapter on the covenant. Beza's remarks on the covenant in his *De praedestinationis doctrina* (1582) differ from Calvin's view as well as from the view Beza offered in earlier works. In that work, Beza denied that the covenant was established with all of Abraham's posterity but taught that it was established only with the elect. He was not clear on whether the covenant was conditional or not (3.8).

Although Beza did not use the terminology of visible/invisible church, he did use the concept: the church is generally called the congregation of all those who profess true religion, whether genuine or hypocritical, but in particular the term is used for all those whom God has elected and whom he calls. While Calvin explicitly stated that he had to see all members of his congregation as believers, according to the judgment of charity, Beza was cautious, only "hoping for the best" for all members of the congregation (3.8).

A final difference with Calvin that needs to be mentioned is that Beza had a different view of faith and assurance. Calvin never addressed the questions that could arise from his view of faith as the conviction that one's sins are forgiven, the duty of all to believe, and predestination. Neither did Beza. Yet it is remarkable that his view of faith and assurance does not raise the same questions. Assurance should be gained by recognizing faith and sanctification within oneself. Here Beza differs again from Calvin, who had taught that assurance is to be gained by looking to Christ as the mirror of election. There is no clue that predestination was the reason why Beza differs from Calvin on faith and assurance (3.12).

Despite these differences between Calvin and Beza on doctrines that are related to predestination and calling, there was no difference between them on the direct relation between predestination and the call. Predestination did not prevent them from calling all who heard their sermons to repentance and faith. The Gospel was preached to all, even if God intended salvation only for the elect. Faith in Christ was required as a condition for actual salvation, and this faith was given by God to his elect. In Calvin's theology, conditionality was the answer to questions concerning the general external call of the Gospel and particular election. In

Beza's theology, he used the concept of conditionality but did not explicitly relate it to these questions himself (3.10).

It is not easy to answer the question of continuity or discontinuity between Calvin and Beza. Should the differences between Calvin and Beza be regarded as shifts or as developments? And what about developments in Beza's own thinking? In my view, there is continuity at some points despite differences and discontinuity at other points. Their treatments of the doctrine of predestination do show continuity. Beza's and Calvin's ideas on predestination are basically the same. Beza's use of Bullinger's distinction between *propositum* and *excecutio* is a difference in accent rather than content. Beza's explicit supralapsarianism can be regarded as an elaboration of some statements in Calvin's *Institutes* on people being created for salvation or damnation, although Calvin did not develop Beza's ideas of the lump in Romans 9 in his own works. With respect to reprobation, Calvin stated that God's reasons for election and reprobation were always just, while the younger Beza stated that God choose to hate without cause and hence without justification other than his free will. This would lead to the conclusion of discontinuity, if not for the fact that Beza himself changed at this point. The view of the mature Beza was that God predestined the reprobate to righteous hate, which is closer to Calvin than his initial view (3.6).

Whether God is the cause of sin and unbelief was a question both Calvin and the younger Beza affirmed. The older Beza denied it. Nonetheless, this shows continuity since Beza was compelled to find the correct expression of the view that, on the one hand, God controls all things and that nothing, not even sin, can or will happen without his will, and that, on the other hand, God is not the author of sin. This basic idea remains the same in the theology of both Calvin and Beza. The difference is that Calvin and the younger Beza accepted God as cause of sin as an acceptable expression of the fact that sin cannot happen without God's will, and the older Beza thought it inappropriate (3.11).

The notion that Christ was subordinate to the decree was a new element in Reformed theology rather than a departure from a former view (3.4).

The older Beza's ideas on the relation between the covenant and election show discontinuity both with his former ideas and with Calvin. Calvin and the younger Beza thought the covenant was established with more people than just the elect, while the older Beza restricted the covenant to the elect (3.8).

The differences between Calvin and Beza concerning election and atonement are the most difficult to evaluate. A decision here depends on the actual formulation of the question. If the question is whether Christ's death applies to the whole world, both elect and reprobate, Calvin would answer yes and the older Beza no. That entails discontinuity. If the question is whether Christ's death was intended to save the whole world or the elect alone, both Calvin and Beza would deny the former and affirm the latter. That entails continuity.[227] Calvin and Beza differ on the atonement, but the direction Beza went was already implied although not fully present in Calvin. So, there is not much of a difference between them (3.7).

Beza's increasing use of scholastic material has often been regarded as a departure from Calvin, and hence as discontinuity. Yet, as Muller has argued, Calvin himself made use of scholastic material.[228] That Beza did so more extensively should not be regarded as a shift but as a development. Beza's use of scholastic distinctions, like between kinds of necessity enabled him to prevent the Reformed doctrine of reprobation becomming a christian version of fate and to teach both God's sovereignty and human responsibility.

In conclusion, I think there is more continuity than discontinuity between the theologies of Calvin and Beza. Most differences between Beza and Calvin are a development of the same basic ideas rather than departure from basic ideas. The obvious exception is Beza's idea of the covenant being established solely with the elect.

3.15 Beza's Sermons on the Resurrection of Christ
3.15.1 Predestination

In 1593, Beza published a series of sermons on the resurrection of Jesus Christ.[229] This series is sufficient to get an impression of how Beza deals with issues concerning predestination and preaching in his sermons.[230] It

---

227 Blacketer stresses the agreement between Beza and Calvin on the latter question, but he largely ignores the weight of Beza's denial of Christ having died sufficiently for the whole world. According to him, this was only a "minor development." Raymond A. Blacketer, "Blaming Beza". See also 4.4 note 28.

228 Richard. A. Muller, *The Unaccommodated Calvin: Studies in the Foundation of a Theological Tradition* (Oxford: OUP, 2000) especially pp. 39-61.

229 *Sermons svr l'histoire de la resurrection de nostre Signeur Iesus Christ* (Geneva: Ian le Prevx, 1593). (Quoted as *Sermons*.)

230 Beza published two more volumes of sermons earlier: *Sermons sur les trois premiers chapitres du Cantique, de Salomo* (Geneva 1586) and *Sermons sur l'histoire de la passion et Sepulture de nostre Seigneur Iesus Christ* (Geneva, 1592). These sermons show the same characteristics as his sermons on the resurrection, so this series can be regarded as representative for how Beza preached. For Calvin, we looked at more series to see if there was any development in his sermons that reflected disputes on predestination in the period between the series. Since Beza was not involved in a dispute on predestination between 1586 and 1593, there is no need to examine another volume of his sermons.

is not exactly known when Beza preached these sermons. Most likely, they were preached immediately after his sermons on the passion and burial of Christ, which were published in 1592. Since Beza once remarked that the Reformation in Geneva had begun some 50 years prior to that date, the sermons must have been preached approximately 1586.[231] Hence, these sermons reflect the older Beza.

Predestination is not dominant in Beza's sermons on the resurrection. Indeed, there are sermons in which words like predestination and election are not even mentioned. Beza heeded his own advice not to begin with predestination in sermons. For instance, in his preface, he mentions creation and the Fall and eternal salvation without referring to predestination in any way, referring instead to those who will be saved as "those who take refuge in him."[232] This does not mean that predestination is absent from Beza's sermons – as we will see below – but it never assumes a prominent place.

Beza mentions *election* in connection with atonement, ecclesiology, sanctification, glorification, and assurance. We will look at atonement and ecclesiology in separate sections. *Sanctification* is regarded as a testimony to justification and election, from which it is inseparable.[233] *Glorification*, or sitting at Christ's right hand in heaven, is the certain destiny of the elect.[234] *Assurance* and *perseverance* are fruits of election: a child of God cannot be lost.

> The reason is that this is founded entirely upon the eternal and immutable decree of God and not upon us, either totally or partially, Eph. 1:11, and the ordination of God cannot take any effect, Rom. 9:6... The eternal decision for election, the call that is the declaration and exhibition of it, the justification and finally the glorification of those who are predestined to salvation are things that are inseparably joined together, Rom. 8:29.[235]

---

231 *Sermons*, 326.
232 *Sermons*, epitre, no page number (x): "D'avantage au lieu de ce monde bas premierement benit pour l'habitation de l'homme, & depuis, à cause du pechê dicelui, assuieti à vanité telle que nous experimentons tous les iours, il a dressé, pour ceux qui auroyent recours à lui une habitation celeste ..." (*Instead of this lowly world, which was in the beginning blessed to be the habitation of human beings and was afterwards, because of sin, subjected to such vanity as we experience every day, he has prepared a heavenly habitation for those who take refuge in him.*) (All translations of quotations from the *Sermons* are mine.)
233 *Sermons*, 26.
234 *Sermons*, 48.
235 *Sermons*, 118-19: "La raison est, d'autant qu'elle est entierement fondee sur le decret eternal & immuable de Dieu, & non pas sur nous, ni en tout, ni en partie, Eph. 1.11.

Beza usually uses the doctrine of election in his sermons to console his congregation, as in the example above. He also uses it sometimes to make his congregation humble – a use of the doctrine that Calvin also employed.[236]

There are just a very few instances where he gives a more doctrinal treatment of predestination. In the first sermon, on Matthew 28:1-4, Beza states that the spiritual union of "those who are his (*les siens*) is proper to those whom the Father had given him (*proper a ceux que la Pere luy a donnes*) and, hence, it is necessary that only they be resurrected by the reviving power (*necessairement que ceux-la seuls ressuscitetor par la vert vivisiante*) of Christ.[237] In the sermon on Mark 16:10-11 and John 20:15-17, Beza remarks that God is our Father since he has ordained us to salvation. And yet even here the pastoral motive is not absent, for, since we are elected in Christ, Beza says, the Father loves us as much as he loves Christ.[238]

Beza does not use the word *reprobation* in his sermons on the resurrection. But the concept does occur sometimes. The seventh sermon, on Matthew 28:11-15, contains a remarkable passage in which Beza not only uses the concept of reprobation but also speaks of Christ as executing it. While Christ played no role on the side of reprobation, in his *Tabula*, here Beza tells his congregation that it was the risen Lord who darkened the vision and blinded the eyes of the guards of the tomb and the priests and elders who gave them money to be silent, thus showing that he reigns in the midst of his enemies.[239] A second instance in which Beza mentions the

---

ne pouvant iamais dechoir l'ordonance de Dieu, Rom. 9.6... L'arrest donc eternel de l'election, la vocation qui en est la declaration & exhibition, la Iustification, & finalement la glorification des predestinés à salut, sont choses inseparablement conionctes, Rom. 8.29." (see also. p. 278)

236 *Sermons*, 204: "[C]e n'est pas qu'il nous trouve preparés ne bien disposés, mais une infinie grace & misericorde qui l'ensmeut à commencer, à continuer, & à parachever son oeuvre, en ceux qu'il luy plaist de choisir." *([When God speaks to us] it is not because he finds us prepared or well disposed but out of the infinite grace and mercifulness by which he was moved to start, to continue, and to perfect his work in those it has pleased him to choose.)*

237 *Sermons*, 13.

238 *Sermons*, 179: "Et quant à nous, il nous est Pere entant que c'est en ce Fils qu'il nous a ordonnés à salut, nous unissant à icelui spirituellement par la vertu de son S. Esprit & par l'instrument de la foy, pour estre ses enfans adoptifs, Ieh. 1 v. 12. nous communicant la mesme dilection de laquelle il aime ce Fils, pour nous glorifier finalement en & par icelui, Ieh. 17.24."

239 *Sermons*, 192-93: "Car qui les a ici tant aveuglés, tant endurcis, & mis du tout en sens reprouve pour manifester sa gloire; Rom. 1.21 & Exod. 9.26. sinon ce ressuscité pour dominer au beau milieu de ses ennemis." *(For who has so blinded them here, so hardened, and given over to an ungodly mind to manifest his glory, if not the risen Lord in order to reign in the midst of his enemies.)*

concept of reprobation is the 19th sermon, on John 21:15-17. Here, having quoted the text that states that there are more who are called than who are elect, Beza states that God had even sent his servants to those for whom the Word would only serve to harden them.[240]

3.15.2 The Atonement

In 3.7 we saw that Beza explicitly stated at the Montbéliard Colloquy in 1586 that Christ died for the elect alone. Since his sermons on the resurrection were published later, it is no surprise that this view of the atonement of the older Beza can be found in them. The statement or even the suggestion that Christ died for the whole world, as found in several places in Calvin's works and sermons, is absent in Beza's sermons. Beza did not state, in a negative way that Christ did not die for the reprobate, but he does state several times either explicitly or more implicitly that he died for the elect alone. For example, in his preface, Beza states that God has crucified all the elect (*tous ses esleus*) in Christ.[241] In the ninth sermon, on Luke 24: 22-28, Beza remarks that Christ,

> having accomplished the payment, brought the crown of glory for him and for those whom he has obtained… taking with him those for whom he has responded and paid, Heb. 2:10.[242]

If there is just one clear difference between Calvin's sermons and Beza's, it is that Beza did not use phrases that Christ died for all people or for the world, as Calvin did. Beza's position concerning the atonement affected his sermons. Calvin was dissatisfied with the classic distinction that Christ died sufficiently for the whole world and efficiently only for the elect, but he nevertheless used universal language concerning the atonement in his works and sermons. Beza's concrete criticism on the content of the distinction, due to his view of a closer relation between election and atonement, resulted in abandoning this universal language while preaching. But since he used the first-person plural to address his congregation, just as Calvin did, it is likely the congregation did not notice this.

---

240 *Sermons*, 569: "[V]oire mesmes quelque fois le grand Pasteur envoye ses serviteurs vers ceux ausquels ceste parole ne sert que d'endurcissement."
241 *Sermons*, "epitre," no page number (xii).
242 *Sermons*, 264: "[A]yant accompli ce payement en rapporte la couronne de gloire pour soy & pour ceux qu'il a acquités … amenant avec soy ceux pour lesquels il aura respondu & payé Heb. 2.10."

At least, this change had no consequences for the way Beza addressed or exhorted his congregation.

3.15.3 The Covenant and Church

Unlike his earlier works, in his later work *De praedestinationis doctrina* (1582) Beza seems to have held a different view of the covenant than that found in Calvin. It is therefore remarkable that we can find a slight trace of his former view of the covenant, which was similar to Calvin's, in these sermons by the older Beza. For instance, he remarks:

> For although, under the old covenant, the Lord sent the light of his knowledge to his elect, first to the Patriarchs, afterwards to the people descended from Abraham, which he has not done to other nations ...[243]

Although no clear view of the covenant is present here, the use of the concept of "the elect" (*ses esleus*) for the descendants of Abraham in distinction from other nations, and of the word covenant (*alliance*) in this context suggests that Beza, like Calvin, could use "the elect" in a broader sense than only for those elected unto salvation and that this "first step of election," as Calvin called it, held a middle place between the world and God's children in the more narrow sense of the term.[244] This is also indicated by how Beza addresses his congregation: he uses the words "we" and "us," just like Calvin, and he implicitly or even explicitly states that "we" are elect.[245] He can thank God that he led "us" away from the wide gate and put us on the narrow road to life.[246]

Yet Beza also makes it clear that this did not entail that he believed that all his hearers would be saved and, hence, he did not believe that all his hearers were elect in the narrower sense of the term. For instance, he states that there are hypocrites among the members of the congregation.[247] Elsewhere, he tells them that there are indeed a great number of people listening to God's Word, but as in Isaiah's time, they approach God with their lips but not with their hearts. Beza continues by praying that God would convert Geneva soon or take him away from the city so that he

---

243 *Sermons*, 38-39: "Car combien que le Seigneur, sous l'anciene alliance, eust envoyè la lumiere de sa cognoissance à ses sesleus, à savoir premierement aux Patriarches, puis à ce people issus d'Abraham, n'aya(n)t pas fait ainsi à toute nation."
244 See 2.6.
245 *Sermons*, 25: " [I]l nous à predestines ..."
246 *Sermons*, 239.
247 *Sermons*, 100: "[L]es hypocrites & les mocqueurs..."; cf. p. 374.

would not perish with them.[248] He tells his congregation that if "we" say we are the Reformed church, we are lying for the most part, for we are more foolish and rebellious than ever. He warns the members of his congregation that the door to salvation would be closed for them.[249]

Here again Beza, like Calvin, uses the word "we" both in a positive and in a negative sense: "we" are elect, and "we" are rebellious. Moreover, on the one hand, Beza addressed his congregation as a whole as God's children but, on the other, made clear that not all individuals were God's children. Although Beza had not developed a clear view of the covenant, his practice in his sermons was the same as Calvin's.

3.15.4 Conditionality

In Calvin's theology, conditionality was the key concept for unlocking the paradox of particular election and the universal call of the gospel. This conditionality was also a fundamental part of his view of the covenant. Again, Beza thought and taught like Calvin on this point.[250] He tells his congregation that "we" have no reason to fear, but all that is required of us is "that we act like true and loyal subjects."[251] He also mentions faith or embracing Christ as a condition according to the covenant, though he does not use that precise word.[252]

Conditionality plays a role not only in public preaching but also in personal pastoral care. If a guilty person clearly repents and believes, a pastor can proclaim him forgiven simply and categorically; if he does not repent and believe, the pastor can proclaim his condemnation just as simply and categorically. But if a pastor has reason to doubt, this sentence is spoken conditionally, viz. absolution is given if the sinner repents and

---

248 *Sermons*, 373.
249 *Sermons*, 574: "Nous di-ie qui nous appelons l'Eglise reformee, mentans saussement devant les hommes, pour la pluspart. Car sommes nous pas au contraire autan insensés qua iamais? autant rebelles?" Similar expressions can be found in the sermons on the Song of Solomon; see Maruyama, *The Ecclesiology of Theodore Beza*, 156-57.
250 Beza even mentioned a conditional decree, such as that concerning Nineveh and Hezekiah. *Sermons*, 268.
251 *Sermons*, 49: "Seulement donc peut portons nous comme ses vrais & loyaux subiects."
252 *Sermons*, 112: "Quelle peur donc peut ou doit avoir le vray Chrestien, ayant embrassé ce payeur par vraye foy, selon la teneur de l'alliance promise aux Peres, & finalement exhibee au monde, & ratifice par l'oblation parfaicte, & une fois faicte de ce pleige & respondant? *"(What fear can or should a real Christian have who has embraced this Redeemer with a sincere faith, according to the content of the covenant that was promised to the fathers and finally displayed to the world and ratified by the perfect sacrifice and at one time done by the surety and substitute?)* See also p. 461.

believes but condemnation is proclaimed if he does not.[253] Although Beza uses the word "conditionally" here only in cases of doubt and states the other proclamation simply and categorically, in actuality, the absolution or condemnation by a pastor is conditional anyway. A pastor can proclaim them simply and categorically when he is convinced that the condition has been met. If he is not convinced, not only is the sentence conditional, but the proclamation of it is as well. In the first case, it is the pastor who decides if the condition is met; in the latter case, it is the sinner himself who has to be clear on this point. The conditionality in preaching does not mean that Beza restricted the Gospel to a certain group, i.e., to believers, let alone to the elect. Pastors should invite all who want to hear and even those who have "lost all taste."[254]

3.16 Summary: Theory and Practice

Beza's sermons are consistent with and cohere with his systematic theology. In his systematic works Beza insisted that predestination should be preached. He added several warnings concerning, for instance, how to bring up this doctrine in sermons. A preacher should begin with the signs of election and then move upward to election itself. Beza stressed that the preacher not start with predestination. In the sermons we have studied, predestination is neither dominant nor absent. There are sermons in which words like predestination and election are not even mentioned. Beza heeded his own warning not to begin with predestination in sermons. He usually introduced the doctrine to comfort his congregation

---

253 *Sermons*, 462: "Quelquesfois aussi en cas de iuste doute, ceste sentence se prononce conditionnellement, à savoir, sentence d'absolution donnec au ciel, si ceux desquels il est question, se repentent & croyent: ou de condemnation, s'ils ne se repentent, & s'ils ne croyent: à quoy les a absous ou condamnés, doivent penser en eux mesmes." (*Sometimes, in the case of justified doubt, this sentence is pronounced conditionally, viz. a sentence of absolution in heaven, if the person in question repents and believes; or of condemnation, if he does not repent and does not believe. The absolved or condemned should examine themselves with respect to these sentences.*)

254 *Sermons*, 570: "[V]oila pourquoy quand il est question du saint ministere, il ne saut pas prendre ce nom de brebis si estroitement: mais faut que les Pasteurs, laissans à la providence de Dieu la secrete & exacte cognoissance particuliere des vrayes & des fausses brebis, presentent la pasture indifferemment à tous ceux qui veulent ouir, voire mesmes leur devoir est d'en metre en appetit les plus desgoustés." (*That is the reason why, concerning the holy ministry, this name of sheep should not be taken so strictly, but the pastors, leaving to God's providence the hidden and exact particular knowledge of the real and the false sheep, should present the pasture without discrimination to all those who want to hear, yes, they even have to provoke the taste of the most disgusted.*)

and sometimes to keep it humble. But he rarely gave a more doctrinal treatment of predestination in a sermon. The word reprobation does not occur, though there are some references to this doctrine.

Beza addressed his congregation as a whole and usually as elect believers. Nevertheless, he also stated that not every individual member was a believer, but never drew the conclusion that not every member was elect. How he addressed his congregation was similar to how Calvin addressed it, even though, in Beza's case, this had no theological foundation in a clear and consistent view of the covenant.

Beza's message was the explanation of the text or pericope for that service. As in Calvin's sermons, this meant that predestination was usually mentioned only when the text gave occasion to do so. In the sermons of Beza we looked at, Christ is mentioned more often than in Calvin's sermons. We cannot conclude that this is true for all their sermons. The sermons by Calvin we looked at were on books or chapters (Micah and Genesis) in which Christ is not often mentioned, so not mentioning him in sermons was a result of the view of preaching held by Calvin and Beza. The sermons by Beza we looked at were on the resurrection of Christ, which, given the same view of homiletics, led to Christ being given a central place in those sermons.[255]

Election was frequently mentioned in Beza's sermons, and the concept of reprobation sometimes. His view of faith as a condition comes up, not as a means to restrict the message of the Gospel to a certain part of the church but to stress the necessity of personal faith in order to be saved. Also, Beza's conviction that Christ died for the elect alone can be heard in his sermons. The greatest difference between the sermons of Calvin and Beza is that Beza did not use expressions to the effect that Christ died for all people or for the world, as Calvin did. But it is not likely that his congregation noticed this difference since Beza addressed them in the first-person plural. Hence, he could say with Calvin that Christ died for "us." The development in Beza's thinking on the atonement had no practical consequences for those who heard him preach.

As with Calvin, a nuanced answer should be given to the question whether or not predestination influenced the theory and practice of the call of the Gospel in preaching. Predestination and the call were closely related. The call belongs to the execution in time of God's eternal decree. The call

---

255 The other volumes with sermons are on the passion and death of Christ, in which, of course, Christ is also mentioned often, and on the Song of Solomon, which is explained by Beza as a song about Christ (the Bridegroom) and his church (the bride). Hence, Christ is central in these sermons too.

and *electio ipsa* are even more or less the same regarding this execution in time. Notwithstanding this close connection between the two, the external call in Beza is not dominated by predestination, neither in its address nor in its content, despite the fact that Beza refrained from stating that Christ died for all. The external call to eternal life is addressed to all who hear it, and its is the complete message of Scripture, of which predestination is only a part.

4. Geneva and the Synod of Dort - John Diodati and Theodore Tronchin

4.1 Diodati, Tronchin, and the question of Predestination and Preaching

The theologians the church of Geneva sent to the Synod of Dort, John Diodati and Theodore Tronchin, did not leave any systematic-theological works nor volumes of sermons behind.[1] Therefore, we cannot use the same method to study them that we used for Calvin and Beza and will use to look at Turretin and Pictet. Since, however, the Synod of Dort is a landmark in the history of Reformed theology and its conclusions in the *Canons* were very influential, even in Geneva, where the *Canons* were accepted, we cannot omit the Genevan contribution to Dort concerning predestination and the external call. Moreover, in their assessments of the Remonstrant theses, Diodati and Tronchin made some important decisions that affected the Genevan development of the doctrine of predestination. Moreover, the conclusions concerning the relation of the delegates to older and later Genevan theologians in previous research need examination.

In the Netherlands, which was at war with Spain from 1568 to 1648 except for the interruption by the "Twelve Years' Truce" from 1609-1621, serious difficulties arose during this truce between two professors at the Academy in Leiden: Arminius and Gomarus. In the process of the struggle between Arminians and Gomarists, the former wrote a remonstrance containing five articles about their teachings. These articles spoke of (1) election based on faith; (2) Christ having died for all people; (3) the necessity of a new birth through the Spirit; (4) resistible grace; (5) the possibility of

---

[1] Tronchin left three funeral orations, which are not "ordinary" sermons for a congregation. The reason why neither of the two left any sermons behind might be that they regarded their professorship at the academy their primary responsibility, and were reluctant to accept a pastorate. See Karin Maag, "From Professors to Pastors: The Convoluted Careers of Jean Diodati and Théodore Tronchin," in Jordan J. Ballor, David S. Sytsma, and Jason Zuidema (eds.), *Church and School in Early Modern Protestantism: Studies in Honor of Richard A. Muller on the Maturation of a Theological Tradition* (Leiden: Brill, 2013), 243-54. That neither of them left any systematic works might be because they considered the *Theses* of their predecessors Beza and Fayus sufficient or the pastorate both accepted in 1608 took up too much of their time.

falling from grace.² Due to this document, the Remonstrance, the Arminians were also called Remonstrants. The Gomarists wrote a Contra-Remonstrance, hence they were called the Contra-Remonstrants.

For a long time, the government refused to organize a national synod. In the end, however, it agreed to do so. Since the difference between Arminians and Gomarists was judged to be an issue of more than regional or national importance, churches in other countries were invited to send delegates to the synod. The many foreign divines made this synod "a Reformed ecumenical council."³ When the Dutch States General decided to invite foreign delegations, Geneva was neglected at first, due to Remonstrant influence. The Remonstrants did not expect any support from Geneva. Whereas other foreign theologians had been invited by mid-July 1618, the invitation to the Genevan theologians was not received until the end of September or the beginning of October, due to the growing influence of Prince Maurice of Nassau, who supported the Contra-Remonstrants. These events show that the church in Geneva was supposed, by friend and foe, to be opposed to the Remonstrants. And, indeed, the Genevan church was predisposed against them.⁴ It decided to send John Diodati and Theodore Tronchin, whom the *Compagnie* charged to represent the views of the church of Geneva. They had to promise not to demean the Genevan church and to preserve the memory of Calvin and Beza.⁵ The *Compagnie* did not explicitly charge them to preserve the doctrine of predestination as taught by Calvin and Beza.

---

2 The complete text in 17th century Dutch, Latin, and English is in P. Schaff, *Creeds of Christendom*, III, 1877, http://www.ccel.org/ccel/schaff/creeds3.iv.xv.html.

3 For the history of the ecclesiastical and political struggles of this period, as well as the synod itself, see: B. Glasius, *Geschiedenis der Nationale Synode in 1618 en 1619 gehouden te Dordrecht in hare voorgeschiedenis, handelingen en gevolgen* (Leiden: P. Engels, 1860). A concise introduction to the synod of Dort is H.J. Selderhuis "Introduction to the Synod of Dort (1618-1619)" in Donald Sinnema, Christian Moser and Herman J. Selderhuis, *Acta et Documenta Synodi Nationalis Dordechtanae (1618-1619)*. Vol. I. *Acta of the Synod of Dort* (Göttingen: Vandenhoeck&Ruprecht, 2015), xv-xxxii. Different aspects of the synod of Dort are studied in A. Goudriaan and F. van Lieburg (eds.) *Revisiting the Synod of Dort (1618-1619)* (Leiden: Brill, 2011). For an extensive study to the issue of reprobation at the synod, as well as of the history of this doctrine before the synod, see Donald Sinnema, *The Issue of Reprobation at the Synod of Dort (1618-19) in Light of the History of this Doctrine* (Toronto, PhD thesis, 1985).

4 Nicolas Fornerod, "'The Canons of the Synod Had Shot Off the Advocate's Head': A Reappraisal of the Genevan Delegation at the Synod of Dort," in Goudriaan and van Lieburg (eds.), *Revisiting the Synod of Dort*, 189-91, 195, 203. See also Fornerod's 'Introduction' in *Registres de la Compagny des Pasteurs de Genève*, Tome XIV et dernier (1618-1619) (Geneva: Droz, 2012), vii-ciii. Quoted as *Registres*.

5 Fornerod, *Registres*, 194.

John Diodati or, in its original Italian, Giovanni Diodati (1576-1649) was born in Geneva on June 6, 1576, to a family that had left the Italian city of Lucca because of their Reformed beliefs. He studied theology at Geneva and Herborn, and his progress in the biblical languages was such that he was – at Beza's recommendation – appointed professor in Hebrew in 1596, at the young age of 20. He started to translate the Bible into Italian, his family's mother tongue, and this translation was published in 1603. Diodati became famous for this translation. In 1607, he published a second edition, complete with notes, the *Annotationes in Biblia*. His language skills enabled him to translate the Bible into French as well (1644). In 1606, Diodati was appointed professor of theology and was ordained as a minister of the Genevan church in 1608. The next year he succeeded Beza at the academy. Diodati was sent on a mission to France in 1614 and was sent as a delegate to the Synod of Dort in 1618-1619, where he was appointed as one of the six divines to formulate the conclusions of the synod regarding the Remonstrant articles. He retired from his professorship at Geneva in 1645 and died on October 3, 1649.[6]

The parents of Theodore Tronchin (1587-1657) had fled from France to Geneva after St. Bartholomew's Night's Massacre in 1572. Theodore was born on April 17, 1587. Theodore Tronchin's godfather was Theodore Beza, and Tronchin went on to study theology in Geneva and Leiden. In 1606, he became professor in oriental languages at Geneva, and two years later a pastor in the Genevan church. In 1618, he was appointed professor of theology, and the same year the *venerable compagnie* sent him and Diodati to Dort to represent the Genevan church at the synod. Tronchin was sent on diplomatic missions several times by the Genevan state and church. He aimed to unify the Lutherans and the Reformed, to which end he even wrote a – never printed – harmony of confessions. Tronchin died on November 19, 1657.[7]

4.2 Earlier research

The Genevan theologians and theology at the time of Dort have been subject to research by William McComish, who presents biographical material of the theologians discussed in this chapter and describes their theological

---

6 The most complete recent biography of Diodati was written by William A. McComish, *The Epigones: A Study of the Theology of the Genevan Academy at the Time of the Synod of Dort, with Special Reference to Giovani Diodati* (Allinson Park, PA: Pickwick Publications, 1989), 1-31 and 167-208. Short surveys of his life can be found in Campi, *Shifting Patterns*, 241-58, and in Andrea Ferrari, *John Diodati's Doctrine of Holy Scripture* by (Grand Rapids: Reformation Heritage Books, 2006).

7 The most recent biographical sketch of Tronchin can be found in McComish, *Epigones*, 32-34.

endeavors.[8] He does of course pay special attention to the Genevan contribution to the Synod at Dort and concludes that the view expressed by the Genevan delegates is not as close to Beza than that of several other delegates.[9] He also concludes that the Genevan delegates were unique at the synod in presenting a non-Anselmian doctrine of the atonement.[10]

Joel R. Beeke examines the Genevan thinking on the order of decrees from Beza to F. Turretin, which includes research on Diodati and Tronchin. According to Beeke, the Genevan delegates were supralapsarians.[11] Nicolas Fornerod made an important contribution to our knowledge of the labors and sentiments of the Genevan delegates. He read some personal writings by Diodati (his correspondence) and Tronchin (his journal) and analyzed them in an article in *Revisiting the Synod of Dort*.[12] Emidio Campi studied Diodati, primarily as a Bible translator, in which he, like Beeke, assumed that Diodati was a supralapsarian.[13] Andrea Ferrari's book on Diodati's view of Scripture does not deal with his ideas on predestination.[14]

4.3 The Genevan Remarks on the First Article

The proceedings of the synod were laid down in the *Acta*, which are not minutes of each session but summaries or indications of what was done in each session, the publication of which was completed by the written responses of each delegation to the five articles of the Remonstrants.[15] The delegates at the Synod of Dort made assessments of the articles of the Remonstrants. Tronchin presented his feelings on perseverance in session 94, whereas Diodati

---

8   McComish, *Epigones*.
9   McComish, *Epigones*, 80-81
10 McComish, *Epigones*, 104-05
11 Beeke, "The Order of the Divine Decrees at the Genevan Academy: From Bezan Supralapsarianism to Turretinian Infralapsarianism," in Roney and Klauber, *The Identity of Geneva*, 63-65.
12 Fornerod, "Genevan Delegation", 181-215.
13 Campi, "John Diodati (1576-1649), Translator of the Bible into Italian," in idem, *Shifting Patterns*, 241-58.
14 Ferrari, *John Diodati's Doctrine of Holy Scripture*.
15 *Acta Synodi Nationalis … Dordrechti habitae Anno 1618 et 1619: Accedunt Plenissima, de Quinque Articulis, Theologorum Judicia* (Lugduni Batavorum [Leiden]: Isaac Elzevir, 1620). (Quoted as *Acta* 1620). Recently a new edition of the Acta was published, completed with the Acta Authentica and the Acta Contracta, but without the Judgements of the Delegations. Donald Sinnema, Christian Moser and Herman J. Selderhuis, *Acta et Documenta Synodi Nationalis Dordechtanae (1618-1619). Vol. I. Acta of the Synod of Dort* (Göttingen: Vandenhoeck&Ruprecht, 2015). The jugements are planned for vol. V of this series.

gave his view of the same subject in session 106.[16] Diodati was appointed a member of the committee that was to prepare the conclusions of the synod concerning all the articles of the Remonstrants in session 128. He was also the means for conveying the thoughts of the French theologian Pierre du Moulin, whose views he read aloud in session 143.

The first article of the Remonstrance dealt with predestination. The response of the Genevan delegates gives a summary of their thoughts on this subject. Tronchin and Diodati divided their answer into three parts, the first on election in eight theses, the second on reprobation in five theses, and the third on the rejection of Remonstrant errors, in seven theses.[17]

Beza and Fayus[18]	Subject	Diodati and Tronchin[19]
13.	God chooses in Christ whom he willed out of the fallen human race and calls them, gives them faith, justifies, and glorifies them.	1, 4.
14.	The election is not based on foreseen worth or good works, which are not a cause but the effect of election.	2, 3.
1, 2.	The decree is firm and irrevocable.	5.
-	All the elect, coming of age, will be assured of their election.	6.
-	Election in the Old Testament was the same as under the New Testament.	7.
15.	Assurance of election can be obtained from the gifts and marks proper to the elect.	8.

Table 1: *The theses of Diodati and Tronchin on election compared with those of Beza and Fayus.*

---

16 Tronchin's discourse is in *Registres*, 440-455; Diodati's discourse is lost. Campi, *Shifting Patterns*, 244-45, suggests that, "thanks to the contribution of Diodati," the doctrine of perseverance appeared for the first time in a Reformed confession. This suggestion is mistaken, for perseverance, or the possibility of apostasy by a true believer, was a point of discussion due to the Remonstrance. According to the Acta Contracta, Diodati's speech, which is missing, also addressed the questions how often the Spirit works in the hearts of the reprobate, and what is the difference between justifying faith and temporal faith. The Acta Contracta are more extensive here than the Acta Authentica and the published Acta. Sinnema e.a., *Acta et Documenta*, Vol. I, 444.
17 *Acta* 1620, II, 46-54.
18 Beza and Fayus, *Theses theologicae*, XI, pp. 16-19. *Theses de aeterna praedestinatione*.
19 *Acta* 1620, II, 46-51. *De primo articulo, qui est de Electione ad vitam aeternam.*

There is a remarkable similarity between this assessment by Diodati and Tronchin and the theses on predestination in the theological handbook of the Genevan Academy, *Theses Theologicae* by Beza and Fayus. As shown in Table 1, all the theses of the delegates, except for six and seven, are mirrored in this set of theses on predestination.

Because the agreement between Beza and his students is evident from this table, their differences should be indicated. The delegates omitted the end of the decree (the glory of God) and God's attribute of mercy in their first thesis. Beza's warning not to try to derive assurance of election from searching God's decree, is omitted in their eighth thesis, as well as Beza's detailed description of the steps to be taken to obtain assurance. On the other hand, the delegates add some themes not mentioned by Beza in his theses. In their fifth thesis, they state explicitly that no elect person can become reprobate. This could inevitably be concluded from Beza's words, but he did not state it explicitly. This addition seems to have been important for Diodati and Tronchin, for they repeated it twice (thesis four on reprobation and the third rejected thesis). In the sixth thesis on election, the delegates state explicitly that all the elect, or at least those who have reached the age of reason, are or will be assured of their election; a statement that is not found in Beza. Nor did Beza mention election in the Old and New Testaments, as the delegates did in their seventh thesis.

Turning to Beza's and the delegates' theses on reprobation, table 2 shows great similarity between them. Here again there is a theme mentioned by Beza but not by Diodati and Tronchin: God's glory as the ultimate purpose in Beza's 16th thesis. Also, we again see a theme mentioned by them but not by Beza: the impossibility mentioned in the fourth thesis for a reprobate to become elect.

Beza and Fayus[20]	Subject	Diodati and Tronchin[21]
16.	God decided to leave others in their sin and corruption. These people are either not called or called but not regenerated.	1, 2.
4, 8, 9, 19.	God's passing people over is not a cause of sin.	3.
1, 2.	This decree is firm and immutable.	4.
15.	The general call to the church is not a sign of election.	5.

Table 2: The theses of Diodati and Tronchin concerning reprobation compared with those of Beza and Fayus.

---

20 Beza and Fayus, *Theses theologicae*, XI, pp. 18-19. *Theses de aeterna praedestinatione.*
21 Acta 1620, II, 51-53. *De reprobatione.*

Having stated what they taught on the themes of election and reprobation, the Genevan delegates rejected seven theses.[22] The rejected theses 1-4 and 6 simply follow from the former positive theses. Diodati and Tronchin reject the fifth thesis that God wills the salvation of all, gave the Mediator for all, and ordained all to obtain salvation by faith, offers salvation to all, and grants all the necessary means to be saved.[23] This follows from Beza's doctrine: he had stated these things in various places.

The seventh rejection, which denies that there are multiple decrees, deserves more attention.[24] It is obviously a rejection of the Remonstrant's multiplication of God's decrees and their distinctions. Beza had distinguished between the decree to elect and election itself, but the delegates did not use this distinction. Although Beza's distinction between the decree to elect and to reprobate *(propositum eligendi / reprobandi)* and election or reprobation itself *(electio /reprobatio ipsa)* was not actually a distinction between decrees but between the eternal decree and its execution in time, the terms he used could be confusing. It is possible that the Genevan delegates did not use this distinction to avoid a likely objection by the Remonstrants against this seeming "multiplication of decrees" which was "not clearly founded in Holy Scripture." They thus left it unclear as to whether they referred to the purpose or to the execution. Indeed, they even left it unclear as to whether they accepted this distinction or rejected it. In stating that God's passing over some people was not a cause of sin, damnation, or creation, they followed the views of the mature Beza (see 3.11).

---

22 *Acta* 1620, II, 53-54. They reject the following: 1. that election is due to faith; 2. that God's benevolence is nothing more than that he chose faith instead of another means; 3. that an elect person can become reprobate and vice versa.; 4. that there is no assurance of election, save a special revelation of perseverance; 5. that God wills the salvation of all, gave Christ for all, has ordained all to obtain salvation by faith, offers salvation to all ,and gives all people the necessary means to salvation; 6. that a better use of universal grace is the cause of the Gospel being preached somewhere, while a worse use is the cause of the Gospel not being preached. 7. that the decrees of God are manifold.

23 *Acta* 1620, II, 54: "Generali voluntate Deus omnium salutem desiderat: omnibus Mediatorem dedit: omnes ad salutem ex fide obtinendam ordinat, omnibus eam offert: mediaque necessaria & sufficientia administrat."

24 *Acta* 1620, II, 54: "Multiplicationes decretorum & distinctionum, cum ad suffulcienda isthaec ἑτερόδοξα tantum inventae sunt, & Scripturae sacrae vel plane non innitantur vel adversentur, a nobis rejiciuntur." *(The multiplications of decrees and distinctions, which are only invented to support this heresy and are not clearly founded in Holy Scripture or opposed by it, are rejected by us.)*

The Genevan statements on the first Remonstrant article are clear about some points but leave other important questions unanswered. It is clear that most of the statements are in accord with Beza's teachings, for example, the firmness and unconditionality of the decree of election and reprobation. The delegates followed Beza rather than Calvin on obtaining assurance of election from the fruits of election rather than by looking to Christ. Most of their theses show agreement with Beza's theses on predestination. There are differences on minor points, such as the Genevans addressing election in the Old Testament and stating that all the elect who can think rationally will be assured of their election before death. A question that is not answered is whether Diodati and Tronchin accept Beza's distinction between the decree to elect and to reprobate on the one hand and election and reprobation itself on the other.

4.4 The Genevan Remarks on the Second article

The Remonstrants had argued in their second article that Christ died for all people, although only believers actually enjoy the forgiveness of their sins. Beza had rejected the classic formula of sufficiency and efficiency at the Colloquy of Montbéliard. The judgment of this second article shows the view of Genevan delegates on this question. They formulated their judgment in eight statements, which can be summarized as follows:

1. Christ is given by the Father to be Head and Mediator for a certain number of people, who are his spiritual body, according to election;
2. Christ intended to die for the elect and to add to the limitless worth of his death a very powerful and specific intention of his will;
3. Christ is the cause and foundation of the call and all other special blessings of the elect;
4. Faith in Christ is a work of the Spirit of regeneration, bestowed by Christ himself;
5. Faith is a condition of the new covenant regarding the certain order made by God, but it is also a promise and gift of the new covenant and an effect of being engrafted in Christ;[25]

---

25 This opinion on faith as both a condition and a gift is also expressed by Tronchin in his discourse on perseverance, *Registres*, 442-446. Tronchin there declared that he used conditionality in preaching. Not, like Calvin, as a means to make predestination and the universal call agree with each other, but to promote piety. "Quod igitur respondent Remonstrantes in Collatione Hagiensi : « In promissione Dei, in Spiritus Sancti obsignatione etc. subesse conditionem fidei et poenitentiæ, quæ a nobis requiruntur ». Nos hoc non tantum libenter damus sed et ore pleno prædicamus. Pia non est doctrina quæ pietatem non commendat. Perseverantia sanctorum electorum in gratia Dei, connexam habet perseverantiam in fide et sanctitate, via enim est hæc electionis

6. The universal verses in the Scripture do not mean that Christ died for each and every person but refer to all members of Christ's body or to the dispensation of the new covenant, in which all different people and nations are accepted by the Son and hence the grace of preaching is given to all people and nations, which is the foundation of the universal call of the gospel;
7. The distinction between obtaining and appropriation is to be accepted in that there is a decree in God to be gracious to the elect because of Christ, even before the elect exist, but election is always the cause of the appropriation in the elect;
8. But this distinction ought not to be used to say that God is reconciled to all men because of Christ's death and wills their salvation if they simply desire it, for this is Pelagianism.[26]

There is again great harmony between the theses of Beza and those of the Genevan delegates concerning the atonement, although the similarity is not so great that we find corresponding theses in Beza for most theses of the delegates. It would exceed the scope of this chapter to prove the harmony with respect to every single thesis; hence, we will look at the differences.

It is difficult to compare thesis five to Beza's view. While Beza did call faith a condition in one way and a gift in another, he did not link this to the doctrine of the covenant.[27] And although Beza held that faith was a result of election, he did not state that it was the result of being engrafted into Christ, but he did not deny this either.

---

ad salutem (Eph. 2, 10)." *(What the Remonstrants answered at the Colloquy of The Hague: "Behind the promise of God, the sealing of the Holy Spirit etc., is the condition of faith and repentance, which are required from us," this we readily not only grant but we also preach it fully. For it is no pious doctrine which does not recommend piety. The perseverance of the elect saints in God's grace is connected to perseverance in faith and sanctification, for this is the way from election to salvation (Eph. 2.10). Registres, 445.* Yet in answering the Remonstrants, the accent was laid on the unconditional part. "«*Vobis gratis datum est in Christum credere* » non tantum dat posse credere, sed fidem operatur (Phil. 29 .) ; *fides est donum Dei* non oblatum tantum, alioqui fides esset omnium ex sensu Remonstrantium, sed et collatum." *("To you it is given to believe in Christ," not only the possibility to believe is given, but a working faith (Phil. 1.29): faith is a gift of God, not only an offer, like faith only would be in the opinion of the Remonstrants, but also a bestowing.) Registres, 444.* The pun of *oblatum* (from 'ob-ferro', literally 'to carry before') and *collatum* (from 'con-ferro' literally 'to bring together' is lost in the translation.

26 *Acta* 1620, II, 100-03.
27 See 3.10. Cf. Beza, *Quaestionum et Responsionum Christianarum Libellus* (fifth edition, Geneva: Eustathius Vignon, 1577), 117.

It is clear that Diodati and Tronchin agreed with Beza's view regarding the extent of the atonement. While Calvin used the classic formula with respect to sufficiency and efficiency, the later Beza and the Genevan delegates did not. They limited the scope of Christ's death to the elect alone. However, a clear refutation of the classic formula in words similar to that of Beza is not given, not by the Genevan delegates nor by any other delegation - at least, nothing can be found on this in the written judgments. It is probable that the classic formula was discussed since several sessions were devoted to the second article. In session 74 the synod dealt explicitly with the distinction between sufficiency and efficiency. But we know nothing more about the content of this session. The phrase that Christ died for the whole world was used in the written *judicia* of several delegations as well as in the letters of David Pareus and Piere du Moulin, which were publicly read (the latter even by Diodati), while at the same time all delegates denied in their judgments that God intended the death of Christ for the salvation of the whole world.[28] It can be concluded that the synod's view concerning the scope of the effect of Christ's death was the same as Beza's but that an important part of the synod did not assume that the phrase that "Christ died for the whole world" suggested a divine intention to save the whole world.[29]

For a long time, Diodati thought that the doctrine of the extent of the atonement would not lead to great doctrinal difficulties. He tolerated the hypothetical universalism of the English delegates since they taught a particular application based on the doctrine of election and the individual gift of the Spirit. The committee that was to draft the *Canons*, which included Diodati, did not spare any effort to satisfy the British delegation.

---

28 That means that the larger part of the synod used the phrase in the same way that Calvin did (see 2.5). Blacketer's argument (to suggest that Calvin's and Beza's view on the extent of the atonement are virtually the same) that the debate on the extent of the atonement would become clearer in the later Remonstrant controversy does not hold up since most of the delegations did not reject the classic formula, as Beza had done. Rather, modifications by the British and Bremen delegates were approved by the synod: they stressed *pro omnibus* part of the classic position.

29 The second article was much discussed. The British delegate Balcanquall treated it in session 72, and a general discussion followed in session 74. A defense of Article 2 by the Remonstrants was read (and probably discussed) in sessions 82, 92, 93, and 95. Pareus' examination of the first two articles was read in session 99. In session 101, the *judicia* of all delegations were handed over. The *judicia* of the second article were read in sessions 110, 111, 113, 114, and 115. The final canon concerning the second article was discussed in session 127, 129, and 128. This was the only canon in which the *Acta* mentions that the synod decided to make some "minor changes" before approving it. *Acta*, I, 195, 196, 199, 201, 204-32, 234-35, 238-39.

Considering Beza's heavy criticism of the classic formula following the failed Colloquy with the Lutherans, it is remarkable that his student Tronchin without comments noted that modifications proposed by the British and Bremen delegates were approved.[30]

Nevertheless, the exact phrase that Christ "died sufficiently for the whole world" cannot be found in the final version of the *Canons*. Instead, it says that the death of Christ is "of infinite worth and value, abundantly sufficient to expiate the sins of the whole world."[31] While this might seem a very minor change, it was important enough to make this canon acceptable for those who agreed with Beza's criticism. Given the way the phrase "died for the whole world" or similar phrases were used by members of the synod, the change seems to have been occasioned by those who doubted the orthodoxy of the phrase, even when there was no reason to doubt the orthodoxy of those members of the synod who used it. Nonetheless, the delegation, i.e., Diodati and Tronchin, that was expected to raise this objection did not include it in their written *judicia*. No conclusion can be drawn from this, however, for the *Acta* are not minutes but simply indications of the subjects discussed. We do not know, therefore, what the exact position of the Genevan delegates concerning this very phrase was. Fornerod is definitely right when he concludes that

> [a] detailed analysis of the period of the redaction of the Canons remains to be undertaken, both in order to grasp the import of the nuances that the delegates were willing to introduce into the Canons and to determine with precision where the points of doctrinal disagreement between the majority and the dissenting theologians lay.[32]

4.5 Less Bezan than Others? McComish's Thesis Examined

According to McComish, the Genevan delegates differed in some measure from their teacher Beza on some points, whereas other delegates were closer to him. First, McComish stated that Diodati and Tronchin "diminish the importance of the divine decree in favor of a doctrine of Trinitarian providence. This doctrine is more explicit about the role of Christ." Second, they do not mention the final cause of predestination. Third, they do not mention mercy and justice as the qualities of God that were behind salvation and damnation. According to McComish, the delegates of Switzerland,

---

30 Fornerod, "Genevan Delegation," 211-13.
31 *Canons,* Chapter II, article 3: "Haec mors Filii Dei est ... infiniti valoris et pretii, abunde sufficiens ad totius mundi peccata expianda."
32 Fornerod, "Genevan Delegation," 215.

Nassau, and Bremen reflected Beza's ideas more closely concerning this article.³³

His first observation is related in part to the first article in which the Genevans mentioned Christ. The question is whether this really differs from Beza's view. McComish compares the *judicia* of the Genevan delegates with Beza's tract *De praedestinationis doctrina*, but it has been demonstrated that the *judicia* of the Genevan delegates show a strong resemblance to another work by Beza, his *Theses theologicae*. At Dort, however, the delegates did not actually comment on a work by Beza but on an article written by the Remonstrants in which they mention Christ. Both the resemblance and the difference between the first part of Remonstrant Article 1 and the first thesis of the Genevan delegates is obvious when placed alongside each other:

The first article of the Remonstrants reads:

> That God, by an eternal, unchangeable purpose in Jesus Christ his Son, before the foundation of the world, hath determined, out of the fallen, sinful race of men, to save in Christ, for Christ's sake, and through Christ, those who, through the grace of the Holy Ghost, shall believe on this his Son Jesus, and shall persevere in this faith and obedience of faith, through this grace, even to the end …³⁴

The first thesis on predestination by the Genevan delegates reads:

> God has from eternity, merely out of the good pleasure of his will, determined in Christ, through Christ and for Christ's sake, certain persons, out of the seed and posterity of Adam, fallen in and with him, guilty and corrupt, out of this same pleasure of his will, destined unto this end individually by the Father, to call gracefully and effectively, to give them faith, to justify them, to sanctify them by the regeneration of the Spirit, and by these and after all these things, finally to glorify them.³⁵

---

33 McComish, *Epigones*, 80-81.
34 Translation taken from Schaff, *The Creeds of Christendom* III, 545: "Deus aeterno et immutabili decreto in Christo Jesu Filio suo, ante jacta mundi fundamenta, statuit ex genere humano in peccatum prolapso, eos in Christo, propter Christum, et per Christum salvare, qui per gratiam Spiritus Sancti in eundem Filium suum credituri, inque ea ipsa fide et obedientia fidei, per eandem gratiam, usque ad finem essent perseveraturi."
35 *Acta* 1620, II, 46: "Deus ab aeterno, ex mero beneplacito voluntatis suae, certas personas, ex semine & posteris Adae, in, & cum eodem lapsas, reas & corruptas, decrevit in Christo per & propter Christum, ex eadem εὐδοκίᾳ in hunc finem ipsis singulariter

What the Genevan delegates did here is to change a document of not Beza but the Remonstrants. The latter stated that God decreed in, by, and because of Christ to save those who would believe and persevere, leaving open who would do so, and if anyone would do so. The Genevans state that God decreed in, by, and because of Christ, to save *certain persons* by actually *making* them believe and persevere. It is obvious that the formulation of the Remonstrants was decisive for the Genevans to mention Christ at the very beginning of their response.

Moreover, there is more agreement with Beza than might be initially apparent. Beza usually starts his systematic treatises and theses on election with general remarks on predestination, and there he, indeed, did not mention Christ. But he did distinguish between predestination as the purpose to elect and election itself *(electio ipsa)* and he does mention Christ when speaking about *electio ipsa*. When Beza's thesis on election is compared with thesis one of the Genevan delegates, the agreement is obvious:

> Out of this bondage, God (who is bound unto no man) according to His eternal predestinated election in Christ, whom He has willed himself to choose merely out of His own mercy, out of that same mercy (whenever He provides it) calls, enlightens, and having bestowed faith upon them and having regenerated them, He freely justifies them in the same Christ, and finally in glorifying them He will lay open the most high glory of His mercy.[36]

Here one can see that Beza, when speaking about election itself, spoke about election in Christ and election out of bondage. It is clear that the Christological emphasis in thesis one of the Genevan delegates is not a deviation from Beza. In his *De praedestinationis doctrina*, he even called Christ the foundation of election.[37]

McComish's second argument, i.e., that the Genevans differ from Beza in not mentioning the final cause, is true as such. Beza does refer to the final

---

à Patre destinatum, gratiose & efficaciter vocare, fide donare, iustificare, per Spiritum regenerationis sanctificare, & per haec, & post haec omnia, tandem in aeternum glorificare."

36 Beza and Fayus, *Theses theologicae*, XI, 13: "Ex hac servitute Deus nemini debito, secundum aeternam suam in Christo praedestinatam electionem, quos ipsi libuit, ex mera sua misericordia seligere, eadem sua misericordia, quando ipsi visum est, vocat, illuminate, fide donatos & regeneratos gratis in eodem Christo iustificat, in illis tandem glorificandis summam summae misericordiae gloriam suam patefacturus."

37 Beza, *De praedestinationis doctrina*, 11. However, Beza called Christ the foundation of election itself, not of the decree to elect.

cause in his specific thesis on election, whereas Diodati and Tronchin do not, nor do they mention the final cause in other theses at the synod, while other delegates do. It is not clear why they leave this out of their theses, but this does not necessarily suggest a deviation from Beza. There was no disagreement with the Remonstrants concerning the final cause of election. Moreover, one should not argue from silence. The same holds for McComish's third observation. Beza actually mentions God's mercy as the fountain of salvation, while the delegates do not. Again, this should not be seen as a deviation from Beza since the subject of their first thesis was not salvation but election. Neither God's qualities nor the final cause was a theme in the discussion with the Remonstrants at the Synod of Dort. That other delegates actually cite these themes is of no great importance here. McComish does not mention a delegation that is closer in general to Beza than the Genevan delegation but refers to three delegations that were closer to Beza only on some of the themes McComish mentioned. This is not enough to argue that the Genevan delegates were not as close to Beza in general than other delegations. For instance, the opinion of the Bremen delegation on the extent of the atonement differs greatly from Beza's.

As for the second article, McComish pays a great deal of attention to the term used by the Genevans to the effect that Christ is "Head" of the elect, which besides them only the delegates of Zeeland use.[38] Yet the question is whether the use of this single word indicates a different theology, as McComish suggests.[39] Beza also used the term "Head" for Christ in his *Ad Acta*.[40] Hence, there is no need nor even a reason to speak about a different theology.

We can conclude that, although there were some delegates who addressed themes that Beza discusses but are not mentioned by the Genevan delegates, there are no grounds for saying that other delegations were altogether more Bezan than the Genevans. The similarities between their theses and Beza's theology are too great to allow this conclusion. Some apparent differences between Beza and the Genevan delegation on themes McComish mentions can be eliminated by comparing the delegates' thesis on election with those on predestination from other works by Beza than the one McComish used, while others do not actually or necessarily suggest a deviation.

---

38 McComish, *Epigones* 85-105.
39 McComish draws this conclusion from the almost unique use of this term.
40 Beza, *Ad Acta,* 218: "[I]llis servandis, Christum suum qui est illorum caput ..."

4.6 Supralapsarianism or Infralapsarianism? Beeke's Thesis Examined

It is remarkable that McComish, in listing some differences between Beza and the Genevan delegates does not mention the question of supra- and infralapsarianism. Beza was supralapsarian concerning God's decree of predestination, but Diodati and Tronchin seem to have taken the infralapsarian stance.[41] This can be argued from their first thesis on election, in which they stated that some were elect out of the fallen human race, and from thesis one on reprobation, which states that God decreed leaving some in sin and corruption, which means that the Fall preceded election and reprobation.[42] Moreover, in thesis three on reprobation, Diodati and Tronchin explicitly deny that reprobation is the cause of creation, which might suggest that in God's decree, creation preceded reprobation.[43]

Although these theses seem to reflect infralapsarianism, Beeke states that both Diodati and Tronchin were supralapsarians.[44] Campi also assumes that Diodati was a supralapsarian.[45] Concerning Diodati, Beeke offers two arguments. The first is that the supralapsarian chairman of the synod, Johannes Bogerman, praised Diodati's address to the synod on the topic of perseverance. The second consists of three quotes from Diodati's annotations on Romans 9.[46] Both arguments fail to prove Beeke's conclusion. Being praised for an address on perseverance by a supralapsarian does not necessarily make the speaker a supralapsarian himself. The annotations quoted by Beeke do not suggest any preference for, let alone indicate, supralapsarianism.

Moreover, there are other annotations by Diodati, even on the same chapter, Romans 9, which point to an infralapsarian stance. For instance, on the words *neither having done any good or evil* in vs. 11, he commented that Jacob and Esau were considered by God "in their natural state, wherein they were both the sonnes of *Adam,* equally sinners and corrupt,

---

41 According to Fornerod, Gomarus's concept op predestination followed the supralapsarian scheme of Beza. Fornerod, "Introduction", xiii.
42 *Acta* 1620, II, 46: "Deus ab aeterno ... certas personas, ex semine & posteris Adae, in, & cum eodem lapsas, reas & corruptas, decrevit ..." Idem, 51: "Deus ab aeterno ... certas personas, in & cum Adamo lapsas, reas & corruptas, statuit apud sese, in statu peccati, & corruptionis suae propriae relinquere ..."
43 *Acta* 1620, II, 53: "Praeteritio ista, non est causa peccati, nec damnationis, multo minus creationis."
44 Beeke, "The Order," 63-65. After a personal conversation with him, Beeke changed his mind. Joel R. Beeke, *Debated Issues in Sovereign Predestination: Early Lutheran Predestination, Calvinian Reprobation, and Variations in Genevan Lapsarism* (Göttingen: Vandenhoeck & Ruprecht, 2017), 10, 197-206.
45 Campi, *Shifting Patterns,* 244.
46 Beeke, "The Order," 63-64.

having done no actual good nor evil ..."⁴⁷ According to Diodati, the word *election* in the same verse refers to that "by which he had determined to chuse the one, and leave the other," while he remarked on verse 16 that election was out "of pure mercy." The clay mentioned in verse 21 is seen by Diodati as "humane nature in its universal corruption."⁴⁸ One can safely conclude from these annotations that Diodati was infralapsarian since verse 11 was always used by supralapsarians as an argument for their position. His teacher Beza had explained the lump of clay as being the human race not yet created or fallen.

Another argument in support of the view that Diodati was infralapsarian is that the Remonstrants judged him to have dealt with the topic of reprobation in more moderate terms than the Contra-Remonstrants did. This is striking, for most Contra-Remonstrants at the synod were infralapsarians, and Diodati seems to have been more moderate in the eyes of the Remonstrants. Diodati opposes the view of the supralapsarian Piscator, that the reprobates were created for damnation.⁴⁹ He is even inclined to condemn Piscator for this view but in the end acknowledges that a condemnation of Piscator on this point ran the risk of damaging the reputation of some Reformed theologians who were supralapsarian.⁵⁰ He might have been thinking of Calvin and Beza.⁵¹ He did not openly oppose supralapsarianism, but he did not hide his disproval of the "horrid" supralapsarian position of Gomarus.⁵²

Beeke offers one argument for Tronchin's supposed supralapsarianism: his work on original sin.⁵³ But since he does not refer to any quotation or page number in this volume, it is difficult to examine this argument. He refers to Armstrong's work on Calvinism and the Amyraut heresy to state that "supralapsarianism was the common position in the Genevan Academy throughout the first half of the seventeenth century."⁵⁴ Beeke does not take into account the contribution of the Genevan delegates

---

47 Diodati wrote his annotations in Italian. I used the anonymous English translation, John Diodati, *Pious and Learned Annotations upon the Holy Bible* (London: Mile Flesher for Nicholas Fussell, 1648).
48 Diodati, *Annotations*, NT, 167.
49 Piscator agreed with Calvin here; see 2.4 and *Institutes*, III, xxi, 5.
50 *Registres*, 257.
51 The Genevan consistory advised the Genevan delegates to be very prudent and remembered them their assignment to keep the names of Calvin and Beza in honour. *Registres*, 73-74.
52 Fornerod, "Genevan Delegation," 206-09.
53 Beeke, "The Order," 64.
54 Beeke, "The Order," 64, n .47.

to the Synod of Dort. There is no reference to the *Acta* in his section on Beza's successors. This is a strange omission, given that the *judicia* on the Remonstrant theses of the delegates are obviously the best source for determining their standpoint concerning predestination. Tronchin seems to have concealed his view for a long time. Some delegates were not sure he had the same view as Diodati. Tronchin had no problem in subscribing to the infralapsarian view of the majority of the synod but would never have accepted a condemnation of supralapsarianism. According to him, the synod did not touch on the question of the order of decrees. As Fornerod noted, the definitions of election and reprobation in the *Canons* have a strong infralapsarian orientation, but they still left open the question of the precise order of the eternal divine decrees made before creation. Only in 1647, when asked by the *Compagnie* whether he agreed with Beza on this matter, did he answer that he did not but did not deem it useful to refute it in public.[55] Thus, both Diodati and Tronchin were infralapsarians, the latter with more toleration of supralapsarianism than the former.

4.7 From Supralapsarianism to Infralapsarianism

In his article, Beeke wonders "when the winds of infralapsarianism began to blow through the Genevan Academy." He asks how it came about that Beza's supralapsarian position gave way to Francis Turretin's infralapsarianism.[56] Since Diodati and Tronchin were infralapsarians, it seems that this question can be answered with some exactness: in the years of "the epigones," as McComish calls them.

That infralapsarianism was the ruling view at the Genevan Academy after Beza's death is clear from a work by Friedrich Spanheim (1600-1649), who studied under Diodati and Tronchin in the years 1619-1620, just after the synod, and who succeeded Benedict Turretin in 1631 as professor of theology in Geneva.[57] Spanheim offered three views on the object of predestination: first, humans not yet created at all; second, humans created but not fallen; and finally:

> The patrons of the third opinion take predestination in the strict sense for the decree either of mercy, or of sovereignty and justice concerning fallen men,

---

55 Fornerod, "Genevan Delegation," 209-11.
56 Beeke, "The Order," 64.
57 Friedrich Spanheim (1600-1649) was born in Germany, studied in Heidelberg and Geneva, succeeded Benedict Turretin as professor in theology in Geneva in 1631 and was given a similar position in Leiden in 1642. For him, see D. Nauta, "Spanheim, Fri(e)dericus," in D. Nauta et al. (eds.) *Biografisch Lexicon voor de geschiedenis van het Nederlandse protestantisme*, vol. II (Kampen: Kok, 1983), 410-11.

whereof the object certainly is man, considered as fallen, which meaning for the word "predestination" was wisely used by the Synod of Dort and by us here with her.[58]

Spanheim not only took the infralapsarian position himself but also ascribed it to the *Canons of Dort*. Nevertheless, Spanheim is known as the theologian who "used to say that when he lectured in a theological classroom, he was a supralapsarian, but when speaking to his congregation he was an infralapsarian." This statement was widely publicized by Herman Bavinck[59] and has been repeated by several authors but was never examined. It needs to be corrected. Bavinck's source is a work by Comrie and Holtius, but these authors gave no source for their statement that they "heard from someone who had heard that Spanheim used to say …"[60] This cannot be used as an authoritative argument. Moreover, since, in the next sentence, Comrie and Holtius quote from the *Syntagma* of what they call "the old Spanheim," it is plausible that the statement quoted by Bavinck refers to the younger Spanheim, which makes even more sense when we take into account the year Comrie and Holtius published their statement (1756).[61] That the older Spanheim was an infralapsarian is clear from the quote above.

One should not think that the move from supralapsarianism to infralapsarianism attracted a great deal of attention in Geneva. It was never a controversial issue in Geneva. Calvin's works contain both supra- and infralapsarian statements. Beza was a supralapsarian when he wrote about the eternal purpose to elect and to reprobate. But when he wrote on election and reprobation itself, he used infralapsarian language. Since

---

58 F. Spanheim, *Disputationum Theologicarum Syntgama*, I (Geneva: Petrus Chouët, 1652), 180. "Tertia sententiae fautores praedestinationem stricte sumunt pro decreto vel misericordiae, vel libertatis & justitiae circa hominem lapsum, cujus sane objectum est homo consideratus ut lapsus, quo significatu praedestinationis voce usa fuit sapienter Synodus Dordracena & nos hîc cum illa."

59 Herman Bavinck, *Gereformeerde Dogmatiek* II (Kampen: J.H. Bos, 1908), 398.

60 Alexander Comrie and Nicolaus Holtius, *Examen van het ontwerp van tolerantie …*, VII (Amsterdam: Nicolaas Byl, 1756), 296. "Ook heb ik eenen Ouden Doctor, nu in de ruste, wel hooren verhalen, dat hy van zynen Vader, die Regent in het Staaten Collegie te Leyden was, gehoort had, dat de wydvermaarde Spanheim pleeg te zeggen, dat hy op de Katheder een *Supralapsarius*, of bovenvaldryver was, maar in het onderwyzen der Gemeinte een *Infralapsarius*, of benedenvaldryver. En de oude Spanheim, aanmerkende …"

61 Bavinck did not make it clear which Spanheim he meant. Frederic Spanheim jr. (1632-1701) was a son of Spanheim the elder; he was born in Geneva and became professor of theology in Heidelberg (1655) and Leiden (1670). For him, see Nauta, "Spanheim, Fri(e)dericus, filius," Nauta et al. (ed.) *Biografisch Lexicon*, 411-13.

Beza urged his readers and students to start with the things that happen in time (like faith and repentance) and then take up eternal predestination, rather than beginning with eternal election and reprobation, it is not likely that Beza insisted on supralapsarian terminology nor that he himself used it often, save when speaking about the eternal decree.[62] An illustration of the way he dealt with predestination is the way this doctrine is introduced in the *Gallican Confession*. This confession was initially drafted by Calvin and then revised and ratified by the Synod of La Rochelle over which Beza presided. Predestination is mentioned in the twelfth article:

> We believe that from this corruption and general condemnation in which all men are plunged, God, according to his eternal and immutable counsel, calleth those whom he hath chosen by his goodness and mercy alone in our Lord Jesus Christ, without consideration of their works, to display in them the riches of his mercy; leaving the rest in this same corruption and condemnation to show in them his justice. For the ones are no better than the others, until God discerns them according to his immutable purpose which he has determined in Jesus Christ before the creation of the world.[63]

The confession starts with God calling people out of the general corruption (this seems to be infralapsarian) but then points back to the eternal and immutable decree, thus leaving it open as to whether this decree has a supra- or an infralapsarian structure. There is hardly any difference between this article of the *Gallican Confession* and the *judicia* of the Genevan delegates on the first article of the Remonstrants or the first chapter of the *Canons of Dort*. The transition from Beza's supralapsarianism to Turretin's infralapsarianism was not abrupt but fluid.

---

62 The statement incorrectly attributed to Spanheim, that when he lectured in a theological classroom, he was a supralapsarian, but when speaking as a pastor, he was an infralapsarian, could have been correctly attributed to Beza.

63 The translation is taken from "Confessio Fidei Gallicana" in Schaff, *Creeds of Christendom* III, 366-67. "Nous croyons que de cette corruption et condamnation générale, en laquelle tous hommes sont plongés, Dieu retire ceux lesquels en son Conseil éternel et immuable il a élus par sa seule bonté et miséricorde en notre Seigneur JÉSUS-CHRIST sans considération de leurs œuvres, laissant les autres en cette même corruption et condamnation, pour démontrer en eux sa justice, comme aux premiers il fait luire les richesses de sa miséricorde. Car les uns ne sont point meilleurs que les autres, jusques à ce que Dieu les discerne, selon son Conseil immuable qu'il a déterminé en JÉSUS-CHRIST devant la création du Monde."

4.8 The *Canons* on Predestination

Having seen in what sense Diodati and Tronchin's views agreed with and on some points differed from Beza, we should now look at the *Canons*. These *Canons* were not the result of the reflections of the Genevan delegates alone but of many delegates. This section will investigate how much of the Genevan view features in the *Canons* and whether there are differences between the *Canons* and the theology of the Genevans. Diodati himself was one of the delegates who edited the final *Canons*, so one can expect to find some influence of Genevan theology.

Concerning the first article of the Remonstrants, the synod decided not to start its answer in chapter 1 with eternal predestination or election in time but with the dark background of God's grace: human sinfulness (1). Then they mention John 3:16 on God's love manifested in sending his son (2), and the preaching of this Gospel (3). Those who do not believe it remain under God's wrath (4) by their own guilt (5). Yet faith in Christ is a gift of God (5).

This is quite atypical for Beza's approach in his more systematic-theological works and for Diodati and Tronchin in their *judicia*. They started their theses on predestination with the decree. This approach, however, echoes Calvin's opening sentences of his chapter on election in his *Institutes*, where he introduced this decree in order to explain why some believe the preaching of the Gospel and others do not. The *Canons* do likewise in stating that God granting faith to some and not to others is rooted in his decree of election and reprobation (6). This difference in structure however, does not imply any difference in content.

Election is described as

> the unchangeable purpose of God, whereby, before the foundation of the world, he hath, out of mere grace, according to the sovereign good pleasure of his own will, chosen, from the whole human race, which had fallen through their own fault, from their primitive state of rectitude, into sin and destruction, a certain number of persons to redemption in Christ, whom he from eternity appointed the Mediator and head of the elect, and the foundation of salvation. This elect number, though by nature neither better nor more deserving than others, but with them involved in one common misery, God hath decreed to give to Christ to be saved by him, and effectually to call and draw them to his communion by his Word and Spirit; to bestow upon them true faith, justification, and sanctification; and having powerfully preserved

them in the fellowship of his Son, finally to glorify them for the demonstration of his mercy, and for the praise of the riches of his glorious grace ..."[64]

In this definition, one finds the Bezan theme that was ignored in the theses of the Genevan delegates: God's glory as the ultimate goal of election. As for the rest, its content is generally in agreement with what these delegates had stated in line with Calvin and Beza.

The *Canons* proceed to state that election is not manifold but one and the same in the Old and New Testament (8). Election is not because of any good quality but is directed to good qualities (9). It is based solely in God's pleasure (10). It is immutable (11), and the elect will be assured of it by seeing the fruits of election in themselves (12). These are all themes addressed by the Genevans, and their content is in accord with their remarks. The *Canons* chose the line of Beza and the Genevan delegates concerning assurance as based on the fruits of election rather than Calvin's view that assurance should be obtained by looking to Jesus.

The *Canons* explicitly state that predestination should be preached (14). This theme was not touched on by the Genevan delegates in their written judgement, but their predecessors Calvin and Beza had written similar statements, and it is likely the delegates agreed with them. Having stated what those should do who lack assurance of election (16), the first chapter concludes with some themes not mentioned by the Genevans: What should one think of children of believers who die in infancy (17), and an answer to those who reject the doctrine of predestination (18).

---

64 *Canons*, I,7, Schaff, *Creeds of Christendom,* III, 553: "Est autem electio immutabile Dei propositum, quo ante jacta mundi fundamenta ex universo genere humano, ex primæva integritate in peccatum et exitium sua culpa prolapso, secundum liberrimum voluntatis suæ beneplacitum, ex mera gratia, certam quorundam hominum multitudinem, aliis nec meliorum, nec digniorum, sed in communi miseria cum aliis jacentium, ad salutem elegit in Christo, quem etiam ab æterno Mediatorem et omnium electorum caput, salutisque fundamentum constituit; atque ita eos ipsi salvandos dare, et ad ejus communionem per verbum et Spiritum suum efficaciter vocare ac trahere; seu vera et ipsum fide donare, justificare, sanctificare, et potenter in Filii sui communione custoditos tandem glorificare decrevit, ad demonstrationem suæ misericordiæ, et laudem divinarum gloriosæ suæ gratiae ..." The English translation is taken from the same volume, p. 582.

Genevan Theses	**Subject**	Corresponding articles
Election 1	Definition of election	I, 7
2	Distinguishing the elect as under the same guilt as others	I, 6, 7
3	No good qualities in humans preceding their election	I, 6, 7, 9
4	Effectual calling and faith as means granted by God	I, 5, 6, 7, 9
5	The decree is immutable; no elect person can become reprobate	I, 11
6	God gives his elect assurance of their election	I, 12
7	Election is the same in the Old and New Testaments	I, 8
8	One should strive to know his election	I, 16
Reprobation 1	Definition of reprobation	I, 15
2	No call and/or no regeneration of the reprobate	I, 15
3	This decree does not cause sin	I, 15[65]
4	The decree is immutable; no reprobate can become elect	-
5	Election to and reprobation from the external means of grace can be temporary	-
Rejection 1	Election due to foreknowledge of faith	I, 7,9, r1,3,4,5,[66]
2	God choosing faith as a condition is the content of election	I, r3
3	An elect person can become reprobate, and vice versa.	I, 11, r6
4	No assurance of election	I, 12, 16, r7
5	God wills that all people be saved	I, r8
6	A better use of common grace as a reason for preaching of the Gospel	I, r4, 9
7	Multiplication of decrees and distinctions	I, 8, r2, 5, 6

Table 3: The Canons *on predestination compared with the Genevan theses.*

---

[65] The *Canons* accept only the statement that reprobation is not a cause of sin; it did not mention, as did the Genevans, that it is not a cause of damnation and creation.
[66] 'r' stands for the rejection of errors.

When the theses of the Genevans are compared with the *Canons*, it turns out that almost all their theses are incorporated into the final canons as adopted by the synod, as can be seen from Table 3. This table makes clear that only the fourth and fifth of the Genevan theses on reprobation did not find their way into the *Canons of Dort*. But their fourth thesis on reprobation is almost the same as their fifth on election, which is explained in I, 11. The content of their fifth thesis on reprobation is incorporated in chapter V on perseverance. Hence it turns out that the content of Canon I is in harmony with Genevan theology. The articles in Canon I, which the Genevan delegates did not address do not oppose anything they stated. That means that Genevan theology on predestination was generally representative for European Reformed theology on the topic of predestination at the time of the Synod of Dort.[67]

4.9 The *Canons* on the Atonement
The second chapter of the *Canons* shows a similar pattern when compared with the Genevan theses. Whereas the Genevans started immediately with the question of the extent of the salvific value of Christ's death, the *Canons* again start with the background of this question. They first point out the necessity of satisfaction (1) and the impossibility of satisfying God's justice, which is why God sent his own Son (2). Christ's death, being perfect, is of infinite power and value and sufficient to satisfy for the sins of the whole world (3) since Christ is both human and God (4). The promise of the Gospel is that whoever believes in Christ will not perish, a promise that should be preached with the command to repent and believe (5). That many of those who are called do not believe is not because of a lack of power on the part of Christ's death (6), but that some do believe is a matter of God's grace (7). Only after that do the *Canons* address the question of whom Christ died for. The eighth article of chapter two states that it was God's purpose to extend the benefits of Christ's death only to the elect by bestowing on them the faith that was purchased for them by Christ. The last article (9) states the firmness of this purpose. Then follows the rejection of errors.

---

67 This does not mean that the content of the *Canons* was marked by the Genevan delegates, nor that Genevan theology was normative but only that there was a great deal of agreement among the Reformed concerning the content of the doctrine of predestination and that Genevan theology was representative for the mainstream of Reformed theology.

Genevan Theses	**Subject**	Corresponding article
1	Christ is given by the Father for the elect	II, 8, r1
2	Christ had a special intention in dying	II, r2, 3
3	Christ is the foundation of all special blessings for the elect	II, 8, r3, 4
4	Faith is a work of the Spirit, bestowed by Christ himself	II, 8, r3
5	Faith is a condition of the new covenant, but also an effect of being engrafted in Christ	II, 5, 8, r3
6	Universal verses in Scripture do not prove universal salvation	II, 5
7	Proper use of the distinction between obtaining and appropriation	II, r6
8	Bad use of this distinction	II, r6

Table 4: The Canons *on the atonement compared with the Genevan theses.*

A comparison of the second chapter of the *Canons* with the theses of the Genevan delegates shows again that the content of all the theses of the Genevans return in the *Canons*, as is clear from Table 4. McComish points to the fact that at least two important themes mentioned in the *Canons* cannot be found in the Genevan theses: the all-sufficiency of Christ's death and Anselmian language concerning the necessity of the atonement.[68] Yet there is no reason to suppose that they were opposed to the latter doctrine. The necessity of the atonement was not questioned by the Remonstrants and hence not addressed by the Genevan delegates.

McComish has a point in addressing the all-sufficiency of Christ's sacrifice. The Genevans did not mention this at all, even though the second Remonstrant article gave them occasion to do so. Since the article in the *Canons* on all-sufficiency is in agreement with how Beza understood it, however, it is plausible that his students and successors agreed with this article. This is all the more likely since the sufficiency of Christ's death for the whole world was not stated in the *Canons* in the classic sense that Christ had sufficiently died *for* the whole world, but in the sense that Christ's death was "abundantly sufficient to expiate the sins of the whole

---

68 McComish, *Epigones* 104-05.

world."⁶⁹ The difference is small but important, for the word "for" *(pro)* is omitted, and it was this very word that made Beza criticize the classic formula. The difference is that the *Canons* did not state that Christ died for the whole world, including the reprobate, as did the classic formula.

Beza's criticism of the classic formula was as such not adopted by the majority of the synod. Many delegates used this phrase since they considered it orthodox. Yet the final version of the *Canons* adapted the formula, most likely to make it acceptable to those who agreed with Beza. It is not certain what role Diodati and Tronchin played in this process, if at all, but, given that Diodati was a member of the committee that was to prepare the conclusion of the synod concerning all the articles of the Remonstrants, this is a plausible hypothesis.

4.10 Predestination and the External Call in the *Canons*

The Genevan delegates did not say much on predestination and preaching. But the *Canons* made some remarks, and given that the *Canons of Dort* were accepted in Geneva, they are important for this study. In the order of subjects, the preaching of the Gospel preceded the doctrine of election in the first chapter (I, 3-4; I, 6-11). The doctrine of election should be preached discretely and without curiosity (I, 14). In the second chapter, the all-sufficiency of Christ's death and the universal preaching of the Gospel preceded the particular application of Christ's death in the order of subjects (II, 2-4; II, 5; II, 8). The *Canons* made a short but important statement on the content and extent of the Gospel in II, 5, viz.

> the promise of the gospel is, that whosoever believeth in Christ crucified shall not perish, but have everlasting life. This promise, together with the command to repent and believe, ought to be declared and published to all nations, and to all persons promiscuously and without distinction, to whom God out of his good pleasure sends the gospel.⁷⁰

---

69 Schaff, *Creeds of Christendom* III, 561, 586: "abunde sufficiens ad totius mundi peccata expianda."
70 Schaff, *Creeds of Christendom* III, 561, 586: "Caeterum promissio Evangelii est, ut quisquis credit in Christum crucifixum, non pereat, sed habeat vitam æternam. Quæ promissio omnibus populis et hominibus, ad quos Deus pro suo beneplacito mittit Evangelium, promiscue et indiscriminatim annunciari et proponi debet cum resipiscentiæ et fidei mandato." An earlier version had "under condition of faith and repentance" (sub conditione fidei et resipiscentiæ). Fornerod suggests that the modification of this article was due to British influence but it is not clear why *sub conditione* was changed in *cum mandato,* since both terms can be interpret as having the same as well as as having a different meaning. The matter of concern for the British as well as

This canon states that, notwithstanding the doctrine of predestination and of the particular application of Christ's death to the elect alone, the Gospel should be preached to all nations and persons without distinction. In the first sentence, for instance, the conditional structure used by Calvin can be seen. The promise of the Gospel is neither that all people will have everlasting life, nor that all the elect will have it, nor that all who hear the Gospel will have it. The promise is that only those who believe in Christ will have everlasting life. This promise should be preached together with the command to believe. This was how both Calvin and the Synod of Dort could maintain the doctrine of particular election as well as a preaching of the Gospel to all indiscriminately.

4.11 Conclusions

Most elements of Beza's teaching on predestination were incorporated into the *Canons*. This does not mean that this was due to Beza's influence through his students and successors, for most elements of Beza's doctrine were not uniquely Bezan but were generally accepted among Reformed theologians. With respect to election as the source of all grace and of salvation, there is no difference between the two delegates at Dort and their predecessors in Geneva. Nor do they differ from the *Canons*. Unchanged components are election on the basis of free grace, directed to and not based upon faith and good works, and *praedestinatio gemina* or adhering to election and reprobation as two sides of the decree of predestination (4.3, 4.8).

One specific distinction in Beza's doctrine was not used by Diodati and Tronchin. They did not mention his distinction between the purpose to elect or reprobate on the one hand and election and reprobation itself on the other. They seem to have applied Beza's theses on election and reprobation to the eternal decree of predestination. This is the most important shift between Beza and his successors concerning predestination, and there is no trace of Beza's distinction in the *Canons* either. Related to this shift is the move from the Beza's supralapsarianism to the infralapsarianism of Diodati and Tronchin. Beza was supralapsarian concerning the decree to elect and to reprobate and rejected infralapsarism as false with respect to God's purpose. Yet he used infralapsarian terminology when speaking about election and reprobation itself, i.e., election and reprobation in time. At Dort, his pupils only used the latter terminology and applied that to the eternal decree. Diodati showed himself clearly to be an infralapsarian in his

---

for the Bremen delegation seems not to have been the question whether or not faith and repentance were conditions, but the necessity to preach the gospel to all men. Fornerod, "Introduction", lvii, *Registres* 342 n. 779.

Annotations and was even opposed to supralapsarianism; Tronchin declared himself to be an infralapsarian years after the synod. Although this change from supra- to infralapsarianism did probably not attract much attention in Geneva, it is nevertheless an example of discontinuity in Genevan theology (4.3, 4.6, 4.7).

Concerning the extent of the atonement, Diodati and Tronchin followed Beza and maintained that Christ died with the intention to save only the elect. The *Canons* did not use the precise classic formula concerning the extent of the atonement either, avoiding the suggestion that it was the intention of God or Christ to save all people, despite the fact that many delegates had no objection to the classic formula nor questioned its orthodoxy (4.4, 4.9).

In themes related to the doctrine of predestination, Genevan theology was representative for Reformed thought at the time of the Synod of Dort. There was less unanimity among the Reformed on the doctrine of the atonement. The synod found a formula that was acceptable to all. It seems that Beza's critique of the classic formula influenced the formulation of the *Canons of Dort*, even though a majority of the synod did not adopt his critique and even though it stressed the all-sufficiency of Christ's sacrifice (4.8, 4.9).

Concerning the preaching of the Gospel promises, little can be concluded, but as far as we know the thinking of Diodati and Tronchin, it seems that they agreed with Calvin on conditionality. This can be derived from their 5th thesis on the second article, as well as from Diodati's discourse on perseverance (4.4).

In short, there was great harmony and continuity between Beza, the Genevan delegates, and the *Canons of Dort* on the question of predestination. There seems to be harmony and continuity between Beza and his successors on the the extent of the atonement as well, but on this subject there was less harmony with – let alone influence on – many other Reformed theologians. While Beza rejected the phrase that Christ died for the whole world and while Diodati and Tronchin did not use it, many other delegations saw it as orthodox (4.9). However, this difference is not as great as it seems since all delegations agreed with Beza that Christ's sacrifice was intended for the elect, and the *Canons* adapted the classic formula in a way acceptable to those who agreed with Beza. The agreement is greater than the difference. Geneva's position was not an extreme one against the background of early 17th-century Reformed theology. Rather, it took a middle position between strict supralapsarians like Gomarus and Piscator on the one hand and the forerunners of hypothetical universalism like the theologians from Bremen and Britain on the other.

5. High Orthodoxy - Francis Turretin

5.1 Turretin and the Question of Predestination and Preaching
5.1.1 Historical Developments: Saumur

The *Canons of Dort* were accepted by churches all over Europe as being orthodox, even when they were not given any confessional status. They were adopted in 1623 by the French Reformed churches. Eleven years later, however, a conflict on predestination broke out in these churches.[1] Moyse Amyraut, professor at Saumur, published a treatise on predestination.[2] In a nutshell, Amyraut taught that, in sending his Son to earth, God intended salvation for all, on condition of faith.[3] This construction made his universalism hypothetical, for salvation would only be universal on the hypothesis of universal faith. As argued in earlier chapters, the Genevan Reformed used the concept of conditionality to solve the problem of particular election and reprobation, and the free offer of the Gospel. But Amyraut made conditionality a part of God's decree. This sounded like the Arminian view that Christ died for all and every person, with the difference that only the believers enjoyed the fruit of his death.

Amyraut was not an Arminian. He taught that human beings were so corrupt that no one would accept the offer of Christ's grace. God foresaw that nobody would believe in his Son and hence that nobody would be saved. His first (general) decree, to give Christ for the salvation of all people on condition of faith, would hence fail. Therefore, he said, God made a second (particular) decree, viz., to give some people faith, while passing over others.[4]

This second decree accords with the traditional Reformed view of predestination. In Amyraut's theology, this doctrine was neither supra- nor infralapsarian with respect to order but was placed after redemption by

---

[1] For developments among the Reformed in France, see Tobias Sarx, "Reformed Protestantism in France," in Selderhuis, *Companion*, 227-250.

[2] Moyse Amyraut, *Brief traité de la predestination et de ses principales dependances* (Saumur: Lesnier & Desbordes, 1634). There is an unpublished English translation by Richard Lum: *Brief Treatise on Predestination and its Dependent Principles* (n.p. [Dallas?], 1985).

[3] Amyraut, *Brief Treatise*, 35, 36, 38, 41, 42. Amyraut himself pointed to Calvin, but, although Calvin used the classic distinction and maintained that Christ had died sufficiently for all, he did not teach that salvation was intended, much less destined, for all.

[4] Amyraut, *Brief Treatise*, 45-58. Although Amyraut labored to convince others that he was in agreement with Calvin, he was closer to Bullinger on this point.

Christ, hence the name "postredemptionism." But the decree to send Christ for the whole world was also part of predestination. Hence, Amyraut taught two decrees of predestination, while Dort had condemned those who teach more than one kind of predestination to salvation. Amyraut's view gave new impetus to the question whether God intended to save all people by Christ's sacrifice or ordained his Son to the cross without intending to save certain individuals. Both positions had been rejected at Dort.[5]

Moreover, Amyraut thus implicitly denied that the gift of faith was merited by Christ. Christ died with the intention to save all people on condition of faith, and predestination to faith was only decreed when God foresaw that nobody would believe and accept Christ's completed work. Christ was not sent to save all those who were elect. Rather, it was the reverse, according to Amyraut, God elected people in order to save some of those for whom Christ died.

A consequence is that Amyraut taught that God first decreed saving all people but was satisfied later with only a small number of people being saved. Hence, his thoughts on predestination and the atonement had consequences for the doctrine of God, i.e., on the unchangeability of God and his decree.[6]

Whether Amyraut can be included in Reformed orthodoxy has always been subject to dispute. He always viewed himself as Reformed and even as a better student of Calvin than the Dort Reformed. But their opponents viewed him and his students as semi-Arminians.[7]

---

5 See the *Canons of Dort*, Chapter II, rejection of errors 1 and 2.
6 For a survey of the theology of Amyraut and the Amyraldians, see B.G. Armstrong, *Calvinism and the Amyraut heresy. Protestant Scholasticism and Humanism in Seventeenth-Century France* (Madison, WI, and London: University of Wisconsin Press, 1969).
7 An anonymous person described the theology of Saumur ironically as a formula for a panacea to unite the Reformed and the Arminians:

| *Doctrina absoluta Electionis quantum potest Redemptionis Universalis in toto Foederis gratiae conditionalitatis ana Cum Liberi Arbitrii quantitate tam exigua ne discernetur.* | Take as much as possible from the doctrine of absolute election, everything of universal redemption just as from the conditional covenant of grace, and so much from free choice that it will not be discerned. |

(Quoted in Alexander Comrie and Nicolaus Holtius, *Examen van het ontwerp van tolerantie ...*, Tweede samenspraak (Amsterdam: Nicolaas Byl, 1753), 114 (Reprint in two volumes, Houten: Den Hertog, 1993).)

The disputes among the Huguenots spread to other European churches, especially to The Netherlands but also to Switzerland, and Geneva in particular.[8] The *venerable compagnie* of Geneva wrote a letter to the French churches in 1637 expressing their concern about new teachings in France.[9] It seemed best to keep silent on these points, but if this was not an option, then people should adhere to the confessions and to the conclusions of Dort.[10] Between 1646 and 1649, the churches of several Swiss cities, as well as Geneva, sent three letters showing increasing concern to the consistory of Paris, stating that Amyraut should not be allowed to speak on the issue and that the theology of Saumur should not be tolerated.[11] In the meantime, individual Genevan theologians corresponded with French and Dutch theologians on Amyraut's theology and the events in France. Geneva was clearly interested in what happened in the French churches and distanced itself from the teachings of Saumur.[12] It was primarily Francis Turretin in Geneva who opposed the ideas of Amyraut from the moment of his appointment as professor of theology.

5.1.3 Turretin's Life and Works
Francis Turretin (original: François Turrettini; Latin: Franciscus Turrettinus) was the son of the Genevan preacher and professor Benedict Turretin (1588-1631).[13] He was born on October 17, 1623 in Geneva, where he

---

8   For the historical development of these disputes, see F.P. van Stam, *The Controversy over the Theology of Saumur, 1635-1650: Disrupting Debates among the Huguenots in Complicated Circumstances* (Amsterdam/Maarssen: APA-Holland University Press, 1988).
9   Although often used to denote the same set of views, "Amyraldism" and the "theology of Saumur" are not identical. The former refers to the views of Amyraut concerning predestination and atonement. The latter refers to both these views as well as those of two other Salmurian professors, Louis Cappel (1585-1658) and Josué de la Place (?-1655). Cappel taught that the Hebrew vowel points were not original to the text. De la Place taught the mediate imputation of Adam's transgression. The aversion against each of these three views mutually intensified each other. All three were condemned in the *Formula Consensus Helveticarum Ecclesiarum*.
10 Van Stam, *Controversy*, 102-03.
11 Van Stam, *Controversy*, 291-328.
12 A striking fact is that F. Spanheim, a fanatic opponent of Amyraut during his period in Leiden, edited the complete works of Cameron, the Saumur professor from whom Amyraut seems to have derived his views, when Spanheim was in Geneva before. See Van Stam, *Controversy*, 165-66.
13 Benedict Turretin or Benoit Turrettini was a descendant of a silk-producing family from Lucca, Italy. His father had fled the country because of the persecution of Protestants. The family eventually settled in Geneva where Benedict began studying theology in 1602. He was ordained as the pastor of the Italian congregation at Geneva in

was educated and began his theological studies under John Diodati, Theodore Tronchin, and Friedrich Spanheim. After finishing the Genevan curriculum in 1644, he studied at several European universities, viz. Leiden (again under Spanheim, Amyraut's opponent in Leiden) and Utrecht in The Netherlands, and in Paris, Saumur (under Amyraut), Montauban, and Nimes in France. In 1648, he returned to Geneva and became the pastor of the Italian congregation. For a short time, he served the Reformed church Lyon (France) as pastor before being appointed professor of theology at the Academy of Geneva in 1653. In 1675, he was one of the co-authors of the *Formula Consensus,* a document intended to prevent the influence of Salmurian theology in Switzerland and Geneva. Turretin was sent several times by the city of Geneva with a special mission. An attempt to appoint him to a Dutch university failed, and he remained a professor in Geneva for the rest of his life. He died on September 28, 1687.[14]

Turretin's most important work is his *Institutio Theologiae Elencticae.*[15] Although Turretin confined himself to controversial points in this work, it covers so many themes that it is almost a complete systematic theology. Nevertheless, the elenctic character can give the impression that he stressed the controversial issues more than the less disputed ones. Anyone studying Turretin's *Institutes* should be aware that the goal of elenctic theology is to defend some points of doctrine against adversaries and not to give a complete systematic theology – even if Turretin's *Institutes* cover

---

1611 and in the same year was appointed professor at the Academy. Benedict was a respected professor: from 1620 to 1625 he was rector of the Academy and represented both the Genevan church and the Genevan state on different occasions, traveling internationally in these years, notwithstanding the fact that it was not until 1627 that he was given the rights of a Genevan citizen. For him, see William A. McComish, *The Epigones: A Study of the Theology of the Genevan Academy at the Time of the Synod of Dort, with Special Reference to Giovani Diodati* (Allinson Park, PA: Pickwick Publications, 1989).

14 For a survey of Turretin's life, completed with biographical information, see Erich Wenneker "TURRETTINI, François" in *Biographish-Bibliographisches Kirchenlexicon,* Band XII (Herzberg 1997), 735-38. James T. Dennison Jr. added an article on "The Life and Career of Francis Turretin" to his edition of the translation of Turretin's *Institutes,* III, 639-58. For a complete biography, see Eugène de Budé, *Vie de François Turrettini, théologien Genevois (1623-1687)* (Lausanne, 1871) and Gerrit Keizer, "François Turrettini: Sa vie et ses œuvres et le consensus" (Diss. Lausanne, 1900).

15 *Institutio Theologiae Elencticae, in qua status controversiae perspicue exponitur, praecipua orthodoxorum argumenta proponuntur et vindicantur et fontes solutionem aperiuntur* (Geneva, 1679-1685).

almost all themes of Reformed theology.[16] Some other disputations by Turretin, on the satisfaction of Christ and concerning the necessity of seceding from the Roman Catholic Church were published separately.[17] Turretin also published two volumes of sermons.[18]

Turretin is a good example of a theologian of the era of High Orthodoxy. His system is detailed and has a very high theological and technical level. He combined great clarity and resolution with a courtesy that was remarkable for that time. His influence has been great: his *Institutio* was used directly and indirectly. Benedict Pictet's (1655-1724) work in systematic theology depends greatly on Turretin's work. The Dutch theologian Leonard Ryssen (ca. 1636-1700) made a summary of Turretin's work, which was used in Scotland.[19] In the 19th century, the Scottish theologian William Cunningham (1805-1861) republished the *Institutio*, while in the United States Charles Hodge (1797-1878) used it when writing his own *Systematic Theology*. Hodge also persuaded G.M. Giger (1822-1865) to translate it into English, which translation was published at the end of the 20th century.[20]

---

16 J. Mark Beach, *Christ and the Covenant: Francis Turretin's Federal Theology as a Defense of the Doctrine of Grace* (Göttingen: Vandenhoeck & Ruprecht, 2007), 213-14. Beach's distinction between Turretin's explaining the doctrine of the covenant and defending it is inadequate. The *Institutes* are completely elenctic. In the topics on the covenant, only the discourse on the meaning of related biblical words (XII, 1) is an exception, necessary for the right understanding of his defense of what Turretin thought to be the Reformed doctrine of the covenant.

17 *De satisfactione Christi Disputationes cum indicibus necessariis*, Geneva, 1667 (Keizer and Worldcat.org have 1666 as year; yet the title page of my copy has 1667, without indicating that it is a second printing); *De necessaria secessione nostra ab ecclesia Romana, et impossibili cum ea syncretismo disputationes*, 1687 [1691]. Both series were published in one volume in Leiden and Utrecht in 1696. The disputations on Christ's satisfaction did not touch upon the Amyraldian question of the extent of the atonement but are dedicated to the necessity, truth, and perfection of Christ's satisfaction. The first two doctrines were denied by the Socinians, the latter according to Turretin by the Catholics.

18 Francois Turretin, *Sermons sur divers passages de l'ecriteure sainte* (Geneva: Samuel de Tournes, 1676). Idem, *Recueil de sermons sur divers passages de l'ecriteure sainte* (Geneva: Samuel de Tournes, 1686).

19 Ryssen's work was the doctrinal manual during the study of Thomas Boston (1676-1732) under George Campbell (?-1701) at Edinburgh. Thomas Boston, *Memoirs* (Edinburgh and London: Oliphant, Anderson & Ferrier, 1899; Reprint Edinburgh: Banner of Truth, 1938), 21.

20 Francis Turretin, *Institutes of Elenctic Theology*, transl. G.M. Giger, ed. J.T. Dennison Jr. (Phillipsburg, NJ: P&R Publishing, 1992-1997).

5.1.3 Turretin against Saumur

Although Turretin lived in turbulent times with respect to philosophical and political developments, his main concern was to oppose the theology of Saumur on predestination and related subjects.[21] Among other places, Turretin also studied at the seminary of Saumur, where Amyraut was his teacher. Nevertheless, he opposed Amyraldism as soon as he was in the position to do so. Just one year after being appointed pastor at Geneva in 1648, he successfully insisted on pastors and candidates subscribing to some anti-Saumur theses.[22] Turretin denied Amyraut's assertion that the difference was only a matter of method.[23]

Despite Geneva's disapproval of Amyraut's convictions, he did have sympathizers in that city. In 1649, Alexander Morus (1616-1670), professor of theology at the Genevan Academy, was accused of unorthodox teachings that resembled those of Saumur. The consistory drew up some theses he refused to sign, and he was thus forced to leave Geneva.[24] Geneva seemed to have resisted the Salmurian ideas, but the conflict burst out again twenty years later in 1669, when Turretin insisted that the French student Charles Maurice subscribe to the theses of 1649. Philippe Mestrezat (Alexander Morus' successor) and Louis Tronchin (son of Theodore Tronchin, the delegate to Dort and Turretin's mentor) opposed this.[25] Turretin prevailed, but everyone now knew that the professors of

---

21 Important developments during his life were the rise of Cartesian philosophy (which even affected theology) and the revocation of the Edict of Nantes by Louis XIV in 1685. It is remarkable that the elenctic theologian Turretin did not oppose Cartesianism, although his opponent Chouet taught Cartesian philosophy at the Genevan academy. Dennison states that according to Turretin, orthodoxy could 'sanctify' cartesianism, James T. Dennison, Jr., "The Twilight of Scholasticism: Francis Turretin at the Dawn of the Enlightenment," in Carl R. Trueman and R. Scott Clark, *Protestant Scholasticism. Essays in Reassessment* (Carlisle, UK: Paternoster Press, 1999), 253. Kaiser wrote that Turretin even took a positive interest in Descartes's natural philosophy and only objected to the application of his methodical doubt to theological issues, Christopher B. Kaiser, *Creational Theology and the History of Physical Science. The Creationist Tradition from Basil to Bohr* (Leiden: Brill, 1997), 220. See also Michael J. Heyd, "Orthodoxy, Non-Conformity and Modern Science", in M. Yardeni (ed.), *Modernité et non-conformisme en France à travers les ages* (Leiden: Brill, 1983), 104.
22 See Timothy R. Philips, "The Dissolution of Francis Turretin's Vision of *Theologia*: Geneva at the End of the Seventeenth Century," in Roney and Klauber, *The Identity of Geneva*, 78.
23 Turretin, *Institutio*, IV, 17, xi.
24 For Morus, see "More, Alexander" in William B. Hunter (ed.), *A Milton Encyclopedia*, vol. V (Bucknell: BUP, 1979), 153. Morus was also charged with immorality.
25 Philippe Mestrezat (1618-1690) was a nephew of Jean Mestrezat, pastor at Charenton in France, who sympathized with Saumur. For him, see Marco Jorio (ed.), *Historisches*

theology were divided. Tronchin's faction prevailed in exempting philosopher Jean-Robert Chouet from signing the theses.[26]

The majority of the Swiss and Genevan theologians feared the influence of Saumur so much they decided to draw up a new formula of orthodoxy: the *Formula Consensus Ecclesiarum Helveticarum Reformatarum*.[27] It was written by Johann Heinrich Heidegger (1633-1698) of Zurich, assisted by Lucas Gernler (1625-1675) of Basel and Francis Turretin of Geneva.[28] Written in 1675, it took three years for it to be adopted in Geneva; a sign that its adoption was not a formality. Its influence in Geneva was restricted by the many French refugees arriving there after the revocation of the Edict of Nantes in 1685. No French synod ever repudiated the theology of Saumur, so many of these refugees adhered to it or at least tolerated it.

The views of Amyraut and the *Formula Consensus Ecclesiarum Helveticarum* dealt with, among other things, the themes of predestination, the extent of the atonement, the natural and moral inability of humans to believe, and the doctrine of the covenant. These themes proved to be important for the discussion of predestination and preaching in the preceding chapters. Even more important, Turretin devoted several topics in his *Institutes* to subjects related to predestination and to preaching, even one to the question whether the reprobate are called with God intending to save them. This makes him a good subject for investigating the relation between predestination and the external call in Genevan theology during the period of high Reformed orthodoxy.

Lexikon der Schweiz (Basel: Schwabe, 2002-2014) http://www.hls-dhs-dss.ch/textes/d/D26062.php.

Louis Tronchin (1629-1705) studied in Geneva and Saumur and became professor of theology in 1661. He preferred Cartesianism to Reformed scholasticism. For him, see *Historisches Lexikon der Schweiz*, http://www.hls-dhs-dss.ch/textes/d/D11339.php.

26 Chouet was a nephew of Louis Tronchin. For him, see Michael Heyd, *Between Orthodoxy and the Enlightenment: Jean-Robert Chouet and the Introduction of Cartesian Science in the Academy of Geneva* (The Hague: Martinus Nijhof, 1982).

27 *Formula Consensus Ecclesiarum Helveticarum Reformatarum circa Doctrinam de Gratia Universali & Connexa, aliáque nonnulla capita* (n.p., n.d.). Cited as *Formula*.

28 For the history of the *Formula*, see P. Schaff, *Creeds of Christendom*, I (1877, reprint Grand Rapids: Baker, 1977), 477-489, available online at http://www.ccel.org/ccel/schaff/creeds1.ix.ii.xi.html, Martin I. Klauber, "The Helvetic Formula Consensus (1675): An Introduction and Translation," in *Trinity Journal 11:1* (Spring 1990), 103-23 or Keizer, *François Turrettini*, 96-123.

For Heidegger, see *Historisches Lexikon der Schweiz*, http://www.hls-dhs-dss.ch/textes/d/D10459.php. For Gernler see *Historisches Lexikon der Schweiz*, http://www.hls-dhs-dss.ch/textes/d/D10631.php .

5.2 Earlier Research

J. Mark Beach gives a complete survey of literature on Turretin.[29] This section mentions only publications that are relevant to the theme of this study. Two biographies of Turretin were written at the end of the 19th century by Eugene de Budé and Gerrit Keizer: both are still good sources of biographical information.[30] Half a century passed before a new work on Turretin was finished: John. W. Beardslee III's dissertation on Francis and Jean-Alphonse Turretin.[31] Another dissertation was finished in 1988 in which Paul T. Jensen compares Calvin's and Turretin's soteriologies.[32] He concluded that there was great continuity between Calvin and Turretin and that, although Turretin said much that Calvin had not, he said nothing that Calvin would not have agreed with, and that Turretin represented Calvin's doctrine of election "in every essential."[33]

The number of publications on Turretin increased after the edition of the first volume of the English translation of his *Institutio* in 1992 by James T. Dennison Jr.[34] Joel R. Beeke examined Turretin's doctrine of predestination in an article in which he remarked that Turretin was the first infralapsarian at the Genevan Academy.[35] Dennison wrote about Turretin's position in 17th-century Geneva.[36]

J. Mark Beach's dissertation on Turretin's federal theology was published in 2007.[37] Over against modern interpretations, Beach denied that the covenant was "swallowed up" by the doctrine of election in Turretin's theology. According to Beach, Turretin hardly mentions the doctrine of predestination in expounding the doctrine of the covenant. When predestination is mentioned, it is in connection with "the scope of divine grace, not its character." He argues that reprobates can be members of the covenant, though in a different way than the elect.[38] According to Beach,

---

29 Beach, *Christ and the Covenant*, 67-73.
30 De Budé, *Vie de François Turrettini*; Keizer, "François Turretini."
31 John W. Beardslee III, "Theological Development at Geneva under Francis and Jean-Alphonse Turretin (1648-1737)." (Ph.D. diss. Yale University, 1956). According to Beach (*Christ and the Covenant*, 68), this dissertation was "mired in numerous discredited assumptions regarding Protestant scholasticism, besides being infected with a polemic against the Princeton theology."
32 Paul Timothy Jensen, "Calvin and Turretin: A Comparison of their Soteriologies," (Ph.D. diss. University of Virginia, 1988).
33 Jensen, "Calvin and Turretin," 74, 104.
34 Turretin, *Institutes of Elenctic Theology*.
35 Beeke, "The Order," 57-75.
36 Dennison, "The Twilight of Scholasticism," 244-55.
37 See 5.1.3 note 16.
38 Beach, *Christ and the Covenant*, 213-14.

Turretin says it "is to be taken for granted … that God entered into a covenant relation with a class of persons from whom he demands a fulfillment of the covenant's conditions but unto whom he does not confer the fulfillment of those conditions in and for them."[39] His general conclusions concerning predestination are that Turretin's federal theology integrates and includes the doctrine of election without compromising the covenant scheme. In Christ, election and covenant intertwine and interpenetrate, but predestination is not the controlling idea nor a "central dogma." Regarding the continuity between Calvin and Turretin he argues that Turretin's federal theology shows continuity with Calvin regarding the doctrine of grace.[40]

Turretin's doctrine of predestination was treated only by Jensen and Beeke,[41] his doctrine of the covenant only by Beach, and that of the atonement only by Jensen. These themes were never investigated in their mutual relation. Nor has any attention been paid to his sermons. This chapter is intended to fill these gaps.

5.3 Predestination

Turretin included the doctrine of election among the fundamental articles of faith in his topic on theology.[42] He located the doctrine of predestination in the fourth topic of his *Institutes*, the decrees of God,[43] and devoted 18 *quaestiones* to the decree, 13 of which to predestination. Having stated that the decrees belong essentially to God and are hence eternal, the question follows whether or not there are conditional decrees. In opposition to the Socinians, Remonstrants, and Jesuits, Turretin denied.[44] He did not deny that there are decrees that have a condition attached to them, but in that case "condition" is a less proper word for "means." Such means are a condition for the execution of the decree but not for the decree itself. There are no decrees in God that depend upon something

---

39 Beach, *Christ and the Covenant*, 232.
40 Beach, *Christ and the Covenant*, 330-37.
41 Jensen, "Calvin and Turretin," 62-104, Beeke, "The Order," 65-67. Due to Turretin's great clarity, it is hard to misinterpret him. Beeke and Jensen have both given a good survey of his thinking on predestination, the former briefly, the latter at length.
42 Turretin, *Institutio*, I, 14, xx. Turretin mentions election, not predestination.
43 The first three topics were: Theology, Scripture, and the Trinity. The *Formula* does not contain any separate canon for the decrees in general.
44 Turretin, *Institutio*, IV, 1-3. Turretin did not mention Saumur here. An application of Turretin's remark concerning the unconditionality of God's decrees in general to the decree of election as a conditional will to pity the whole human race is given in IV, 17.

outside of him. One of Turretin's arguments here is the immutability of God and his decree.⁴⁵

Turretin affirmed that God's decree necessitates future things but denies that God's decree is the cause of all things. He made several distinctions with respect to necessity. The word "necessity" means "that which cannot be otherwise." Things cannot be otherwise either absolutely *(absoluta)*, or necessary in themselves, like God's incorruptibility, or hypothetically necessary on the hypothesis from God's decree *(hypothetica ex hypothesi decreti divini)*, being dependent on God's will, like the existence of the earth. This hypothetical necessity is again divided into three kinds. 1. First is physical or internal necessity, like burning is necessary for fire. This physical necessity is hypothetical since it depends on God's decree, but God has decreed that fire cannot act otherwise than as burning. 2. Second is the necessity of coercion, when something external acts with violence. 3. Third is the hypothesis of the event or of dependence *(hypothetica eventus seu dependentiae)*, by which a thing, although mutable and contingent by nature, cannot but be, according to God's ordination of things. For instance, to die is contingent but becomes necessary once the heart is wounded.⁴⁶

The necessity of events because of God's decree is of this third kind. It is a hypothetical necessity or a necessity of the consequence *(necessitas consequentiae)*. It is neither an absolute necessity nor a physical necessity (at least not in all cases), nor a necessity of coercion, for God decreed future things to take place in accordance with their own nature. Free agents act freely. Hence, Adam sinned necessarily with respect to God's decree but freely with respect to his own will. God's decree and human freedom and responsibility are not opposed to each other but cooperate. God is not the author of sin, for, although sin necessarily follows the decree, it does not flow from the decree. In other words, it is a consequence of the decree but not an effect of the decree. The difference is that a consequence (necessarily or not) follows the antecedent without being caused by it, while an effect always is caused by the antecedent.⁴⁷ Concerning the nature of God's decrees (and hence of the decree of predestination), their unconditionality and their relation to human responsibility,

---

45 Turretin, *Institutio*, IV, 3, ii-iii, ix; IV, 12. In thesis IV, 3, vii.
46 For these and more distinctions used by Turretin to comment on free will in his *Institutio*, X see: W.J. van Asselt e.a. (eds.), *Reformed Thought on Freedom. The Concept of Free Choice in Early Modern Reformed Theology* (Grand Rapids: Baker Academic, 2010), 171-200.
47 Turretin, *Institutio*, IV, 4, IV, 14, xxvii, IV, 16, v.

Turretin agrees with Beza, although he is more detailed and technical than Beza.

In his *Institutes* (1679), Turretin does not provide any concise definition of predestination but does so in his sermon on the call and election (1676). In this sermon, he defines election as the

> decree of God, completely wise, completely free, completely merciful, by which he, foreseeing in the light of his eternal prescience, all people being fallen in Adam, and culpable of curse and death, resolved merely from his good pleasure and only for his mercifulness, to choose a certain number out of the corrupted mass, neither better, nor more excellent as the others, to save them by Jesus Christ and to make them forever blessed in him.[48]

The *Formula Consensus* (1675) to which Turretin contributed, states:

> Canon IV: Before the creation of the world, God decreed in Christ Jesus our Lord according to his eternal purpose (Eph 3:11), in which, from the mere good pleasure of his own will, without any prevision of the merit of works or of faith, to the praise of his glorious grace, to elect some out of the human race lying in the same mass of corruption and of common blood, and, therefore, corrupted by sin. He elected a certain and definite number to be led, in time, unto salvation in Christ, their Guarantor and sole Mediator. And on account of his merit, by the mighty power of the regenerating Holy Spirit, he decreed these elect to be effectually called, regenerated and gifted with faith and repentance. So, indeed, God, determining to illustrate his glory, decreed to create man perfect, in the first place, then permit him to fall, and finally pity some of the fallen, and therefore elect those, but leave the rest in the corrupt mass, and finally give them over to eternal destruction.[49]

---

48 François Turrettini, *Sermons sur divers passages de L'Ecriture Sainte* (Geneva: Samuel de Tournes, 1676), 448 (henceforth quoted as *Sermons*): "Decret de Dieu, tout sage, tout libre, & tout misericordieux, par lequel prevoyant dans la lumiere de sa prescience éternelle, tous les homes tombez en Adam, & coûpables de la malediction, & de la mort; Il a resolu de son pur bon plaisir, & de sa seule misericorde, d'en choisir un certain nombre de cette masse corrumpuë, qui n'étoyent ny meilleurs, ny plus excellents, que les autres pour les sauver par Iesus Christ, & pour les render éternellement bienheureux en luy.'

49 *Formula*, IV. The translation of the *Formula* is taken from Klauber, "The Helvetic Formula Consensus," 103-23. The original *Formula* was published in both Latin and German. Only the Latin text will be quoted in the footnotes.
IV: "Deus ante jacta mundi fundamenta in Christo Jesu, Domino nostro fecit πρόθεσιν αἰώνιον *propositum seculorum,* in quo ex mero voluntatis suae beneplacito, sine ulla meriti operum vel fidei praevisione, ad laudem gloriosae gratiae suae elegit certum

These definitions remind of those formulated by the Genevan delegates to the Synod of Dort and the *Canons* of that synod in their infralapsarianism and deviation from Beza's supralapsarianism.[50] In accordance with Calvin and Beza, these definitions excluded all human merit or properties as causes of predestination. Over against the teachings of Amyraut, the *Formula* described Christ as the Guarantor *(Sponsor)* of election, instead of taking the view that election guarantees that the merit of Christ for all is accepted by some. The next canon stated explicitly that the sacrifice of Christ "was to proceed from the zealous love of God the Father toward the world of the elect."[51]

Although Turretin offers no concise definition in his *Institutes*, he does treat the doctrine of predestination in detail. He describes the meaning of several Greek words relating to or denoting predestination, just as Beza had done.[52] "To predestinate" was defined by Turretin as

> to determine something concerning things before they take place and to direct them to a certain end.[53]

Turretin presents three ways in which the word "predestination" can be understood: 1. as synonymous with "providence"; 2. as God's counsel concerning fallen people to be saved or damned; 3. as referring to election alone or as the predestination of the saints. Turretin took the word in

---

ac definitum hominum in eadem corruptionis massa, & communi sanguine jacentium, adeóque peccato corruptorum numerum, in tempore per Christum Sponsorem & Mediatorem unicum ad salutem perducendum, ejusdémque merito, Spiritus S. regenerantis potentissima virtute, efficaciter vocandum, regenerandum, & fide ac resipiscentia donandum. Atque ita quidem Deus gloriam suam illustrare constituit, ut decreverit, primo quidem hominem integrum creare, tum ejusdem lapsum permittere, ac demum ex lapsis quorundam misereri, adeóque eosdem eligere, alios vero in corrupta massa relinquere, aeternoque tandem exitio devovere."

50 Cf. *Canons of Dort*, I, 7. Turretin shows his infralapsarianism at several other points in his sermons. For instance, *Sermons*, 27.
51 *Formula*, V.
52 In denoting the relational order of the words, he even presents almost the same order as Beza does.

Turretin's order (IV, 7, xiii)	Beza's order (*De Praedestinationis*, 1-2)
prothesis or *eudokia*	*prothesis*
prognosis or *ekloge*	*prognosis*
proorismos	*proorismos*
	electio et reprobatio

53 Turretin, *Institutio*, IV, 7, ii: "Praedestinare ... est de rebus antequam fiant aliquid definire, easque ad certum finem dirigere."

the second sense: predestination embraces both election and reprobation. Indeed, election of some implies the rejection of others.[54]

The only cause of election is God's good pleasure. Neither Christ and his merits, nor foreseen faith, nor foreseen works are the cause. Christ's merit is the cause of salvation, and faith and sanctification are the means, but all – merit, faith, and sanctification – are effects of election.[55] Nor are sin and unbelief causes of reprobation. To make human acts the cause of election and reprobation would turn predestination into post-destination.[56] Here Turretin agrees with Beza in making Christ as Mediator subject to the decree of election.

Predestination is not only the destination of the end but also that of the means. Although faith and sanctification as means to salvation are effects of election, Turretin rejects the view that sin and unbelief as means to damnation are likewise effects of reprobation. Turretin's infralapsarian concept of the decree of reprobation presupposes sin; hence, it cannot be an effect. Unbelief and hardening in sin follow reprobation and are therefore consequences but not effects. Likewise, the destruction of the sinner follows necessarily on the decree of reprobation but is caused by sin, not by reprobation.[57] Again, Turretin agrees with Beza here. Reprobation consists in two acts: first, the negative act of preterition and desertion, or the choice by God, as supreme Lord, to leave some people in their sin and guilt; second, God's positive act of hardening and damnation by God as supreme Judge.[58]

An original contribution by Turretin to the development of the doctrine of election in Geneva is the way he linked the different Greek words denoting this doctrine to both the Trinity and the order of salvation. The words *protheseos* and *eudokias*, which denote the counsel and good pleasure of God, refer to the first cause and its immutability as well as to the purpose of the decree. This is the Father's role, who from eternity decreed to glorify the elect. The words *prognosis* and *ekloge*, which denote the separation of certain persons from others to be saved, refer to the object of the decree. This is the role of the Son in whom the elect are predestined

---

54 Turretin, *Institutio*, IV, 7, ii-xv. In *Formula*, VI, this is used as an argument against Amyraldism: "[T]he Scriptures do not extend unto all and each God's purpose of showing mercy to men, but restrict it to the elect alone, the reprobate being excluded even by name, as Esau, whom God hated with an eternal hatred (Rom 9:11)."
55 Turretin, *Institutio*, IV, 10 and 11; Turretin attacked Saumur in IV, 11, viii, naming Testard and Cappel.
56 Turretin, *Institutio*, IV, 14; 15; 16, v.
57 Turretin, *Institutio*, IV, 14, xxvii and xxiii; IV, 15, v; IV, 16, v.
58 Turretin, *Institutio*, IV, 7, ii-vii, xi; IV, 14, iv-ix.

and justified. The word *proörismos* refers to the means decreed to bring the elect to glory. This involves the Holy Spirit, who provides the means, like the call and sanctification and makes them efficacious.[59]

Turretin differs from both Calvin and Beza in that he takes what is called an infralapsarian standpoint from the beginning, while Calvin was more ambiguous initially and Beza was a supralapsarian on the decree of election and reprobation. Turretin agrees with the Genevan delegates to Dort but moves beyond them by explicitly rejecting supralapsarianism. Turretin did not think was supralapsarianism was "absolutely repugnant to the foundation of salvation and the analogy of faith," but nonetheless objected to it and was convinced that infralapsarianism was better. One of his arguments is that creation and the Fall cannot be the means for the execution of predestination, which was taught by Beza. Turretin refers to Calvin as holding the same infralapsarian position. Although he provides a quote that seems to imply Calvin's infralapsarianism, this claim is doubtful, for Calvin also stated that some people were created as preordained for damnation.[60] Yet Turretin does not call himself an infralapsarian. He uses his own definition of infralapsarianism to denote the position of those who thought that the object of predestination was not only the human being as fallen but also as redeemed through Christ and as believing or unbelieving. That means that, in Turretin's works, infralapsarianism is synonymous with Arminianism. He describes his own position as a middle ground, seeing fallen humankind as the object of predestination – in other words, what is commonly called infralapsarianism.[61]

Turretin utterly rejects as heretical the view of the semi-Pelagians and the Arminians that the object of predestination was the human being

---

59 Turretin, *Institutio*, IV, 7, xiii-xiv.
60 Turretin, *Institutio*, IV, 9, iv-xxx; IV, 18, iv-v, xxi-xxv. Cf. Calvin, *Institutes* 1559, III, xxi, 5. Cf. 2.4 above. Turretin acknowledges that we can only speak about an order in the decrees with respect to our manner of understanding but not with respect to the decree itself, since that is "a single and most simple act," IV, 18, xxiv.
61 Turretin, *Institutio*, IV, 9, ii; 18. He distinguishes between three positions. The first is that of those who go back beyond the fall *(supra lapsum)*, viewing the object of predestination as neither created nor fallen. The second is that of those who take the starting point of predestination as occurring on this side of the Fall *(infra lapsum)*, viewing the object of the decree as those created, fallen, and redeemed by Christ and as either believing or unbelieving (which is usually called postredemptionism). The third position finds its starting point in the Fall *(in lapsu)*, viewing the object of predestination as both created and fallen. Turretin gives no name to this last position, but it is usually called "infralapsarianism." In IV, 18 he distinguishes between Arminianism and Amyraldism, but in IV, 9, ii he places them both in the second position, which regarded the object of predestination *infra lapsum*.

created, fallen, and redeemed by Christ, either as believer or as unbeliever. Turretin argues that this was in fact Pelagianism. Contra Scriptura, it would make predestination referring to qualities of people instead to an individual human being, and it would exclude the gift of faith from election.[62]

Turretin also rejects a third position, that of "those among the Reformed who hold to universal grace." Without naming them, it is obvious that he is referring to Amyraut and the Amyraldians here. Although he calls them Reformed, he thinks there are sufficient reasons why the Reformed churches cannot accept their teaching, listing five objections to this "method."[63] The first is that their general and their special decrees are contradictory and cannot be reduced to one and the same decree, as is possible with the orders found in supra- and infralapsarianism. In Amyraut's system, God loves all in the general decree but hates some in the special decree. Second, in this system God decrees the means before decreeing the end, or God sends Christ (the means to salvation) without having a certain end (salvation being hypothetical at that moment in the structure of the decree). Third, according to this method, faith is not merited by Christ. Fourth, the call would precede election, whereas Scripture testifies that God ordained the preaching of the Gospel to gather the elect. Fifth, the distinction between God as Lawgiver and God as Father does not apply to election and his sending Christ because these things are part of the evangelical covenant and not to the legal covenant.[64]

According to Turretin, the common view among the Reformed concerning the order of the decrees is that God's first decree has to do with the creation of humankind, and the second with the permission for the Fall to occur.[65] The third concerns the election to salvation of some, leaving others in their corruption. The fourth deals with the sending of Christ as Mediator for the elect, and the fifth with the effectual call by the Gospel and the Spirit. The first decree was about providence and nature, and the last three about redemption and grace. Between the first and the last three is the decree to permit the Fall.[66]

---

62 Turretin, *Institutio*, IV, 9, xxxi; IV, 11; IV, 18, vi-xii.
63 Note that Turretin's use of the word "method" concerns the content, not the form.
64 Turretin, *Institutio*, IV, 18, xii-xx. Cf. *Formula*, VI.
65 Turretin denies that God only permitted the Fall. God is not the cause of sin, but his providence nevertheless governed it in several ways: 1. as prescience, because God foreknew it; 2. as decree, because God decreed that the Fall would happen; 3. actual permission in time.
66 Turretin, *Institutio*, IV, 18, iii, xxi-xxv.

In general, Turretin agrees with Beza in his *De praedestinationis doctrina* and also with Calvin. All held to a *praedestinatio gemina,* the eternity and immutability of the decree and its independence from human acts or worth. All warned that the decree was not to be separated from the means for its execution.[67] Yet some differences should be noted. Whereas Beza held to supralapsarian decrees and infralapsarian acts of election and reprobation, Turretin says that "from what mass in time God calls a man" (which Beza would have called "actual election") "from the same mass he elected him from eternity" (which Beza would have called "the decree to elect") "and the same order we observe in the execution of the decree, should have been before God in the decree itself."[68] For his infralapsarian views, he refers to Calvin, but that reference is doubtful. Turretin was more technical than Calvin and Beza were. He made more use of scholastic distinctions to clarify his positions and to answer objections.[69]

5.4 Predestination and the Extent of the Atonement

Turretin dealt with the question of the extent of the atonement in his topic on the mediatory office of Christ. The 14th question is whether Christ died for each and every person universally or only for the elect. Turretin affirms the latter and denies the former position, which was held, with respective differences, by Pelagians, Jesuits, Lutherans, Arminians, and universalists. With 54 subsections, this is one of the longest answers in his *Institutes.*

The issue is not what the nature and power of Christ's death in itself are but what the Father's purpose was in appointing him to die and Christ's own purpose in submitting. Turretin retained the classic distinction that Christ died "sufficiently for all but efficiently for the elect only" insofar this is understood with respect to the dignity of Christ's death. But it is "less accurate" if used to refer to the will and purpose of Christ and the Father. Turretin modified Beza's criticism here but retains its core since Beza did not deny the sufficiency of the worth of Christ's death but

---

67 Cf. 3.6 and Beza, *De praedestinationis doctrina,* 1-7.
68 Turretin, *Institutio,* IV, 9, xv. "Nam ex qua massa in tempore Deus hominem vocat, ex eadem ab aeterno eum eligit, et qualis observantur in executione decreti, talis debuit Deo obiici in ipso decreto." Nevertheless, Turretin himself distinguishes between (the decree of) reprobation and the act of reprobating in time in IV, 14, i.
69 It is plausible that the elenctic genre of Turretin's work forced him to use these scholastic distinctions. His focus on defending Reformed theology and showing the faults of alternative positions demanded more distinctions than an exposition of Reformed theology for a Reformed public, in which alternative positions did not have to be explained or rejected.

understood the word *pro* to refer to the will and purpose of God. Turretin accepted Beza's doctrine but found a way to retain the classic formula.[70]

Turretin presents several arguments to prove his position that God and Christ intended his death for the elect only. He argues on the basis of Scripture that Christ did not die for all since many texts restrict his death. Other texts, which seem to extend the atonement to all, speak of all classes of individuals, not of all individuals of classes.[71] Another argument is that the death of Christ is restricted to those who were given him by the Father. Christ is given to the same people as were given to him. This gift was unconditional,

> for although faith is proposed as a means and condition necessary to the reception and enjoyment of this benefit, yet it does not follow that it was a condition to the giving of Christ (since it is itself a gift of grace and a fruit of this giving).[72]

Sending Christ to produce faith on the condition of faith would be useless. Christ is given to the elect as a Surety to obtain salvation, but he is also given as Head to apply salvation to them. Christ died for the same people for whom he was raised and for whom intercedes. He did not die for the sins of all people but only died to justify believers and intercedes

---

70 Turretin, *Institutio*, XIV, 14, ix. This was perhaps because at the Synod of Dort (and probably thereafter) the majority of Reformed theologians did not object to this formula, although the same majority agreed that it was Christ's and God's intention to save only the elect. Turretin saw no need to reject the formula as sharply as Beza had done.
71 Turretin, *Institutio*, XIV, 14, xii-xvii.
72 Turretin, *Institutio*, XIV, 14, xix. "Licet enim fides proponatur ut medium & conditio necessaria ad receptionem & usum istius benefici ; Non ideo potest censeri conditio praesupposita dationi Christi; cum ipsa sit donum gratiae & fructus istius dationis. See also *Formula* VI: "Quamobrem neque eorum suffragamur sententiae, qui docent, Deum φιλανθρωπία seu praecipuo quodam generis humani lapsi amore motum Electioni praevio, voluntate quadam conditionata, velleitate, Misericordia prima, uti vocant, desiderio inefficacy omnium & singulorum, conditionatè saltem, si videlicet credant, salute, intendisse: omnibus & singulis lapsis Christum Mediatorem destinasse." (*[W]e can not agree with the opinion of those who teach: 1) that God, moved by philanthropy, or a kind of special love for the fallen (of the) human race, did, in a kind of conditioned willing, first moving of pity, as they call it, or inefficacious desire, determine the salvation of all, conditionally, i.e., if they would believe; 2) that he appointed Christ Mediator for all and each of the fallen.*) (Transl. M. Klauber). Klauber translates "the fallen of the human race," but the Latin *generis humani lapsi* provides no justification for using the words "of the." Though grammatically correct, it is not in line with any theology of that time and deviates from old French, Dutch and German translations of the text.

only for the elect in order to give them faith. Turretin continues to argue this on the basis of the gift of the Spirit, who is given to the same people for the application of salvation as the Son is given to obtain it. Furthermore, Christ did not atone for the sin of unbelief of all people.[73]

Turretin denies that everyone is commanded to believe that Christ died for him. One should believe this only when he believes and repents.[74] In short, Turretin restricts the death of Christ to the elect in the same way Beza and the Genevan delegates to the Synod of Dort had done.

5.5 Predestination and the Covenant

Turretin wrote about the covenant in the twelfth topic of his *Institutes*. He regarded the doctrine of the covenant to be of "the greatest importance" in theology.[75] I will discuss only those parts of his view of the covenant that are important in relation to either predestination or preaching. The covenant involves God's election in choosing people and people choosing God.[76] It is called a covenant because it is an agreement between God and humans, and there are conditions on both sides. It is also called a testament because an inheritance is promised that benefits only the heirs, not the Testator, and because the execution of the conditions on both sides is entrusted only to the Testator. Both relations should be given attention.[77]

To grasp the structure of Turretin's doctrine of the covenant, two distinctions should be considered. The first is the distinction of a twofold pact within the covenant of grace.[78] One pact is between the Father and the Son, another between God and the elect.[79] This implies that there are three instead of two parties in the covenant: God offended but appeased, people having offended but believing by virtue of God's election, and Christ the

---

73 Turretin, *Institutio*, XIV, 14, xviii-xxxv. Cf. *Formula*, XIII, XIV, XVI.
74 Turretin, *Institutio*, XII, 6, xxii. Cf. section 5.10.
75 Turretin, *Institutio*, XII, 1, i.
76 Turretin, *Institutio*, XII, 1, ii.
77 Turretin, *Institutio*, XII, 1, iii, vi, ix.
78 Turretin, *Institutio*, XII, 2, xii: "Et certum est *duplex* hic *pactum* necessariò attendum esse, vel unius ejusdemque pacti duas partes." *(There are not two covenants, but a twofold pact or two parts within the single covenant of grace.)*
79 Beach's remark (*Christ and the Covenant*, 213-14) that Turretin hardly mentions the doctrine of predestination in his exposition of the Gospel covenant except to argue that Christ is the Surety for the elect, is doubtful and at least a matter of interpretation. In Topic XII, predestination or election is mentioned in question 1, section ii, question 2, sections iii, x, xii, xiv. Although a fourfold mention of predestination could be viewed as "hardly," Turretin makes it clear that the covenant is made in Christ with the elect. Nevertheless, Beach's main argument, viz. that the doctrine of predestination does not swallow up the covenant, is true.

Mediator, reconciling the offended God to the offending people. The second distinction is between the internal essence *(essentia interna)* and the external dispensation *(externa dispensatio)* of the covenant.[80]

In the pact between the Father and Son, the Father demands obedience unto death and promises that the Son will be the Head of the elect, his mystical body. He committed the work of salvation to the Son. The Son promised faithful obedience to the Father, became Surety, and demanded the kingdom promised to him. This part of the covenant was from eternity, although it was executed in time, when Christ reconciled God and humans by his incarnation and death, thereby making God their God and them his people.

Since Christ is the Mediator between God and people, he ought to act with both. He acts on behalf of people with God by making satisfaction for their sins, by interceding for them, and in that way by obtaining the Spirit and his gifts for them. He acts on behalf of God with people by declaring God's good will towards them, demanding faith in the promises and obedience to his commands, promising in return all the benefits of the covenant. He sealed this with his blood. Thus, through his death Christ reconciled God to humans and obtained the Spirit to convert and sanctify people and, by converting them, he reconciles people to God. As the Mediator between God and humans, Christ is both the foundation of the covenant and its content.[81]

The *Formula* explicitly states that Christ "was made Guarantor of the New Covenant only for those who, by means of the eternal election, were given to him as his own people, his seed, and inheritance."[82] In his *Institutes*, Turretin hardly speaks of the elect with respect to the pact between Father and Son. Yet there is nothing that contradicts the statement of the *Formula*. The covenant of grace was entered into by God with the elect in Christ after the Fall.[83] Here an important difference with Calvin appears. The latter viewed the covenant as a kind of middle ground between the world and the elect, whereas Turretin restricts the essence of the covenant to the elect alone.

Over against Remonstrants, Lutherans, and Salmurians, Turretin denies that the covenant is universal. According to him, the covenant is as particular as saving grace and is restricted to the elect with respect to its internal essence. In this regard, the covenant corresponds with the internal call and

---

80 Turretin, *Institutio*, XII, 2, ix-xii; 6, v.
81 Turretin, *Institutio*, XII, 2, vii, xiii-xxvi.
82 *Formula*, XIII.
83 Turretin, *Institutio*, XII, 2, ii, x. Cf. *Formula*, XXIII.

the invisible church of the elect. Turretin denies that the covenant was made only with those who had the conditions set before them but not effected in them. They have only the external dispensation, but the elect are partakers of the covenant according to God's intention.[84] One of Turretin's arguments for denying the universality of the covenant is that there is no universal will in God to have mercy on the entire human race but only a particular will to select a certain number. Another argument is Christ's satisfying death as particular. Turretin ties election, the atonement, and the covenant closely together.[85]

In this covenant, God promises to be our God. This involves the blessings of reconciliation and union with God, the communion of goods, conformity to God, in perpetuity. God in turn requires people to be his people. This involves consecration to God, obedience, and the principal duties of faith and repentance. The former embraces the promises; the latter fulfils the command. These duties or conditions of the covenant are also promised gifts of the covenant merited by Christ.[86]

If the word "covenant" is taken in its outward dispensation, it is restricted to the promulgation and presentation of the covenant by the

---

84 I disagree with Beach here. Beach takes Turretin's words in XII, 6, x, "Quia gratis supponitur foedus gratiae cum illis etiam initum esse, à quibus Deus conditionem illi annexam exigere tantùm vult, non verò in illis efficere ..." to mean: "It is to be taken for granted, that God entered into a covenant relationship with a class of persons from whom he demands a fulfillment of the covenant's conditions but unto whom he does not confer the fulfillment of those conditions in and for them." But the words "Quia gratis supponitur" cannot be translated as "It is to be taken for granted," at least not in this context, for four reasons.

First, Turretin is defending the particularity of the covenant, which he argues on the basis of its determination for the elect in thesis vii *(certum numerum eligendi),* on the basis of particular atonement for the elect and the gift of the Spirit to the elect for regeneration and faith in thesis viii (cf. thesis v), and on the basis of the particularity of the promises of the covenant for the elect in thesis ix. Then, in thesis x, he answers an objection to this particularity for the elect. Turretin would have been inconsistent within one thesis if he had affirmed here that the covenant was entered in with more people than the elect.

Second, the word *gratis* is used in a negative way: *gratis supponitur* means that something is presupposed without proof. Turretin means: "It is an unfounded supposition."

Third, Turretin immediately adds in the same sentence, *quod foederis gratiae naturae repugnat,* (which is repugnant to the nature of the covenant of grace), thus rejecting the supposition indicated in the first part of the sentence as repugnant to the nature of the covenant.

Four, Turretin elsewhere uses these words to express his disagreement, for instance to reject a conditional gift of Christ in XIV,14, xix, "Quia gratis supponitur talem dationem esse conditionatam, cum nuspiam Scriptura istius conditionis meminerit."

85 Turretin, *Institutio,* IV, 18, xxiii; XII, 6, v, vii-x, cf. xvi. Cf. *Formula,* XXIII, in which the covenant is likewise restricted to the elect.

86 Turretin, *Institutio,* XII, 2, xvii-xxx.

external call. Turretin admits that the covenant was the property of the people of Israel, if it is restricted to their being called to the covenant of grace. The ministers of the Gospel are ambassadors by whom God invites us to the covenant.[87] Several blessings attend this presentation of the covenant, like the preaching of the Word and the administration of the sacraments. In this sense, it is extended to many reprobates within the visible church and hence can be called "more general" (*generalior*) but still not universal. Over against those who maintained universal grace, Turretin denies that there is a universal call to salvation through the works of nature.[88] He seems to deny here what he has stated elsewhere, viz. that the covenant is made with the elect only, yet it should be noted that he takes the word "covenant" in a different sense here, i.e., its external dispensation. Although Turretin does not deny that the word "covenant" can be taken in this sense, his theses on the extent of the covenant of grace suggest that he prefers to use the word to denote the internal essence. The difference between the external dispensation and the internal essence of the covenant is that in the former God only sets forth the condition of faith and repentance and promises eternal life to those that believe and repent, while he himself effects these conditions in the elect. The internal essence includes the acceptance of all the federal benefits that belong to the elect only, who are called internally and form the invisible church.[89]

---

87 It is important to note that what Turretin calls "external administration of the covenant" in his *Institutes* is termed "the call to salvation" (*vocatio ad salutem*) in the *Formula*. In canon XVII, the same things are ascribed to it as are ascribed to the external administration in the *Institutes*. These words are used by Turretin as synonyms.
88 Turretin, *Institutio*, XII, 6, v, vi, xii, xvii, xxi, xxiv. *Formula* XVIII and XX. Klauber's translation of XVIII is incomplete and incorrect. Klauber translates: "So they might learn the mystery of salvation through Christ and be without excuse ..." But the *Formula* reads (after quoting Rom. 1:20): "[N]on arcanum beneplacitum in Christo; neque etiam hunc in finem, ut inde mysterium salutis per Christum perdiscerent, sed ut sint ἀναπολόγητο, *inexcusabiles*." A correct translation is: "[N]either [God's] secret good pleasure in Christ nor this [viz. the seeing of God's power and divine nature] have the purpose that they [viz. the heathen] should learn the mystery of salvation by Christ from them but that they should be inexcusable." Cf. the German translation of canon XVIII in the original *Formula*: "[N]icht aber sein verborgenes Wohlgefallen in Christo werde von der Erschaffung der Welt an ersehen ... Und zwar nicht zu dem Ende, dass sie daher das Geheimnuss unserer Seligkeit durch Christum erlerneten, sonder damit sie keine Entschuldigung hätten."
89 Turretin, *Institutio*, XII, 2, viii; 6, v, xi, cf. 12, xii. Though the doctrine of baptism is not a part of this study, it is interesting to note that Turretin differs with Beza and Calvin here on the reason why children of believers should be baptized. For Calvin, it is because of the covenant of which they are members by birth. Beza, however, argues that it is because we have to suppose they are regenerated or elect. Turretin argues

Turretin notes that the question whether the covenant was conditional divided the Protestants. But he thought it was easy to reconcile both views by making the correct distinctions.[90] According to Turretin, faith and repentance are conditions of the covenant in some way but not in another. They are not meritorious *a priori* conditions or impulsive causes, for the covenant is wholly based on grace. Yet they are *a posteriori* conditions or instrumental causes, for the promises of the covenant are received through them. The promises of the covenant regarding its end (salvation) are under condition of faith and repentance, but the promises of the covenant regarding these means or instruments (faith and repentance) are absolute. The covenant is absolute regarding its first confirmation in Christ but conditional regarding its application to the believer. Since the conditions are produced by effective grace, in the end the covenant depends on God alone and in that way is unconditional.[91] In the same way the promises of salvation are both conditional and unconditional. In the outward dispensation, they are proposed conditionally to all who hear them. But for the elect they are absolute since Lord promises to fulfill the conditions. That means that, in a proper sense, the promises belong to the elect only. That they are not universal does not do away with the foundation of consolation since they are presented to all believers. By knowing one is a believer, one can know that the promises pertain to him.[92]

That faith is a condition does not mean that faith causes salvation by itself but rather that God made a connection between faith and salvation. Faith "necessitates" salvation by a hypothetical necessity of the event or dependence by which something, although mutable and contingent by nature, has no option but to be, according to God's ordination of things. In other words, faith does not save in the same way that fire burns, but only because salvation is promised on condition of faith.[93]

5.5.1 Turretin's View of the Covenant Compared with Calvin's

If we compare Turretin's view of the covenant with Calvin's, several differences become apparent. In connection with predestination, the most

---

that God can give grace to children as well as to adults. Baptism seals saving grace to true believers only, but for hypocrites (there was no third category between true believers and hypocrites), baptism is nothing more than a badge of profession that distinguishes them from Jews, Turks, and heathens. XIX, 20, xx-xxi.
90 Turretin, *Institutio*, XII, 3, i.
91 Turretin, *Institutio*, IV, 18, xvii; XII, 3, ii-v, vii.
92 Turretin, *Institutio*, XII, 6, ix-x, xvi, xxxi.
93 See 5.8.

important difference is that, according to Turretin, the covenant of grace is restricted to those elected to salvation, while, according to Calvin, the covenant is a middle position between election and reprobation and was extended to more people than the elect.[94] Nonetheless, Turretin acknowledges that the covenant in its outward dispensation is extended to more than the elect. The question is whether the difference is as great as it might seem at first sight.

Calvin's and Turretin's views of the relation between covenant and election can be presented in a diagram of three concentric circles. Both place the reprobate in the outermost circle, the elect or the invisible church in the innermost circle, and a mixture of both elect and reprobate in the visible church in the middle circle. Both state that the middle circle of the visible church is characterized by conditionality, whereas God promises salvation upon condition of repentance and faith. Both agree that God works these conditions in the elect.

They differ on the question whether there actually is a covenant with the reprobate or not in the second circle. Calvin calls this middle position "the covenant," even when the conditions are not fulfilled (2.6), whereas Turretin argues that there is a covenant (in the full meaning of the word) only when the conditions are fulfilled.[95] This coheres with their view of the relation of Christ to the covenant. For Calvin, Christ is the Surety of the covenant in the sense that he assures that God will give salvation to those who fulfill the conditions of the covenant by faith and repentance. In Turretin's theology of the covenant, Christ is the Surety also in the sense that he has merited faith and repentance for the elect. Calvin holds the same view concerning the benefits of Christ's death but does not relate this to his doctrine of the covenant. Turretin states that there was a pact between Father and Son in the Godhead, but this notion is not found in Calvin.

Turretin quotes Calvin to prove his view on the extent of the covenant, yet these quotations deal with the question whether God wills the salvation of all people, something that Calvin denies since God did not have the Gospel preached to the whole world. But Calvin does not use this to claim that the covenant was made with the elect only, as Turretin does.[96]

---

94 For a survey of developments in Reformed thought on the covenant, see. R. Scott Clark, "Christ and the Covenant: Federal Theology in Orthodoxy," in Selderhuis, *Companion*, 403-428. Scott Clark does not describe the development of the relation between covenant and predestination in Reformed orthodoxy.
95 When Turretin admits that the "covenant" is extended even to some of the reprobate, he takes the word in the restricted sense of "the outward dispensation" or the outward call. See the section above.
96 Turretin, *Institutio*, XII, 7, xxxii.

In short, Calvin stresses that the covenant is a mutual pact between God and the visible church, and that it is conditional in its essence, although God effects the fulfillment of the conditions in the elect. Turretin stresses that the covenant is a unilateral testament of God for the elect, unconditional in its essence, although its external dispensation is conditional. Whether the agreement or difference affected the practice of preaching will be seen in the section on Turretin's sermons below.[97]

5.6 Predestination and the Church

The doctrines of the covenant and the church are closely related in Turretin's theology. God wished to have a church in every age to cherish communion with him and instituted that communion by means of a covenant that outlines a mutual approach of both parties to each other.[98] Hence, covenant and church are in some way synonymous in his theology. This also appears in the correspondence of the internal essence of the covenant with the invisible church and the outward dispensation of the covenant with the visible church. Nevertheless, he devotes a single topic to the doctrine of the church.

Since the covenant has an internal essence as well as an external dispensation, so the church has an invisible and a visible form. Properly speaking, the church is a congregation of elect believers. Turretin did not say that all the elect are members of the church since one becomes a true member only by faith. Those who are elect but are not yet believers are not yet members of the church. The church of elect believers is both visible and invisible. It is visible in the preaching of the Word and in the profession of faith. It is invisible by reason of the internal call and the communion with Christ by faith. The church is the body of which Christ is the Head and Savior and is united by the Spirit. Since there are also wicked and hypocritical people in the visible church of those who are called externally, the visible church is wider than the invisible church, for many are called but few are chosen. The essential form of the church is neither the external profession of faith nor the elect as such but the internal truth of faith that is restricted to those who are elect and efficaciously called.

Turretin admits that reprobate infidels can be called members of the church regarding its external state. Nonetheless, unbelievers are spiritually dead, have no communion with Christ, and are destitute of the Spirit. They are not the bride of Christ, they do not belong to his sheepfold, nor

---

97 See also 7.5.
98 Turretin, *Institutio*, XII, 2, i.

do they have Christ as their foundation. They are not members of Christ but of the devil instead.[99]

This does not always mean that the invisible church is smaller than its outward form. Believing catechumens are true members of the church, even if they have not yet entered its outward form through baptism. One enters the visible church through baptism but the invisible one through faith. It is even possible for someone who is excommunicated from the visible church, to be a true member of the invisible church.[100]

5.7 God's Purpose and the Preacher's Purpose in Preaching

If many are called but only few are chosen, what is God's purpose with the call of those who are not elect? Turretin denies that it was God's design to save them all, but he also denies that God does not deal with them seriously. Turretin distinguishes a twofold call, external and internal, which correspond to the different aspects of the two states of the church: visible and invisible. The external and internal calls both have God as their author, are both addressed to people who are lost and dead in sin, both proceed by the instrument of the Word, and both have as their end the glory of God and the salvation of people. Yet they differ in that in the external call God only commands, while in the internal call he also gives strength to perform the duty commanded. The external call proceeds via the Word only, while the internal call proceeds also by the Spirit. The external call is extended to the elect as well as to many of the reprobate, but the internal call is issued only to the elect. The external call can be inefficient, while the internal is always efficient. The external call is temporal and revocable, but the internal call is immutable. The external call constitutes the visible church, while the internal call constitutes the invisible church.[101]

Turretin denies that God calls the reprobate with the intention of saving them. The purpose of the external call is salvation, but God intends this for the elect alone. The call is intended primarily for them, and it is for their sake that the ministry of the Gospel was instituted. The reprobates only share in the external call accidentally since they are mixed with the elect and because the external call is addressed to all indiscriminately. This is just like a fisherman who intends to catch good fish but indirectly also catches the bad fish in his net since they are mingled with the good.[102]

---

99 Turretin, *Institutio*, XVIII, 2, vii-x; 3, i-xxii; 7, iv-xxiii.
100 Turretin, *Institutio*, XVIII, 4.
101 Turretin, *Institutio*, XV, 1, 1-vii.
102 Turretin, *Institutio*, XV, 2, ii-iii.

Turretin distinguishes the purpose of the call itself from God's purpose of the call. The purpose of the law itself is life by the law, but since the Fall, God's intention with the law is not that people should attain life by it but rather to lead people to Christ. In the same fashion, the purpose of the Gospel in itself is the salvation of people, but God's purpose with the Gospel is not the salvation of all who hear the Gospel but only that of the elect. God's purpose through the preaching of the Gospel in general is to demonstrate the mode and means of salvation and the promise of salvation to those who believe and repent. God's special purpose with the elect is their salvation, and hence he works not only imperatively in them but also operatively. God's special end with the reprobate is their conviction and inexcusability, not their salvation. God cannot intend the salvation of those whom he reprobates.[103]

Nevertheless, Turretin argues, God acts in a serious and sincere fashion when he calls the reprobate. He shows them the only way of salvation (i.e., faith in Christ and repentance toward God), exhorts them to follow it, and promises salvation to all those who follow it, and bestows salvation according to the promise. Salvation is not offered to them absolutely but under a condition. God wills them to believe and repent by his commanding will. Since he promises salvation to those who repent and believe, and since it pleases him that the called do come, he wills their salvation in that way. Turretin uses the Greek word *euarestia* to denote that God is pleased when people perform what he commands. *Euarestia* or the approving will is related to the commanding will *(voluntate praecepti)* and is distinguished from the *eudokia* or will of the decree *(voluntate decreti)*.

Although God wills the sinners to come to him through his commanding will, he does not will to give reprobate sinners the power to come through his decreeing will. A serious call does not require the intention to draw those who are called but only a constant will of commanding duty and the bestowing of the promised blessing on those who perform it. Since the commanding will is our rule of life, the unbelief of the reprobate cannot be excused, even if their rejection of the Gospel is in accordance with God's decreeing will.[104]

Like Calvin, Turretin uses the concept of conditionality to solve the problem of the calling of the reprobate. Both Calvin and Turretin maintain that the external call is serious because to those who hear the Gospel salvation is not promised in an absolute way but in a conditional way, viz. under

---

103 Turretin, *Institutio*, XV, 2, iv-xiii. Cf. *Formula*, XIX.
104 Turretin, *Institutio*, III, 15, viii-xii; IV, 14, xxv, xxx; 16, viii-ix; 17, viii, xx, xxx-viii-xxxix, xli-xlvi; XV, 2, xiv-xviii, xxv-xxviii. See also *Formula*, XIX.

condition of faith and repentance. That the reprobates do not fulfill this condition is their own fault. That the elect do fulfill it is God's grace. Turretin refers to and quotes Calvin on the key passages Ezek. 33:11 and 1 Tim. 2:4.[105] These elements are also in Beza's theology, although he did not relate the conditionality clearly to God's sincerity in calling the reprobate.

If God does not intend the salvation of all who hear the Gospel, does the preacher have to distinguish the elect from the reprobate? According to Turretin, they do not have to and are even unable to do this. They should address all with the Gospel, indiscriminately. They cannot promise salvation in an absolute way to all but only in a conditional way: those who believe and repent will be saved; this is a message that is true for all. They have to call all people to faith and repentance; this is God's command to all. As long as they preach the Gospel this way, they can preach it to anyone.

Although preachers should not intend the salvation of the reprobate, they may intend the salvation of all who hear them since they do not know who is elect and who is not. Prompted by love, they may (or ought to) desire the salvation of all and they should not despair of the salvation of anyone. The ministers of the Gospel are even bound to perform their duty towards all sinners indiscriminately. They will incur great guilt if they can be accused of the neglect of duty in the perdition of any.[106] Here Turretin agrees with Beza and Calvin.

5.8 The Mode of Preaching the Gospel

Our discussion above shows how Turretin thought the Gospel and its promises should be preached. Preaching the Gospel is showing the way of salvation to sinners. This way to salvation is faith in Christ and repentance toward God. Christ has merited salvation by his most perfect obedience and promises salvation to all who repent and believe. This Gospel is to be preached to everyone. The promises of the Gospel are to be preached conditionally, in such a way that the promises are for those who fulfill the condition, i.e., only the believers. This conditionality does not exclude anyone from the message of the Gospel nor from the call to flee to Christ by faith. Believing is a condition, but there is no condition to believe. All sinners are indiscriminately called to faith and repentance to be saved, but salvation is promised only to those who believe and repent.

Calvin sometimes calls being aware of sin or knowledge of one's misery a condition. This suggestion can be found in Turretin's works as well, although

---

105 Turretin, *Institutio* IV, 17, xxxiii-xxiv, xxxvii, XII, 7, xxxii.
106 Turretin, *Institutio* IV, 17, xlvii; XV, 2, xxii-xxiii.

– as in Calvin – there is no systematic treatment of it. In his view of the acts of faith, the first act is knowledge of both our misery and God's grace. This first act is in some way a condition for the next acts. When he writes about the act of reception, Turretin remarks that "God freely offers his own Son in the gospel to the sinful soul, burdened and cast down and broken by a sense of his sins." Christ is promised "to all those weary with the sense of sin, those flying to and sincerely receiving him."[107] Elsewhere, he even states that

> they who are ordered to believe are not all men simply, but relatively (to wit, "the weary" and heavy laden with the burden of sin, Mt. 11:28; "the thirsty" and they who feel their need of drink, Is. 55:1, i.e. who are penitent and feel their misery.)[108]

Turretin never called this a "condition." The conditions of the covenant, proposed in the preaching of the Gospel, are always faith and repentance. Throughout his *Institutes*, Turretin never uses the word "condition" in the sense of a restriction of the Gospel offer but only as a means to attain salvation. Knowledge of sin and misery and being burdened is not in itself a means to salvation. Yet it is connected to faith and repentance. Without knowledge of sin, there is no knowledge of the need to repent nor knowledge of the need to believe in Christ. In this sense, one's knowledge of misery is not a condition for faith but a consequence of the first act of faith.[109] Although this might be called a condition for the next acts of faith (as a *conditio sine qua non*) it is not a condition or predisposition preceding faith and the call to faith altogether.

That Turretin wrote in one place that God *offers* his Son to the burdened and heavy-laden does not mean that he says that God did not offer it to others. Instead, he states elsewhere that all people are called to believe the Gospel offer. This differs with the *promise* of Christ to those who are weary with the sense of sin. Although all are called to believe the offer of the Gospel, according to Turretin, the promise is not made to everyone but only to believers. Since Turretin thinks that the knowledge of sin that

---

107 Turretin, *Institutio*, XV, 8, v, ix, x: "Ut enim Deus animae peccatrici oneratae ac sensu peccatorum suorum dejectae & contritae, Filium suum, & Christus seipsum cum omnibus beneficiis suis & plenitudine salutis quae in ipso residet gratis offert in Evangelio." "Cum enim promissibus sit omnibus fatigatis sensu peccati, & ad ipsum confugientibus, & sincere eum recipientibus …".
108 Turretin, *Institutio*, XIV, 14, xlv: "Unde qui jubentur credere non sunt omnes & singuli simpliciter, sed secundùm quid, nimir. *onerati* & pondere peccatorum pressi Matth. 11.28 *sicientes* & sua ariditatis conscii Isa. 55.1. id. poenitentes & miseriam suam agnoscentes."
109 See 5.10.

makes a person flee to Christ belongs to saving faith, he can write that Christ was promised to them who have this knowledge.

The quote, which seems to state that only those "who are penitent and feel their misery" are called to faith seems to be a greater problem. This statement does not fit into Turretin's theology of the call to believe issued to all who hear the Gospel. The discrepancy is easily resolved, however, if one takes into account the fact that Turretin is dealing here with those who say that everyone should be called to believe that Christ died for him. In the statement quoted, Turretin takes the command to believe in this sense. While he denies that everyone should believe that Christ died for him, he does state that everyone should believe, i.e., that everyone should flee to Christ by faith.[110]

5.9 Predestination and the Response to Preaching

The Gospel is either received by faith or rejected in unbelief. Because fallen humankind is spiritually dead in sin, the natural state of human beings is unbelief. Sufficient grace is not given to each and everyone to answer God's call. Without saving grace, no one will respond to the Gospel in faith and repentance. Since the reprobate are and will be destitute of saving grace, they will never believe. This is not due to any insufficiency or defect in the Gospel, however – it is only because of the fault of people that it is not efficacious. Neither is reprobation the cause of unbelief: the only reason for unbelief is human sinfulness, by which the Gospel becomes a savor of death. Unbelief is a consequence of reprobation but not an effect.[111] Unbelief and sin in reprobates are an example of how God's free decision is executed by man acting in freedom of coercion, although not in freedom of sin and misery.[112]

The response of the elect to the preached Gospel is faith and repentance. They are called not only externally but also internally and effectually. Christ has merited faith and repentance for his elect and also sends the Spirit to apply the merited salvation to them. The Spirit gives life to those who are spiritually dead and renews the will. In regeneration, the Spirit infuses supernatural habits in the soul of the elect. This is followed

---

110 See 5.10.
111 Turretin, *Institutio*, IV, 14, xxi. VI, 7, xxviii; X, 4; XV, 3. Cf. IV, 4. See 5.3 for the distinction between consequence and effect in Turretin's thought.
112 The reprobate act in freedom when they reject to repent and believe. They are not coerced to sin and unbelief by anything outside of them (for instance by God or his decree), but their moral state of sinfulness makes it necessary that they voluntarily choose to be sinners and unbelievers. See Van Asselt e.a. (eds.), *Reformed Thought on Freedom*, 171-200.

immediately by human action in faith and repentance.[113] The Spirit in regeneration acts mediately through the Word, but also immediately with the Word on the soul. Both Word and Spirit are necessary. The Word is needed to know what and who to believe and toward whom one should repent, and the Spirit is needed to give power to human faculties and to renovate them so as to make the soul believing and repenting.[114]

In Turretin's theology, the doctrine of predestination does not make preaching superfluous. Election needs the Gospel to be preached. But the preaching of the Gospel needs the grace flowing from election to be effective.

5.10 Predestination, Faith, and Assurance

Turretin distinguishes between a general and a proper or specific object of faith. The general object of faith is the written Word of God. But the faith that is a condition of the covenant has as its proper object the teaching concerning Jesus Christ and the promise of the remission of sins and of salvation in his blood. As the object of faith, Christ is joined with God: God as the supreme good in whom we are to be made happy, Jesus Christ is the means by which we are led to God.[115] The object of faith is not "Christ having died for me." Not all those who hear the Gospel are bound to believe that Christ died for them. Rather, the impenitent and the unbelieving, while in that state, should not believe that Christ died for them. Only those who repent and believe should believe this. Telling all people indiscriminately that Christ died for them would be telling a lie. The object of faith is Christ as a Mediator between God and humans, and as the only way to be reconciled to God, and the promise of the Gospel is that all will be saved who repent and by faith flee to Christ. Whoever gives assent to this by faith will flee to Christ and rest in him to obtain pardon and salvation. Whoever hears the Gospel may and should be urged to this act of faith, and all who believe and repent may believe Christ died for them.[116]

We have seen that there was a tension in Calvin's theology between his definition of faith as a sure knowledge of divine favor towards humans and his doctrine that God did not show favor to all people since all are called to faith. This tension is not found in Beza's theology because he did

---

113 In his sermon on the foundation of God, Turretin speaks about the possibility of habit *(habitude)* without acts *(actes)* of backsliding believers. *Sermons*, 346.
114 Turretin, *Institutio*, XV, 4, x-xxviii (especially xxiii). Cf. *Formula*, XXI.
115 Turretin, *Institutio*, XV, 11, ix-xv; XV, 12.
116 Turretin, *Institutio*, XIV, 14, xlv-liii.

not include assurance in his definition of faith.[117] Turretin defines saving faith as a faith "which involves a fiducial apprehension of Christ and his benefits, called 'justifying and saving faith.'"[118] The nature of this saving faith can be perceived when its actions and object are known. Its object – Christ and the promise of the Gospel – has been discussed above. As to the acts, Turretin mentions that the more common view recognizes three acts in faith, viz. knowledge, assent, and trust *(notitia, assensus, fiducia)*, yet he offers some further distinctions in the act of faith.[119]

A first distinction is that between a direct act and a reflexive act. A direct act is occupied with the object, while the reflexive act is concerned with the direct act. By the reflexive act one knows one is a believer and hence that Christ has died for him or her, that the promises of salvation are for him or her and that he or she is elect.[120]

Next, Turretin distinguishes among seven acts of faith, five of which belong to the direct act and two to the reflexive act. All acts reflect either knowledge, assent, or trust. The first is the act of knowledge *(actus notitiae)*. This knowledge concerns all things that people are to believe, whether with respect to our misery or to God's grace.[121]

Turretin distinguishes two acts within the act of assent. The first of these and the second act in faith is theoretical assent *(assensus theoreticus)* in which knowledge is received as true and divine. The third act is fiducial and practical assent *(assensus fiducialis & practicus)*, which is the persuasion of the practical intellect that the Gospel is not only true but also the highest good; that its promises will bestow salvation upon all believers and penitents "and so also upon me if I shall believe and repent."[122]

The act of trust is divided into two acts. The first (being the fourth act of faith) is an act of taking refuge *(actus refugii)*, which flows naturally from the last act of assent. Since all people desire to be happy, a person who knows he is miserable and that salvation is found nowhere else than in Christ alone and that he cannot obtain this salvation without coming

---

117 See 2.12 and 3.12
118 Turretin, *Institutio*, XV, 7, iv: "[E]am, quae fiducialem apprehensionem Christi & beneficiorum ejus importat, quae *fides justificans* & salvifica dicitur."
119 Turretin, *Institutio*, XV, 8, ii-iii.
120 Turretin, *Institutio*, XV, 8, iv.
121 Turretin, *Institutio*, XV, 8, v.
122 Turretin, *Institutio*, XV, 8, vi-vii: "… promissiones gratiae de remissione peccatorum & salute conferenda omnibus credentibus, atque adeo & mihi si credidero …" In XV, 9, iii, vii, Turretin takes this fiducial assent as part of trust; this is understandable since the *assensus fiducialis & practicus* and the following *actus refugii* are closely related and inseparable.

to Christ, cannot not come to Christ by desiring him, seeking him, fleeing to him and endeavoring to posses him. This is followed by a fifth act of reception of or adhesion to and union with Christ *(actus receptionis sive adhaesionis & unionis)*. By this act, Christ is not only sought but also apprehended, received, embraced, applied to ourselves, adhered and united to, as he offers himself with all his benefits in the Gospel. This is the formal and principal act of justifying faith *(formalis & praecipuus fidei justificantis actus)*.[123]

Next comes the sixth act of faith, a reflexive act *(actus reflexus)*. The believing soul, seeing the direct acts of persuasion, refuge, and reception in itself, concludes that it believes and hence that Christ with all his blessings belong to him and that Christ has died for him and will save him.[124]

Turretin adds a seventh act of faith that is not part of its essence but flows from it as a necessary consequence and effect. It is an act of consolation and confidence *(actus consolationis & confidentiae)*, consisting in joy, peace, and delight that arise from the knowledge of possessing Christ.[125]

Elements of faith	Corresponding acts of faith		
		essential acts	
knowledge	*notitia*	1. act of knowledge	*actus notitiae*
assent	*assensus*	2. theoretical assent	*assensus theoreticus*
		3. fiducial and practical assent	*assensus fiducialis & practicus*
trust	*fiducia*	4. act of refuge	*actus refugii*
		5. act of reception and adhesion	*actus receptionis sive adhaexionis & unionis*
		6. reflexive act	*actus reflexus*
		non-essential act	
		7. act of consolation and confidence	*actus consolationis & confidentiae*

Turretin's distinctions helped him answer the Romanists who denied that trust belonged to faith and to solve a dispute among the Reformed as to whether trust belonged to the essence of faith or not. As the seventh act of faith, trust does not belong to the essence of faith, says Turretin, but as

---

123 Turretin, *Institutio*, XV, 8, viii-ix.
124 Turretin, *Institutio*, XV, 8, x.
125 Turretin, *Institutio*, XV, 8, xi.

fiducial assent, coming to, and receiving Christ, trust surely belongs to the essence of faith.[126]

It also helped him solve the problem we met in Calvin's theology concerning the call to faith. Turretin understood that if God does not show favor to all, not all can be called to believe he will show favor to them. Moreover, since Turretin claims that Christ did not die for all people, he understands that not all people can be called to believe that Christ died for them. Yet he does acknowledge that trust is essential for faith. His distinctions allow him to maintain both that trust is essential to faith, even the trust that Christ died for me, as well as the general call to faith, without it being a call to everybody to believe that Christ died for them. The faith all men are called to is the faith of knowledge, assent, refuge, and reception. The reflexive act whereby the believer knows he or she believes follows logically from the act of faith and is there immediately *(statim)* with the direct act. All men are called to the direct act of faith but not immediately to the reflexive act.

We ought to know whether our faith is a true faith. But this can only be known *a posteriori*, from its operations, not *a priori*. Although Turretin does not mention the question here, it is in fact an answer to the question whether one ought to know his election prior to believing in Christ. Because Christ is preached to all who hear the Gospel, hearing the Gospel is not a sure sign of election. One can know the sincerity of his faith at any moment if there is love for and assent to Christ in the present, to receive the offered grace "today" when we hear the voice of Christ. A second mark is that we do not receive Christ as Redeemer only but also as Lord, and we should do this without reservation.[127]

Believers can be sure of their election. Turretin agrees with the delegates at Dort that all believers are persuaded in this life that they are elect. Turretin took a middle position between Calvin and Beza with respect to how this certainty is acquired. Calvin said it was obtained by looking to Christ, whereas Beza held that it was to be gained from the fruit of effective calling. Turretin asserts that certainty comes through faith in Christ but distinguishes two acts in that faith: a direct act going out to Christ and the promises and a reflexive act coming back to the believer. By this reflexive act, the believer knows he believes and thereby knows he is elect.[128] It is impossible to be assured of one's reprobation.[129]

---

126 Turretin, *Institutio* XV, 10.
127 Turretin, *Institutio* XII, 3, xiii-xiv.
128 Turretin, *Institutio* IV, 13; XII, 3, xiii-xiv.
129 Turretin, *Institutio* IV, 14, xxi.

5.11 Preaching the Doctrine of Predestination

Because the question whether predestination should be preached was a question that had been asked throughout history and was answered in the affirmative by, for example, Augustine, Calvin, and Beza, Turretin could not avoid this question in his elenctic theology. Just like Calvin and Beza, he holds that the doctrine of predestination should be preached, but soberly.[130] It should be preached since Christ and the apostles did so and because it is one of the primary doctrines and foundations of faith. It produces many good fruits: gratitude, humility, confidence, consolation, piety, and holiness. These are the same arguments Calvin used. Turretin adds another. The adversaries of the Reformed doctrine of predestination have surrounded and covered the doctrine with errors and calumnies. Therefore, the Reformed need to free it from their incriminations and display it as it truly is. Then it will become clear that predestination is not a fatal necessity, does not extinguish religion, does not lead to despair or to security in profanity, and does not make God either the author of sin or cruel and hypocritical. The abuse of this doctrine does not cancel out its use.[131]

Predestination should be preached soberly. It is a mystery. We do not know the "why" of predestination but only the fact. We should not be silent on what God has revealed nor investigate what he has hidden out of curiosity. The preacher should have regard for his audience, the places, and the times when he deals with the doctrine of predestination. Since some parts of it are more useful, like election, they should be more frequently discussed than other parts, like reprobation. It should not be taught in the churches in the same way as in the schools. In applying the doctrine of election to the congregation, one should not descend from causes to effects but ascend from effects to causes. One cannot read the book of life to see if his or her name is written in it, but one can and should read the book of his or her conscience to see whether he or she has faith and repentance as fruits of election.[132] Turretin agreed with Calvin and Beza concerning the "what" and "how" of preaching predestination.

5.12 Summary: Predestination and Preaching

Turretin is more detailed and technical than Calvin and Beza. The distinctions he makes allow him to solve problems and answer questions from both outside and within Reformed orthodoxy. In Turretin's *Institutes*, the

---

130 Turretin, *Institutio,* IV, 5, i-iii.
131 Turretin, *Institutio,* IV, 5, iv-viii.
132 Turretin, *Institutio,* IV, 5, ix-xi; 13.

loci are much more closely related to and intertwined with each other than in Calvin's *Institutes* or in Beza's *Theses*. This is not unique to Turretin, but common to Reformed academic theology in his time. The different doctrines were seen in their mutual relations, a development that was often forced because of the criticism of their opponents. Calvin was forced by Pighius and Bolsec to think in more detail about the relation between predestination and the call of the Gospel in general (2.1). Beza was forced by Andreae to think in more detail about the relation between predestination and the extent of the atonement (3.7). Reformed theologians from all over Europe were forced by the Remonstrants to think about the relation between predestination and the atonement, the state of fallen humankind and perseverance (4.1). Turretin was forced by the opponents of Reformed theology as well as by the theologians at Saumur to think in great detail about all these themes and also about the relation between predestination and the covenant (5.1, 5.5). That predestination became intertwined with many Reformed doctrines was not the result of it being an inner principle or central dogma of Reformed theology but the result of ongoing criticism of the Reformed doctrine of predestination by Romanists, Socinians, Lutherans, Remonstrants and Amyraldists.

Nevertheless, Turretin's theology is not a predestinarian system. The doctrine of predestination is related to other doctrines but does not absorb them. Even when Turretin asserts that the covenant is essentially with the elect only, it remains a true bilateral covenant with serious conditions and promises. The nature of the covenant was not affected by predestination. And even when Turretin asserts that God only intends the salvation of the elect in the external call of the Gospel, it remains a serious call to all who hear it (5.7, 5.8).

Turretin agrees with Calvin, Beza, and the delegates to Dort on the *praedestinatio gemina* as an unchangeable and eternal divine decree. Scholastic distinctions between kinds of necessity and causality allow him to hold that God is not the cause of sin or unbelief, even when sin and unbelief are included in his decree (5.3, 5.9). There is continuity with Beza here and with Calvin, just as there is continuity between Calvin and Beza, although Calvin states that God was the cause of unbelief (2.11, 3.11). With respect to the order of the decrees, Turretin firmly defends what is known as infralapsarianism, although he does not call himself an infralapsarian since he defines infralapsarianism as what is now commonly called postredemptionism. In this choice, he consciously deviates from Beza (3.6.2) and chooses the line followed by Tronchin and Diodati (4.6).

The doctrine of the covenant is an important element in Turretin's theology. Various subjects come together and are intertwined with each other in this doctrine: for instance, God's decrees (predestination), soteriology (the atonement, call of the Gospel), and ecclesiology. According to Turretin, the covenant is essentially established with the elect but at the same time the covenant is administered to more people than simply the elect (5.5). Here he agrees with the later Beza and differs with Calvin who taught that the covenant is made with all who are baptized and are members of the church, be they true believers or not (2.6, 3.8). Another difference with Calvin and Beza is that Turretin traces the covenant of grace back to an eternal pact between God the Father and God the Son. This is not found or at most in a latent, undeveloped form in the theology of his Genevan predecessors. A final difference with Calvin concerns the conditionality of the covenant. According to Calvin, conditionality is part of the essence of the covenant, while election guarantees that the conditions are fulfilled in and by the elect. According to Turretin, the essence of the covenant of grace is unconditional since the fulfillment of the conditions in the elect is included in the promises of the covenant. Only the administration of the covenant was conditional, not its essence (5.5). Turretin's doctrine of the church is in line with his doctrine of the covenant. The visible church consists of various people, congruent with the administration of the covenant, but the invisible church consists of the elect only, congruent with the essence of the covenant (5.6). Turretin is in agreement with Calvin and Beza on the church.

Like the later Beza, Turretin holds that redemption by Christ was particular, i.e., that Christ had died with the intention to save the elect only, even if the extent of the value of his sacrifice was great enough to save the whole world. Nevertheless, Turretin can use the classic formula that Christ had died sufficiently for the whole world since he understands this phrase as referring to the dignity of Christ's death (5.4).

Faith is connected to election since faith is a gift of God given to the elect. In contrast to Calvin's theology, predestination does influence Turretin's view of the object of faith. He denies that the object of faith is that "Christ died for me." Calvin would not have objected to this formulation, but Turretin's doctrine of particular redemption forced him to disagree with it. Since Christ intended his sacrifice for the elect only, not all can be urged to believe that Christ died for him. Predestination influences Turretin's view of the object of faith by means of the doctrine of the atonement (5.10).[133] Predestination affects his view of the nature of faith in the same way. If not all can be urged to believe that Christ has died for them,

---

133 Beza held the same view with respect to the object of faith but did not relate it explicitly to predestination or the atonement.

how can assurance of salvation be essential to faith? Turretin has difficulty showing how this is consistent. He manages it by distinguishing several acts within the act of faith and saying that those who do not believe at this moment are urged to perform the first acts (knowledge, assent, and fleeing to Christ) and only then to the last act, viz. the reflexive act of assurance (5.10).

Turretin agrees with his predecessors that only the elect will, by God's grace, give a positive response to preaching (5.9). Like Calvin, he solves the problem of God's sincerity in calling the reprobate to salvation by means of the concept of conditionality: God calls all who hear the Gospel, elect and reprobate, to faith and repentance and thus to salvation. This conditionality does not hinder exhortations and the invitation to believe but supports them. The promises of salvation are unconditional for the members of the covenant since God works the condition in them. But they are offered to the whole congregation and to whoever hears the Gospel in a conditional way: whoever repents and believes will be saved (5.8). Although he differs with Calvin on the extent of the covenant, Turretin and Calvin agree with respect to the practice of applying the promises. The condition is not meritorious, but it is a hypothetical condition or cause according to God's ordination. Turretin is more detailed and technical in describing the nature of conditions than Calvin and Beza are, but the concept remains the same. Like Calvin, Turretin stresses the need of knowledge of misery. He does not call this a condition and, in the context of his theology, it appears that he did not regard it as a necessary condition before one is called to believe but a knowledge that accompanies or flows from the first acts of faith (5.8). God works faith and repentance in his elect; the purpose of preaching is their salvation. In the reprobate, God will not work this faith and repentance; the end of preaching for them is to render them inexcusable (5.7, 5.9). But there are not different messages for the elect and the reprobate in the congregation. Despite his knowledge that there is a decree of predestination, a preacher does not know who is elect and who reprobate. He is obliged to labor for the salvation of all who hear him preach (5.7).

It is difficult to determine to what extent his historical context influenced Turretin's theology, but some of its influences can be traced. For instance, Turretin's staunch infralapsarianism seems to be a result of the formulation of the *Canons of Dort* and of the teachings of his predecessors and teachers Diodati, Tronchin and Spanheim. The growing influence of the teachings of Saumur in Geneva led him to reject them in both the *Formula* and in his *Institutes*, but whether this affected only the quantity of words spent on them or their quality or content as well is uncertain.

Despite these differences, there is continuity on the issue of predestination and the external call. Calvin, Beza, and Turretin agree much more than they disagree. All hold to the notion of a *praedestinatio gemina;* all hold that the Gospel can and should be preached indiscriminately to all who can hear it; all use the concept of the promise of salvation under the condition of faith and repentance; all teach that one should start not with predestination but with the call and with Christ. The differences make clear that the continuity was not complete and that each theologian made his own choices within the framework of the more important subjects on which they agreed.

5.13 Turretin's Sermons

Somewhere between 1630 and 1675, the Genevan consistory abandoned the *lectio continua*. From then on, preachers were free to choose the texts they wanted to preach on.[134] Two volumes of sermons by Turretin's father, the Genevan theologian Benedict Turretin, published in 1623 and 1630, were still sermons on successive texts.[135] We will see that Francis preached on texts from different books of the Bible. Since the *lectio continua* was

---

134 The first to offer a new approach to preaching in Geneva was Calvin's student Lambert Daneau (1530-1595). He was professor of theology at Geneva from 1572-1580 and published a book on preaching: *Methodus Sacrae Scripturae in publicis tum praelectionibus tum concionibus utiliter atque intelligenter tractandi* (Geneva: Petrus Santandreanus, 1579). His method and its consequences are described by Amy Nelson Burnett as follows: "The practice of slowing the pace at which the preacher proceeded through a book of Scripture had the practical result of virtually ending the older form of homily or expository sermon. No longer was the pastor discussing the larger context or explaining a train of thought. Instead, he now used the single verse as a springboard to expound on the theological truth he believed was contained in the verse. As Daneau explained, each verse was to be described first in terms of its rhetorical function (such as statement of argument, definition, explication or summary), then of its dialectic function or manner of argumentation (whether from authority, on the basis of distinction and division, or using any of the other topics of dialectical invention: adjuncts, antecedents, consequences, etc.). This was preparatory to the discussion of the locus *theologicus* or substance of what was taught in that verse. Daneau listed ten precepts to follow in explaining the doctrine drawn from the text, including comparison with other portions of Scripture, refutation of heresies drawn from 'papist doctrines,' and, if the text gave opportunity, discussion of the differences between the regenerate and unregenerate." Amy Nelson Burnett, "How to Preach a Protestant Sermon: A Comparison of Lutheran and Reformed Homiletics," in *Theologische Zeitschrift* 63/2 (Basel: 2007), 115-16.
135 Benedictus Turretini, *Sei homilie sopra le parole di Iesu Christo, Luc. XII. v. 5.6. & c.* (Geneva: Pietro Alberto, 1623), Idem, *Profit des chastimens, ou, Sept sermons sur l'exhortation contenue en l'Epist. Aux Hebrieux chap. XII. v. 5. 6. 7. 8. 9. 10. 11.* (Geneva: Pierre Aubert, 1630).

introduced to give the preacher no occasion to touch on subjects that were not in the text, it will be interesting to see whether the doctrine of predestination occurs more frequently in sermons from then on, even when the text does not present an occasion to preach on it.

Unlike those of Calvin and Beza, Turretin's sermons do not follow the *lectio continua*. His volume *Sermons sur divers passages de L'Ecriture Sainte* contains sermons on texts from various books of the Bible.[136] Several of these texts are related to a theme that has proven to be important in the systematic part of this chapter. The first sermon, which is on Ps. 33:12, has election, and the concept of God as the God of his people as its main theme.[137] The second sermon is on Christ weeping over Jerusalem: this relates to the question whether Christ intended the salvation of the city that rejected him.[138] The third sermon is on the call to awaken from sleep and rise from the dead. This has to do with the external and internal call of the Gospel.[139] The fifth sermon concerns the firmness of the foundation of God, having the seal that he knows those who belong to him.[140] The seventh sermon is on making one's calling and election sure.[141] The ninth is on the broken spirit as a sacrifice of God: Turretin sometimes seems to regard a broken spirit to be a condition.[142]

The abandonment of the *lectio continua* caused or was accompanied by a shift in the form of the sermon. Calvin and Beza were more exegetical, preaching through books or chapters and explaining the text verse by verse. This method prevented them from elaborating on themes not arising directly from the text. Turretin did not really elaborate on subjects that were not at all connected with the texts but was still able to address many more subjects than would have been possible following the method of Calvin and Beza. His method was more systematic.

---

136 François Turrettini, *Sermons sur divers passages de L'Ecriture Sainte* (Geneva: Samuel de Tournes, 1676). Quoted as *Sermons*.
137 "Le Bonheur du Peuple de Dieu, Ou Sermon sur le Pseaume XXXII v. 12," *Sermons*, 2-75.
138 "Les Larmes de Iesus Christ sur Ierusalem, Ou Sermon sur S. Luc. Ch. XIX v. 42," *Sermons*, 76-160.
139 "Le Réveil, & la Ressurrection du Pécheur, Ou Sermon sur le Chap. V. de l'Epître de S. Paul aux Ephes. v. 14," *Sermons*, 161-221.
140 "La Fermeté du Fondement de Dieu, Ou Sermon sur le v. 19 de la II Epitre de S. Paul à Timothée," *Sermons*, 304-77.
141 "L'Assermissement de la Vocation, & de l'Election du Fidele, Ou Sermon sur le Chap. I. de la II. Epître de S. Pierre v. 10," *Sermons*, 435-94.
142 "Le Sacrifice du Coeur froissé, Ou sermon sur le Ps. LI. v. 19," *Sermons*, 572-653.

5.13.1 Predestination

Predestination is frequently mentioned in Turretin's volume of sermons. Yet there are great differences in how he addresses it. If the text mentions a word like "election," Turretin expounds that word and gives a short or lengthy survey of the doctrine of election. If a text does not contain the word as such, Turretin sometimes simply uses the word or even says nothing about it. This was also the method Calvin and Beza followed. Yet it is obvious that Turretin's volume of sermons mentions election more often and more extensively than their sermons do. There are at least two reasons for this. The first is that Turretin, just as in his *Institutes,* intertwines the several doctrines with each other. His approach in sermons was more systematic than Calvin's and Beza's. From this point of view, the increase in the mention of predestination was not due to the doctrine itself nor to an increasing importance being ascribed to it. Other doctrines also received more attention in Turretin's sermons.[143]

Another reason is that the texts of the sermons chosen by Turretin to be published in this volume are relatively often related to predestination: three out of ten. It seems that this was not representative for Turretin's choice of texts in general; in his other volume, none of the twelve sermons is on a text relating to the doctrine of predestination.[144] The first volume of sermons offers the opportunity to investigate how Turretin preaches on predestination both in sermons on texts that do mention the doctrine and in sermons on texts that do not. Two sermons have election as their main theme and will be discussed separately; the other sermons will be looked at together to see how the doctrine of predestination functions in them.

5.13.1.1 The Sermon on Making One's Calling and Election Sure

Peter's exhortation in 2 Peter 1:10, to make one's calling and election sure, is the only text containing the word "election" and also the only sermon having this word in its title in the *Sermons*. Turretin introduces his sermon by pointing to the objection to the doctrine of grace, that it opened a door to ungodliness by proclaiming free forgiveness of sins and the immovable firmness of God's election. He answers that grace instead sup

---

143   For instance, in his sermons on Ps. 33: 12 and on 2 Tim. 2: 19 he expounds the Trinity. Both the covenant and human responsibitlity are mentioned frequently. Sanctification is stressed in several sermons.

144   *Recueil de sermons sur divers passages de l'ecriteure sainte* (Geneva: Samuel de Tournes, 1686).

ports good works and that assurance of election is impossible without sanctification.[145]

Calling and election are the two principal graces. They belong together as decree and execution. Election is the eternal call and the call is temporal election.[146] Turretin acknowledges that Peter started with calling since one should ascend from calling to election, but, since we cannot understand the calling if we do not understand election, he himself chooses to talk about election first. That election is a mystery is no reason not to preach about it in the church since the apostles themselves wrote about it. What is revealed should be preached. Moreover, election is a doctrine of consolation.[147]

In this sermon, he presents the definition of predestination that we quoted in 5.3. Having mentioned some other terms for election, Turretin expounds his definition. He states why election is both free and merciful. It is free because all people are equally culpable and there is no reason for God to elect the one above the other. It is merciful because God elects some miserable and culpable people to be saved. Taking the example of the election of Jacob and the reprobation of Esau, he explains to his congregation that the only basis for election is God's good pleasure. Grace is the basis of election when election is viewed in itself. Liberty and good pleasure are the causes when viewed with regard to the one person or the other. One is not elect because he is better nor because he is more miserable than others. Turretin rejects the error of the Pelagians who taught that God elected on the basis of foreseen faith.[148]

Calling is the execution of election. God separates his elect by calling them out of the corrupt world and brings them into communion with him. One should not be deceived into thinking this call is of only one kind: there is a twofold call – one external by the Word alone and the other internal, by the Word and the Spirit. By the former one is joined to the external, visible church, by the latter into internal communion with the Lord Jesus Christ. The first has no effect on the ungodly and the hypocrites in the church who have no part in salvation and in Christ. The other is effective since it is the fruit of election. The calling that should be affirmed or made sure is the internal call. The term "calling" is used to show us several things. First, it shows us our misery, as far from God and unable to come back to him

---

145 *Sermons*, 435-39.
146 *Sermons*, 443. "[L]'Election est une Vocation éternelle, & la Vocation, une Election temporelle."
147 *Sermons*, 442-47.
148 *Sermons*, 449-53.

unless he calls us. Next, it shows us the dignity he calls us to since "calling" is also used for being called to an office in the church. Most of all, it shows us the means whereby the Spirit works, viz. the Word. This Word provides internally what it commands externally. It is a calling from death to life, as powerful as it is sweet, invincible yet without constraint. It is a call that must be answered. It is this internal call that should be affirmed.[149]

Now this calling is in itself sure and firm, just like election. The affirmation of both means the assurance of calling and election in the mind of believers. They often doubt whether they are among the elect and among God's children. Actually, it is the work of the Spirit to affirm the sense of calling and election in believers. God made the decree of election in heaven but writes a copy of that decree on our hearts. Yet the Spirit wants us to labor with him.[150]

Believers affirm their calling and election through sanctification. Then we confirm to others our identity as Christian and our calling and election to ourselves, when we glorify God by good works. Good works are like the seals that confirm the truth of the credentials accorded by princes to their ambassadors. They are like images since we show the image of God through them. They are like good fruits that reveal the nature of the tree. They are means because there is no salvation without sanctification. They are ends because election is for sanctification. All these observations are reasons to be diligent in making one's calling and election sure, to be, in other words, diligent in sanctification.[151]

Turretin makes a practical application in the conclusion to his sermon. He exhorts his congregation, whom he addresses as "brothers," to be thankful for God's merciful election, when they are just as worthy of condemnation as others and others are reprobate indeed, even though they are no worse than us. He exhorts them to rejoice in God's calling and election, for nothing and no one can impede their salvation. He exhorts them to walk worthy of their calling. That is how they will make their election and calling sure. They do not need to ascend to heaven. If they simply see the seal and the fruit of election and calling, i.e., sanctification, they do not need to doubt whether they are partakers of God's grace. Turretin consoles those who finds this seal in their hearts but warns those who do not, not to flatter themselves that they are called internally. They should not abuse the doctrine of election by thinking they will be saved if they are elect, no matter how they live. There is an inseparable bond

---

149 *Sermons,* 453-58.
150 *Sermons,* 458-66.
151 *Sermons,* 466-80.

between sanctification and salvation. Sanctification should not only be external but be in one's heart. He indicates some marks by which believers can know they are not hypocrites, answers an objection based on their own sinfulness, and consoles them by quoting Paul's statement that all things work together for good to those who love God.[152]

In this sermon, Turretin speaks extensively about the doctrine of election. If we compare this sermon with the fourth topic of his *Institutes*, on the decrees of God in general and predestination in particular, it turns out that most subjects treated in the questions occur in his sermon. Only the questions on the decrees in general, on the end of life, on the predestination of angels, on Christ not being the foundation of election, the different specific questions on reprobation, and the order of the decrees are left unmentioned. The questions of the eternity and the unconditionality of the decree of election, on whether the decree necessitates future things, on whether predestination ought to be publicly taught, on the different words for predestination in Scripture, on the object of predestination, on foreseen faith not being the basis for election, on the certainty of election, on the question whether believers can be certain of their own election, and on reprobation in general are touched on or expounded. What Turretin tells his congregation concerning election is completely in line with what he tells his students on the same topic. Nonetheless, this very agreement means he did not follow his own advice. He wrote in his *Institutes* that, in sermons, one should ascend from the effects of grace to their cause, but in this sermon, he descends from election to calling, despite the fact that Peter mentions calling first.[153]

5.13.1.2 *The Sermon on the Firm Foundation*
Another sermon on a text that is directly related to predestination is the sermon on the firm foundation of God. Actually, this is one of a series of two sermons on 2 Timothy 2:19. The first part of this verse is a "cure against desperation" (explained in the first sermon), the second part against "carnal security" (explained in the second sermon). Just as in his sermon on making one's calling and election sure, Turretin keeps election, calling, assurance, and sanctification closely connected.[154]

---

152 *Sermons*, 480-94.
153 Turretin's sermon on Abraham's call shows a similar pattern. Explaining the meaning of "being called" (*étant appelé*), he starts with a short exposition of election as the foundation of being called. *Recueil*, 448-50.
154 *Sermons*, 304-07.

In this sermon, he intertwines the doctrines of the Trinity and the satisfaction of Christ. Three parts can be distinguished in God's foundation of salvation. The first is the destination of salvation from eternity or election: the foundation of the Father. The second part is the acquisition of salvation in time by Christ: the foundation of the Son. The third part is the daily application of salvation by the call and faith in the hearts of believers: the foundation of the Spirit. Election is the first foundation. Acquisition rests upon it, and application rests upon both election and acquisition. Election, redemption, and the call should not be considered separately but as inseparable links in a chain.[155]

Turretin assures his congregation that this foundation is sure and hence that there is no reason to doubt "our" salvation. Election stands because it is irrevocable, for God does not change. Redemption stands because Jesus has satisfied God's righteousness with a price of unlimited worth and constantly intercedes for those for whom he died. The covenant between God and in Christ with believers stands, for it is an eternal covenant, founded on God's eternal love and the merit of Christ. Hence, the things promised to us in this covenant stand, even the things promised conditionally, for its condition is promised in unconditional promises. This includes calling and faith; therefore, the application stands as well, for God's gifts of grace are irrevocable.[156]

The firmness of the foundation of salvation does not take away the necessity of faith and sanctification as a means to obtain salvation. Its firmness refers to God's counsel and promises, not to the will and nature of the believer or to his sense of assurance of salvation. The sins of the saints do not cancel out this foundation for the saints always repent, even of the most heinous sins. They may lack the acts but never the habit of faith. The fact that there are apostates does not cancel out this doctrine either, for they were never built on this foundation by faith and love.[157]

The seal of this foundation has two forms, one referring to God as knowing those who are his children, the other as referring to the sanctification of people. It is impossible to know the former without the latter. The knowledge of God meant in this verse is not his knowledge of all people as God the Creator, but a special knowledge of the elect by God the Redeemer. Only he has this knowledge; humans do not.[158]

---

155 *Sermons*, 307-17.
156 *Sermons*, 317-40.
157 *Sermons*, 340-48.
158 *Sermons*, 348-66.

Turretin concludes this sermon with the exhortation to take some "fruits" from the firm foundation. The first is that the perseverance of saints can be maintained. The second is that we can rest on God's sure promises. He consoles the believers by saying that God, having begun a work of grace in them, will never abandon it. He warns the hypocrites against imagining that they share in God's grace as long as they do not show the seal of sanctification, even though they have external communion with the church and use the sacraments.[159]

This warning is the theme of the second sermon on the same text. Turretin keeps the threefold foundation and sanctification closely connected. Election is for sanctification. Christ redeems his people to sanctify them. They are called to sanctification by faith. Repentance is a condition for living, for sin is connected with death.[160] Turretin's doctrine of election and calling did not promote passivity.

5.13.1.3 Other Sermons

A third sermon on a text that refers to predestination is the one on Psalm 33:12, the second part of the text mentions that God has chosen a people for his inheritance. Since the covenant of grace is the main theme of this sermon, we will summarize it in the section on the covenant. Turretin did not expound the doctrine of election here as profoundly as in the two sermons discussed above. He speaks about election in the context of God being the fountain of the covenant of grace since fallen human beings will never choose God. God chose or elected people in Christ. The calling in time is the effect of this election from eternity, and this election is not based on something good in the elect. Turretin warns his congregation against the errors of those who say that election is based on foreseen faith.[161]

In most of the other sermons, predestination is mentioned only in passing.[162] In the sermon on Christ's tears, election is referred to in the answer to the question whether or not Christ intended Jerusalem's salvation, and in the remark that, although the complete city would be destroyed, there would nevertheless be a remnant as a result of election.[163] In the sermon on the victory over death, based on 1 Cor. 15:55-57, Turretin remarks that the unfaithfulness of the people of Israel could not bar

---

159 *Sermons*, 366-77.
160 *Sermons*, 397-404
161 *Sermons*, 27-32.
162 It is not mentioned at all in the sermon on Hebr. 13: 10. In other sermons, the word occurs occasionally.
163 *Sermons*, 111-13, 126.

the faithfulness of God's promises regarding his elect. He called Paul an elect vessel and described Jesus Christ as saving the vessels of election from Satan's power.[164] In the sermon on the awakening and rising up of the sinner, he mentions election only once, when he asserts that exhorting dead sinners is useful since God gives what he commands to the elect by his Spirit, together with the preaching of the Word.[165] He mentions it once in the sermon on the faithfulness that is rewarded with the crown of life (Rev. 2:10), in the sentence that we are predestined to be conformed to the image of Christ.[166] He also mentions it in his sermon on Ps. 51:17 in describing the difference between the contrite heart of the elect and believers, and the proud heard of the reprobate and ungodly.[167]

5.13.1.4 Conclusions

Of the ten sermons in Turretin's volume, only one does not mention predestination at all. It is mentioned in five other sermons, once, twice, or three times in each. In two sermons, Turretin speaks explicitly about election, and in one sermon it is the main theme, together with the internal call. The three sermons in which Turretin deals explicitly with election are all on texts that refer to it in some way.

Turretin's sermons are consistent with his doctrine of predestination. Nowhere in his sermons does he say anything that does not agree with it. Turretin also heeds his own warnings concerning predestination in sermons save in the sermon on making one's calling and election sure. He mainly addresses those themes that served to edify the church. The doctrine of election was preached to exhort believers to give the glory of their salvation to God alone and not to themselves in any way. It also serves to assure them of their salvation since God's decree cannot fail. That Turretin preached about predestination to edify the church is clear in his sermon on the firmness of God's foundation. Turretin addresses the congregation as believers who should not doubt God's eternal love since they are elected by him.[168]

Turretin usually restricts himself to election: reprobation is seldom mentioned explicitly. One sermon in which the word *(reprouvé)* occurs is the one on making one's calling and election sure; this sermon has election

---

164 *Sermons,* 663-64, 687, 693.
165 *Sermons,* 184.
166 *Sermons,* 223. "[P]redestinez à étre rendus conformes à son image ..."
167 *Sermons,* 599.
168 *Sermons,* 304-07; cf. 59.

as its main theme.[169] Another one is the sermon on the covenant where Turretin says that the care of God intended in the text is not the general care for all people, including the ungodly and the reprobate, but a special care for his people.[170] He refers to it implicitly in other sermons. He does not put the "elect" and the "reprobate" over against each other but "God's people" or "God's inheritance" over against "all people." Only an insider could make a link to the doctrine of reprobation.

Comparing Turretin with Calvin and Beza, we can see that he did not shun touching on the doctrine of election in his sermons, just as they had not. All three preached about it when the text gave occasion to do so and touched on it sometimes in other sermons. Yet the doctrine of election is somewhat more prominent in Turretin's sermons as a result of his different style of preaching. Whereas Calvin and Beza touch on the doctrine of predestination insofar as the text gave occasion, i.e., if there was an exegetical reason, Turretin expounds the doctrine of the *locus* to which a text belongs, i.e., insofar as there is a systematic reason. He addresses the subject extensively and systematically, saying much more than only those things the text gives occasion to.

This refers only to his sermons on texts that mention election. In other sermons, he does not differ with Calvin and Beza on the number of times and how election is mentioned. Although election is the main theme of one sermon and an important subject in two others, predestination is far from being the all-embracing theme of his sermons. As stated above, in Turretin's other volume of sermons, none is on a text that mentions election.

5.13.2 *The Extent of the Atonement*

Turretin's doctrine of particular redemption does not occur in his sermons. Even in preaching on Christ's tears, he does not mention that Christ died only for his elect. Nor does he say anything anywhere that might suggest that Christ died for the whole world. In that sense, Turretin's *Sermons* are consistent with his *Institutes*. Since he saw his congregation as a congregation of believers, he could say that Christ died for "us." Obviously, he did not deem it edifying to tell his congregation that Christ did not die for the reprobate.

The atonement is sometimes mentioned within the framework of election – for instance, in his sermon on the firm foundation. Election for salvation is the first part of the threefold foundation of salvation. Acqui-

---

169 "L'Assermissement de la Vocation, & de l'Election du Fidele, Ou Sermon sur le Chap I. de la II. Epître de S. Pierre v. 10," *Sermons*, 435-94.
170 *Sermons*, 9.

sition rests upon it, and application rests upon both election and acquisition. Election, redemption, and calling should not be considered separately but as inseparable links in a chain.[171] Here the context suggests particular redemption, even when it is not stated explicitly.

5.13.3 *The Covenant*

The first sermon in Turretin's volume is on Psalm 33:12, on the blessedness of the people whose God is the Lord, who are chosen by God for his inheritance. Turretin tells his congregation that this text has to do with God's covenant. This sermon is a more popular version of the doctrine of the covenant presented in Turretin's *Institutes*. That God wants to be the God of his church is the greatest and center of all Gospel promises; it is the soul of the covenant and the marrow of the Gospel. This does not refer to God being the God of all as Creator nor, strictly speaking, to the privilege of the people of Israel since that form of the covenant has been abrogated.[172] It refers to the church and implies reconciliation and union with the nature and attributes of the Persons of the Triune God, which again implies many blessings.[173]

In relation to the second part of the verse, Turretin gives a short exposition of the doctrine of election, as discussed above.[174] With respect to the word *inheritance,* Turretin repeats what he says about the covenant: it does not refer to all people as created by God nor to the privilege of the people of Israel, which had only the letter but not the spirit of the covenant. It refers to the church.[175] The people whose God is the Lord are truly blessed *(bonheur)* since nothing can harm them and God will give them all they need. Moreover, this covenant is eternal: God's blessing cannot be lost.[176]

Turretin then urges his hearers to apply this word of God to themselves. Above all else, they need to know whether they really are included among the number who partake of this advantage. Otherwise, this promise cannot give them consolation. How they can get this knowledge is described in the section on assurance of election. This knowledge should cause them to show admiration, humility, consolation, self-denial, confidence, sanctification, and thankfulness.[177]

---

171 *Sermons,* 307-17.
172 *Sermons,* 6-11, cf. 38.
173 *Sermons,* 13-27.
174 *Sermons,* 27-32.
175 *Sermons,* 32-39.
176 *Sermons,* 39-53.
177 *Sermons,* 53-75.

Almost all subjects mentioned in this sermon are also treated in Turretin's *Institutes*. There is no discrepancy between his sermon on the covenant and election and his theology of the covenant and election concerning the essence of the things said. Yet there are important differences in form and with respect to things he does not say. The form or genre of the sermon is different from the form of the *quaestio* in the *Institutes*. Turretin is compact and technical in his systematic-theological work but extensive and non-technical in his sermon. Many subjects on the covenant mentioned in the *Institutes* are not mentioned in the sermon. For instance, he does not mention the pact between the Father and the Son, the conditionality of the covenant, and the differences concerning the economy or dispensations of the covenant. When he says that the covenant was not made with all people, he does not restrict it abstractly to the elect but, concretely, to "us," i.e., to believers.

Regarding the question of predestination and preaching in relation to the covenant, we see some interesting differences as well as similarities between Calvin, Beza, and Turretin. Like Calvin, Turretin addressed his congregation as members of the covenant.[178] In Turretin's covenant theology, this meant that he addressed his congregation as elect. Indeed, he told his congregation that God had chosen them from eternity.[179] Calvin did likewise but, with his doctrine of the covenant, he could address both the threats as promises of the covenant to his congregation. Turretin, with his doctrine of the covenant, could address only the promises of the Gospel to them.

Nevertheless, Turretin is convinced that not all members of his congregation were indeed members of the covenant. He urges them to discover whether they are included among the people whose God is the Lord. In this sermon, however, he addresses only those who conclude that they are. He has no message for members of the congregation who could conclude that they are not; he only addresses the elect believers. This means that in his sermon on the covenant Turretin only addresses those who have already believed and repented. The conditional structure, which was fundamental in Turretin's doctrine of covenant, predestination, and calling, does not at all occur in this sermon on the covenant and election.

In the other sermons, the covenant is mentioned frequently, but not expounded,[180] though the conditional structure frequently appears in

---

178 *Sermons*, 14.
179 *Sermons*, 30.
180 For instance, Turretin mentions the covenant in his sermon on calling and election, saying that it is a great benefit of the covenant of grace that God's children not only

various sermons. It is all the more strange that the conditional structure, so important for the doctrine of the covenant in his *Institutes,* does not occur in his sermon on the covenant. This structure will be explored in a separate section.

5.13.4 *The Congregation*

Turretin addresses his congregation as a congregation of believers, just as Calvin and Beza had done. He usually addresses them in the first-person plural, saying that "we" are elect, redeemed, and sanctified, that Christ died and intercedes for "us," that "we" do not have to fear the curses of the law, etc.[181] Again just like Calvin and Beza, Turretin sometimes makes clear that this does not mean that all members or hearers are believers in fact. This happens more frequently in Turretin's sermons than in theirs, however. Turretin says at one point that only a small number of his hearers are real Christians: "Although we all bear the name of Christ, it is not less true, that there are very few who have the truth of it."[182]

Several sermons are concluded by addressing two kinds of people: on the one hand, sinners, apostates or hypocrites and, on the other, believers.[183] He warns the hypocrites against imagining that they share in God's grace as long as they do not show the seal of sanctification, even though they have external communion with the church and use the sacraments. The most extensive warning to hypocrites and apostates is found in the sermon on the faithfulness that is rewarded with the crown of life. He addresses them at length, exposing their inexcusable sin, and only at the end does he exhort them to faith and conversion in a few words.[184]

On the other hand, he consoles the believers. The unbelievers are always addressed as "you," while the believers are addressed as "we" and as "brothers."[185] Calvin had addressed both as "we." Turretin does not account for this difference, but it seems to reflect his view of the covenant.

---

possess the supreme good but even that they know they possess it. *Sermons,* 465-66.
181 *Sermons,* 15-16, 275, 304-07, 523, 699.
182 *Sermons,* 425: "Mais quoy que nous portions tous le nom de Christ, il n'est que trop vray pourtant, qu'il y en a fort peu, qui on ayent la verité." See also 137-38; 560-61.
183 Cf. Daneau, *Methodus Sacrae Scripturae,* 5.13 note 134.
184 *Sermons,* 285-96. Since Turretin addresses them as having served the "Anti-Christ" and adored the "Beast" and suggests they might object that they did so by constraint, to save their lives and to acquire the favor of their Prince, he seems to address members of the congregation, or at least listeners to his sermon, who had attended Roman Catholic services. Doing so for their Prince suggests that this sermon was not delivered in Geneva but more likely in Lyon.
185 *Sermons,* 296, 366-77, 411, 425-30, 558, 658.

Whereas Calvin regarded even hypocrites as members of the covenant, Turretin regards them only as having external communion with the covenant, not belonging to its essence. The reason why he calls believers "brothers" is explained by Turretin in his sermon on calling and election. Believers in the new covenant are brothers in the Spirit, bound together by the spiritual bond of grace.[186] This clarifies why Turretin addresses only believers as brothers.

Apart from the more systematic way Turretin speaks of election in his sermons, this is one of the greatest differences between his sermons and those of Calvin and Beza concerning predestination and preaching. It seems to be a result of his view of the covenant. Yet this difference, despite its relative importance, was so slight that it is questionable whether the members of the Genevan church noticed it. They might have noticed, however, that Turretin addresses and warns unbelievers more often, even when the text gives no occasion to do so.

5.13.5 *The Assurance of Election*

In the first sermon, Turretin tells his congregation that they can know whether they are members of the covenant. This knowledge can be gained, not by ascending to heaven but by descending into their own hearts. When they see God's calling and their own response in faith, if they stand by the knowledge of salvation given them by God and if they honor God as Father, they should not doubt that they are included among the people whose God is the Lord. This knowledge should cause them to show admiration, humility, consolation, self-denial, confidence, sanctification, and thankfulness.[187] He deals with this subject exactly as he himself advises in his *Institutes*.

In other sermons, Turretin exhorts his congregation in the same way to become sure of their salvation by searching for the fruits of election and calling, i.e., to search for sanctification. The assurance of election is profitable: since the foundation of salvation is sure, there is no reason to doubt "our" salvation. Election is irrevocable, for God does not change.[188]

---

186 *Sermons*, 441.
187 *Sermons*, 53-75.
188 *Sermons*, 317-40. Other arguments are that redemption stands since Jesus has satisfied God's righteousness with a price of unlimited worth and intercedes continually for those for whom he died. The covenant between God and the believers in Christ stands, for it is an eternal covenant, founded upon God's eternal love and the merit of Christ. Hence, the things promised to us in this covenant do stand, even the things promised conditionally, for the condition is promised in unconditional promises. This includes calling and faith; therefore, the application also stands, for God's gifts of grace are irrevocable.

The assurance of election should not give reason for carnal security but for sanctification.[189] Indeed, there is no assurance of calling and election, save by sanctification.[190] In the sermon on making one's calling and election sure, he expounded this extensively. Turretin agrees with Beza, Diodati, and Tronchin rather than Calvin.

5.13.6 God's Purpose in Preaching

The relation between God's will and the purpose of preaching is not addressed directly. In his sermon on Christ's tears over Jerusalem, Turretin makes some remarks relating to this subject. Just like the question whether God is sincere when he calls the reprobate to salvation when he decreed not to save them, one can ask whether Christ's tears were sincere if he had decreed not to save Jerusalem.

The tears of Christ are proof that his human nature was real. They are an assurance of his love. Even though the Jews had abused God's grace, Christ wept over them. He was aware of the evils coming over his enemies. But he also wept over their sins. Jerusalem had rejected the Savior sent to it.[191] Although God complains about the impenitence of his people, Turretin denies that he really desires things he does not effect himself or regrets things he had done. Such passions are ascribed to God by way of accommodation, to show men that he delights in their conversion and salvation and that he is not the cause of their destruction.[192] Christ's tears were real, however. He was weeping not as God, but as a human being. Just as a good servant of God desires the salvation of those to whom he is sent, Christ desired the salvation of Israel and wept over its destruction. His tears were not signs of the secret will or counsel of God but of his revealed, commanding will. As God, Jesus could have converted and saved the people of Israel. But God has decreed that they would be given only the external call, not the internal one; to promise grace if they did their duty but not to give them the power to do so. God still has the right to punish them for their sins since humans always have the duty of obedience, whereas God is not obliged to give grace and humans are unworthy of his grace through their own fault.[193]

Jerusalem could have had peace and happiness according to the constant and inviolable order that God has established, viz., that he will give

---

189 *Sermons*, 304-07, 397-98.
190 The seventh sermon is devoted to this theme.
191 *Sermons*, 94-103.
192 *Sermons*, 104-09.
193 *Sermons*, 109-16.

salvation upon faith and holiness. But it rejected the only One who could save them. "Their day" was the time when Christ came to them; it is the day of the church when God offers his Word. Turretin warns his congregation not to let this day go by but to repent today or be in danger of perishing forever. God has appointed a time, says Turretin, and if that time is past, there is no possibility to come to grace.[194]

If God's will is taken for his revealed will or his commanding will, he wills the believer to take refuge in him and to have a sensible feeling of the punishment he deserves in order to attain the grace promised to him. But those who do not fear but remain hardened and impenitent, will perish. God does not bring about the deserved punishment immediately; he is good and patient and calls people to repentance. Turretin urges his congregation to repent and not be insensitive to Christ's tears.[195] His tears are not proof that God intended the salvation of Jerusalem, but they are proof that God delights in faith and repentance.[196]

Turretin practices what he writes in his *Institutes*, viz. that preachers may wish all their hearers will be saved and that they are obliged to be diligent regarding their salvation. He urges his congregation not to let a day go by without responding to Christ's tears. He compares Geneva to Jerusalem, both in the special blessings received as in sins committed and warns Geneva against falling into the same sin and hardening itself. Rather it should repent sincerely.[197] Paraphrasing Moses in Deut. 30:15-20, he says

> See, we have set before you today life and death, good and evil. Therefore, choose life, that you might live, and love the Eternal your God, and be obedient to his voice. Otherwise I declare unto you, if your heart turns away from him, you will certainly perish.[198]

If the inhabitants of Geneva desire God to make them partakers of the grace he had promised them, they should do all God demands of them. Turretin addresses the magistrates to care for God's glory and pure reli-

---

194 *Sermons*, 116-26.
195 *Sermons*, 76-80.
196 In the doctrinal terms of the *Institutes*, they are signs not of God's *eudokia* but of his *euarestia*.
197 *Sermons*, 126-52.
198 *Sermons*, 129-30: "Regardez, nous avons mis aujoud' huy devant vous la vie & la mort, le bien & le mal. Choisissez donc la vie, afin que vous viviez, en aimant l'Eternal vôtre Dieu, & obeisant à sa voix: Autrement je vous declare, que si vôtre Coeur se détourne de luy, pour certain vous perirez."

gion, the observance of worship and Sabbaths and the punishment of the ungodly. He urges pastors to labor so that their flock might make peace with God, to preach the Gospel without neglecting to oppose sin. If anyone perishes because of unbelief, their blood should not be on the heads of the pastors. The latter should be examples in doctrine and life. Fathers and mothers are urged to rule their families according to piety. In general, all people are warned to repent and to acknowledge what serves their peace so that Christ, seeing their faith and repentance, will rejoice in them and lead them into the heavenly Jerusalem.[199]

This is an extended example of what Turretin says in other sermons. He does not speak about the question of God's intentions, but he almost always exhorts his congregation to repent. Here again, Turretin's sermons are in accordance with his doctrine. Although he acknowledges that God did not decree to save all people, he urges all his hearers to repent. The conditional structure and the distinction between *eudokia* and *euarestia* in God's will regarding those who do not (yet) believe allows him to exhort all people in his congregation to seek salvation through repentance without being inconsistent with his doctrine of predestination.

5.13.7 Conditionality

The conditions of the covenant, faith and repentance, or sanctification frequently occur in Turretin's sermons. In several sermons, he stresses the relation between the condition and salvation.[200] For instance, he says that we are partakers of Christ's victory over death when we embrace it by faith.[201] He sometimes explains the difference between condition and cause.[202]

If election is more prominent in Turretin's sermons, so the exhortations to fulfill the conditions are also more prominent. In almost all his sermons, he exhorts his congregation to repent and to live in accordance with their calling. He tells them about the plagues they have to fear if they do not and about the grace they had to hope for if they do repent and

---

199 *Sermons*, 154-60.
200 *Sermons*, 39-40, 64-68, 116, 151, 246, 661, 663.
201 *Sermons*, 707.
202 *Sermons*, 231, 270-71. See section 5.8 on this difference. In his *Institutes*, Turretin distinguishes between (1) impulsive causes as meritorious *a priori* conditions and (2) instrumental causes as *a posteriori* conditions, so condition and cause are synonyms there. He does not use or explain this distinction to his congregation but equates (1) with causes and (2) with conditions in his sermon, accommodating himself to the level of his congregation.

believe.²⁰³ Most often, the exhortations are for repentance and sanctification. An implicit exhortation to believe is contained in his sermon on the Christian's altar.²⁰⁴

The conditional structure does not make God's promises feeble in Turretin's sermons, for he tells his congregation that the things promised in God's covenant do stand, even the things promised conditionally, for its condition is promised in unconditional promises. This includes calling and faith.²⁰⁵

It is the conditional structure of his doctrine of covenant and calling that enabled Turretin to exhort his congregation without giving any suggestion of a Pelagian view of a natural power on the part of humans or of a Remonstrant view of common grace and free choice. A significant example that Turretin's doctrine of election and calling did not promote passivity is found in his sermon on sanctification:

> Repentance does not depend upon man. It is a gift of God which he gives to whom it pleases him and when he wills. What do we know, after we have for a long time despised the voice of God, who calls us, and rejected the grace with stubbornness, would he not withdraw it and close the door of salvation to us? ... We can see clearly from that, that one should never defer his repentance, and if one has the design to leave iniquity, such should happen promptly and without delay. ²⁰⁶

Because Turretin sometimes suggests in his *Institutes* that knowledge of one's misery was a condition in some way, we have to see whether or not this occurs in his sermons. The best sermon to read for an answer to this question is the one on the broken or contrite heart. The suggestion that this knowledge is a condition for faith might arise from some statements he makes. For instance, he remarks that God demands a bruised spirit before one can be accepted by God.²⁰⁷ Elsewhere, he says that God promises

---

203 *Sermons*, 90.
204 *Sermons*, 540, 569.
205 *Sermons*, 317-40.
206 *Sermons*, 419-20: "La repentance ne depend pas de l'homme; c'est un don de Dieu, quil donne, à qui il luy plait, & quand il veut. Que savons nous; si après avoir longtemps méprisé la voix de Dieu, qui nous appelle, & rejetté sa grace avec opiniatreté, il ne la retirera point, & nous fermera la porte de sa misericorde? ... Ce qui nous fait bien voir, qu'il ne faut jamais disserer sa repentance, & que si on a dessein du se retirer de l'iniquité, il faut que cela se fasse proptement & sans delay." See also p. 150
207 *Sermons*, 625: "C'est la disposition, que Dieu demande du pecheur, pour luy agreer."

forgiveness of sins and the enjoyment of grace only to repenting souls, and rest only to tired and burdened souls, etc.[208]

Although such statements indicate that knowledge of one's sins and misery, i.e. a broken heart, is in some way a condition for salvation, they do not state that this knowledge is a condition or predisposition for believing or being called to believe. Rather, it is a fruit of faith. Just like the other sermons, this one is addressed to believers.[209] A broken heart is broken only in a saving way *(salutaire)* when the "beats" of the law are accompanied by the "beat" of the Gospel, which makes us see that God is our Father who gave his Son for us.[210] Our tears should flow from faith and hope.[211] Confidence that God is our Father in Christ is a mark of a broken heart.[212] In the context of Turretin's theology, a broken heart and a bruised spirit are the disposition of those who truly come close to God. They can be called conditions only in the sense that they necessarily accompany faith and repentance and precede some acts of believing, but they are not conditions in the sense of predispositions to believe altogether or to be called to believe. Rather, they are fruits of former acts of faith or of parts of faith in its first acts.

5.13.8 *The External and Internal Call*

Turretin's sermon on the awakening and arising of a sinner shows how he deals with the distinction between the external and the internal call of the Gospel. In the words of Eph. 5:14, Turretin says, we can hear the voice of the Son of God, approaching us in his Word and with the power of his Spirit, to awaken us from death. The sleep and death Paul speaks of concerns not (only) the natural, unregenerate human being, but all people, even believers. It refers to sin working in all people. This prevents people from having knowledge of divine things and a life of piety, unless God brings it about it. Each sinner is dead to good things; hence, Turretin rejected the error of the Pelagians.[213]

Nevertheless, it is not pointless to exhort sinners to repent, he tells his congregation. *First*, there is a difference between the death of the soul and the death of a corpse. The inability of the sinner to repent is not because he cannot use his understanding and will (like a corpse) but because he abuses those faculties. Although it is true that we cannot repent, God is

---

208 *Sermons*, 631-32.
209 *Sermons*, 593.
210 *Sermons*, 592.
211 *Sermons*, 649.
212 *Sermons*, 599-600, 605; cf. 637-38.
213 *Sermons*, 161-81.

just when he requires us to repent. *Second*, there is a difference between the commandments of the law and the exhortations of the Gospel. The law only commands, but with the Gospel God gives the elect power to obey. *Third*, there is a difference between the first moment of calling and later moments. At the first moment, there is no power in the human being to hear and obey God's voice. But God, giving grace in the first moment, wills us to use it and to labor with him. He gives us life in the Spirit and wills us to walk in the Spirit.[214]

Having expounded the meaning of "sleep" and "death," Turretin proceeds to explain what the call to awake and arise means. It is of no avail to awake if this is not followed by arising. This is the act of repentance, when the evil of sin is seen and abandoned in order to return to God. This happens both in the first moment of conversion as well as in the process of sanctification. Again, Turretin explains why it is useful to exhort powerless sinners to arise.[215]

Turretin proceeds to explain the promise added to the exhortation to wake up and arise. Anyone who hears these words of Christ and does them will receive more and more grace from Christ, even the grace of perseverance and eternal glorification. The reason why Paul wrote about Christ shining on them only after they awaken and arise is that Paul wrote about what theologians call "subsequent grace" that follows "prevenient grace." The latter precedes repentance, the former follows and accompanies repentance. The promise of this verse is indiscriminately proposed to all, but only believers are its beneficiaries. But the exhortation to awake and rise, i.e., to believe and repent pertains to all. Turretin exhorts his listeners to hear God's voice and to accomplish what he commands – then the Lord will accomplish what he has promised.[216]

Turretin addresses two kinds of people. The first are sinners who are not yet converted *(pecheurs, qui ne sont pas encore convertis)*. He exhorts them, using the second person *(vous)*, to acknowledge their misery, as being dead in God's eyes, and slaves to sin and death. They have eyes, but they are closed to the Sun of Justice; ears, but they are deaf to God's voice; hands but they cannot lift them up to heaven; feet, but they cannot walk in God's ways. Nevertheless, he exhorts them to seek a way to leave that condition behind, for the Lord calls them to awake from sleep and arise from death.

---

214 *Sermons*, 181-89, cf. 466.
215 *Sermons*, 189-200.
216 *Sermons*, 200-10.

> Open your eyes, sinner, that you might see the misery wherein you have fallen, the grace God offers you, and the salvation he prepares for you. You have been long enough in the darkness of error and ignorance; henceforth it is time, if you do not want to close the door of salvation for you, to awake from this deadly sleep and from this profound lethargy, to think about yourself, and to avoid the final misery that threatens you.[217]

Next, he addresses those who have been called but need to be awakened again, who are called "brethren" *(freres)* and are addressed in the first person *(nous)*. They need this exhortation every day. Many are sleeping and dead in carnal security. If they continue in this way, their judgment is inevitable.[218] Finishing his sermon, Turretin indiscriminately calls all to repentance and exhorts them to pray a humble prayer:

> I know very well, Lord, that you let me hear your voice, and that I am obliged to obey in all ways. But I am feeble and destitute of all power, and of myself, I can not awake myself nor arise, if your grace does not come before me, and if your power is not accomplished in my infirmity. So come to my help, my sweet Savior, and do not be content with making your voice sound in the ears of my body, but let it penetrate into my heart by the power of your Spirit, that it might produce what you demand. Effect in me what you command, then command whatever you want, and you will not command in vain.[219]

The conditional structure of Turretin's view of the covenant and calling is given practical form in this sermon. Indeed, he exhorts unconverted sinners to repent and believe, promising salvation and blessing to those who do. Election is mentioned only when Turretin asserts that exhorting dead sinners is useful since God gives what he commands to the elect by his

---

217 *Sermons*, 190-91: "Ouvre les yeux, pecheur, afin de voir le malheur où tu t'es precipité, la grace que Dieu te presente, & le bonheur qu'il te prepare; C'est assez avoir croupi dan les tenebres de l'erreur & de l'ignorance; il est tems desormais, si tu ne veux te fermer la porte du salut, que tu te reveilles de cet assoupissement mortel, & de cette profonde lethargie, pour penser à toy, & pour éviter le dernier malheur qui te menace."
218 *Sermons*, 210-17.
219 *Sermons*, 219-20: "Je say bien, Seigneur, que tu me fais entendre ta voix, & que je suis obligé en toutes manieres d'y répondre; mais je suis foible & denué de toute force, & je ne saurois de moy-même, ny me réveiller, ny me relever, si ta grace ne me previent, & si ta vertu ne s'accomplit en mon infirmité; Vien donc à mon secours, ô mon doux Sauveur, & ne te contente pas de faire ouïr ta voix aux oreilles de mon corps; mais fais la penetrer dan mon coeur par la vertu de ton Esprit, afin qu'il y produise les devoirs qu'elle demande; fay en moy ce que tu commandes, commande ce que tu voudras, & tu ne le commanderas pas en vain."

Spirit, together with the preaching of the Word. But this by no means frustrated the general call to faith and repentance. Turretin does not tell dead sinners to wait for God's prevenient grace (the internal call), but to answer his (external) call by repentance.

Although Turretin distinguishes between the external and the internal call, he keeps them close connected. The internal call occurs via the preached Word and cannot be made without the external call. The external call can be made without any internal call in individuals, yet it is clear from this sermon that Turretin believed that the Spirit would accompany the preaching and make the call internal for the elect. Knowing that preaching to unbelievers is preaching to spiritually dead and powerless sinners who will not hear nor obey unless God gives them prevenient grace, he notwithstanding exhorts these dead sinners to arise, without mentioning the necessity of prevenient grace at that moment. Not knowing who are elect and desiring the salvation of all, he exhorts all people to repent and believe.

5.13.9 The Object and Nature of Faith

According to Turretin, Christ and the promises of the covenant are the special, particular objects of faith in justification, while God's Word as a whole is the object of saving faith in general. He preached about Christ and the promises in all his sermons, although more about the latter than about the former. Christ is explicitly set forth as Savior in the sermon on the Christian's altar.[220]

As the exhortation to believe is seldom explicit, not much is found in his sermons on his distinctions between the acts of saving faith. One does not find the exhortation "believe that Christ died for you," but neither does one find the explicit exhortation "believe that Christ is the only way to be saved" or "flee to Christ." But Turretin, preaching about Christ or about one of the promises of the Gospel, preached them as the object of faith. In general, since he addressed his congregation as believers, he spoke about Christ as having died "for us," but when he addressed the hypocrites and unbelievers, he usually did not exhort them to believe but to repent.

5.14 Summary: Theory and Practice

Turretin's sermons are as consistent and coherent with his doctrinal views as Calvin's and Beza's sermons were with theirs. He preached predestination and related themes almost the same way he taught them to his students. An exception is his sermon on affirming one's calling and election: here he starts with election, contrary to the view given in his *Institutes*.

---

220 *Sermons*, 510-25.

Turretin's message was the explanation of the text, but he approached it in a more systematic-theological way than exegetically. This might have been caused by abandoning the *lectio continua* – at least these two changes did coincide. One consequence was that a text was more often related to doctrinal subjects than in the sermons by Calvin and Beza, which also means that the doctrine of predestination was more often mentioned in Turretin's sermons than in Calvin's and Beza's.

Turretin usually addressed his congregation as elect believers, in the first-person plural, like Calvin and Beza, or as "brothers." But he did not always do so. Calvin also addressed unbelievers in the first-person plural, but Turretin always addressed unbelievers in the second-person plural. It seems that this was due to the difference in their view of the covenant of grace. Calvin held all members of the congregation to be members of the covenant, but Turretin only the elect believers. The hypocrites were not real members of the covenant and, hence, not heirs of the promises and not addressed as "we" but as "you."

Even though Turretin addressed the subject of predestination more often than Calvin and Beza, his sermons were not dominated by this doctrine. He extended the call of the Gospel to all who heard him, elect or reprobate, godly or ungodly. Yet where Calvin and Beza addressed the congregation by "we," whether a text spoke to the godly or to the ungodly, about the promises or threats of the Bible, Turretin restricted the use of "we" to the godly when speaking about the promises. Important as this might be as an indication of his view on the covenant and its differences with Calvin, it remains a question whether it made any difference for the congregation, given the great similarity in the rest of the way he addressed the congregation.

As with Calvin and Beza, an answer to the question whether predestination influenced the theory and practice of the call of the Gospel in preaching should be nuanced. Predestination and the call were closely related in Turretin's theology. The call belongs to the execution in time of God's eternal decree. Nevertheless, the external call is not dominated by predestination, neither in its address nor in its content. The external call to eternal life is addressed to all who hear it.

6. Late Orthodoxy - Benedict Pictet

6.1 Pictet and the Question of Predestination and Preaching
6.1.1 A Changing Theological Climate

Although Francis Turretin is a representative example of a Reformed theologian during the period of high orthodoxy, he is not a representative example of Genevan theology as a whole during the second half of the 17th century. Turretin succeeded having the *Formula Consensus* adopted at Geneva, but a strong minority in the company of pastors opposed his strict views and promoted a more moderate and tolerant form of orthodoxy. One of the first adherents of this moderate form of theology was Louis Tronchin (1629-1705), son of Theodore Tronchin, the delegate to the Synod of Dort.[1] After his ordination in 1651, Louis studied at Saumur. Having served the Reformed congregation in Lyon, he was appointed professor of theology at the Genevan Academy in 1661 and pastor in 1662. In 1669, he opposed Turretin's insistence on subscribing to the anti-Saumur standards of 1647-1649. According to Tronchin, this was more characteristic of the "papists and antichrist" than of Reformed theologians. Turretin won this battle, yet from then on, the academy and the consistory were divided.[2] Tronchin won another battle in the same year by having his nephew, the philosopher Jean-Robert Chouet (1642-1731), exempted from having to subscribe to these theses before being allowed to teach philosophy in Geneva. Chouet was a Cartesian philosopher and had taught at the academy of Saumur.[3] Louis Tronchin himself integrated Cartesianism into his theology.[4]

---

1   For Louis Tronchin, see O. Fatio, *Louis Tronchin: une transition calvinienne* (Paris: Garnier, 2015).
2   For a survey of this confrontation, see: James T. Dennison Jr. "The Twilight of Scholasticism: Francis Turretin at the Dawn of the Enlightenment," in Carl R. Trueman and R. Scott Clark, *Protestant Scholasticism: Essays in Reassessment* (Carlisle, UK: Paternoster Press, 1999), 250.
3   It is remarkable that Cartesian philosophy could enter the Genevan Academy without problems or opposition since it was opposed by many Reformed and Roman Catholic theologians in Europe. Even a polemical theologian like Francis Turretin did not object to Cartesianism. Yet Pictet showed himself worried about Cartesian doubt, rejecting "pyrrhonism" in religion in his *Quatorze Sermons,* 279. He did not mention Descartes by name, but mentioning "pyrrhonism" as methodical doubt in the early 18th century could hardly be understood in any other way than as referring to Cartesianism.
4   Walter E. Rex, "Bayle, Jurieu, and the Politics of Philosophy: A Reply to Professor Popkin," in Thomas M. Lennon et al., *Problems of Cartesianism* (Kingston, ON: McGill-Queen's University Press, 1982), 83-94.

Turretin achieved victory in getting the *Formula Consensus* adopted in Geneva, although it took three years after it was written to do so. The year it was adopted, 1679, was the same year the Roman Catholic diplomat of the French king, Louis XIV, took up residence in the city and invited Roman Catholic Genevans to his home to celebrate a private Mass. This was a sign that Reformed orthodoxy was losing the upper hand in Geneva. When the Edict of Nantes was revoked in 1685, many French refugees with Salmurian sympathies came to Geneva, threatening the future of the acceptance of the *Formula* in the city. Philippe Mestrezat (1618-1690), another professor of theology, recommended the decisions of the French synods – which neither censured Amyraut nor called him orthodox – be accepted as normative for Geneva.[5] While Turretin constructed the solid bastion of Reformed theology in his *Institutes* and defended it against all kinds of heresies and errors, including Salmurian theology, the Reformed bastion that the Genevan Academy had once been opened its gates for exactly the theology Turretin opposed: Amyraldism. The dominance of strict orthodoxy at Geneva ended with Turretin's death in 1687. Someone wrote to Louis Tronchin about his death: "If we had only heard the same news [of Turretin's death] some thirty years ago, your Church and Academy would have been so fortunate!"[6]

6.1.2 Jean-Alphonse Turretin

Louis Tronchin had to subscribe the *Formula Consensus* himself. He did not publish anything against it during his life, but he had a major influence on his students such as Pierre Bayle (1647-1706) and Jean-Alphonse Turretin (1671-1737).[7] The latter was Francis's son. He was 16 years old when his father died and received his theological education and formation primarily from Louis Tronchin. He became pastor of the Italian congregation of Geneva in 1694, professor of church history in 1697 and of theology in 1705. With his orthodoxy already suspect in 1703, Jean-Alphonse Turretin led the Genevan church through liturgical innovations and in 1706 to the abolition of the *Formula Consensus* for which his own father had been such

---

5 Dennison, "The Twilight of Scholasticism," 251.
6 This was Daniel Chamier (grandson of the famous Huguenot pastor of the same name (1565-1621), who was the founder of the academy in Montpelier). He is quoted by Timothy R. Philips, "The Dissolution of Francis Turretin's Vision of *Theologia*: Geneva at the End of the Seventeenth Century," in *The Identity of Geneva*, ed. Roney and Klauber, 78, and by Dennison Jr. "The Twilight of Scholasticism," 249.
7 For Jean-Alphonse Turretin see: Martin I. Klauber, *Between Reformed Scholasticism and Pan-Protestantism: Jean-Alphonse Turretin (1671-1737) and Enlightened Orthodoxy at the Academy of Geneva* (Selingsgrove: Susquehanna University Press, 1994).

a zealous proponent. Jean-Alphonse found doctrines like the two natures of Christ, the Trinity, and predestination of no importance. A pure Christian life was valued as more important than pure doctrine. Doctrines were only important if they promoted a good moral life.[8] He became the most influential Genevan theologian of the first half of the 18th century. To understand the changed climate in which Pictet lived, it might be good to have a look at Jean-Alphonse's ideas on predestination.

Jean-Alphonse Turretin did not leave a systematic treatise on predestination behind. Nevertheless, it can be concluded that he treated the doctrine of predestination in a different way from his predecessors. In his *Cogitationes et dissertationes theologicae* he dealt with predestination in relation to the question of fundamental articles of faith. He acknowledged the controversies of the Reformed with the Lutherans on the subjects of universal grace, election through faith, resistable grace, and the possibility of falling from grace (which were also differences between the Remonstrants and the Reformed). According to Jean-Alphonse, those who err on these doctrines can nevertheless be very good Christians. Moreover, both Lutherans and Reformed agree on seven points: 1. all good comes from God, and all evil from humans; 2. humans sin freely and are inexcusable; 3. God accepts every individual who believes and repents; 4. those who perish, perish through their own fault; 5. nothing happens in time that has not been decreed to happen, either in an establishing or a permissive decree; 6. God decreed all things in a single act; 7. God will reward everyone according his works. Jean-Alphonse rejected all questions on predestination that did not affect the praxis of piety.[9] He did not investigate the subjects he mentioned as differences between Reformed and Lutheran churches, nor did he formulate a Reformed view on these subjects.

In his posthumously published commentary on Romans, Turretin wrote that in the ninth chapter Paul dealt with the rejection of the unbelieving Jews.[10] He summarized the content of chapter nine as God being

---

8   M.I. Klauber, "The Uniqueness of Christ in Post-Reformation Reformed Theology: From Francis Turretin to Jean-Alphonse Turretin," in Jordan J. Ballor, David Sytsma, and Jason Zuidema (eds.) *Church and School in Early Modern Protestantism: Studies in Honor of Richard A. Muller on the Maturation of a Theological Tradition* (Leiden: Brill, 2013), 709.

9   Johannes Alphonsus Turrettinus, *Cogitationes et dissertationes theologicae ... volumen alterum* (Geneva: Barrilot, 1737), 471-73.

10 Johannes Alphonsus Turrettinus, *In Pauli Apostoli ad Romanos Epistolae Capita XI Praelectiones Criticae, Theologicae et Concionatoriae* (Lausanne & Geneva: M.M. Bouchet & Socior, 1741), 304. (Quoted as *Praelectiones*): "[A]git de rejectione Judaeorum incredulorum ..."

able to call some to knowledge of him and to justify and save them on condition of faith, while those who reject this condition are excluded from God's grace.[11] Romans 9 has always been the classic text for proving the doctrine of predestination and of election as a source of grace. That J.-A. Turretin does not mention this doctrine at all but mentions the condition of faith instead as a part of the content of this chapter – even though it is not mentioned by Paul – indicates that he deviated from both the traditional exegesis of this chapter as well as from the Reformed doctrine of predestination.

With respect to the 13th verse, he remarks that God's hatred of Esau was directed at his posterity and not at Esau himself, and that to hate Esau here (only) means that God loved Esau's posterity less than the Israelites and placed the latter above the former as superior.[12] Jean-Alphonse left out any mention of eternal life or punishment in his remarks on Paul's chapter on election and reprobation. According to him, the cause of rejection is unbelief, while his predecessors had always denied any human basis for the reprobation of individuals.[13]

J-A. Turretin shows himself to be averse to supralapsarianism. His father had rejected this doctrine, though he acknowledged that it was not unorthodox. But Jean-Alphonse wrote that supralapsarianism was unacceptable since it taught that God, according to his supreme authority, could abandon innocent creatures to eternal damnation, without regard for the Fall. Turretin denies that God has this authority.[14] He expresses his view most clearly in some concluding remarks on this chapter in Romans. He also denies that the words of Paul in Romans 9 have anything to do with the last judgment or eternal life. All that Paul said concerning God's freedom relates only to God's dispensation in this present life.[15]

These examples of Jean-Alphonse Turretin's ideas illustrate how much his view concerning predestination differed from that of his father Francis. Even the classic proof for the doctrine was explained in a different way. He denied explicitly that Romans 9 had anything to do with eternal life or death and judged supralapsarianism unacceptable. Notwithstanding, Jean-Alphonse did nothing to attack the doctrine of predestination. Nor did he formally object to the content of the *Canons of Dort* or the

---

11 J-A. Turretin, *Praelectiones*, 304.
12 J-A. Turretin, *Praelectiones*, 313.
13 J-A. Turretin, *Praelectiones*, 318.
14 J-A. Turretin, *Praelectiones*, 319.
15 J-A. Turretin, *Praelectiones*, 323-32 "Quicquid ergo de Dei libertate huc assert Paulus, spectat tantùm ad Dei dispensationes in vita praesente ..."

Formula Consensus. He did not want everyone to agree with them. He was wary of dogmatism but did not attack the dogmas. Nonetheless, his approach to Romans 9 shows that he not only opposed dogmatism but also neglected the dogma. He neither defended nor attacked the doctrine of predestination as such. He apparently simply declared it irrelevant.

6.1.3 Pictet's Life and Works

In a climate changing from Francis Turretin's orthodoxy towards Jean-Alphonse Turretin's moderate theology, Benedict Pictet tried to maintain an orthodox Reformed position. He was born May 19, 1655, to André Pictet and Barbe Turretin, Francis' sister. He studied theology at Geneva, under his uncle Francis Turretin, and at Leiden under Friedrich Spanheim the younger (1632-1701). He became pastor at Geneva in 1680. In 1686, one year before Francis Turretin died, Benedict Pictet was appointed to assist him. After Turretin's death, Pictet became professor of theology in his place. He refused an offer by the academy in Leiden to succeed Spanheim and stayed in Geneva until his death on January 10, 1724.

During his professorship at Geneva, several changes took place. In 1702, the influence of the consistory in appointing professors at the Academy was limited. In 1707, Lutherans were allowed to hold public services in Geneva. In 1711, it was decided to have fewer sermons per week in Geneva, and in 1724, the liturgical form for baptism was modified, softening formulations regarding original sin and the corruption of human nature.[16]

In 1706 Pictet defended the *Formula Consensus.* In that year, Jacques Vial de Beaumont (1678-1746), a minister called to Geneva, refused to subscribe to the document and offered instead not to speak against the *Formula.*[17] The *venerable compagnie* received him on this lesser subscription, but a minority, led by Pictet, protested to the state council. Pictet's conservative party within the *compagnie* had decreased from a majority

---

16 For this period of the Genevan Academy, see Maria-Cristina Pitassi, "From Exemplarity to Suspicion: The Genevan Church between the Late Seventeenth and Early Eighteenth Centuries," in *History of European Ideas*, vol. 37 / 1, 2011, 16-22; Idem, "Arminius Redivivus? The Arminian Influence in French Switzerland, and at the Beginning of the Eighteenth Century," in Marius van Leeuwen and Keith D. Stanglin, eds., *Arminius, Arminianism, and Europe*, Brill's Series in Church History 39 (Leiden: Brill, 2009), pp. 135-57.

17 Little is known about Jacques Vial de Beaumont. See O.H. Selles, "A Case of Hidden Identity," in *The Identity of Geneva*, ed. Roney and Klauber, 93-110; [anonymous], *The Confessional: Or a Full and Free Inquiry into the Right, Utility, Edification and Success of Establishing Systematical Confessions of Faith and Doctrine in Protestant Churches* (London: S. Bladon, 1767), 144-46. These sources contradict each other concerning the place he came from: Grenoble or Neuchâtel.

at the time when Francis Turretin died (1687), to a minority of 12 out of 34 in 1706. This party feared that if the *Formula Consensus* were set aside, the *Helvetic Confession* and the *Canons of Dort* would soon be disavowed as well, that Arminianism would make its entrance, and that Geneva would become separated from Holland as well as Switzerland. Indeed, in 1725, the year after Pictet died, his party had scarcely any adherents, and that year the lesser form of subscription was diminished even more. Ministers were only required to subscribe to the Old and New Testaments and Calvin's catechism. That meant that not only was the *Formula Consensus* set aside, but the *Second Helvetic Confession* and the *Canons of Dort* as well.[18]

Pictet published books in several genres, including chants for the liturgy, a systematic theology, catechisms, sermons, a history of the church, a work on Christian ethics, prayers, and a tract on religious indifference. Pictet was a diligent worker and expected the same from his students.[19] It is interesting to see the chronological order of some of Pictet's publications, compared with the events in Geneva. His first publication was a tract on religious indifference, published anonymously in 1692. A revised edition, with the name of the author, was published in 1716.[20] This book was a response to religious indifference as it arose in the late 17th century.[21] This was an important target for Pictet, for in 1698 he published eight sermons to examine several religions, both Christian and non-Christian.[22] Although this volume contains "sermons" on 1 Thess. 5:21, they are not sermons in the usual sense of the word but lectures on several religions contrasted with Reformed Christianity. These two works show Pictet to be a polemical theologian. Other Protestants were not the target of his polemics, just other religions and Roman Catholicism. Another publication was *La Morale Chrêtienne ou l'Art de Bien Vivre,* a work on Christian life published in 1695.[23] Here Pictet shows himself joining the

---

18 M.I. Klauber, *Between Reformed Scholasticism and Pan-Protestantism,* 146-48.
19 Pictet once reprimanded a student for refusing to work more than thirteen hours a day. Klauber, "Pictet," 95.
20 Pictet, *Traite Contre L'Indifférence des Religions Ou L'On Établit les Fondemens de la vraye Religion, & l'on répond aux principales Objections des Athées, des Déistes, & autres Libertins* (Geneva: Cramer & Perachon, 1716; first edition 1692).
21 For instance, Baruch de Spinoza, a Jew, had published his *Tractato theologico-politicus* in 1670, in which he advocated religious tolerance and argued that Judaism and Christianity were mere historical phenomena. Pierre Bayle, a pupil of Louis Tronchin, advocated religious tolerance, even for atheists.
22 Pictet, *Huit Sermons sur L'Examen des Religions* (Geneva: Societe des Libraires, 1701). Quoted henceforth as *Examen.*
23 Pictet, *La Morale Chrêtienne ou l'Art de Bien Vivre* (Geneva: pour la Compagnie des Libraires, 1695) 2 vols.

majority of his Genevan fellow pastors as well as his predecessors in their concern for a moral Christian life.

Just one year after his *Morale Chrêtienne*, Pictet published his major systematic-theological work: *Theologiae Christiana*.[24] According to his preface, this book was intended for the students to whom Pictet offered a *didactic* theology by himself, after they had gone through the *elenctic* theology written by his uncle Francis Turretin.[25] The scope of Turretin's elenctic theology was to defend Reformed theology against the charges of others and to show the errors of non-Reformed doctrines. The scope of Pictet's didactic theology was to instruct students in Reformed doctrine. To have a didactic theology follow an elenctic theology is quite curious since elenctic theology seems to presuppose knowledge of the theology that is to be defended. Moreover, Pictet hardly offers anything new for those who have mastered Turretin's *Institutes* It could be that Pictet actually had another aim in publishing his *Theologiae Christiana*. Given that the theological climate had changed from domination by Francis Turretin's exclusive Reformed orthodoxy as defended against the views of other Protestant denominations in the direction of tolerance of other Protestants and a distaste for polemics with them, Turretin's *Institutes* should have become increasingly unpopular. In maintaining the positive content and leaving out the negative polemics, Pictet seems to have tried to preserve Turretin's orthodoxy by presenting it in a more acceptable way.

---

24 Pictet, *Theologia Christiana, … Ex Puris S.S. Literarum Fontibus Hausta* (Geneva: Cramer et Perachon, 1696), 2 vols.; it was reprinted by the same publisher in 1716. In 1722 it was reprinted in The Netherlands (Lugduni Batavorum [Leiden]: J.A. Langerak. In 1820 a reprint in one volume was published (Bradford: Inkersley, 1820). The edition used is from 1716, quoted as *TC*.

Unless otherwise indicated, English quotations are taken from the translation by F. Reyroux: Benedict Pictet, *Christian Theology* (London: Seeley and Burnside, 1834), quoted as Reyroux Reyroux's translation should be used with care. In the "Translator's Preface" he wrote that he "omitted a few passages," and has taken "the trifling liberty of throwing several of the shorter chapters into one." Sometimes, this resulted in an alteration of Pictet's order. For instance, Pictet devoted book III to the decrees in general (3 chapters), IV to the decrees of creation and creation itself (7 chapters), V to the decree of permitting the Fall, and the Fall of human beings and angels (10 chapters), and VI to providence (6 chapters). Reyroux took the liberty of "throw[ing] together" books III, IV and VI into one new book III "Creation and Providence" (12 chapters instead of Pictet's original 26), thereby placing the decree to permit the Fall after providence, whereas Pictet placed it before.

25 Pictet, *TC*, "Praefatio," [11]. "[U]t Institutio Theologia Didacticae ipsis traderetur, in qua omissis controversiis, Veritas tantùm nude doceretur."

In 1697, Pictet published a dissertation on the agreements and differences between Lutherans and the Reformed.[26] This work shows his concern for unity among the Protestants and is an example of Pictet as an irenic theologian. The occasion for this work was the revocation of the Edict of Nantes in 1685, when Lutherans, as well as the Reformed, lost their religious privileges. Some of them went to Geneva where they, supported by the King of Prussia, petitioned the Genevan authorities for permission to hold Lutheran services. They were finally given permission and held their first service in 1707. A second edition of Pictet's work on both confessions was published ten years later, in 1717.

Pictet made some popular or abridged versions of his major works. His *Medulla Theologiae*,[27] (intended as a short summary of didactic and elenctic theology) along with his syllabus of controversies[28] should be mentioned. Although these titles raise the expectation that Pictet would be quite polemical in these volumes, he did not engage in polemics at all. The elenctic remarks of the *Medulla* are hardly polemical towards other Protestants, and the *Syllabus* only indicated matters in which other religions or sects differed from the Reformed. For instance, the differences with Arminians are stated by summarizing their five articles, but Pictet does not refute these articles.

He composed a French edition of his *Theologia* himself, which was published in 1702.[29] A reprint with an added third volume was published in 1721.[30] The French edition was more than a translation, containing more chapters and more arguments. The general order is the same, but individual sections in the *Theologia* were expanded to complete chapters in the *Théologie*. It is remarkable that Pictet is often more detailed and more inclined to polemics in the French edition. This might be because Pictet could not presuppose knowledge of Turretin's *Institutes* among his

---

26 Pictet, *De consensu ac dissensu inter Reformatos et Augustanae Confessionis Fratres dissertatio* (Amsterdam: Gallet, 1697). Quoted as *De consensu*.
27 Pictet, *Medulla Theologiae Christianae Didacticae et Elencticae* (Geneva: Societatis, 1711). Quoted as *Medulla*. ("Societatis" probably refers to the Genevan "Société des Libraires.")
28 Pictet, *Brevis Syllabus Controversiarum* (Geneva: Societatis, 1711). Quoted as *Syllabus*.
29 Pictet, *La Théologie Chretienne et la Science du Salut* ... (Amsterdam: G. Gallet, 1702) 2 vols.
30 Pictet, *La Théologie Chretienne et la Science du Salut* ... (Geneva: Cramer, 1721) 3 vols. The third volume was historical rather than theological, containing lists of theological writers, heretics, popes, church councils, a survey of world history and Jewish antiquities. This is the edition used in this study and will be cited henceforth as *TCF*.

French readers, given that this work had never been translated into French.[31] He also published several sermons.[32]

Pictet was both preacher and theologian. Since the doctrine of predestination has always been a part of Reformed theology in Geneva, it seems obvious that Pictet should treat it in his systematic theology. In his time, however, some of his colleagues like Jean-Alphonse Turretin included the doctrine of predestination among the indifferent or non-fundamental doctrines; they did not preach about it and did not teach it at the Academy. Preaching and teaching about predestination was not as obvious for Pictet as it had been for his uncle. Therefore, it was a conscious choice to treat the doctrine of predestination in his *Theologia* and it was also a conscious choice by a minority in the Company of pastors to defend the *Formula Consensus*.

It is a paradox that Pictet defended the *Formula,* which refuted Amyraldian theology and at the same time aimed at union with Lutherans. For the Lutherans of his day differed from the Reformed on several doctrines. Some of these were the same doctrines in which the *Formula* differed from Saumur. For instance, the question whether there is an eternal will in God to save every human person was affirmed by the Lutherans but rejected by the Reformed. Concerning the question whether election depended merely on God's good pleasure or on foreseen faith, the Reformed adhered to the first position, but the Lutherans to the latter. Pictet denied that these differences were fundamental, despite the fact that these Lutheran positions were more alien to the orthodoxy of the *Formula* than the theology of Amyraut.[33]

Pictet tried to write as clearly and simply as possible so that everyone would be able to understand him.[34] In this he was a child of his time:

---

31 In this study, the Latin edition is taken as the primary source, being intended for an academic public and being suitable for comparison with the Latin vocabulary in systematic theology used by his predecessors. Important differences in the French edition, changes, omissions, or additions, will be mentioned.

32 In addition to the *Huit Sermons sur L'Examen des Religions*, he published a sermon called *L'Examen des Chretiens: Ou Sermon sur Apoc. III. v. 1. 2. 3.* (Geneva: Querel, 1716) and some individual sermons. A volume with several sermons is *Quatorze Sermons sur Divers Textes de L'Ecriture Sainte* (Geneva: les Frères de Tournes, 1719), which will be cited here as *Quatorze Sermons.* The first seven sermons in this volume are on Paul's discourse on the Areopagus; the last seven on several texts from the New (6) and the Old (1) Testaments.

33 Pictet, *De consensu,* 46-59.

34 Even in the Latin edition he confessed to having aimed at a style that was plain and familiar and to have abstained from the "barbarous expressions of the school divines" (*scholasticorum*), "being conscious of how unpopular the terminology and distinctions of the scholastics are in the present age." Pictet here made a different choice than his uncle Turretin, who used scholastic terminology and distinctions.

doctrines were regarded as useful only if the laypeople could understand them. That was a reason for other theologians and preachers not to touch on the doctrines of Christ's two natures, the Trinity, or predestination. Nevertheless, Pictet wrote about predestination in his systematic works. We will see whether his approach affected the content of the doctrine of predestination.

Pictet was typical for this period of the transformation of Genevan orthodoxy. He struck a balance between the strict orthodox theology of his teacher Francis Turretin and the enlightened and moderate theology of Jean-Alphonse Turretin. On the one hand, Pictet was a conservative theologian: he defended the *Formula* (though not as vehemently as Francis Turretin did) and adhered to the teachings of his uncle's *Institutes*. On the other hand, he was a progressive theologian who worked with Jean-Alphonse Turretin for liturgical changes. Again, he was an irenic theologian who left out the polemics in his own didactic theological work and aimed at the union of the Reformed and Lutherans. Finally, he was a polemical theologian, though he did not write very much against other Protestant theologies (as Francis Turretin did) but against Roman Catholicism, Judaism, Deism, Mohammedanism, etc. The fronts had changed. Whereas Turretin regarded Amyraldism as a great danger to Reformed theology, Pictet saw indifference toward the above-mentioned religions as a great danger to Christian theology. He even dealt with these different religions in a series of sermons.[35] Pictet's place in Reformed history, his conscious choice to treat predestination in his *Theologia,* and his both defending the *Formula* and striving to unite with Lutherans make him an interesting figure for research. How much did he adhere to the strict orthodoxy of his uncle, and how much was he inclined toward the enlightened orthodoxy of his nephew? Did his approach influence the content of his doctrine of predestination? How did he deal with predestination in his systematic theology, and how in his sermons?

6.2 Earlier Research
The only full biography of Pictet was written more than a century ago by Eugene de Budé, who concluded that Pictet was a defender of Reformed scholasticism who had little in common with enlightened orthodox theo-

---

35 See his *Examen* in which he preached about natural religion, the religion of heathens, Mohammedans, and Jews, and contrasted them with the Christian religion, and in which he defended Reformed doctrine against Greek Orthodox and Roman Catholic criticism.

logians like Jean-Alphonse Turretin.³⁶ Martin Klauber, who has written several articles on Pictet and his times, in particular on Pictet's younger contemporary theologian Jean-Alphonse Turretin, does not agree with De Budé. According to Klauber, Pictet's *Theologia Christiana* does not bear the marks of a scholastic treatise, which is an indication that he moved away from a scholastic methodology to the model of Calvin and the early Reformers.³⁷ His theology is a mediating position between Reformed scholasticism and enlightened orthodoxy.³⁸

Joel Beeke has investigated Pictet's doctrine of predestination. He argues that Pictet was a stout defender of the *Formula Consensus* and the predestinarian doctrine of Francis Turretin, even though he did not employ as much of the scholastic method as his predecessor.³⁹ Beeke had earlier noted that Pictet placed the doctrine of predestination at a different spot than his predecessors had done, viz. at the beginning of Christological soteriology.⁴⁰

6.3 Predestination

Pictet's *Theologia Christiana* deals with predestination in Book 7. Having spoken about God and his Word (Book 1), the Trinity (Book 2), he deals with the decrees in general in Book 3. Then he proceeds to discuss the decree to create, and creation itself (Book 4), the decree to permit the Fall and the Fall itself (Book 5) and providence (Book 6).⁴¹ Only then does he deal with predestination, immediately followed by the means to execute the decree of election, viz. Christ and the covenant of grace (Book 8) and the order of salvation (Books 9-12). His *Medulla* does not have a separate chapter on the decrees in general, but predestination occupies the same place as in his *Theologia*.⁴² As Beeke already noted, the place of predestination in

---

36 Eugène de Budé, *Vie de Bénedict Pictet, théologien genevois (1655-1724)* (Lausanne: Georges Bridel, 1874).
37 Martin I. Klauber, "Family Loyalty and Theological Transition in Post-Reformation Geneva: The Case of Bénedict Pictet (1655-1724)," *Fides et Historia* (Winter/Spring, 1992), 61.
38 Martin I. Klauber, "Reformed Orthodoxy in Transition: Bénedict Pictet (1655-1724) and Enlightened Orthodoxy in Post-Reformation Geneva," in *Later Calvinism: International Perspectives*, ed. W. Fred Graham (Kirksville, Missouri: Sixteenth Century Journal Publishers, 1994), 93-118.
39 Joel R. Beeke, *Sovereign Predestination: Election and Reprobation in Early Lutheran and Reformed Theology* (forthcoming), chapter 16.
40 Beeke, "The Order," 68.
41 This order was changed by Reyroux in his translation. See 6.1.3 note 24. In the French edition, Pictet adds a chapter between the first and the second, on God's virtues.
42 The decrees in general are treated at the end of the chapter on the Trinity; they have

Pictet's theology is different from the place it had in Beza and Turretin. But he was not really original in this respect, for the *Canons of Dort* also placed election after the Fall and even after the call. And Beza's idea of *electio ipsa* also placed election after the Fall. Pictet's order shows him to have been a consistent infralapsarian. This shift in removing predestination from the decrees in general is the most important change. Pictet wrote on almost all subjects Turretin had. The only exception is the question whether predestination ought to be preached, which is omitted from the Latin edition. In this edition, he added some sections on eternity and other properties of the decree, on ideas in God and a chapter on the use and abuse of the doctrine of predestination.

The differences between the Latin and the French edition are remarkable. In the latter, he left out the question whether the end of a person's life is decreed by God. It may have been that he did not think it to be edifying for the average Christian. But he did add a discussion on the question whether predestination ought to be preached and on the view of the ancient church on predestination, and these chapters seem to be more suited for future preachers than to the average Christian. It is quite strange that Pictet, even though he moves the doctrine of predestination to a separate book, keeps a discussion on the order of the decrees concerning predestination in his book on the decrees in general. He did this to make clear why he chose to write about creation, the Fall, and providence before predestination. In this he shows his infralapsarianism, like Turretin and the delegates to Dort did.

Like Turretin, Pictet said that the decrees are essential to God and are eternal, and added that they are most wise, most free, and unchangeable.[43] It follows from this last property that the decree necessitates future things but in such a way that human freedom is not removed, even though we do not know how these two can coexist. Created things are decreed to act in conformity with their nature: rational and free beings act with reason and liberty.[44] Pictet agrees with Turretin and the later Beza here.

It also follows from the unchangeableness of God's decrees that there are no conditional decrees. If the condition is changeable, the decree would be changeable too. Moreover, a conditional decree would mean

---

the same place in the *Medulla* as in the *Theologia*, though they are not given a separate chapter.

43 Pictet, *TC*, III, 1, i-xii. *Medulla*, 46-47.
44 Pictet, *TC*, III, 1, xiii-xiv. In the French edition, an excursus is added on different attempts to harmonize God's decree and human freedom. Pictet rejects all of them all because of their difficulties. *TCF*, IV, 2. *Examen*, 407-13.

that either God does not know if the condition will be performed or he is not able to perform it himself. There are indeed conditional promises and threats, but these do not determine future events, as decrees do. Conditional promises only show what is pleasing to God and what the connection is between the required condition and what is promised.[45] Again Pictet agrees with Turretin.

Pictet sees the order of God's decrees as follows. God first decreed to create the world and humankind (for he could not decree anything concerning humankind before decreeing the existence of humankind), which was also the first decree executed in time. Next, he decreed to permit the Fall and the spread of sin. Third, God decreed that not all people were to be condemned but to have mercy on some. He decreed that Christ would satisfy his justice and his Word and Spirit to apply salvation, to gather the church and to sanctify its members. Lastly, he decreed to crown with eternal glory all those for whom Christ had acquired this.[46] Although this order is usually called infralapsarian, Pictet, like his uncle, did not use this word to describe his position. In Pictet's view, the decree concerning sin is a decree of permitting, although God did not withdraw people from his governance. He rejected all possible answers to the question why God permitted the Fall. We should be satisfied with the knowledge that God is not the cause of sin, even though he reigns over all events.[47] Pictet follows the delegates to Dort and Turretin rather than Beza with respect to the order of the decrees and follows the later Beza in denying that God is the cause of sin.

Pictet agrees with Turretin in almost all things he said, but he does not repeat everything Turretin said. He says nothing about heretical or rejected views but simply gives his own. He rejected neither the supralapsarian nor the Amyraldian view of the order of the decrees. The polemical character of Turretin's *Institutes* is absent in Pictet's *Theologia*. In the French edition, Pictet presents the views of several theologians on the order of decrees but without explicitly rejecting them. Finally, he presents the view of "the majority of the Reformed" as most in accord with Scripture while acknowledging that this view differs from the views of both Beza and Amyraut. He did the same with the question of how God's

---

45 Pictet, *TC*, III, 1, xv. Cf. *TCF* IV, 3. *Medulla*, 47.
46 Pictet, *TC*, III, 3, ii. Cf. *TCF* IV, 4. In the French edition, an excursus is added on different views (both Roman Catholic and Protestant) on the order of God's decrees. Before the first decree mentioned in *TC*, he adds as the first decree God's decision to reveal his properties. This reminds us of Beza.
47 Pictet, *TC*, V, 1, i; *TCF*, VI, 1.

decree and human freedom can coexist. Only with respect to the conditionality of the decree are the views of Socinus and the Remonstrants rejected but in a very polite manner, just by saying he could not agree with them. Pictet was also less technical than Turretin. For instance, he did not use Turretin's distinction between the "consequence of an antecedent," and the "effect of a cause," saying that it is sufficient to deny that God is the author of sin.

Pictet's adherence to the doctrine of *praedestinatio gemina* is clear from the beginning of his chapter on God's decrees concerning the salvation of human beings. God, foreseeing the Fall, "purposed before the foundation of the world to save some of them, and to leave others in their fallen condition."[48]

To understand this decree, four things should be noted. First, we should note that all humans are the object of this decree. Second, the object of this decree is humankind as created, and, third, humankind as fallen. Fourth, Scripture uses different words to denote this decree: (i) *prognosis* or foreknowledge; (ii) *proorizein* or predestination; (iii) *prothesis* or purpose and (iv) *ekloge* or election. Pictet chooses the word election, which he defined as

> the eternal and unchangeable decree of God; whereby, out of the whole race of mankind fallen from primitive innocence into sin and perdition by their own fault, he has, according to the free purpose of his will, and of his mere grace, destined to salvation a certain definite number of individuals, who were neither better nor worthier than the rest, but lay in the same state of sin and misery.[49]

This definition is identical in content to Turretin's, which in turn resembled the definition given in the *Canons of Dort*.[50]

---

48 Pictet, *TC*, VII, 1, i (translation: Reyroux, 228). "[D]e quorundam ex iis salute ante jacta mundi fundamenta cogitavit, aliis in suâ corruptione derelictis." The *Medulla*, 85, has exactly the same phrase.
49 Pictet, *TC*, VII, 1, v (translation: Reyroux, 230): "Electionem esse immutabile et aeternum Dei decretum, quo è toto genere humano ex primaevâ integritate, in peccatum et exitium suâ culpa prolapso, secundum liberrimum suae voluntatis propositum, ex merâ gratiâ, certam quorundam hominum multitudinem, aliis nec meliorum, nec digniorum, sed in communi miseriâ cum aliis jacentium ad salutem destinavit." Cf. *Examen*, 333.
50 See 4.8 and 5.3.

In a next section, Pictet explains this definition. Election concerns "a certain definite number," for not all are elected, as the very word indicates. That election is out of grace and involves human beings fallen in misery excludes all foreseen worthiness, faith, or good works. Faith and obedience are effects of election, not causes. Its only cause is God's good pleasure *(beneplacitus)*. In election, God is to be regarded both as a merciful Father and as the sovereign Lord. The reason why God elects is his mercy, but the reason why he elected Peter rather than Judas is because it pleased him to do so.

Election includes both the destination to salvation and the destination of the means to salvation. With Beza and Turretin, Pictet regards Christ as the first means of the execution of the decree of election *(primum medium exequendae electionis)* and the meritorious cause of salvation. His benefits, which include faith and repentance, are the next means.[51] So, although election is not founded on foreseen faith, nonetheless "salvation is decreed to no one but upon condition of faith and repentance," and therefore everyone whom God has elected will assuredly believe before he obtains the salvation that he has been appointed to.[52]

Pictet's choice to use the word "election" instead of "predestination" was no reason to be silent on reprobation. With respect to this subject, he writes at the end of his book on "the decrees concerning the salvation of men." The very title indicates that his focus was on election and salvation. Pictet first proves that reprobation is a fact since election means that not all are elect. Moreover, Scripture testifies to this. Reprobation is defined as

> the eternal counsel of God whereby he has decreed, out of the will of his good pleasure, not to have mercy on some men lying in the same corrupt mass with others but to abandon them in the corruption in which they are lying, and to condemn them, because of the sins they will perform, by a most righteous judgment, to eternal destruction.[53]

---

51 Pictet, *TC*, VII, 1, vi-vii; *CTF*, VIII, 2, 3. The French edition is more extensive, containing answers on several counterarguments and exegetical questions that are also treated in the *Examen*, 375-81. The *Medulla*, 85-89 is almost as extensive as the *TC*.

52 Pictet, *TC*, VII, 1, vii: "[S]ed tamen salutem nemini decretam, nisi sub conditione fidei et poenitentiae, ... Deus itaque neminem eligit, qui non sit crediturus, antequam consequatur salutem, ad quam destinatus est ..."

53 Pictet, *TC*, VII, 4, iv: "Reprobatio itaque est aeternum Dei consilium, quo ex voluntatis suae beneplacito quorundam hominem in eadem cum aliis corruptionis massâ jacentium, misereri noluit, sed eos in eâ, in qua jacebant, corruptione, relinquere, et propter peccata, quae patraturi sunt, justissimo judicio, aeterno exitio mancipare decrevit" (translation mine). Reyroux omitted this definition in his translation, as well as the sections surrounding it.

There is a twofold act of reprobation. The first is a decree to neglect some and leave them in their misery *(praeteritio)*. This is not a denial of all grace but only of all saving and life-giving grace. The second act is the decree to give these people, who are abandoned in their misery and spontaneously abuse the light either of nature or of the Gospel, their deserved punishment. This is called predamnation *(praedamnatio)* and includes the destination to the ultimate judgment as well as the means for that, as hardening and blinding.[54]

As in election, so in reprobation God is to be regarded in two respects: here not as loving Father and as sovereign Lord but as sovereign Judge and sovereign Lord. When God passes someone over, he is acting as sovereign Lord, but when he condemns him, he is acting as sovereign Judge. Sin is the reason why God passes some people over, but sin is not the reason why he passes some over and not others (since all are equally sinners). The reason, rather, is his sovereign pleasure. Yet the reason for damnation is sin alone. The acts and presuppositions of election and reprobation are different. Election presupposes misery and is an act of mercy; reprobation presupposes sin and is an act of justice. People have no reason to complain why God elected some and not others since he is free to have mercy. People have no reason to complain about damnation since damnation is caused by their own sin.[55]

Pictet wrote a separate chapter on the use and abuse of the doctrine of predestination. A first abuse is to make it an occasion of despair when one thinks: "If I'm not elect, eternal destruction awaits me, whatever I do." Pictet answers that no one should despair of his salvation as long as he lives. Although no one can know his election before he is conscious of his faith and sanctification, there is no reason to regard himself as reprobate, "since God daily calls him in the Gospel, and knocks at the door of his heart by his Spirit." One who thinks "If I'm reprobate, I will perish even though I believe and pursue holiness," is going contrary to the promise of the Gospel that whoever believes will have everlasting life. Instead of an occasion to despair, it offers comfort in times of temptation and affliction, and believers should use it this way.[56] Another abuse is to make it an occasion for licentiousness when one thinks that if he is elect, he will be saved, whatever he does. Such thoughts arise from an ungodly heart because a believer who knows his election cannot offend the God who

---

54 Pictet, *TC*, VII, 4, v; *TCF*, VIII,6; *Medulla*, 90-91.
55 Pictet, *TC*, VII, 4, vi-ix; *TCF*, VIII,6.
56 Pictet, *TC*, VII, 5, iii: "Deus in evangelio quotidiè vocat, et cujus cordis ostium Spiritu suo pulsat." *TCF*, VIII, 7.

loves him and cannot conclude he is allowed to lead a life satisfying his carnal appetites since he is predestinated to a heavenly life. Moreover, it is false that an elect person will be saved whatever he does, for God has not only predestined him to salvation but also the means for that salvation. The fact of an elect person's salvation depends not only on his predestination to such but also on the faith and holiness he displays and thus on his fulfillment of the conditions of the new covenant. The right use of the doctrine of predestination will lead one to holiness, for it gives rise to love for God, sanctification, leads to humility, fills believers with the full assurance of salvation and causes us to work out our salvation with fear and trembling.[57]

The distinction between the reason for predestination in general, and the reason for the predestination of individuals is an original contribution by Pictet.[58] The place predestination received in his theology is remarkable but not original. Pictet did not add much to the doctrine of predestination. In contrast, he omitted some things, not so much with respect to the content and the core, but with respect to the method and the details. Pictet just states his view without explicitly rejecting other views, either in the Latin or the French edition. His explicit choice for one position shows that he thought this was the best, but he does not say the views of other Protestants were to be rejected. The absence of polemics is as characteristic of Pictet's *Theologia* as was its presence was of Turretin's *Institutio*. Calvin and Beza were not as polemical as Turretin, but they did not shun polemics as Pictet did in his *Theologia*. The content of the chapter on the use and abuse of predestination is in accordance with the theology of Turretin, Beza, and Calvin. But Pictet devotes a separate chapter to this subject, which Calvin and Turretin had not done. He also added a chapter on God hardening people and other passages in Scripture that seem to make God the cause of sin.[59] This might be because Pictet could have been faced with more questions from members of his congregation about this subject.[60] Another, perhaps more plausible reason is that Pictet was urged to do so because of criticism by his colleagues in the consistory and the Academy on the doctrine of predestination as not useful but dangerous for Christians.

---

57 Pictet, *TC*, VII, 5, iv; *Examen*, 173-74; *TCF*, VIII,7. The French edition is again verbose, but here without adding anything to the content.
58 Although Francis Turretin had made some similar remarks in a sermon, see 5.13.1.1.
59 *TC*, VI, 6.
60 Richard Muller: "Not everything which presents itself in a historical text as a doctrinal problem necessarily has a doctrinal cause or a doctrinal solution." Quoted by Carl Trueman, "The Dogma Is Not Necessarily the Drama," in Ballor et al. (eds.), *Church and School in Early Modern Protestantism*, xxvii-xxx.

6.4 Predestination and the Atonement

The next book after the one on predestination is on "the means to execute election, viz. Christ and the covenant of grace." Here, Pictet is not as clear on particular redemption as the title suggests. He summarizes the preceding chapters on election as "we have seen that God took pity on the human race" *(videmus Deum generis humani misertum)*. The first means Pictet describes is Christ as Mediator between God and humankind and the means to satisfy God on behalf of humankind.[61] Pictet does not state that Christ died for the elect. He seems to have avoided this subject since there is no chapter on the extent of the atonement.

In the chapters on Christ's humiliation and exaltation, and with reference to his offices of prophet, priest, and king, Pictet writes that Christ's work was for "us" or for "mankind" and that Christ's works were signs of "God's love toward mankind."[62] Only with respect to Christ's intercession does Pictet remark that this expresses Christ's constant desire to save the elect.[63] In the French edition, he adds a remark on the three parts of Christ's priestly office, viz. sacrificing, praying, and blessing. These three parts, Pictet writes, have the same scope. Christ did not pray for the world but for those given to him by the Father in order to shed his blood for them. He does not use the precise term "elect," but any other interpretation is impossible in the context of Pictet's theology. The same holds true for what Pictet writes about Christ's sacrifice. He offers himself for "his church," which consists of "true believers"; they are those "given him by the Father," who "obey him," of which he is "head and surety."[64] He does not write anything about the extent of the atonement in the *Medulla*. He seems to be most clear in his *Syllabus* on this subject, stating that the Arminians differ from the Reformed in saying that Christ died for all in accordance with God's intention.[65] This implies that Pictet rejected this thesis, but it is not a clear statement of particular redemption.

That Pictet in his *Theologia* usually spoke of God's love for humankind is not inconsistent with his rejection of general atonement. In the French chapter on predestination, Pictet answers an objection based on John 3:16. The statement that God so loved the world that he gave his Son is in accord with the doctrine of election, he said. There Christ teaches that

---

61 Pictet, *TC*, VIII, introduction and 1, i.
62 Pictet, *TC*, VIII,15-23.
63 Pictet, *TC*, VIII, 22, iv and *Medulla*, 120 both have the expression "Voluntatem constantem servandi electos."
64 Pictet, *TCF*, IX, 36.
65 Pictet, *Syllabus*, 94.

God could have damned all people, that God could not save anyone without sending his Son into the world, and that the means to share in salvation is faith. Pictet illustrates this by a tale of two cities that both rebel against their ruler. This prince decides to completely destroy one of the cities while saving some people of the other city and sends his son to this latter city. One can say that the prince loved the second city, even if he just saved some of its inhabitants.[66] This same illustration can serve particular redemption, which was likely Pictet's view. Why Pictet was not explicit in stating particular atonement will be discussed in the next section.

6.5 Pictet's Ambivalence on Predestination and the Atonement

Pictet abstains from polemics in his *Theologia* and even rejected polemics on this subject between adherents of the Reformed confessions and those of the *Augsburg Confession*. Both parties, he acknowledges, differed on the question whether God has an eternal will to save all. He denies that this difference concerned something fundamental since both parties agreed that only believers will actually be saved; that Christ's death is of unlimited worth; that people from every age, race, gender and nation are saved; that God has a general love for humankind, and bestows many benefits upon all; that God imposes on all mortals the duty to believe, repent, and to be saved; and that God delights in the repentance and life of the sinner, rather than his death. Hence, Lutherans and the Reformed should not abstain from communion because of the Reformed doctrine of predestination.[67]

Pictet's tolerance of Lutherans in a book published in 1697 and republished in 1717 is quite paradoxical, considering his defense of the *Formula* in 1706. Canon VI of the *Formula* said that "we cannot agree with the opinion of those who teach that God, moved by philanthropy, or a kind of special love for the fallen human race, did, in a kind of conditioned willing, first moving out of pity, as they call it, or inefficacious desire, determine the salvation of all, conditionally, i.e., if they would believe."[68] What Pictet rejected in defending the *Formula* was hardly different from what he tolerated in Lutherans. The Salmurian theologians would have agreed with Pictet on all points where he thought there was consensus between the Reformed and Lutherans. Even the Remonstrants could have agreed with what Pictet wrote in his *De consensu* on this point.

---

66 Pictet, *TCF*, VIII, 2.
67 Pictet, *De consensu*, 46-52.
68 *Formula*, VI, transl. M.I. Klauber. See 5.4. note 72 for the Latin.

Pictet is as ambivalent regarding the foundation of election and reprobation. He acknowledged that the Reformed believe that predestination depends on God's good pleasure, whereas the Lutherans believe that election is based on foreseen faith and reprobation on sin. According to Pictet, these differences are not fundamental. For both parties agree that nothing happens in time that is not decreed from eternity; that there is election and reprobation from eternity; that nobody will be saved apart from faith and outside of Christ; that nobody will be damned if not because of sin; that God is not the author of sin; that faith arises by the grace of the Spirit and a gift of God with respect to its origin, progress, and perseverance; and that the gift of grace of the Spirit flows from the decree to give that grace for faith. Hence, Pictet concludes, the foreseen faith in the theology of the Lutherans is a faith that is given by God out of grace. Therefore, the difference is not fundamental. Here again, we see a tension between Pictet's tolerance of the adherents of the *Augsburg Confession* and his defense of the *Formula*. The latter document excluded "any prevision of the merit of works or of faith"[69] from election. Pictet tolerated in Lutherans the same doctrines he rejected in the Amyraldians. Even Remonstrants might have agreed with what Pictet says about the agreement between the Reformed and Lutherans.

With respect to reprobation, Pictet explains the two acts of *praeteritio* and *praedamnatio*. According to the Reformed, *praeteritio* presupposes sin, but sin is not the reason why some are not elect. According to the Lutherans, *praeteritio* presupposes sin and also unbelief, and this foreseen unbelief is the reason why they are not elected. "Who will say this dissension is fundamental?" Pictet asks.[70]

On the doctrine of the atonement, Pictet shows the same ambivalence as on predestination. On the one hand, he presents his own view clearly. He defends the *Formula*, which states "that the appointment and giving of Christ, our Mediator, was to proceed from the zealous love of God the Father toward the world of the elect," and denies that God "appointed Christ Mediator for all and each of the fallen [human beings]."[71] On the other hand, in his *De consensu* he does not see it as a fundamental dissension that the Lutherans teach that God, in line with his general will to save all human beings, gave his Son, who procured justice and life for all and each by his death.[72]

---

69 *Formula*, IV, transl. M.I. Klauber. Cf. *Canons of Dort*, I, 9 and rejection of errors 5.
70 Pictet, *De consensu*, 52-59.
71 *Formula*, IV, VI, transl. Klauber.
72 Pictet, *De consensu*, 46.

What moved Pictet to defend the *Formula Consensus* and the *Canons* of the Synod of Dort, that reproved Amyraldians and Remonstrants, and at the same time to be so tolerant of Lutherans that Amyraldians and Remonstrants might have agreed with his proposal of communion? According to Martin I. Klauber, there are three reasons for this. Pictet's major reason for defending the retention of the *Formula* was its usefulness for defending the fundamentals against the onslaughts of heterodoxy by providing a very conservative creed. Another argument was that it served the uniformity of belief because all graduates of the Genevan and the Swiss Reformed Academies had to subscribe to it. Pictet, says Klauber, feared that abrogating the *Formula* would open the floodgates to revising the Reformed faith and be a prelude to the abrogation of the *Canons of Dort*.[73] Klauber's first argument seems implausible since – as he himself acknowledges – Pictet did not think any of the doctrines of Saumur, and hence any of the doctrines of the *Formula*, to be fundamental. The second reason seems more plausible, for the orthodoxy of the Genevan Academy became suspect in that very period. Retaining the *Formula* was necessary for being recognized as orthodox by the Swiss Reformed academies. Moreover, the Swiss and Genevan churches could retain the *Formula* without abstaining from communion with churches in countries where the *Formula* was not signed. The third argument might be true, but then the question arises as to why Pictet feared the *Canons of Dort* would be abrogated since he confessed to the Lutherans that the differences between them and the *Canons* were not fundamental.

In addition to the arguments offered by Klauber, the most plausible reason for Pictet to defend the *Formula* and the *Canons* while being tolerant of dissension on the same doctrines among the Lutherans seems to be that, on the one hand, Pictet was convinced that the content of the *Formula* and the *Canons* was true and was the best expression of biblical doctrine concerning predestination, while, on the other hand, he thought that the doctrines of these documents were not fundamental, so that other, less appropriate expressions were to be tolerated and should not be an obstacle to communion with churches in other cities and countries, even if they should not be propagated or taught in Geneva. Pictet shows himself to taking a position between the two Turretins. He agrees with Francis that the Reformed doctrine of predestination was true (which is more than Jean-Alphonse stated concerning this doctrine), but he agrees with Jean-Alphonse that it was not fundamental. Although Pictet's position might have been consistent in his own eyes, his behavior was ambivalent

---

73   Klauber, "Pictet and Enlightened Orthodoxy," 108.

and paradoxical. Defending the *Formula* while at the same time explaining that its content is not fundamental and should not hinder communion with those who retain other creeds, like the *Augsburg Confession*, is far from convincing, especially since the Lutheran king of Prussia and the Anglican Archbishop of Canterbury judged the *Formula* as the major stumbling block to union with the Swiss Reformed Churches.[74] Given Pictet's ambivalence concerning the *Formula* and the importance of the doctrine of predestination, as well as the influence of the ecumenical movement at that time, it is not surprising that he could not convince the other party.

6.6 Predestination and the Covenant

Pictet's predecessors dealt in different ways with the doctrine of the covenant of grace. Calvin has no separate chapter or treatise on this subject, but from his works one can reconstruct a consistent and coherent doctrine of the covenant. In Beza's systematic works, the covenant was treated in different ways. Turretin regards the covenant as very important and dedicates a separate *locus* with twelve *quaestiones* to it, prior to the *locus* with twelve quaestiones on Christ. Pictet wrote on the covenant in his book on the execution of the decree of election, after he had written about Christ. His first remark is that it is "not useless" to note that Scripture mentions a pact between the Father and the Son. This pact is nothing more than the will of the Father to give the Son as the Head and Redeemer of human beings *(homines)* and the will of the Son to give himself as a surety for them.[75] Again, it is striking that Pictet talks about "human beings" and not about the elect.

After having entered into a covenant with Jesus Christ, God was pleased to enter into a covenant with us as well, in Christ, our Surety. There are three parties to this covenant. First, there is God, the author of the covenant, the offended but merciful Father who wants to be reconciled with offending humans. The second party consists of human beings as sinful creatures but aware of their misery.[76] The third party is Christ as the Mediator of the covenant. God promises reconciliation and communion with him, and the communication of all necessary goods, like holiness, life, and immortality. He requires us to be his people, which involves

---

74 Klauber, "Pictet and Enlightened Orthodoxy," 108.
75 Pictet, *TC*, VIII, 24, ii; *TCF* IX, 46. The *Medulla* is silent on the *pactum salutis*.
76 The French edition adds: "qui sent sa misere, qui est chargé et travaillé par ses pechez qui en a un vif sentiment & qui est pénetré de son état." *(whoever feels his misery, is burdened by his sins, a vital awareness of them penetrating his being)*. Pictet, *TCF,* IX,46.

faith, repentance, worship, and obedience, which he produces in us by his Spirit.⁷⁷

Pictet's refraining from mentioning election in his chapters on the covenant gives rise to the question as to whether his view of the covenant is more like Calvin's or more like Turretin's. There are convincing arguments to conclude that Pictet shared Turretin's view concerning the relation between election and covenant. These arguments can be found in his chapter on the sacraments and on baptism. If Pictet had extended the covenant to include more than the elect, one would expect this to be explicitly stated with respect to the baptism of children. But it is precisely in connection with baptism that Pictet writes:

> *Fourthly*, the *subjects* of baptism are all that are in the covenant, whether they be really such, or are reckoned as likely * such, either on account of their outward profession and communion with the faithful, or on account of their being born of Christian parents, without any distinction of sex, age, or nation, although we must confess that baptism belongs to the elect only.⁷⁸

Pictet extends baptism to all who are in the covenant and at the same time restricted it to the elect. This indicates that covenant and election concern the same people. This idea was formulated by Pictet in the French *Théologie Chrétienne*:

> Baptism, like the Holy Supper, does not belong to anyone else than to the elect and to the believers, for since it is a sign and a seal of the covenant, by which God destines and communicates to those who are in it, the saving goods of his grace and his glory, it follows that those who have no right to these goods, neither have right to the seal of this covenant before God's court. But since they who have to administer those sacred things cannot distinguish those who are elect from those who are not, they administer baptism to all who are born of Christians.⁷⁹

---

77 Pictet, *TC*, VIII, 24, iv-v; *TCF* IX,46.
78 Pictet, *TC*, XIV, 4, 2. "Quarto, subjectum baptismi sunt omnes qui sunt in foedere, sive verè sint tales, sive tales probabiliter censeantur, aut ob externam professionem et cum fidelibus communionem, aut ob nativitatem ex parentibus Christianis, absque ullo discrimine sexus, aetatis, gentis, quamvis faciendum ad solos electos pertinere baptismum" (transl Reyroux, 486). At the * Reyroux inserted the words "to become." I do not think Pictet is talking about the probability that those are to be baptized will become true partakers of the covenant. Rather, he is talking about those who might be partakers, although the preacher is not sure.
79 Pictet, *TCF*, XV, 12: 'Le Batême, comme la Sainte Cène, n'apartient qu'aux élus & aux

Here Pictet follows Beza but differs from Calvin and Turretin.[80]

In a chapter on the efficacy of baptism, he defended the connection between election and covenant against Forbesius, who argued that the sacraments are seals of God's covenant and not of God's counsel.[81] Pictet answers that the covenant is nothing more than the execution of God's counsel and that justification by faith, which is sealed by the sacraments, is only for the elect.[82] Here Pictet gives a clear answer to the question whom the covenant is established with: the elect and believers only. Yet the question remains as to why he was so clear on this only in his chapter on baptism and not in his chapters on the covenant itself.[83]

Nothing is said about conditionality in Pictet's definition of the covenant. But when he talks about the covenant of grace in the period of the Old Testament, he writes about conditions as if the topic is a familiar one. One of his proofs that the covenant is the same in the Old and the New Testament is that the condition was the same: faith. He adds penitence as

---

Fidéles; car puis que c'est un signe & un seau de l'alliance, par lequel Dieu destine & communiqué à ceux qui sont entrez les biens salutaires de sa grace, & de sa gloire, il s'ensuit que ceux qui n'ont point de droit à ces biens, n'en ont aussi aucun au seau de cette alliance, devant le tribunal de Dieu; cependant comme ceux qui dispensent les choses sacrées, ne peuvent pas distinguer ceux qui sont élus, d'avec ceux qui ne le sont pas, quand ils administrant le Batême à tous ceux qui sont nez de Chrétiens." Pictet's reason for baptizing not only believers but their children as well is that their children are reckoned as likely being included in the covenant. He distinguishes four kinds of baptized children: first, those who never repent and believe – for them, baptism is ineffective *(nihil obsignat, nihilque exhibet baptismus)*; second, those who repent and believe long after having been baptized – their baptism acquires saving power only when they convert; third, those children who show signs of piety and faith as they grow up – their baptism seals that God forgives them their original sin and gives them his Spirit. Fourth, those who die before they have grownup, whose baptism is a seal of their salvation. Pictet, *CT,* XIV, 4, iv; *CTF,* XV, 17.

80   See 5.5 note 89.
81   Pictet gives no source for this statement. Some chapters prior to this he mentions John Forbes of Corse (1593-1648), *Instructiones historico-theologicae de doctrina christiana et vario rerum statu: ortisque erroribus et controversiis, jam inde a temporibus apostolicis ad tempora usque seculi decimi septimi priora* (Amsterdam: Elzevir, 1645), also included in his *Opera, pars alterum* (Amsterdam: Westenius, 1702). It is likely that Pictet is referring here to the same author.
82   Pictet, *CTF,* XV, 17. "[M]ais cette aliiance de grace n'est que l'éxécution du décret eternal de Dieu, & la justice de la foi, dont les Sacremens sont les seaux, & qui est promise par l'alliance, n'apartient qu'aux élus."
83   Moreover, it is remarkable that in this chapter on the efficacy of baptism in the French edition, he repeats the connection between election and covenant (see, for one example, the note above) and, unlike in his Latin work, explicitly rejected the opinion of Amyraut concerning regeneration and the sanctification of children.

a second condition in the *Medulla*. Again, when speaking about faith in his *Theologie Chretienne*, he introduces it as a condition of the covenant.[84] There is no excursus on conditionality. Pictet writes about conditions as if they are simply a matter of course. In the French edition, he adds answers to several objections to his argument that the covenant of grace was the same under both Testaments but not to its conditions. This might be because Pictet knew of no objections to the point, but this is hard to believe, given the remark of his teacher Turretin that this very question divided the protestants.

Other things Pictet does not mention are Turretin's distinction between the outward administration and the internal essence of the covenant, and a discussion on the extent of the covenant. Yet they function in the same way, considering his remarks on the sacraments quoted above, and his view of the visible and invisible church.

6.7 Predestination and the Church

Pictet distinguishes between three uses of the word "church" in the Bible, the first in reference to its internal communion with Christ, the second to its external profession, and the third to its rule or government.

> In the first point of view it [the church] may be defined to be, a religious society of elect persons, whom God effectually calls by his Word and Spirit, and who not only profess to believe in Christ but really believe in him, and prove their faith by newness of life. In the second view it is defined to be a religious society of men called by the preaching of the gospel. In the third it is an assembly of the rulers and pastors of the church …[85]

The two first definitions correspond to Turretin's distinction between the invisible and the visible church. The invisible church consists of the elect who are effectually called. There are two classes of people in the visible church: those who are real Christians and those who are Christians only

---

84 Pictet, *TC*, VIII, 25, iii: "conditionem foederis, nempe fidem"; *Medulla*, 123: "Eadem conditiones requirebantur, *Fides & poenitentia*," *TCF*, X, 8: "[la foy est] la condition de l'alliance de grace." See also *TCF*, X, 9, ii.

85 Pictet, *TC*, XIII, 2, iv: "Primo respectu definitur, Societas religiosa hominum electorum, quos Deus per verbum et Spiritum efficaciter vocat, quique non tantùm in Christusm credere profitentur, sed et revera credunt, ac vitae novitiate fidem suam probant. Secundo respectu definitur, Societas religiosa hominum praeconio evangelii vocatorum. Tertio respectu definitur, Coetus rectorum et pastorum Ecclesiae …" (Transl. Reyroux, 425.) In the *Medulla*, 189, the order of the first two is inverted. *TCF*, XIV, 1 inverts all three.

in terms of an outward profession. In this respect, he compares the church to a threshing-floor where chaff and wheat are mingled or to a net in which both good and bad fish are caught.[86]

In the second chapter of his book on the church, Pictet explains his first definition of the church and demonstrates that the real members of the church are believers. He agrees with Turretin that only the elect who are effectually called are true members since election alone is not enough to be a true member: faith is a necessary condition. Although hypocrites and reprobates[87] can have external communion with the church, they are not members of the church since the true church is the body of Christ, animated by the Spirit of Christ, and Christ cannot have members who will be condemned. Only true faith makes one a true member. Hence, unbaptized persons who have faith belong to the true church, even though they are not members of the visible church. Again, excommunicated persons can be true members of the church if they have true faith. Their excommunication can be either unjust or even just, but they can still be members if they only retain the seed of faith and repentance.[88] According to Pictet, the church exists in a twofold state: the one external and visible, the other internal and invisible. It is visible with regard to people, who constitute it, the preaching of the Word, and the administration of the sacraments. It is invisible with regard to faith, hope, and charity as well as in regard to those who have true faith. The preaching of the Word free of heresy, idolatry, and superstition are the marks of a true church, for God nowhere preserves the public ministry of the Word without having some of his elect there.[89] Compared to Turretin, Pictet agrees with him in all he wrote. The only thing he does not mention is the relation between covenant and church. But he expresses the relation between church and election in the same way as Turretin did.[90]

6.8 God's Purpose and the Preacher's Purpose in Preaching

Like his predecessors, Pictet distinguishes between an external and an internal call.[91] His ideas on this subject are exactly the same as Turretin's.[92]

---

86 Pictet, *TC*, XIII, 2, iii; *TCF,* XIV, 1; *Medulla,* 189.
87 Reyroux translates *reprobi* by "unconverted", 426; the *Medulla* and *TCF* have *reprobi* and *reprouvez.*
88 Pictet, *TC*, XIII ,2, ii-iii; *TCF,* XIV, 2-3; *Medulla,* 189-91.
89 Pictet, *TC*, XIII, 4, i; XIII,6; *TCF,* XIV, 3, 8; *Medulla,* 192.
90 See 5.6.
91 Pictet rejected the teachings of Testard and Amyraut that there is a third kind of call to salvation, i.e., by nature and providence. *TCF,* X, 2; *Medulla,* 130-31.
92 Pictet, *TC*, IX, 1; *Medulla,* 129-30. Cf. 5.7.

God has a twofold purpose with respect to those who are outwardly called. He calls the elect to make them partakers of salvation but does not call the reprobate with this intention, for then he would fail in his purpose, which is inconsistent with his perfection. Rather, the reprobate are called since they are mixed with the elect. God has the right to prescribe them their duty, and it is a great kindness on his part to point out the way of salvation. Another reason why the Gospel is preached to them is to restrain their corruption. Although God does not at all *(minimè)* intend the salvation of the reprobate, he deals very *(maximè)* seriously with them in calling them. Pictet quotes the *Canons of Dort* to the effect that God seriously calls all who are called by the Gospel, for God shows to all people what is acceptable to him (viz. that those who are called will come unto him) and seriously promises rest and eternal life to all those who actually come to him by faith.[93]

Again, all Pictet says on this subject is in accordance with Turretin's theology, although, again, he says less than the latter did. Pictet does not distinguish between the purpose of the call and God's purpose with the call. Although he offers the same conditional structure as Turretin had done, he does not stress this, nor does he use the words *euarestia* and *eudokia* to explain God's purpose with the call.[94] Pictet's sections on this subject can be seen as a summary of Turretin's *quaestiones* on it.[95] That he agreed with him on conditionality as well is clear from his remarks on conditionality in his chapter on election.[96]

Neither in his *Theologia Christiana* nor in his *Medulla* does Pictet address the question of the preacher who does not know who is elect and who is not and nevertheless has to preach the Gospel. In his *Théologie Chrétienne*, he adds a few remarks on this subject to what he writes on God's intention in calling the reprobate, although this very subject seems to be more suitable for students who read Latin. On the one hand, the ministers of the Gospel should invite all who hear their preaching to repent and believe, according to God's command. At the same time, a preacher must have no other intention than to save the elect for which they are commissioned. But they do not know who are elect and may

---

93 Pictet, *TC*, IX, 2, vi-x; *TCF*, X, 2; the *Medulla* is silent on the purpose of preaching with regard to election.
94 The content of these words is found in *TCF*, X, 3, where Pictet says that the outward call does not show what God has decreed but what he wants people to do and that it is very agreeable to him that people do their duty.
95 See 5.7.
96 Pictet, *TC*, VII, 1. v.i. See 6.3 note 52 for a quotation.

wish all their hearers to be saved.⁹⁷ This is a summary of what Turretin wrote on this issue. One can recognize Turretin's conditional structure, but, again, Pictet does not use this word nor explain the conditional way in which salvation is promised.⁹⁸

6.9 The Mode of Preaching the Gospel

In his *Theologia*, Pictet writes that the call occurs via the Gospel, but in his *Medulla*, he says that the preaching of both law and Gospel has salvation as its purpose.

> That God uses his Word to our salvation, both the law, which imposes duty, convinces of sin, threatens punishment, vexes the conscience and [is] a pedagogue unto Christ, as well as the gospel, which offers a Mediator, teaches the means whereby we become partakers of him, promises salvation to him who accepts the Mediator duly, and produces faith.⁹⁹

The Gospel tells us: believe and you will be saved. It announces and presents to us a Savior. It is a ministry of reconciliation, assuring us that there is no condemnation for those who are in Christ, promising everything to those who repent sincerely.¹⁰⁰

Pictet does not address the question how the Gospel and the promises should be preached in his systematic works. There are only some remarks scattered throughout his works that indicate that he agrees with Turretin on this subject. For instance, what he says about conditionality regarding the execution of election and the covenant indicates that he holds that the promise of salvation is for those who fulfill the conditions of faith and repentance. He confirms this in his remarks on the Gospel above, and in a single remark on the difference between the sacraments and preaching:

> In the gospel, God says in general that those who repent will not be condemned, and that their sins will be forgiven, but in the sacraments God applies his promises in particular to each believer ...¹⁰¹

---

97 Pictet, *TCF*, X, 2.
98 See 5.8.
99 Pictet, *TC*, IX, 1, v; *Medulla*, 129: "[Deus] Verbo suo uti ad nos salvandos, tum lege, quae officium injungit, peccati convincit, poenam interminatur, conscientiam pungit & paedagogus ad Christum, tum Evangelio, quod Mediatorem offert, medium docet quo ejus compotes fiamus, salutem promittit ei qui Mediatorem rite precipit, fidemque gignit."
100 Pictet, *TCF*, X, 2.
101 Pictet, *TCF*, XV, 4: "Dans l'Evangile Dieu dit en général, que ceux qui se repentent

Pictet distinguishes between conditional and unconditional promises when speaking about the perseverance of the saints. The promises regarding salvation are conditional, but the promises regarding the means to obtain salvation are unconditional.[102] Nowhere does he speak of a condition of knowledge of one's misery. Investigating his sermons will show how Pictet preached the Gospel to his hearers and whether and how conditionality functioned in his preaching.

6.10 Predestination and the Response to Preaching

The external call comes to both the reprobate and the elect. The former make the Word ineffective by their corruption. The latter are also called internally, with the Spirit making the call effective.[103] Pictet did not explicitly write on the relation between reprobation and unbelief. In view of his doctrine of predestination, reprobation is far from being a cause of unbelief.

When the call reaches someone, that person is dead in sin and impotent of doing any spiritual good. God first disposes those whom he wants to save to conversion, by having the law and Gospel preached to them, by temporal blessings or chastisements, by terrifying their consciences with a sense of his displeasure, by presenting holiness to them in its most attractive form and by implanting in them a desire to convert. This disposing grace is given to more than just the elect and is not sufficient to save. Sufficient grace is given to the elect only, who are granted the gift of faith and are drawn by the Father. The preaching of the Word is the instrument, for God acts in a way that is suited to a rational creature. But there is also an immediate operation of the Spirit to produce faith and regeneration, for it is not enough to set light before a blind man if his organ of sight is not restored. Likewise, the revelation of the doctrine in the Word is not sufficient unless the corrupted inner faculty is healed and disposed to receive the object. The Spirit does not act without the Word but with the Word: the object outwardly proposed is internally impressed on the mind by the Spirit.[104]

---

ne seront Point condamnez, & que leurs péchez leur seront pardonnez; mais dan les Sacramens Dieu applique en particulier à chaque Fidéle ses promesses ..." *TC*, XIV, 2, v only reads *promissa evangelii sunt generalia,* but the French edtion clarifies that this "general" does not mean each and all people but all who repent.

102 Pictet, *TCF,* X, 9, ii.
103 Pictet, *TC,* IX, 1, vii-ix; *TCF,* X, 1.
104 Pictet, *TC,* IX, 3, v-vi; *TCF,* X, 3-5, 8. The French edition contains the explicit remark that converting grace flows from God's election and that the elect and the converted have the same scope. *Medulla,* 133-34.

In the first moment of conversion, the individual is spiritually dead and hence passive. Yet the Spirit does not work in lifeless, inanimate blocks of wood and stones, for he does not act without the Word but he makes the Word effective and impresses it upon the mind. He not only acts on the understanding but also on the will and the affections. He not only gives the power to believe and to do good works but gives the very acts themselves. Efficacious grace does not depend in any measure on human free will but only on the virtue of grace, which is so powerful that a person cannot conquer it. It is at the same time delightful and does no violence to natural liberty, for it operates by the illumination of the understanding and the persuasion of the will.[105]

That faith is a fruit of election is a source of great consolation, for since election is irrevocable, believers are never in danger of losing their faith. Pictet argues the same on the basis of the firmness of the covenant of grace, of which faith is a condition. If one could lose one's faith, the covenant would be broken, which is impossible. Hence, it is impossible to lose one's faith.[106]

Most of what Pictet says was said by Turretin. Pictet does not mention Turretin's distinction between the consequence and the effect of reprobation. There are two differences between uncle and nephew: Turretin writes that the Spirit infuses supernatural habits in the soul of the elect while Pictet writes that the corrupt human faculty should be healed, which seems to give nothing supernatural to the soul. According to Turretin, the infusion of supernatural habits is immediately followed by the human acts of faith and repentance, while Pictet wrote that the Spirit produces the very acts themselves.[107]

6.11 Predestination, Faith, and Assurance
Like Turretin, Pictet distinguishes between a general and a special object of faith. The general object is the complete Word of God, and the special object is the doctrine of Jesus Christ and the promise of salvation in him. God's veracity is the foundation of faith, but the proper object of saving

---

105 Pictet, *TC*, IX, 3, xi-xvii; *TCF*, X, 5-6, 8; *Medulla*, 134-35. *TCF* X, 5 contains a discussion with and rejection of the view of Pajon, who taught that the preaching of the Word in the right circumstances was enough for conversion. In his French edition, Pictet adds many proofs, answers to objections, explanations, and a chapter on the view of the ancient church concerning saving grace. Obviously, he regarded a correct doctrine of calling and regeneration very important for his French readers, perhaps because of Pajon's teachings. For Pajon, see Albert Gootjes, *Claude Pajon (1626-1685) and the Academy of Saumur: The First Controversy over Grace* (Leiden: Brill, 2014).
106 Pictet, *TC*, IX, V, 1; *TCF*, X, 9, ii.
107 I leave these differences for what they are, since they are not related to predestination and preaching.

faith is the special promise of mercy in Christ. If it is not, then it would not differ from the faith of devils.[108] Pictet omits Turretin's notion of God being the object of faith to which the believer is led through Christ. He does not deal with the question whether "Christ died for me" is the object of faith, which Turretin had rejected. In the French edition, Pictet adds a short remark that nobody should believe that his sins are forgiven, except he who repents from his sins and takes recourse in Christ. Speaking of the nature of faith, he explicitly denies that one should believe immediately that Christ died for him and that his sins are forgiven unless he finds the first acts of faith in himself. Those who do not take refuge in Christ and do not repent of their sins but are filled with their own righteousness should not flatter themselves that Christ died for them.[109] This makes it clear that he did not regard "Christ died for me" as the object of faith.

According to Pictet, faith is the first effect of the inward call and the first act of the new man. It is the bond of our union with Christ, the condition of the covenant of grace, the fruit of election, the beginning of sanctification and the infallible means of salvation.[110] This short commendation contains two elements that Pictet otherwise seldom mentions: a relation between election and the conditionality of the covenant of grace. These elements are explained in the course of his chapter on faith.

Before explaining the acts of faith, Pictet observes that the idea of faith includes knowledge *(notitia)*. This is remarkable, for it means that Pictet, though including knowledge in faith, did not regard it as an act of faith, as Turretin had done. The French edition even states that faith (pre)supposes *(supose)* knowledge, which seems to imply that knowledge is not a part of faith but precedes it.[111]

While Turretin distinguishes seven acts of faith, Pictet reduces this number to four. In the *first* act, we give assent *(assentimur)* to the complete Word of God and especially to the promises of the Gospel that persuades us that Christ is the Savior. This first act (corresponding to Turretin's second and third act) is common to both humans and demons. Pictet's *second* act is that act in which we are persuaded that Christ is the Savior of all who repent and seek righteousness and salvation in him, and consequently that he is our Savior if we repent and seek refuge in him. Demons cannot perform this second act (corresponding to Turretin's fourth act).

---

108 Pictet, *TC,* IX, 4, ii; *TCF,* X, 8; *Medulla,* 135.
109 Pictet, *TCF,* X, 8.
110 Pictet, *TC,* IX, 4, i; *TCF,* X, 8 and *Medulla,* 138 add that faith is a fruit of Christ's death.
111 Pictet, *TC,* IX, 4, x; *TCF,* X, 8.

The third act of faith as described by Pictet comprises the acts of reception and adhesion as described by Turretin, viz. hunger and thirst after the righteousness of Christ out of a sense of our misery and inability, praying the Father to impute Christ's obedience to us, surrendering ourselves to Christ and being united to him. This act is the proper act of justifying faith. The last act (comprising Turretin's last two acts) is a reflexive act, whereby we behold in ourselves the conditions Christ requires of those whose Savior he is and hence we conclude that he is our Savior. This act is attended with consolation and the peace of conscience.[112] Pictet does not use the word *fiducia* for this last act. Rather, he inquires whether *fiducia* (trust or assurance) belongs to the essence of faith or an effect of faith. Pictet answers that if this *fiducia* refers to the act by which we depend and rely on the merits of Christ, it is part of the essence of faith. But if the term is understood as a firm persuasion of reconciliation with God, it is an effect of faith with respect to the direct acts (the first three) but part of the essence of faith with respect to the reflexive act. Pictet argued that this persuasion is not an essential act of faith, for no one can assure himself that he is reconciled to God without discovering through reflection that he has true faith. Hence, this persuasion presupposes saving faith already existing in the heart. It is the property of a strong and confirmed faith but not of a weak faith.[113]

Elements of faith		Turretin on the acts of faith	Pictet on the acts of faith
knowledge	*notitia*	*Essential acts of faith* 1. act of knowledge	Faith presupposes knowledge
assent	*assensus*	2. theoretical assent 3. fiducial and practical assent	1. act of assent
trust	*fiducia*	4. act of refuge 5. act of reception and adhesion 6. reflexive act	2. act of refuge 3. act of reception and adhesion 4. reflexive act; essential in the sense of relying on Christ
		Non-essential act of faith 7. act of consolation and confidence	non-essential in the sense of persuasion of reconciliation.

---

112 Pictet, *TC*, IX, 4, x-xiii; *TCF*, X, 8; *Medulla*, 136.
113 Pictet, *TC*, IX, 4, iii; *TCF*, X, 8.

According to Pictet, it is easy to define the nature of faith from its acts. Yet he does not offer his own definition in his *Theologia* but offers several definitions given by others.[114] In his *Medulla*, he needed to be brief, and there he offers his own definition of justifying faith:

> It is a living persuasion of the veracity and of the promises of the gospel, which makes us take refuge in Christ and to search after his justice and salvation, and to embrace him, and which at the same time changes our heart and urges it to be obedient to Christ.[115]

In his *Théologie Chrétienne*, Pictet describes faith in two ways. Regarding the first three acts, faith is a persuasion by which we give assent to the truth of the Gospel and to its promises, take refuge in Christ, and seek salvation in him. Regarding the last act, faith is a firm assurance that God gave us his Son and that our sins are pardoned. But one should not believe immediately that Christ died for him and that his sins are forgiven unless he finds the first acts of faith within himself.[116]

A person can be sure of his faith and hence of his salvation and election, but only after a thorough self-examination. Assurance can be obtained if we perceive a sense of our corruption in ourselves, hatred of sin, and the pursuit of holiness, love of Christ, embracing him not only as Priest but also as King and following him not only in his triumph but also in his sufferings, if we feel peace and unspeakable joy, and if we love to read and meditate upon the Word and love to pray.[117]

Pictet agrees with Turretin on most things, but there is no theme on which Pictet differs from him more than on the nature of faith. Pictet includes knowledge *(notitia)* in faith but does not see it as an act, as Turretin had done. Moreover, Pictet excluded the reflexive act from the essence of faith. He thereby excluded the trust that "Christ died for me" from the essence of faith. This is a paradox in Pictet's theology. On the one hand, he does not stress the doctrine of particular atonement, not even mentioning it in his chapters on Christ's suffering and death and on his priestly office. In this regard, he seems to have been more moderate than Turretin. On the other hand, he excludes the trust that "Christ died

---

114 Pictet, *TC*, IX, 4, iii.
115 *Medulla*, 136-37: "Est persuasione viva veritatum & promissionum Evangelicarum, quae nos ad Christum confugere, & in eo justitiam, & salutem quaerere, eumque amplecti facit, simulque cor nostrum immutat, & ad Christo obediendum impellit."
116 Pictet, *TCF*, X, 8.
117 Pictet, *TC,* IX, 6, i-ii; *TCF,* X, 10.

for me" from the essence of faith, while Turretin tried to include this trust in the essence of faith. In this respect, he seems to have been stricter than Turretin.

Pictet also deals with assurance in his book on election. Election is immutable and hence certain. The names of the elect are written in the book of life in heaven.[118] Believers can be certain of their own election, not by ascending to heaven to read this book of life but by descending into their own hearts to read the book of their conscience and discover the fruits of election. These fruits are true faith, hatred of sin, a sincere pursuit of holiness, an unfeigned love for God, love for our neighbors, even our enemies, and a heart that despises the world and longs for heaven.[119] There is no reason for despair if one lacks this certainty. Although believers can be certain of their election, they are not always certain of it. On the other hand, being sure of salvation is not a sure mark of true faith. There are people who boast about their certain election, who do not possess faith and repentance. All true believers will receive the assurance of their election at one time or another, but it cannot exist without the pursuit of holiness. The certainty of election can exist with "fear and trembling" if this is a filial fear and not a servile fear. This doctrine of the individual assurance of election offers great comfort.[120] Pictet's view of the assurance of election is in accordance with Beza, the delegates, and Turretin.[121]

6.12 Preaching the Doctrine of Predestination

Pictet does not answer the question whether predestination ought to be preached in his *Theologia Christiana* nor in his *Medulla*. All he does is make some remarks relating to it. For instance, the doctrine of the assurance of election should be set forth "cautiously and prudently" for the sake of comforting afflicted consciences, not for the encouragement of the ungodly. It should never be enforced without enjoining the pursuit of repentance and sanctification.[122] The French edition contains a short discourse on this question. Pictet answers affirmatively since the apostles spoke about God's decrees concerning the end of human beings. Some

---

118 Pictet, *TC*, VII, 2; *TCF*, VIII, 5. The French edition contains answers to objections against the doctrine of the certainty of election.
119 Pictet, *TC*, VII, 3, i-ii. In the French edition, the doctrine of the individual assurance of salvation is not treated in the book on predestination but in the book on faith, since one can only be certain of his election through faith; *TCF*, X, 10.
120 Pictet, *TC*, VII, 3, ii.
121 See 3.12, 4.3 and 5.10.
122 Pictet, *TC*, VII, 3, ii.

may abuse this doctrine, yet it is very useful and offers comfort. But it should be preached with prudence. We should only think of what God has revealed and leave the hidden things to God. Predestination should not be taught to those who do not yet know the clearest truths of the Christian faith. They should be taught as Christ taught Nicodemus: he told him that whoever believes will not perish but have eternal life, and that he who does not believe is already condemned. It is not necessary to tell people about the different views concerning predestination. One should only use the words of Scripture. Moreover, one should not preach about it frequently but only occasionally, as when the order of texts preached about requires it or when there is great discord in the church between those included among the holiest – a circumstance Pictet thought Paul was facing in 2 Timothy 2:19 – or when believers in times of persecution are afraid they will not persevere but perish.

In teaching this doctrine, one should first state that God has the right to punish us all eternally and, second, that it is out of God's great goodness that he does not want everyone to perish. It should be pointed out, third, that we should not strive to know whether we are elect but be persuaded that we are saved if we have faith and love. Lastly, one should state that those who are predestined to eternal life have no reason to boast and that those predestined to damnation have no reason to complain since the latter are getting what they deserve.[123]

In most things Pictet agrees with Turretin. Some less important differences are that he does not write about the necessity of preaching predestination because of the calumnies of its opponents nor that it should not be taught in the churches in the same way as in the schools. Pictet leaves out the question of the way in which predestination should be applied (from effects to causes), but he explains this in his chapter on the assurance of election. There is also an important difference to be noticed, and one omission that might be an important indication. The difference is that Pictet holds that predestination should not be preached often. The omission is that Pictet did not repeat Turretin's view that predestination is one of the primary doctrines of the Gospel and foundations of faith. The combination of this difference and this omission is especially an indication that Pictet, after all, regarded the doctrine of predestination as less important for preaching than Turretin did.[124] This might also explain why

---

123 Pictet, *TCF*, VIII, 1.
124 Another indication for this hypothesis is that he does not mention predestination in his catechisms. Pictet, *Cinq Catechismes pour Instruire les jeunes gens dans la Religion Reformée* (Geneva: Jean Antoine Querel, 1715).

he does not mention election in several chapters where one might expect it, as has been concluded in several preceding sections.

6.13 Summary: Predestination and the External Call

Pictet stated that he wrote his *Theologia Christiana* as a didactical addition to Turretin's *Institutes*. Whether or not this was his real or most important reason (6.1.3), this statement indicates that he presupposes at least knowledge and probably approval of Turretin's theology. This makes it difficult to evaluate the differences between the two, for it is not always clear whether the differences in their works really reflect differences in their views. There are differences on several levels. One difference concerns the technical level. Turretin's *Institutes* are very technical, making use of distinctions and scholastic instruments at a high level. He was also very detailed in writing about his subjects. Pictet's *Theologia Christiana* is less technical and less detailed. Klauber's correction of De Budé was right: Pictet does not follow Reformed scholasticism insofar as this concerns method and techniques (6.2). Nonetheless, Pictet was a defender of Reformed theology as propagated by his predecessors with respect to the content of theology.

Another difference concerns how predestination is intertwined with other doctrines. Pictet does not do this explicitly, which suggests that predestination has a lesser place in his theology than in Turretin's, but in several places, he clearly agrees with Turretin or presupposes Turretin's position (6.3). This quantitative ambivalence in dealing with predestination in relation to other doctrines corresponds to Pictet's ambivalence concerning the value of the doctrine of predestination and related doctrines. On the one hand, he defends the *Formula Consensus,* which did not tolerate Salmurian theology, and, on the other hand, he himself wrote a book in which he argues for tolerance of Lutheran theology, even though Lutherans held ideas rejected in the *Formula* Differences with Lutherans on predestination were not fundamental to him. (6.5).

Pictet's ambivalence regarding the doctrine of predestination is best explained by the hypothesis that he accepted this doctrine as formulated in the *Canons of Dort* and in the *Formula* as true and as the best expression of the biblical teaching on this matter but did not deem this doctrine to be so fundamental as to be an obstacle to union with Lutherans. Moreover, defending the *Formula* was a means to keep up the good name of the Genevan Academy and to retain unity within the Genevan church. Besides, Pictet saw dangers greater than the theology of Saumur: he saw indifference concerning religion in general, as if all religions, either Christianity or Mohammedanism or Judaism, etc. were all the same in essence. In such a situation, it seemed best to him not to argue against other forms of Protestant Christianity but to aim at unity and to stress the fundamental consensus of the various Protestant religions and confessions. Hence, in his book on consensus with the Lutherans, he modifies the doctrine of predestination in such a way that even Remonstrants might have agreed with most of it. Last but not least, Pictet worked and preached in a time in which Genevan orthodoxy was declining. Most of his colleagues were less orthodox than he was. Pictet himself held to the old doctrines concerning predestination, while his colleagues were more indifferent. Although Pictet defended the theology laid down in Turretin's *Institutes*, he had to work with his more moderate colleagues, and he knew that he was in a minority. He was not in a position to polemize against the majority of his colleagues. This could explain why Pictet did not engage in polemics in his *Theologiae Christiana* (6.1, 6.5).

With respect to the content of Pictet's doctrine of predestination, there is no difference between Turretin and him. The *praedestinatio gemina* as an unchangeable and eternal decree of God, the infralapsarian order of the decrees, the way assurance of election can be gained – these are all themes on which Pictet completely agrees with his uncle. Yet it is paradoxical that this complete unity in doctrine was accompanied by a very different estimation of the value and importance of the doctrine. It was fundamental to Turretin, but not to Pictet (6.3).

Pictet has no separate book on the doctrine of the covenant in his *Theologia*.[125] Combining all his remarks on this subject however, it again turns out that he agrees with Turretin. But at first sight, his *Theologia* gives a different impression. Pictet does not explicitly intertwine the doctrine of predestination with his doctrine of the covenant. Only in his chapters on baptism and its efficacy does he explicitly remark that the covenant was established with the elect. In the chapter on the covenant, this can only be inferred. With respect to the church, Pictet was more explicit in relating it to the doctrine of election. Only the elect believers are true members of the church (6.6, 6.7).

With respect to the doctrine of atonement, we see a pattern similar to what we see with the doctrine of the covenant. Again, looking at all his remarks together, it turns out that Pictet agrees with Turretin, although his *Theologia* gives another impression. Pictet does not devote a separate chapter to the extent of the atonement. He does not explicitly state that Christ died for the elect, but for humankind. In his remarks on the death

---

125 A book and a chapter in Pictet's *Theologia* are comparable with resp. a *locus* and a *quaestio* in Turretin's *Institutio*.

of Christ, the only reason to suppose Pictet adhered to particular redemption is because those remarks are part of a chapter on the execution of election. An explicit doctrine of particular redemption can only be derived from remarks concerning Christ's intercession which has the same extent as his sacrifice, viz. those given to Christ by the Father. These are of course the elect, but even here the precise word is not used. Again, it seems that Pictet agrees with Turretin concerning the content of this doctrine but gave it a different status (6.4, 6.5).

Faith is connected to election since God gives the elect the power to believe. Pictet agrees with Turretin that "Christ died for me" is not the object of faith. He argues that one can only believe that Christ died for him after one has discovered the first acts of faith within him and not immediately. This presupposes particular redemption, but Pictet does not mention this. On the nature of faith, Pictet even argues that the assurance that Christ died for me does not belong to the essence of faith (6.11).

Pictet agrees with Calvin, Beza, the delegates to the Synod of Dort, and Turretin that only the elect will, by God's grace, give a positive response to preaching. There is no conscious reflection on the question of predestination and the general call of the Gospel in Pictet's works and (hence) no section on conditionality. Again, combining data from several chapters, it turns out that Pictet agrees with Turretin on this subject. He does not stress the necessity of knowing one's misery, as his predecessors had done (6.10).

The historical context has been important for the way Pictet deals with the doctrine of predestination. Although agreeing with the staunch Reformed doctrines of Turretin, he had to cooperate with more moderate colleagues who did not preach or teach on predestination. Pictet's theology is ambivalent, maintaining Turretin's orthodoxy for himself and if possible for the Genevan church but not deeming it fundamental enough to obstruct union with or toleration of those who held other views. Pictet's theology is an example of Reformed theology between strict orthodoxy and enlightened orthodoxy (6.1).

6.14 Pictet's Sermons

Pictet published several sermons. Some were published as single sermons, others in volumes of collected sermons.[126] A remarkable volume is his series of sermons on different religions in which he examines several religions and compares them with Reformed Christianity.[127] Another vol-

---

126 See 6.1.3.
127 Pictet, *Huit Sermons sur L'Examen des Religions* (Geneva: Société des Libraires, 1701) (first published in 1698). Quoted as *Examen*.

ume consists of a series of seven sermons on Paul's discourse on the Areopagus and seven sermons on various texts.[128] These two volumes will be subject of our investigation here. The latter volume, containing several sermons on various texts, can give an impression of Pictet's approach to preaching. The first is quite atypical for Genevan sermons, yet it is interesting to see how Pictet deals with the doctrine of predestination in speaking to his congregation.

6.14.1 The Examination of Religions
The volume with sermons on the examination of religions was published in 1698. It is a series of sermons on 1 Thessalonians 5:21: *Test everything. Hold on to the good.* Pictet used this admonition by Paul to test several religions. This is necessary, he says in the first sermon, because many people do not search for the truth and only adhere to the Christian religion because they are born into it. He answers the question why the God of truth permits so many errors and false religions in the world. We should not penetrate into the counsel of God since he did not reveal why he permitted sin. God is not the author of sin and error. Errors serve to manifest God's justice and to reveal the true disciples of Jesus. But why, is the next question, does God not give true knowledge to all people? Pictet's answer was a quote from Paul, i.e., that God has mercy on whom he wills and hardens whom he wills (Rom. 9:18), and from Jesus, who thanks the Father that he had hidden these things for the wise and prudent and revealed them to little children (Lk 10:21). We know this is the will of God, but we should not ask why it is his will. We should labor to distinguish the truth of God from the errors of the devil. These observations urged him to exhort his congregation not only to examine religions but to examine themselves in the first place as to whether they really are children of God, as they claim.[129] Without mentioning election or reprobation by name here, Pictet actually preaches about them. God's will is the reason why some people receive the truth and others do not. Pictet immediately tells his congregation not to search for the hidden reason behind God's will but to search the revealed truth. In addressing unbelievers, and believers who just believe the Christian doctrine because they are born Christians without ever examining the truth of their religion and presenting 18 items his hearers can use to examine the truth of their being Christian – repeating the exhortation to examine oneself 18 times – he

---

128 Pictet, *Quatorze Sermons sur Divers Textes de L'Ecriture Sainte* (Geneva: les Frères de Tournes, 1719). Quoted as *Quatorze Sermons*.
129 Pictet, *Examen*, 10-11, 52-59.

clearly manifests his fear that some or even many of his hearers might not be true Christians.[130]

In the second sermon, Pictet contrasts natural, pagan, Islamic, and the Judaic religion with Christianity. In the third sermon, he answers several objections to Christianity, like the mysteries of the Trinity and the incarnation. One of these mysteries concerns election and reprobation, in which the inference is drawn that it is of no use to do anything to be saved, for whoever is elect will be saved, even if he lives in sin, and, conversely, whoever is reprobate can do whatever he wants – he will be damned.[131] It is hard to imagine a heathen, Jew, or Mohammedan making this objection to a Genevan preacher. It is likely that Pictet took the occasion to answer a question or objection he encountered among Genevan Christians. Pictet answers that it is true that God predestined a certain number of people to glory, but he does not give them this glory, except on the condition that they work on their sanctification. If Paul had continued in his role as a persecutor of Christians, he would have been damned, elected or not. And if it were possible for a person who is not elect to live a life of complete holiness, he would infallibly obtain salvation.[132] Here Pictet uses the conditional structure to answer the question about predestination and responsibility. His language is even more bold than that of his predecessors theirs, when he says that Paul would have been damned had he continued to persecute Christians. In the context of his theology, it is impossible for Paul, as elect, to have continued persecuting Christians, yet Pictet did not deem it necessary to say so in his sermon. All stress is laid on the condition of sanctification. This is where he differs from his predecessors, for they usually cited the conditions of faith and repentance, with sanctification as more or less a synonym of the latter. Pictet leaves out the condition of faith and only refers to the condition of sanctification. It seems Pictet was a child of his times in laying so much stress on sanctification.

In this sermon Pictet introduces two cases not seen in the sermons or writings of his Genevan predecessors.

> There are people who say that they want to believe. But what will they do in order to believe? *Faith is a gift of God*, but they never ask for it. *Faith comes by*

---

130 In the second sermon, Pictet refers to the increasing number of unbelievers in his day. Cf. *Examen*, 178.
131 Pictet, *Examen*, 173.
132 Pictet, *Examen*, 173-74.

hearing, and hearing by the Word of God, but these men neither read nor listen to the Word.[133]

The doctrine of election is not mentioned as the reason why these people who say they want to believe do not actually believe. Pictet points to human responsibility. The second new case is related to the first. It is the question what one should do in order not to be included among the miserable unbelievers. Pictet answers that such a person should do several things. He should ask the Spirit to illuminate him, to produce faith in him, to mortify his flesh, to subdue his pride, and to make all thoughts captive to the obedience of Christ. He should do this constantly. He should hear, read, and meditate on the Word. He should read books that help him understand divine truths. He should examine the right faith. He should examine whether he exhibits pride, libertinism, or anything else that leads him to pernicious thoughts. If everyone would do this, the number of unbelievers would not increase. But if there is someone "among us" with an evil and unbelieving heart, he should think about the words of the Gospel: whoever believes the Son has eternal life, but the wrath of God rests on whoever does not believe.[134]

These are two types of unbelievers who say they want to believe. Calvin, Beza, and Turretin did not mention these types. Pictet also addresses believers in another way. While Calvin, Beza, and Turretin addressed the congregation in general by "us" and as believers, and Turretin consistently used "us" and "brothers" for believers and "you" for unbelievers, Pictet thinks that there could be someone "among us" with an evil and unbelieving heart. In general, he addresses the congregation as "brothers" *(freres)*, but, in the application of the third sermon, he addresses the Christians who are convinced of the divine truths as "you." Instead of offering consolation, he simply warns them. It is not enough to believe in God if "you" live like an atheist. It is not enough to believe that Jesus Christ came to save repenting sinners, if "you" do not repent and if sin reigns over "you." It is not enough to believe he will come to judge, if "you" do not prepare for this judgment by a sanctified life. The faith that saves is not an historical faith but a faith working through love; it is a purifying faith, a regenerating faith. "Let us all ask for this faith from God, let us pray that he will increase it day

---

133 Pictet, *Examen*, 180: "Il y a des gens qui dissent qu'ils voudroient bien croire. Mais que sont-ils pout cela? *La foy est un don de Dieu*, mais ils ne la lui demandent jamais. *La foi vient de l'ouïe, & l'ouïe de la Parole de Dieu*; mais ces gens ne lisent ni n'écoutent Point la Parole."
134 Pictet, *Examen*, 180-82.

by day in us."¹³⁵ This way of addressing the congregation, not as believers but as potential unbelievers, was new for Geneva.

The fourth sermon is devoted to the examination of the Catholic Church, the fifth to that of the religion of the Greek or Eastern Church and that of the Protestant churches. Examining the Reformed faith, he gives a summary of doctrines that is in fact a summary of his *Theologia*.¹³⁶ In this sermon, confession, or summary of Reformed doctrine, Pictet mentions God's decrees in general, election, atonement, vocation, and faith, all themes related to the question of predestination and preaching. With respect to God's decrees, Pictet tells his congregation that the eternal God has decreed from eternity everything that would happen on earth. These decrees are eternal, most wise and immutable.¹³⁷ He proposes the doctrine of election by saying that all men, being sinful and meriting death, would never reach salvation, if God had not, before the foundation of ages, chosen or elected some whom he predestined to glory, while he left all the others in their corruption.¹³⁸ No mention is made of election in connection with the atonement. Christ is said to have died for "us" and for "our sins." Election is mentioned both in relation to the atonement and the call in article 23, on the call.

> We proclaim with Saint Paul that all those who are predestined and for whom he did not spare his own Son are called, and that by this call God revives them from being dead, which they were.¹³⁹

---

135 Pictet, *Examen*, 183-84: "Demandons tous à Dieu cette foi, prions-le qu'il l'augmente tous les jours en nous …"
136 This summary looks like a confession with articles, but it is not a literal quotation of any confession. The order of the articles in this sermon is the same as the order of books in his *Theologia*, save the article on providence: Book I, God and Scripture: Art. 1-6; Book II, the Trinity: Art. 7-9; Book III, God's decrees in general: Art. 10; Book IV, Creation: Art. 11 and 13; Book V, the Fall and sin: Art. 13-15; Book VI, Providence: Art. 12; Book VII, Predestination: Art. 16. Book VIII, Christ: Art. 17-22; Book IX, Vocation and faith: Art. 23-25; Book X, Justification: Art. 26. Book XI, Sanctification: Art. 27-30; Book XII, Glorification: Art. 31; Book XIII, Church: Art. 32-36; Book XIV, Sacraments: Art. 37-40.
137 Pictet, *Examen*, 330: "Nous croions, que ce Dieu eternal, Pere, Fils & S. Esprit arête de toute éternité tout ce qui doit arriver dans le monde, & que ses arrest sont eternels, trés sages & immuables …"
138 Pictet, *Examen*, 333: "Nous croions en suite, que tous les homes étans pecheurs & meritans la mort, il n'y en auroit aucun de bienheureux, si Dieu, avant la foundation des siécles, n'en avoit choisis ou élus quelques uns qu'il a predestinez à la gloire, tandis qu'il a laissé tous les autres dans leur corruption …"
139 Pictet, *Examen*, 337-38: "Nous annonçons avec S. Paul, que tous ceux que Dieu a predestinez, & pour lesquels il n'a point epergne son Fils, sont appelez, & que par cette vocation, Dieu les vivifie, de morts, qu'ils étoient …"

In the next articles Pictet confesses that, since human nature is dead in offences, no one will come to Christ unless the Father draws him. God effects the willing and the doing in us, taking away the heart of stone and giving us a heart of flesh. Faith is a gift of God by which believers are persuaded of the veracity of God's promises and take refuge in Christ.[140] The church is described as a religious and spiritual society of all persons who are called by the Word and Spirit, in accordance with God's purpose of election.[141] A doctrine missing from this summary of Reformed faith is the doctrine of the covenant. Obviously, Pictet did not regard it as very important, for he had also paid little attention to it in his *Theologia*. What Pictet tells his congregation regarding predestination is in accordance with what he wrote in his systematic theology. He does not leave out this doctrine in this sermon. In contrast to some of his contemporaries, he did not deem the doctrine of predestination to be of little or even no use. He did not even hesitate to mention the doctrine of reprobation.

In the sixth sermon, Pictet answers several objections from Roman Catholics to Reformed doctrine. One of those objections was to the Reformed doctrine of predestination. Pictet answers by proving the doctrine of election from Ephesians 1 and that of reprobation from Romans 9. He defends the concept that God elects men without foreseeing faith or good works in them but merely by his good pleasure *(par son pur bon plaisir)*. Faith and good works are not reasons for our election, but fruits. Pictet explains to his congregation the distinction between sin as the reason for reprobation in general, but God's will as the reason for reprobation of the one and the election of the other. Although it is God who damns sinners, sin is the cause proper of damnation, not God. One can be assured of one's election if, after serious examination, one is conscious of a true faith and a serious repentance.[142]

The fifth and sixth sermons are both followed by applications in which Pictet again shows himself to be distressed about his congregation. In the sixth sermon, he answers several objections by Roman Catholics but mentions one objection to the Reformed in the application that he could not answer satisfactorily: the objection that our lives are not worthy of those who profess to be disciples of Christ.[143]

---

140 Pictet, *Examen*, 338-39.
141 Pictet, *Examen*, 343: "[S]on Eglise, qui n'est autre chose, qu'une societé religieuse & spirituelle de plusieurs personnes appellées par la parole de Dieu, & par l'efficace interieure du S. Esprit, selon le propos arête de l'election de Dieu …"
142 Pictet, *Examen*, 375-81.
143 Pictet, *Examen*, 432-36.

Pictet's sermons on the examination of religions are in complete accordance with his view of the doctrine of predestination and related doctrines. What he tells his congregation about predestination, assurance, atonement, and the church is an echo of what he writes about these subjects in his theological works. It is remarkable that he does not say anything about the covenant. He does not pay too much attention to this doctrine in his *Christian Theology* but leaves it out in these sermons, even in his summary of Reformed doctrine. Another remarkable point is that Pictet makes clear the relation between the atonement and election, not when he preaches about the atonement but when he preaches about the call. These sermons display nothing of Pictet's ambivalence concerning the status of the doctrine of predestination. Rather, he presents it boldly in all the aspects he had written about in his systematic works.

Although Pictet regarded the church as a society of all those who are called by the Word and the Spirit, he did not regard all members of his congregation, at least not all who heard him preach, as being effectively called by the Word and the Spirit. His approach to the congregation is quite negative. Though he addresses the congregation as brothers *(freres)*, he doubted the faith and repentance of many. In this, he was preceded by Calvin, Beza, and Turretin, although it is more prominent in Pictet's sermons than in theirs.

6.14.2 The Fourteen Sermons
Unlike the *Huit Sermons sur L'Examen des Religions*, where a text of the Bible was only an occasion to speak about several religions, the 14 sermons in Pictet's other volume are ordinary sermons in the sense that Pictet expounds and applies a text in them. This makes this volume more interesting with respect to the question how Pictet put his theories regarding predestination into practice and the question how he addressed the congregation. Among these sermons are some of special interest, like the fifth sermon on God's voice inviting people to repent, the seventh on the Gospel, rejected and despised by profane people but received by the elect, the tenth on the picture of Christ's servants, preached at the ordination of two ministers, the eleventh on the parable of the invitation to the banquet, the twelfth on the marvelous effects of the preaching of Peter at Pentecost, and the thirteenth on being drawn to Christ by grace. The first seven sermons are on Paul's discourse on the Areopagus. They call to mind more the *lectio continua* practiced by Calvin and Beza than Turretin's sermons. Pictet gave a word-by-word explanation of the text.

None of the sermons in Pictet's volume are on a text that mentions predestination. This makes it difficult to compare him with his predecessors, given that Calvin and Turretin did publish sermons on such texts. We do not know how Pictet dealt with the doctrine of predestination in such sermons, although the way he spoke about it in the *Examination of Religions* suggests that he would have explained the doctrine to the congregation on the basis of such texts.

Pictet's sermons correspond with those of his predecessors in that he seldom mentions predestination if the text gives no occasion to do so. He differs slightly here from his teacher Turretin, who mentioned predestination somewhat more often because he treated texts in his sermons in a more systematic-theological way. Pictet's reluctance to speak about predestination is evident in passages where one would expect him to speak about it. For instance, in the beginning of the sermon on Acts 17:30, Pictet mentions that God left all people, save that of Israel, in the darkness of ignorance and corruption. God illuminated the smallest part of the world, even abandoning the larger part of Abraham's posterity. Pictet uses similar words to describe the doctrine of reprobation in his theological works. But in this sermon, he does not mention reprobation or predestination. Instead, he speaks of God's providence, which dispenses its benefits as it deems right.[144] In another place, Pictet sums up some virtues of God in the work of salvation. He does not mention God's freedom or sovereignty there.[145] And when he lists some heresies, he does not mention any error concerning the doctrine of predestination. Nor does he speak about predestination when he urges preachers to preach openly the doctrines that are attacked today.[146]

This does not mean that he declines to use words like predestination or election at all in his sermons. When he states that the number of believers is much smaller than the number of the wicked, he quotes the text that states that many are called but few are chosen and says that nobody is ordained to eternal life other than believers. Though the number of the elect is not the greatest, it is the choicest (*plus choici*).[147] In his sermon on the effect of Peter's sermon on the day of Pentecost, Pictet remarks that not all were pricked in their heart. It is not given to all to believe, but faith is for the elect. Only those who were ordained to eternal life believed Peter. God left the others in their blindness, for they themselves did not

---

144 Pictet, *Quatorze Sermons*, 167-168. "Adorons la Providence, qui dispense ses bienfaits, comme elle le juge a propos, ..."
145 Pictet, *Quatorze Sermons*, 342-43.
146 Pictet, *Quatorze Sermons*, 406-08, 424.
147 Pictet, *Quatorze Sermons*, 271.

want to open their eyes.[148] Pictet explains the words "so that my house will be full" (Luke 14:23), as meaning "till the number of the elect is full."[149] He answers a question concerning children who were taken away from believers to be raised and educated in superstition and idolatry by saying that such children will be saved notwithstanding, if they are elect.[150] He mentions that "we" are elected in Christ.[151]

What Pictet tells his congregation about predestination, is in agreement with his theology. He sometimes mentions the content of the doctrine without using the words predestination, election, or reprobation.

Pictet pays little attention in his sermons to questions concerning the assurance of salvation or election. Such a phrase occurs only once. If a Christian wants to know whether he will be saved, he should see if he exhibits the image of Christ.[152] Likewise, little attention is paid to the question of whom Christ died for. There is no suggestion of particular or universal atonement. All Pictet said about it was that Christ died for "us," just as Calvin, Beza, and Turretin had done.[153] The question of the extent of the atonement had been a reason for divisions between Protestants, but Pictet argues that being bought by the blood of Christ is a reason instead to pursue the communion with other Christians.[154]

The congregation is addressed as "you" *(vous)* and as "brothers" *(freres)*. Pictet does not follow Turretin's distinction in addressing the unconverted hearers as "you" and true believers as "we" and "brothers." Pictet's way of addressing his congregation shows great similarity to Calvin, who addressed both the promises and the threats of the Bible to the whole congregation. Pictet, on the one hand, said that "we" are happier than the heathen since "we" behold with uncovered face the glory of the Lord. On the other hand, however, "we" will be more miserable than the heathen if "we" despise the knowledge of God and the Savior, if "we" do not do his will. On the day of judgment, Christians will be treated more rigorously than others, Protestants even more rigorously, but "we" the most rigorous of all.[155] Pictet was obviously very critical of and worried

---

148 Pictet, *Quatorze Sermons*, 494.
149 Pictet, *Quatorze Sermons*, 451.
150 Pictet, *Quatorze Sermons*, 331.
151 Pictet, *Quatorze Sermons*, 522.
152 Pictet, *Quatorze Sermons*, 381.
153 Pictet, *Quatorze Sermons*, 79, 117.
154 Pictet, *Quatorze Sermons*, 117.
155 Pictet, *Quatorze Sermons*, 195-202. This indicates that he did indeed think that the Genevan confession, including the *Formula*, was the best summary of biblical doctrine.

about his congregation. He thanks God for giving the knowledge of the true God to Geneva, but he acknowledges that there is "a great number among us who render themselves unworthy of this grace." There are atheists and libertines, there are those who are persuaded of the truth of natural religion but who despise the Christian religion, there are those who are not eager to be instructed by Christ, those who dispute some fundamental doctrines like the Trinity, those who think all religions are the same, and those who are superstitious. Pictet exhorts his "brothers" to know God as he has revealed himself.[156] Seeing many people who did not practice the Christian faith anymore, even though they were educated in the truth, he tells his congregation that such people are not true children of the church and not worthy of its tears. The church should be happy that God has sifted the tares from the wheat.[157] Even when Pictet speaks about the response to preaching, he shows himself to be critical. There are always three kinds of people, he tells his congregation, who hear the Gospel: those who mock, those who doubt, and those who believe. The latter include those who believe without knowing why. Others believe just because they are brought up among Christians. Some say they believe but live as if they do not believe. One should not be astonished on hearing that someone who has risen to a position of dignity has abandoned the truth. The number of true believers is very small *(tres petit)*. When people complain that they are not edified by Pictet's sermons, the reason is that they do not receive them with faith. Hence, many exhortations to repentance have no effect.[158] In general, Pictet worries about the members of his congregation, and hence his warnings and threats against heresy, latitudinarianism, and apostasy are more prominent in his sermons than consolations to true believers.

In his sermons, Pictet says nothing concerning God's purpose in preaching in relation to predestination. The task of preachers is mentioned several times. They have to preach God's Word and his laws and administer his sacraments. Their doctrine should be very pure *(tres pure)*, and nothing should be added to it or mingled with it. They should not

---

156 Pictet, *Quatorze Sermons*, 34-42.
157 Pictet, *Quatorze Sermons*, 331-32.
158 Pictet, *Quatorze Sermons*, 280, 511-12, 515. In the 14th sermon, on pp. 556-58, Pictet distinguishes four kinds of people among those who heard him preach. The first kind consists of those who fear the loss of worldly goods and hence do not seek God's kingdom. The second kind consists of those who vacillate between heaven and earth. The third kind is made up of those who believe and persevere. The fourth kind consists of those who seek the kingdom of God.

ignore any occasion to bring souls to Christ.[159] Pictet did not stress the invitation to Christ or the offer of the Gospel. He simply says that a preacher should preach God's Word faithfully. He stresses the necessity of pure doctrine and reproaches preachers who do not preach about principal truths and mysteries, under the pretext that they surpass our reason or because they were not persuaded about these doctrines themselves. He also reproaches preachers who preach moralistically, just like the heathens, only quoting some texts of Scripture but leaving out specific Christian doctrines. A pure life should be accompanied by pureness of doctrine.[160] Pictet shows himself to be zealous for missions, praying that God would have mercy on the human race *(toute le genre humain)* that Jesus might be known all over the world, by heathens and Jews.[161] This zeal for mission was a new element, hardly seen before in Genevan theology or sermons.

Pictet spoke repeatedly about the response to preaching. A negative reaction to preaching is always due to human corruption, although Pictet sometimes relates it to God's decree. For instance, the people of Capernaum did not believe because it was not given them from the Father. Yet those who do not receive the Spirit have no reason to complain, for God is indebted to nobody. He leaves those in blindness who do not want to open their eyes to the light of the Gospel, against their conscience, and against the admonitions of his servants, and they reject the means offered by God to come to him. To them the Gospel is a savor of death unto death.[162] A positive response in faith and repentance is always due to the work of the Spirit. This is always mentioned by Pictet whenever he speaks of the response to preaching. Because of the Spirit, there will always be some who accept the Gospel.[163] Several times he explicitly traces this back to God's decree or at least to God's sovereignty.

> God is a sovereign free Being, he causes his wind to blow where and when it pleases him; he has mercy upon whom he wants to have mercy.[164] It is not

---

159 Pictet, *Quatorze Sermons*, 391, 405, 426.
160 Pictet, *Quatorze Sermons*, 391, 405.
161 Pictet, *Quatorze Sermons*, 42.
162 Pictet, *Quatorze Sermons*, 494. Cf. 510, 563.
163 Pictet, *Quatorze Sermons*, 135-36; 270-71; 279; 375-77; 383; 423; 533-35, 538, 585.
164 Pictet, *Quatorze Sermons*, 492: "Dieu est un Etre souverainement libre, il fait souffler son vent, où & quand il luy plait, il fait miséricorde à celuy à qui il veut faire miséricorde."

given to all to believe in Jesus Christ and to suffer for him. *Faith is of the elect,* says St. Paul, and only they believed who had been preordained to eternal life.[165]

Pictet pays special attention to the question whether God's work in humans takes away their liberty. Pictet denies this. Instead, the person is set free from the bondage of sin by God's work in him. The way in which the Spirit effects his work is both powerful and sweet, without constraint.[166] Pictet is so eager to deny that the preaching of the Gospel should be done with constraint that he pointed to Christ's question to his disciples "Do you not also want to go away?" (John 6:66) as "the right way to convert souls." So far was Christ from using constraint that he gave his disciples leave to go away.[167]

The Spirit's method is to accompany the preached Word, open the hearts of hearers, and transform them. He convinces us of the truth of the Gospel, leads us to pay attention to it, leads us to behold the glory of the Lord, and creates his image in us, and he gives new objects for our passions and presents to us the perfect example of Christ.[168] In another sermon, Pictet tells his congregation that the first two effects of the work of the Spirit are the remorse of the heart and a desire for salvation.[169]

In Sermon 13, on Song of Solomon 1:4, Pictet's treatment of the response to preaching – as coming to Christ – is the most extensive. Nothing in us tells us how to come to Christ and we would never know this, unless he draws us. To come to him, we need to know our ignorance, our corruption, and how much we need the grace of Christ and the blessing of salvation. To come, we need to be alive, but we are dead. To come, we need to be free, but we are bound to the world. The flesh and the world are obstacles to coming to Christ, and no person is favorably disposed to come to Christ. All favorable dispositions to come to Christ come from God, and he does not give such dispositions to all. Through his Spirit, Christ makes us both willing and able to act, and hence we work out our salvation. For that reason, Scripture teaches us on the one hand that we cannot repent and on the other that we should repent.[170] Pictet was indifferent to

---

165 Pictet, *Quatorze Sermons,* 494: "[I]l n'est pas donné à tous de croire en J. Christ & de souffrir pour luy, *La foy est des élus,* dit S. Paul, & ceux là crurent, seulement, qui avoient été préordonnez à la vie éternelle."
166 Pictet, *Quatorze Sermons,* 138-41,165; 535, 539-40.
167 Pictet, *Quatorze Sermons,* 559.
168 Pictet, *Quatorze Sermons,* 141.
169 Pictet, *Quatorze Sermons,* 482.
170 Pictet, *Quatorze Sermons,* 524-28, 540.

the question whether repentance precedes faith or vice versa. There are arguments for both positions, but he thought the Spirit worked both faith and repentance in us at the same time.[171]

If the conditional structure was less apparent in Pictet's theology than in his predecessors', it is likewise less apparent in his sermons. It does occur only sometimes – for instance, in his sermon on Acts 17:30, where Paul issues a call to repentance. Pictet stresses that repentance is the first thing we are called to and that we should repent immediately.[172] But the conditional structure only becomes apparent in combination with the next sermon, on Acts 17:31, in which Pictet states that sinners who have embraced the Savior by faith, who have truly repented, and who have shown sincere devotion will be pardoned on the day of judgment. For impenitent sinners, there will only be punishment.[173] A conditional structure can be discerned in the introduction to the sermon on Acts 2:37-38. In addition to the first two effects of repentance (compunction of the heart and a desire for salvation) two other things are needed for one to please God: the improvement of one's life and the confession of Christ (by baptism). Peter adds two promises: forgiveness of sin and the gift of the Spirit.[174] Pictet tells his congregation that the Spirit produces improvement and that he is given to those who improve themselves.[175] Unlike Turretin, he does not explain this paradox.

Compared to Calvin, Beza, and Turretin, Pictet places more stress in his sermons on Christ as the object of faith. He does not do this in all his sermons, but there are quite a number of instances in which Christ is presented as the object of faith. In the ninth sermon, especially in the application, he depicts Christ as the glory of the Lord.[176] In the 13th sermon, he presents Christ in his offices of Prophet, Priest, and King as the object of faith.[177] In one sermon he points to Scripture as the object of faith. Scripture is like a mirror in which we behold ourselves and our faults, the means to improve, the perfect example of Christ we should follow, and instructions and consolations.[178]

---

171 Pictet, *Quatorze Sermons*, 531.
172 Pictet, *Quatorze Sermons*, 186-88; 192-94.
173 Pictet, *Quatorze Sermons*, 218.
174 Pictet, *Quatorze Sermons*, 482-83, 508.
175 Pictet, *Quatorze Sermons*, 510. See also 531, where he says that the bride was already drawn to Christ yet prays to be drawn.
176 Pictet, *Quatorze Sermons*, 335-83, especially 381-83, 589.
177 Pictet, *Quatorze Sermons*, 523, 554.
178 Pictet, *Quatorze Sermons*, 380.

6.15 Summary: Theory and Practice

Pictet's sermons are consistent with his theology concerning predestination, the church, and the call. When he mentions predestination in his sermons, he adheres to the Genevan doctrine of his predecessors. He does not even hesitate to mention reprobation. Though he does not use this precise term, he does state openly that some do not believe since God does not give them faith. On the other hand, Pictet sometimes does not mention predestination or election at times when it would have been obvious to mention them. This ambivalence in Pictet's sermons is consistent with his systematic writings.

A conditional structure is less apparent in Pictet's sermons, just like in his theology. It can be found, but not as plainly as in, for example, Turretin's or Calvin's sermons. In the Pictet's sermons, the Person of Christ as the object of faith receives greater importance than it does in the sermons of his predecessors. Concerning the place of Christ, Pictet is more consistent than his predecessors were. He also shows himself more eager to preach the Gospel to all people, even to the heathen.

Pictet addresses the congregation as "you" *(vous)* and as "brothers" *(freres)* in a way similar to Calvin, who addresses both the promises and the threats of the Bible to the whole congregation. He does not make any distinction between believers ("we") and hypocrites ("you"), like Turretin did. Pictet was very critical of his congregation. Although remarks concerning the (great) number of hypocrites and unbelievers within the congregation were usual in Geneva, they occur more frequently in Pictet's sermons than in the sermons of his predecessors. Although he usually addresses them as believers, he is convinced that only a small part of those who heard him were actually true believers. Pictet also addresses a new group among his hearers: those who said they would like to believe the gospel.

Pictet's sermons reflect the developments in Geneva. His hearers were critical of him and did not find his sermons edifying. He was in turn critical of his hearers and their indifference to Reformed religion in doctrine and life. But Pictet was also affected by his time. His sermons place more stress on the necessity of sanctification. He also shows himself to be more tolerant of other protestant views than his predecessors were. In speaking on how one should deal with heretics, Pictet implicitly distanced himself from (Calvin's part in) the death penalty given to Servetus.[179]

---

179 Pictet, *Quatorze Sermons*, 452-73.

As in the chapters on Calvin, Beza, and Turretin, we can again conclude that, though predestination and the external call are closely related to each other in Pictet's theology, the doctrine does not dominate his sermons nor his ideas on the external call. Pictet showed himself even more eager than his predecessors to have the Gospel preached to all nations, including heathens, and, more than their sermons, his point to Christ as the object of faith.

6.16 Appendix: Later Developments in Geneva

Although this study formally ends with our investigation of Pictet, it is interesting to survey developments in Geneva over the next hundred years. From 1706 on, the *Formula Consensus* was no longer binding for Genevan theologians. The *Canons of Dort* were binding only to the extent that one should not preach or teach anything against them, but theologians and pastors were no longer required to subscribe to it. The year after Pictet died, 1725, the *Canons* were also abrogated.

When Diderot and d'Alembert published the seventh volume of their *Encyclopédie* in 1757, they wrote that the preachers in Geneva were actually Socinians and Deists since they were averse to dogmatism, intolerance, and scholastic discussions, did not use the term "Trinity," and propounded a "reasonable" religion.[180] The Genevan consistory protested against this description, claiming that they maintained Calvin's catechism and did not want to be called Socinians and Deists. This accusation was indeed over the top, but Geneva, as Voltaire had written a year earlier, was no longer the Geneva of Calvin. It held to a rational Christianity: the adoration of a "Supreme Being" joined with a moral life.[181] Calvin's catechism was maintained mainly in name. In actuality, it had been replaced by Osterwald's catechism, which was later changed by Jacob Vernes (1726-1770). Versions that deviated further from orthodoxy were sanctioned in 1788, 1793, and 1802.[182]

The burning of Servetus was condemned by the pastors in the second half of the 18th century, but they themselves burned Rousseau's writings, although more for their anti-aristocratic tendency than for their theological content. Rousseau was angry about that and described the pastors of

---

180 Diderot and D'Alembert, *Encyclopédie, ou Dictionnaire raisonné des sciences, des arts et des metiers*, vol. 7 (Paris: Briasson, David, Le Breton & Durand, 1757), 578A-578D.
181 Hermann Freiherr von der Goltz, *Die reformirte Kirche Genfs im neunzehnten Jahrhundert oder der Individualismus der Erweckung in seinem Verhältnis zum christlichen Staat der Reformation* (Basel/Geneva, 1862), 62-63.
182 Quoted by Van Schelven, *Het Calvinisme gedurende zijn bloeitijd. Genève – Frankrijk*, 116; Van der Goltz, *Die reformirte Kirche Genfs*, 71.

Geneva in 1764 similarly to how Diderot and D'Alembert had done: "You don't know what they believe, nor what they do not believe; you don't even know what they want to seem to believe."[183]

With respect to Geneva, the 18th century is usually seen as a period of theological decline. For instance, Von der Goltz describes the developments in 18th-century Geneva as a reaction to orthodoxy in the church.[184] Preaching about doctrines was even forbidden by a decree in 1742: not doctrine, but life; not dogmas, but morals should be preached. Von der Goltz remarked that the Genevan theologians, in their reaction to dogmatism, eventually lost the dogma itself.[185]

Contrary to Von der Goltz and others, Jennifer Powel McNutt recently offered a more positive approach to 18th-century Genevan theology. According to her, the Genevan clergy in the 18th century tried to make Calvin's teachings relevant for their own time.[186] These two different approaches resulted in different conclusions concerning predestination and preaching. According to Von der Goltz, doctrine had become almost absent from theology and sermons.[187] McNutt, however, studied several sermons and formulated a somewhat more nuanced conclusion: doctrine was less dominant in sermons than it had been in previous centuries, but it was not absent.[188] The examples she quotes do not offer much proof of the doctrine that was preached was actually Reformed teaching. This certainly applies to the sentences on predestination she quotes. For example, J-A. Turretin's phrase that God "destines us for his grace"[189] provides no information as to whether his view of predestination is Reformed or Arminian. The same holds for quotations from Gallatin, Vernet, and Francillon. She recommends further research into 18th-century Genevan sermons on this subject, for she has to concede that there is "minimal mention and explanation of this theological topic." McNutt herself suggests that one reason might have been that "the theological perspective of predestination is assumed in the Genevan context and, therefore, not a matter of extensive explanation." Another reason she suggests is that "the

---

183 Quoted by Von der Goltz, *Die reformirte Kirche Genfs*, 65.
184 Von der Goltz, *Die reformirte Kirche Genfs*, 33.
185 Von der Goltz, *Die reformirte Kirche Genfs*, 42.
186 Jennifer Powel McNutt, *Calvin Meets Voltaire: The Clergy of Geneva in the Age of Enlightnment, 1685–1798* (Farnham, UK: Ashgate, 2013).
187 Von der Goltz, *Die reformirte Kirche Genfs*, 61, 64-65.
188 McNutt, *Calvin Meets Voltaire*, 187-229. She concluded, contra Rousseau, that it was at least clear that the Genevan pastors were Protestant Christians, i.e., that they were not Roman Catholics.
189 McNutt, *Calvin Meets Voltaire*, 218.

medium of preaching may also be the cause for minimal discussion of such a dense theological concern." A third suggestion is that "in their strong desire to move away from scholastic reformed debate ... the ensuing generations of clergy shelved the topic in order to focus more on moral living."[190]

Of these suggestions, only the third is plausible. For their predecessors, predestination had to be preached, even when knowledge of it could be assumed. Knowledge of all doctrines could be assumed for those who had been taught the Genevan catechism. Moreover, predestination was not considered by any earlier Genevan theologian as not being suited to the medium of preaching. It is precisely this that was denied from Calvin to F. Turretin. McNutt's third suggestion corresponds best with the development in Genevan theology. Doctrine was regarded to be less important than moral life. The stress on morality was not new: since Farel's time, the clergy had always stressed the importance of a Christian moral life. What was new in the 18th century was that doctrine was neglected because it was felt to be less important than or even unimportant with respect to morals.

It was not only morals that ousted doctrine from its prominent place. Politics played a role here as well. The political developments, especially in France, compelled the Genevan clergy to be more tolerant of other Protestants. The repeal of the Edict of Nantes in 1685 brought many French Huguenots to Geneva. Many of them would have had Amyraldian sympathies. The French threat to the city of Geneva made the Genevans look for support in Lutheran countries as well as elsewhere.[191] Yet these events do not explain the changed demeanor of the Genevan clergy entirely. Calvin, Beza, and Pictet had always aimed at unity with Lutherans but not at the cost of what they regarded as biblical doctrine, of which predestination was not the least important. It was through regarding doctrine in general and thus also the Reformed doctrine of predestination as irrelevant and by raising Christian morals far above everything else that Geneva developed in the 18th century from a city that was Reformed with respect to the doctrine maintained by the clergy and reforming the morals of the people into a city that was in some way puritan in morals[192] but no longer Reformed in doctrine.

---

190 McNutt, *Calvin Meets Voltaire*, 218-19.
191 McNutt, *Calvin Meets Voltaire*, 47-59.
192 For instance, the clergy opposed the building of a theater in Geneva until the French army invaded the city at the end of the century, McNutt, *Calvin Meets Voltaire*, 171-78.

At the end of the century, the French Revolution had its impact on Geneva. In 1798, the republic of the city of Geneva became part of the French Republic. Now it became the capital city of a canton of which the majority of the population was Roman Catholic. Catholics were permitted to hold public masses in Geneva and became so influential that, within half a century, the majority of the city had become Roman Catholic. It was under these circumstances that César Malan (1787-1864) grew up.[193] He finished his theological education in Geneva in 1810. Looking back on his period as student, he himself remarked that he was taught nothing more than the doctrines of natural religion. He preached in the tradition of the late 18th-century Genevan theology: no dogmas but strict morals. His views gradually changed. At that time, Malan began to visit Robert Haldane (1764-1842), a Scottish Calvinist, who became the father of the Genevan Réveil. Haldane exegeted the Epistle to the Romans in an orthodox Reformed way in private lectures to theological students.[194] Malan, who was not a student but already ordained, visited him privately several times.[195]

Malan's orthodox Reformed convictions became manifest in a sermon on Easter 1817[196] that offended both the congregation and his colleagues. Malan was asked to change his doctrine, which he refused. Since Haldane had other disciples among students and young pastors, the *Compagnie des Pasteurs* decided to forbid any of them to preach on the following four things: how the two natures of Christ are united, original sin, how grace works, and predestination. Malan and several students refused to subscribe to this document. They were removed from the Genevan church and formed their own congregations. Predestination was one of the doctrines on which the 18th-century theologians had been silent, and Malan again preached and wrote on this doctrine, though he did not teach at the Academy and the pulpits of the Genevan church were closed to him. After almost a century of silence on predestination, this doctrine was in the end excluded from Genevan theology and sermons.

---

193 W. van der Zwaag, *César Malan (1784-1864): Prediker van het Frans-Zwitsers Réveil* (Utrecht: De Banier, 1997).
194 This resulted in Haldane's *Exposition of the Epistle to the Romans* (New York: Carter & Brothers, 1853; reprint: Grand Rapids: Kregel, 1992).
195 Van der Zwaag, *César Malan*, 61-72.
196 C. Malan, *L'homme ne peut être sauvé que par Jésus-Christ: Sermon sur: Luc. 19: 10*, (Geneva: Bonnant, 817).

7. Synthesis and Conclusions

7.1 Introduction
The central question formulated in the introductory chapter was whether and how the doctrine of election affected preaching in the theology of Geneva from John Calvin to Benedict Pictet, primarily in systematic theology and secondarily in sermons. This central question is divided into several sub-questions (1.3). The first concerns the doctrine of predestination. The second has to do with the relation between predestination, the covenant, and church as comprise of the hearers of preaching. A third question is how predestination affected the ideas on the extent of the atonement as the heart of the Gospel message. Fourth, did it affect the doctrine of faith to which sermons called people? Next we address the influence of predestination on the doctrine of the external call. Finally, the question is whether the sermons are consistent with the preacher's systematic theology on the way the congregation is addressed, how the Gospel is preached to them, and how predestination is discussed. The answer to these questions will help us answer our central question.

This chapter is structured around these questions. Two other questions that were mentioned in the Introduction, viz. whether historical facts and religious developments have been important for this part of the preacher's theology, and whether or not there is continuity in Genevan theology and sermons on this subject will be addressed in relation to each sub-question.

7.2 Genevan Theologians and Their Involvement in the Question of Predestination and Preaching
Each of the theologians had a more or less different reason to address the question whether and how predestination was related to preaching. John Calvin already mentioned this relation in his *Instruction et Confession de Foy dont on Use en l'Eglise de Genève* (1538) and in the opening sentences of his chapter on predestination in his *Institutes* of 1539. But actual reflection on this question was provoked by the attacks by Pighius in 1542. Calvin denied Pighius' idea that God's purpose in preaching was that all who hear the Gospel might believe and be saved. Calvin's reply to this issue was only published in 1552, after Bolsec had attacked Calvin's doctrine of predestination, using, as Calvin asserted, Pighius's ideas. Calvin's main purpose was to defend what he regarded as the pure truth of the Bible (2.1).

Theodore Beza's theological development started, unlike Calvin's, with reflection on the doctrine of predestination. He intervened in the debate between Calvin and Bullinger on Bolsec. In addition to defending what he regarded as the pure doctrine, Beza also wanted to reach a consensus between Bullinger and Calvin, at least in his early correspondence with both theologians. Although Beza was not especially stimulated to reflect on the relation between predestination and preaching, he addressed this question in the context of his ideas on predestination. Beza was incited to reflect on the relation between predestination and atonement, at the Colloquy of Montbéliard in 1586 (3.1, 3.4, 3.7).

Theodore Tronchin and John Diodati were forced to reflect on predestination as well as on its relation to the external call as delegates to the Synod of Dort in 1618-1619. The controversy between Remonstrants and Contra-Remonstrants revolved around predestination, both as a doctrine and its relation to atonement and vocation (4.1).

While the dispute between Calvin and Beza on the one hand and their opponents on the other was a dispute about teachings eventually condemned as errors, Francis Turretin's combatted a faction within the international Reformed community that was never condemned and gained ground even in Geneva. The theology of Saumur, especially the views of Amyraut, led Turretin to reflect on predestination, which he did in an almost complete way. He even wrote a separate *Quaestio* on the call to the reprobate. Saumur was not his only target: Turretin defended what he regarded as the true Reformed faith over against Remonstrants, Roman Catholics, and Socinians (5.1).

Benedict Pictet actually did not have any border to defend anymore. The views Turretin so vehemently protested against had gained so many adherents in Geneva by that time that Turretin's views, adopted by Pictet, were only held by a minority. Pictet defended those views but did so with ambivalence, tolerating in Lutherans the very views he rejected in Salmurians and stating that questions regarding predestination were not fundamental. When Pictet died, predestination received hardly any attention in Genevan theology, let alone its relation to other doctrines, like the call (6.1, 6.16).

7.3 The Doctrine of Predestination

Calvin's idea of *praedestinatio gemina* was defended throughout the period we have investigated. Beza, the delegates, Turretin, and Pictet all agreed that predestination consisted in both election and reprobation. They also agreed that God's pleasure is the only cause of God's decrees of election and reprobation. There are some minor differences in this respect. Calvin sometimes stated that God had just reasons to reprobate the one and to elect the other, but that these reasons are hidden from humans. Nonetheless, he usually stressed God's sovereignty, as did Beza, Diodati, Tronchin, and Turretin with him. Pictet made a distinction here, stating that the reason why God elected in general is his mercy but why he elected the one and not the other is a matter of his sovereign pleasure. Likewise, the reason why God reprobates in general is sin, but the reason why God reprobates the one rather than the other is again a matter of his sovereign pleasure.

There is less unanimity concerning the order of the decrees. Calvin did not reflect on this subject in a separate section, and both supra- and infralapsarian statements can be found in his writings (2.4.3). Beza took a supralapsarian position concerning God's purpose to elect and to reprobate and rejected infralapsarianism. Yet, with respect to actual election and reprobation, which belong to the execution of the decree as well as to the decree itself, he wrote like an infralapsarian (3.6.2). His students Diodati and Tronchin did not agree with Beza but took an infralapsarian stance and did not use Beza's distinction between God's purpose to elect and election itself (4.6). Turretin and Pictet followed them in this (5.3, 6.3). Francis's son Jean-Alphonse went even further and rejected supralapsarianism as an error, something his orthodox predecessors did not dare to do (6.1.2).

Some Genevan theologians had their own characteristic ideas, which are absent from the theology of others. Calvin distinguished between steps in election: a general election of a covenant community and a special election for the salvation of individuals (2.4.4). Pictet distinguished between the reasons for election and reprobation in general and with respect to individuals (6.3). Beza distinguished between the purpose of election and reprobation and election and reprobation itself (3.6). In Beza's case, it is possible to point to historical circumstances as a plausible reason why he made this distinction. This distinction had been made by Bullinger, and Beza used it, it seems, to present Calvin's ideas on predestination in a Bullingerian scheme and thus to attempt to remove the discord between Bullinger and Calvin on Bolsec (3.4).

The importance ascribed to the doctrine of predestination was the same during almost the entire periods of the Reformation and Reformed orthodoxy. Calvin, Beza, the delegates, and Turretin maintained the doctrine, even if this meant that they could not seek union with other Protestants as they wished. Calvin jeopardized his good relation with almost all the Swiss cities by maintaining his condemnation of Bolsec (2.1, 3.4). Beza, though it seems he tried to make Calvin's ideas on predestination acceptable to Bullinger, did not yield to the reluctance of the latter to speak about eternal predestination, but clearly expressed his supralapsarian convictions (3.6.2). Beza also knew he would be rejected by the Lutherans when he set forth his ideas on predestination and the atonement before them in Montbéliard (3.7). Diodati and Tronchin were tolerant of differences of opinion exhibited by Reformed delegates from other countries but approved the dismissal of the Remonstrants and the refutation of their views (4.3, 4.4). Turretin rejected and refuted an interpretation of predestination held by many French Reformed churches (5.1.3, 5.3). From Calvin to Turretin, predestination was regarded as an indispensable doctrine and became an acceptable reason for Protestants to separate. This changed with Pictet who, though he tried to maintain the *Formula* that refuted Amyraldism, stated that differences between the Reformed and the Lutherans on predestination and atonement were not fundamental (6.3, 6.4, 6.5). Because of that, they did not constitute a reason for separation, even though these differences had been so fundamental for Beza and Turretin that they prevented them from becoming united with Lutherans, and for Tronchin and Diodati as the basis for refuting the Remonstrants. The reason is obviously Pictet's context in which doctrine was more or less despised (6.1). But even then, it is remarkable that someone who defended the Genevan doctrine of predestination as far as content is concerned denied the importance of that same doctrine.

The essence of the doctrine of predestination shows continuity from Calvin to Pictet. But there is discontinuity concerning the order of decrees. Beza's staunch supralapsarianism was rejected by his infralapsarian successors whose attitude to supralapsarianism was even more or less negative. There is continuity on the importance ascribed to the doctrine of predestination up to and including Turretin. With Pictet, a breach appears that eventually resulted in an almost complete neglect of predestination at Geneva.

7.4 Predestination and the Extent of the Atonement

Calvin used the widely accepted formula that Christ's death was sufficient for all but efficient only for the elect. He repeatedly stated that Christ died for the whole world, without the stipulation "sufficient." There is little reflection on the extent of the atonement in Calvin's works. Yet the few remarks he made when he consciously reflected on the issue point in the direction of tending to limit the atonement to the elect alone. Whether Calvin can be regarded as being committed to universal or particular redemption is still a matter of dispute. I argue that Calvin's position is neither universal nor particular but prior to either of these positions. Nonetheless, Calvin's remarks tend more in the direction of particular redemption than that of universal redemption (2.5).

Beza followed the line of thinking to its logical conclusion and, taking Calvin's thinking even further, explicitly denied that Christ died for the reprobate in any way and rejected the literal meaning of "Christ died sufficiently for the whole world." His successors maintained at the Synod of Dort that Christ died for the elect alone but tolerated the phrase that Beza rejected (3.7). Turretin, followed here by Pictet, also stated that Christ died for the elect alone but found a way to interpret the notion of Christ's death being sufficient for all (5.4, 6.4).

It is difficult to conclude anything concerning continuity here. On the one hand, one might argue that there is disagreement between Calvin and Beza on the acceptance of the phrase that Christ died sufficiently for all people and conclude that there is discontinuity. The difficulty with this view is that Beza's successors tolerated or even accepted that very phrase. Hence, there would be also discontinuity between Beza and his successors on this point. But these successors agreed with Beza in that Christ died for the elect alone since it was his intention to die for them and not for others. Turretin explained the phrase as referring to the value of Christ's offering. Beza accepted that the value of Christ's death was infinite but denied that this could be formulated as "sufficiently died for all". It is not clear whether Turretin's interpretation is the same as Calvin's. On the other hand, one could argue that Beza's ideas follow logically from Calvin's few reflections on the extent of the atonement and conclude that there is continuity. The problem here is that Beza actually denied the truth of a phrase Calvin frequently used, viz. that Christ died for the whole world. The differences and similarities that seems obvious at first turns out to be nuanced and subtle. A clear conclusion on continuity or discontinuity seems impossible, although the continuity does seem to be greater than the discontinuity.

7.5 Predestination, the Covenant, and the Church

Calvin's ideas on predestination, the covenant, and the church are closely related. His ideas on each of them can be visualized as three concentric circles:

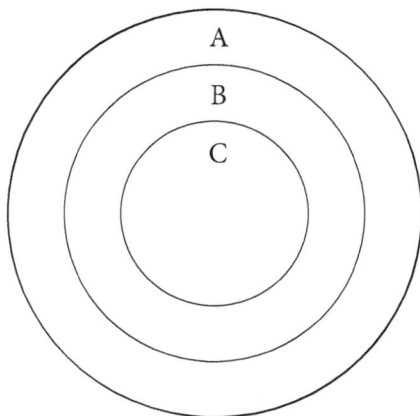

	Predestination	**Covenant**	**Church**
A	The world	The world	The world
B	General election	The covenant	The visible church
C	Special election	The elect believers	The invisible church

The outermost circle is the world, which includes all people. The middle circle includes only those who are included in God's covenant. They belong to the visible church and are generally elect. Salvation is promised to them, on condition that they believe and repent. This circle is a middle position between the world and the true believers of the third, innermost circle. These true believers are elected to salvation by a special election and belong to the invisible church (2.4.4, 2.6, 2.7).

Beza seems to have held the same view of the church as Calvin, distinguishing among the world, the visible church, and the invisible church. But Beza usually does not refer to the notion of a general election. His ideas on the covenant seem to have changed over the years. The younger Beza had the same view as Calvin but seems to have changed in later years, stating that the covenant is established with the elect only (3.8). The delegates to Dort left no clues as to what they thought of this. Turretin and, after him, Pictet seem to have adopted Beza's later view and added a distinction between the essence (C) and the administration (B) of the covenant. This means that the later Beza, Turretin, and Pictet more or less identified covenant and election as involving the same people (5.5, 6.6).

This development, which was not unique to Geneva, but appeared elsewhere as well, made Graafland conclude that in the history of Reformed theology, the doctrine of the covenant became dominated by predestination. This conclusion can be questioned, however, because in the context of the church, Turretin and Pictet actually denied that it is correct to say that the invisible church exists of (i.e. the essence of the covenant of grace is established with) with the elect. The true believers are the invisible church, i.e. members of the covenant (5.5, 5.6, 6.6, 6.7). All believers are elect, but not all the elect are (as yet) believers. So, when Pictet argues that the covenant is restricted in the sense that it is not established with all who are baptized, this restriction is not connected to election but to faith. Moreover, it is obvious that Calvin's ideas on the covenant are no less related to his ideas on predestination and church than Turretin's, albeit in different ways. Besides, both agree on the distinctions concerning the church. The difference is that Calvin identified the covenant with the visible church and general election, whereas Turretin identified the essence of the covenant with special election. Whether this means that the doctrine of predestination dominated the doctrine of the covenant does not depend in the first place on the name given to any part of the covenant and the church but on its function. The function of the three circles remain the same, in both Calvin and Turretin (and Pictet), as is obvious form the table below:

	Church (Calvin and Turretin)	Covenant and election (Calvin)	Covenant and election (Turretin)
A	The world	The world: no part in God's covenant or special grace.	The world: no part in God's covenant or special grace.
B	The visible church	General election or covenant with all who belong to the visible church: revelation of God and grace; conditional offer of saving grace.	Administration of the covenant to all who belong to the visible church: revelation of God and grace; conditional offer of saving grace.
C	The invisible church	Special election: grant of the conditions of the covenant and of saving grace to the elect.	Essence of the covenant: grant of the conditions of the covenant and of saving grace to the elect.

The Gospel is not preached in all the world, and God does not reveal himself to all the world. The Gospel is preached in the visible church, and salvation is promised on condition of faith and repentance – this is so in both Calvin and Turretin. God grants his elect the ability to fulfill these conditions by granting them faith and repentance. They thereby become members of the invisible church. For Turretin, this unconditional grant of saving grace to the elect is the essence of the covenant of grace, while, for Calvin, the general conditional offer of salvation is the essence of the covenant. The difference relates more to the question of what the most appropriate meaning of "covenant" is than to how Calvin's and Turretin's concepts of the covenant function. Hence, I argue that the continuity in the total concept is greater and of more importance than the discontinuity in their definitions of the covenant.

7.6 God's Purpose and the Preacher's Purpose in Preaching

All theologians examined denied that God intended the salvation of all people who heard the Gospel preached. His intention concerning the elect is to save them, and preaching is a means to this end. As far as the reprobate are concerned, his sole intention is to leave them without excuse. Calvin was reproved for this view by Pighius, who accused him of teaching two opposite wills in God. Calvin denied this and pointed out that God wants sinners to repent and promises salvation to those who do. Yet God decreed that he would not grant repentance to all who hear the Gospel. Calvin distinguished between the commanding will of God and the decreeing will of God. He used the conditional structure (God wills the salvation of the repentant sinner) to defend himself against the charge of teaching contradictory wills in God (2.8). This same structure can be seen in Beza (3.10) and the delegates to Dort (4.4), albeit that they did not connect it to the charge of teaching two wills in God. Beza and the *Canons* stressed that God's invitations are serious. Turretin elaborated on the distinction Calvin made concerning God's will, adding a third distinction: the approving will or *euarestia*. God commands all people who hear the Gospel to repent and believe – this is his commanding will. God approves of all who actually repent and believe – the approving will. Yet he decreed that he would not grant faith and repentance to all who hear the Gospel – this is his decreeing will. Furthermore, Turretin distinguished between the purpose of the call (the salvation of those who hear the call) in itself and the God's purpose with the call (the salvation of the elect) (5.7). Pictet used the same conditional structure but did not use the *euarestia* nor the distinction between the purpose of the call and the purpose of God who calls (6.8).

The researched theologians from Calvin to Pictet agreed on what they thought to be God's purpose in preaching. With respect to the elect, preaching is a means by which God brings about their salvation. The sermons acquaint them with the law, their sins, Christ, and with the way to salvation through Christ, viz., faith and repentance. The Holy Spirit produces faith and repentance in the elect. They receive Christ by faith, persist in this faith by the grace of God, and will ultimately be saved, according to God's purpose. With respect to the reprobate, preaching is a means to leave them without excuse. The sermons acquaint them with the same things as the elect, for the message that comes to them is the same. Yet since the Holy Spirit does not grant them the gifts of faith and repentance, they remain averse to God, reject his Gospel, remain unbelieving, become hardened and ultimately condemned because of their sins and unbelief, according to God's purpose.

All theologians studied here deny that it was God's purpose to save all who hear the Gospel. Nevertheless, all affirm that a preacher of the Gospel could and even should want to save all who hear him. The preacher does not know who is elect or reprobate and has the duty to strive for the salvation of all they come across. Calvin quoted, with approval, Augustine to the effect that a preacher who does not know who is elect and who is not should desire to save all those who hear his sermons. All must be exhorted to repentance and faith without distinction and thus to salvation. His successors agreed with him. Turretin added that, although a preacher should not intend the salvation of a reprobate (which would make him oppose God's will), he should nevertheless intend the salvation of all who hear him since he does not know who is elect and who is not. Despite the addition of distinctions by Turretin and Pictet's abandoning of such distinctions, there is obvious continuity in Genevan theology concerning God's purpose and the preacher's purpose in the external call (2.8, 3.9, 5.7, 6.8).

7.7 The Mode of Preaching the Gospel: Conditionally and Unconditionally

All theologians examined here distinguished between an external and an internal call. According to Calvin, in the external call a promise can be either conditional or unconditional and be either general or individual. The promise of salvation can be preached to all who hear the Gospel, but it is offered on condition of faith. It can also be addressed to individual believers, and then the promise is unconditional. Calvin's ideas on the preaching of the Gospel promises correlate with his ideas on the covenant. The promise of salvation is preached to the covenant community on the condition of faith and repentance (the middle circle) but also promised absolutely to the elect (the inner circle). The conditionality of the Gospel made it possible for Calvin to preach the promises of the Gospel to all who heard him without contradicting the doctrine of predestination (2.9, 2.10).

Calvin's successors used similar ideas on the conditionality of the promises of the Gospel in the external call (3.10, 4.4, 5.8, 6.9). Their view on the covenant might have changed, but that did not affect their view of the relation between predestination and the external call. For Calvin, conditionality was essential to the covenant. Turretin held that conditionality was a mark of the administration of the covenant, while the essence itself of the covenant was unconditional. Their agreement is, again, greater than their differences, as the table below shows:

	Calvin	Turretin
The external call	comes to all who hear the Gospel	comes to all who hear the Gospel
	is conditional	is conditional
	belongs to the essence of the covenant	belongs to the administration of the covenant
The internal call	comes to the elect	comes to the elect
	is unconditional	is unconditional
	is the guarantee that the condition of the covenant will be fulfilled	belongs to the essence of the covenant

The difference between Calvin and Turretin only affects the theological relation between the external call and the covenant. It does not affect the practical relation, for both affirmed that the external call comes to whosoever hears the Gospel and that it is conditional. A less important difference is that Turretin actually restricts the promises to those who fulfill the condition, but this seems to be more a matter of accurate language. Calvin teaches a conditional promise of salvation to all who hear the Gospel, and this promise would be fulfilled for those who met the condition. Turretin taught that salvation is promised to all those who met the condition set forth in the preaching of the Gospel.

Although there was a condition of faith and repentance, the preaching of the Gospel was nevertheless not restricted. Nobody is excluded from the call to faith and repentance and thus to salvation. To believe is a condition, but there is no condition for believing. This is the basic idea of all

Genevan theologians from Calvin to Pictet. Yet sometimes there seems to be contradictory views. There is some ambiguity in Calvin concerning humility and the knowledge of one's sin and misery. He could actually state that these things are conditions. Beza, the delegates, and Pictet acknowledged that they were necessary but did not call them conditions. Turretin did not do so explicitly either, yet the suggestion is sometimes so strong that it is hard not to conclude that he occasionally made it a practical condition or restriction for a next act of faith. But for both Calvin and Turretin, it was not a condition that should be fulfilled before salvation could be offered, but before the indiscriminately offered salvation could be received.

7.8 Predestination and the Response to Preaching

From Calvin to Pictet, all ascribed a positive response to the preaching of the Gospel to God's sovereign grace, working by the Holy Spirit in the elect. Preaching was a means used by God to save his elect. Salvation was promised in the preaching of the Gospel to all who repent and believe. It is the Spirit who brings about both repentance and faith in the elect. All theologians here unanimously acknowledged a direct relation between election and a positive response to preaching.

The relation between reprobation and a negative response to preaching is more complex. All acknowledged that there is such a relation, but there are some differences with respect to the form it takes. They all agree on one point: God is not the author of sin and unbelief. Despite this bold denial, Calvin stated just as boldly that God was the cause of unbelief (2.11). This seems to have been the view of the younger Beza as well. But, reflecting on the question how God could be a cause of sin without being its author, he changed his mind and concluded that the decree of reprobation is not a cause in itself but ordains the causes. The true cause of sin and unbelief is human depravity (3.11). The delegates, Turretin, and Pictet followed Beza in his denial that God is the cause of sin by. Turretin added a distinction to answer the question of the relation between reprobation and unbelief, stating that unbelief is a consequence of reprobation being an antecedent, but not an effect of reprobation being a cause, which is actually an elaboration of Beza's notion (4.3, 5.9, 6.10).

The answer to the question as to whether or not there is continuity between Calvin and his successors depends on other questions: Is seeing God as a cause of sin and unbelief to no longer endorsing that view a shift from one basic idea to another, and is Beza's denial of God as the cause of sin a new idea? Or is Beza's denial more of a development and consequence of both his and Calvin's basic conviction that God cannot be the author of sin? I argue for the latter option. It was essential for Calvin that God was not the author of sin, as well as the conviction that nothing happens without God's decree. Beza maintains these two basic notions but regards the idea that God is the cause of everything, even of sin, to be an inappropriate formulation of the second. I therefore argue for continuity here.

7.9 Predestination, Faith, and Assurance

Although the Genevan theologians were convinced that salvation is only for the elect, they were also convinced that the object of faith is not election, but the Gospel, especially the Person of Christ. He should be presented in sermons as the only way to the Father, and everybody should know that whoever comes to him will not be cast out. Election is not an object of faith, but is intended as consolation for believers – it assures them that their faith flows from the unchangeable decree of election, and thus that they surely will be saved. Turretin distinguishes between a general and a proper object of faith. The general object is God's Word, but the proper object of saving faith is Christ and the promise of the remission of sins. It is not "Christ having died for me," for not everyone can be called to believe this since Christ did not die for everyone (5.10).

We saw a tension in Calvin's theology between his definition of faith, the general call to faith, and predestination. Calvin solved the tension between predestination and the general call of the Gospel by the conditional nature of the promises of salvation: only those who have faith will be saved. His definition of faith, however, leads to another tension or contradiction, for, to Calvin, faith is the sure knowledge of God's benevolence towards us. Calvin does not answer the question how everybody can be called to have such a sure knowledge if God has decreed that he will not be benevolent to everybody. Other parts of his theology seem to offer no solution either (2.12). It is not clear whether this contradiction was the reason that Beza defined faith without this sure knowledge of God's benevolence. For him, faith was the means whereby one applies the promises of salvation to himself. The assurance of salvation was more a consequence of faith than part of the essence of faith. Faith was not defined as knowledge but as an act following knowledge (of the promises) and leading to knowledge (of one's salvation). Defined in this way, there is no tension between predestination, a general call, and faith (3.12). Turretin also defined faith as act of apprehension. He went further than his predecessors and distinguishes between several acts of faith. Six of them are direct acts. There is an act of knowledge of the objects of faith, acts of assent, both theoretical and practical, and there are four acts of trust: taking refuge in Christ, accepting him, reflecting on these acts of refuge, and the acceptance of salvation and the realization that one is saved, and a last act of consolation and confidence. Turretin used these distinctions to solve the question of the tension between predestination and the general call to faith. Everyone who hears the Gospel is called to the acts of faith that consist in knowledge and assent and to the acts of taking refuge in, and acceptance of, Christ. But not everybody is called to believe that Christ died for him and that he will be saved. These are indeed acts of faith, according to Turretin, but only those who have performed the first acts of faith are called to these later acts. Turretin combined the ideas of Calvin and Beza by pointing out that faith in Christ is the most important fruit that assures a person of salvation. Pictet summarized and simplified Turretin's distinctions (5.10, 6.11).

With respect to the definition of faith, we see discontinuity between Calvin and his successors. Whereas Calvin saw faith as a sure knowledge of the remission of sins, his successors defined faith more as acts than as knowledge, and assurance more as a consequence than as the essence of faith. Beza taught that assurance was to be gained by perceiving the effects of election in oneself, mainly faith and repentance. Turretin tried to keep both together by distinguishing among several acts of faith, whereby the reflexive, assuring act was essential to faith, just as in Calvin's definition, but not essential to the first acts of faith. It is not clear why Beza and the others did not follow Calvin in his definition of faith, but it is plain that their definition did not raise the same tensions with predestination and the general call as Calvin's definition did.

7.10 Preaching the Doctrine of Predestination

Augustine states that, although there might seem to be good reasons not to preach on predestination, it should nevertheless be preached. He was quoted with approval by both Calvin and Beza, who agreed that predestination was no obstacle to the preaching of the Gospel. They provide several reasons for talking about predestination in sermons. The first is that the Bible itself teaches us about predestination and that the apostles did not avoid it. Preaching this doctrine has several benefits. It teaches that salvation flows from the free mercy of God and hence teaches people true humility. It also offers a sure ground for confidence in one's eternal salvation. Hence, it is a doctrine that serves the godly (2.13, 3.13). Turretin added another reason for preaching on predestination: the insults of the adversaries. A Reformed preacher should free the doctrine from incriminations and explain it in a sound way so that the congregation will understand that predestination is not a fatal necessity, does not extinguish religion, does not lead to despair, or to safety in profanity. Nor does it make God the author of sin and cruel and hypocritical (5.11). Pictet agreed with his predecessors that predestination should be preached, but not very often (6.12).

Calvin warned against giving offense in teaching predestination. Election might be applied to the faithful, to console them, but reprobation should never be applied to any living person. If someone believes, he does so because he is elect. But if someone does not believe, one cannot conclude that he is reprobate. God might give him faith and repentance in the future. Beza added that, when preaching on predestination, a preacher should restrict himself to the words of Scripture. Moreover, he should not start with the eternal decree of predestination and then descend from there but should start in time, with the call, faith and repentance, justification, and sanctification, and then ascend to the eternal decree. Turretin agreed with Beza and stressed the mystery of predestination: we know the fact, but we do not understand it.

7.11 Genevan Sermons and Predestination

In general, the sermons of the Genevan theologians were consistent with their systematic thoughts on predestination. That meant in the first place that predestination, though not neglected, was not a dominant doctrine in their sermons, for their systematic views on predestination included the idea that a preacher should not start with it. The consistency of the sermons with the doctrine is seen first and foremost in the fact that nothing is said that is inconsistent with predestination, and not in that much is said in each sermon that is consistent with it. Using the *lectio continua*, Calvin and Beza hardly mentioned predestination when the text or pericope to be preached on did not give an occasion to do so (2.15-2.18, 3.15-3.16). Turretin, who preached on individual verses, saw such an occasion somewhat more often. His approach, even in his sermons, was more systematic, and he mentioned predestination when he saw a systematic reason to do so. This does not mean that the doctrine of predestination was dominant in Turretin's sermons, for other doctrines, such as the covenant, were also treated more systematically in his sermons. He gave more room to doctrine in his sermons (5.13-5.14). In general, Pictet did not mention predestination as much as Turretin, and his approach to the texts for his sermons was also less systematic. Yet when he addressed this doctrine in his sermons, he also did so systematically (6.14-6.15).

Only secondarily does the consistency regarding predestination between sermons and doctrine mean that talking about predestination in Genevan sermons was consistent with systematic theology. No part of the doctrine was ignored completely, although election was given far more attention than reprobation. But even that contrast was in line with Genevan theology. For instance, although Beza seems to have given as much attention to reprobation as to election in his *Tabula* and other works on predestination, he did not even mention the word in his sermons on the resurrection (the concept seems to occur once, however) (3.15.1). Calvin addressed reprobation explicitly in his sermons on Jacob and Esau, drawing the practical conclusion from this story that godly parents should accept God's acts, even if he reprobates some of their children (2.17).

The sermons were also in harmony with Genevan ideas on the covenant and the congregation, although these ideas changed somewhat over the years. For Calvin, the congregation was a covenant community, occupying a middle ground between the world that did not know God and the elect. The congregation was comprised of both the elect and the reprobate, believers and hypocrites. It is nevertheless addressed as God's people, true believers, according to the judgment of charity. Despite this charitable judgment, the congregation can be addressed as unbelievers and be threatened with temporal and eternal punishment, for the judgment of the preacher is not the same as the judgment of his Sender. Although Beza's ideas on the covenant developed into the conviction that it was established with the elect only, he did not develop his ideas on the congregation in the same way. His view of the congregation was similar to Calvin's. He addressed it as comprised of believers, even though he also made it clear that not all members of the congregation were true believers. Calvin and Beza both addressed their congregation by 'we,' when giving consolation and promising salvation as well as when rebuking the congregation and threatening damnation. Turretin followed Beza both in his view of the covenant as well as in his view of the congregation. He too saw his congregation as comprising believers and hypocrites but addressed the people in the congregation in different ways. He introduced a distinction within the congregation by addressing true believers by 'we' and hypocrites by 'you.' Pictet returned to the practice of Calvin and Beza, usually addressing the congregation by 'we.' None of the theologians we investigated divided their congregation in terms of election and reprobation. All divided their congregation in one way or another in terms of faith and repentance.

Calvin did not link the atonement to predestination in his sermons, since he did not reflect in a critical way on this relation. One cannot find statements in Beza's sermons that one finds in Calvin's, such that Christ died for all people or the whole world. But there is no explicit denial of this either. Rather, Beza stated positively that Christ died for the elect. This is the most striking difference between Calvin's and Beza's sermons.

But it is doubtful whether this had any practical consequence for the congregation, since Beza addressed it as consisting of believers (3.15.2). Turretin and Pictet followed Beza on the extent of the atonement but did not state it as explicitly in their sermons as he did. They confined themselves to the statement that Christ died for "us" (5.13.4, 6.14)

God's purpose in preaching is not addressed explicitly by Calvin. Some passages obviously suggest that this purpose is not to save all, but others just as obviously suggest the opposite. Turretin addressed this question in his sermon on Christ's tears over Jerusalem, denying that it was as God that Christ desired to gather Jerusalem under his wings. He only did so as a man. When he interprets Christ's tears as an indication of God's will, Turretin did not have in mind God's decreeing will, but his commanding will, whereby he urges all people to faith and repentance, and his approving will, whereby he delights in those who do what he commands, that are operative here. There are no clear indications in Beza's and Pictet's sermons with respect to God's purpose in preaching.

Calvin's purpose in preaching does not often emerge very clearly in his sermons. When it does emerge, however, it turns out that Calvin indeed wished all of Geneva to be saved and was greatly disappointed that he did not see much fruit from his labors (2.16.3). Although Beza shared this disappointment with Calvin, he did not make clear in his sermons on the resurrection whether his own purpose through preaching was the salvation of all or only of the elect (3.15). Turretin made his intentions clear in almost every sermon. He urged his hearers to repent and believe and thus to be saved (5.13.6). Pictet's sermons show less zeal in urging Geneva to faith, although repentance is a frequently recurring theme, for pure doctrine and a pure life should go together (6.14).

Regarding the response to preaching, or more broadly, to the administration of the covenant, that faith and repentance were fruits of God's sovereign grace was axiomatic for all. Calvin told his congregation in his sermons on Jacob and Esau that this response is the result of predestination. In their lives, election and reprobation were revealed. Election does not hinder the administration of the covenant but is a guarantee that some of the covenant children will actually believe, whereas all would otherwise reject God's grace (2.17). Beza was also quite explicit, stating that, for some, the preaching of the Gospel would only serve to harden them (3.15.1). Turretin dealt with this subject in his sermon on Christ's tears over Jerusalem (5.13.6). Pictet did so in his examination of religions (6.14.1).

According to all theologians studied here, the object of faith is Christ. One would expect that in line with this view, Christ would be more or less central in their sermons. This is not the case. Calvin and Beza hardly mentioned Christ when the text gave no direct occasion to do so. Christ is absent from most of Calvin's sermons on Micah and Genesis (2.16, 2.17). That he is more present in Beza's sermons seems to be the result of the topic in his sermons we looked at: the resurrection of Christ (3.15). Turretin's sermons all mention Christ and the promises of salvation, although the latter come up more often than the former (5.13). Pictet gave Christ the most prominent place in his sermons (6.14.2).

Themes relating to faith and assurance were not found in the sermons by Calvin we looked at. In one of his sermons, Beza based assurance on God's immutable election but did not indicate how this assurance could be obtained, in contrast to what he did in his more systematic works. Turretin used this method in his sermon on calling and election. Pictet addressed assurance in his quite systematic sermons on the examination of religions and touched on it once in his other sermons, stating that assurance can be gained by discerning the image of Christ in oneself.

In Genevan sermons from Calvin to Pictet, the greatest discontinuity is the shift from *lectio continua* to a free choice of texts. This resulted in a different way of preaching, which entailed a more systematic approach to a text, as part of the whole teaching of Scripture, rather than exegetically, as part of a certain book and periscope (5.13). That predestination received more attention in the sermons of Turretin and Pictet than in those of Calvin and Beza seems largely due to this shift in how the text for a sermon was selected and approached, rather than the doctrine being regarded as more important by Turretin and Pictet. In reality, Pictet regarded the doctrine of predestination as less important than his sixteenth-century predecessors (6.3, 6.5). That means that the increase in attention given to predestination in sermons was the result of homiletical, rather than doctrinal, grounds. Moreover, it was not only the doctrine of predestination that received more attention; other doctrines and the person of Christ did so as well.

No other discontinuities can be detected on other themes in Genevan sermons as far as Genevan theology is concerned. But these differences were probably hardly or not at all noticed by the Genevan church, for Genevan preachers followed a continuous practice of addressing their congregation in the first-person plural, as a congregation of believers. Differences concerning the extent of the atonement and the covenant had no consequences for addressing a church that, according to a charitable judgment, consisted of believers who benefited from the atonement and were members of the covenant.

7.12 General Conclusion

What was the influence of the doctrine of predestination on preaching in Geneva from Calvin to Pictet? That is the central question of this study. The answer is subtle, and the influence is sometimes mutual. That there is a relation between predestination and preaching in Genevan theology from Calvin to Pictet is undeniable. But this relation took shape in different forms and at different levels.

At the doctrinal level, eternal predestination precedes the call and its effects. The external call is a means to implement election and reprobation. Yet, for Calvin, the first Genevan theologian to consciously reflect on this relation in his writings, his experience as a preacher (why the Gospel is not preached everywhere and does not meet the same acceptance wherever it is preached) was one reason to deal extensively with predestination in his *Institutes*; in effect, his experience with the external call was one of the reasons that inspired the development of his ideas on predestination. In other words, for Calvin, reflection on the external call preceded the doctrine of predestination in which he stated precisely the opposite: predestination precedes the external call. His view of the call was not a result of his view of predestination, but the reverse. So, the direction of the relation between predestination and the call is different when it concerns the doctrine itself than when it concerns the configuration of the doctrine. For his successors, the doctrine of predestination of their Reformed predecessor(s) was a fact. But even for them, the relation between the doctrine and the external call was not unidirectional. Beza, for instance, stated with Calvin that eternal predestination precedes the call. But in time, the internal call (which cannot exist without the external call) is election itself *(electio ipsa),* and Turretin, elaborating on this, stated that the call is temporal election and election is the eternal call.

That predestination precedes the call seems to imply a higher status for predestination in Genevan Reformed theology or even domination over the call. Since a decree precedes its execution and in that way determines the execution, predestination in this regard determines the call. But just as Christ was not limited to being the "execution of the decree" by his incarnation in line with the decree, preaching cannot be reduced to being nothing more than an execution of the decree of predestination. For instance, Turretin distinguished between an end of the Gospel in itself (the salvation of all who hear it) and the end of God with the Gospel (the salvation of the elect). So, although predestination in one respect determines preaching, preaching is more than just the implementation of predestination.

Over the course of time, theologians reflected on the relation between doctrinal *loci*, including the relation between predestination and other doctrines. This had to do with the reciprocal relation between doctrines, not the subjection of some doctrines to others. That predestination, as a result of this development, occurred in more *loci* than before is not a convincing argument that predestination dominated others or became a central dogma, for other doctrines also occurred in more *loci* than before. With respect to the church, this development meant that election was linked to the invisible church of true believers. The latter concept was not the result of the doctrine of election, nor was the concept of the visible church or the distinction between the visible and the invisible church a consequence of that doctrine. As far as the covenant is concerned, this resulted in the conclusion by Beza, Turretin, and Pictet that it was established with the true believers or the invisible church, in contrast to Calvin who held that it was established with all who belong to the visible church. That the covenant was restricted by Beza and his successors to true believers who are elect does not necessarily mean that the doctrine of predestination became dominant. While the relation between election and the covenant changed in Genevan theology, the relation between election and the church remained the same, which in effect means that the practice remained the same, as is shown in 7.5. The distinction between the circles remained the same. The names given to these circles relating to predestination and the church remained the same, only the names given to the various circles relating to the covenant changed.

With respect to the external call, Genevan theologians were urged by their critics to reflect on the calling of the reprobate and on the question how God can seriously call them to salvation when he had decreed that they would not be saved. Calvin and Turretin used the concept of conditionality to unravel this knot. God did not promise salvation to everybody but to those who believe, and he delights in those who obey his command to believe in Christ and to repent. In this way, they could maintain both a general call to salvation for all who hear the preaching of the Gospel as well as eternal predestination and sovereign grace as the only cause of salvation. Beza, the *Canons of Dort*, and Pictet did not relate the concept of conditionality explicitly to the question of the calling of the reprobate, but the concept itself is discernable in their works.

When it comes to the content of preaching or the external call, Genevan preachers from Calvin to Pictet agreed that predestination should not dominate sermons. The content of sermons should be the content of the Scriptures, and they spoke of predestination and other doctrines in their sermons insofar as the text gave occasion to mention or explain them. The external call was not restricted to the elect, for the preacher did not know who the elect were. They all agreed on their duty to work for the salvation of all who heard them. The promise of salvation was restricted to the believers, but nobody was excluded from the invitation to believe, to which the promise of salvation was attached.

Historical developments were important at some stages. Calvin's view of predestination was formed and articulated more extensively due to the attacks of opponents outside (Pighius) and inside Geneva (Bolsec) and due to his work on Scripture (Commentary on Romans). But there are no real turning points in his development at which he abandoned a former idea; rather, he elaborated on former ideas. In Beza we can see a development in which he actually changed his mind and developed a more scholastic way of theologizing. Both changes are related to the question whether reprobation can be called a cause of sin and unbelief, a question that Calvin and the younger Beza affirmed. Due to the attacks on this statement by Castellio and his reading of Vermigli in the course of answering Castellio, Beza abandoned the idea that God is the cause of sin and adopted a more scholastic approach. Beza's *Tabula* with its *Brevis Explicatio* were not an example of Reformed scholastic theology. The controversy in The Netherlands between Arminians and Gomarists was an occasion for further reflection in the early 17th century, especially for the Genevan delegates Diodati and Tronchin. The rise of Amyraldism was such an occasion for Turretin, and the knowledge of and indifference toward other religions was one for Pictet.

In general, there was great continuity in Genevan theology from Calvin to Pictet on predestination and preaching. We detected just a few discontinuities in this period, like the development from supra- to infralapsarianism, the question who is included in the covenant, and the question whether God is the cause of sin and unbelief. In the two latter cases, the question is whether the changes actually reflect a shift or a reformulation in the same basic idea. A clear discontinuity can be seen in the evaluation of the importance of predestination. From Calvin to Turretin, this doctrine had been regarded as important and as a valid reason for the Reformed churches not to unite with the Lutherans, for instance. Pictet shows continuity with his predecessors regarding the content of the doctrine, but discontinuity with respect to its importance. This discontinuity is related to another one, viz. whether or not predestination should be preached. Pictet did so, but after his death the doctrine was neglected, both in theology as in preaching. This latter development is not due to Pictet's low estimation of the importance of the doctrine but followed from the same process of devaluing doctrine for the sake of morals and Protestant unity. Predestination was not so much opposed or changed – it was neglected. But this neglect led to deviating views on predestination in the 18th century, and to opposition to this doctrine in the early 19th century.

Briefly summarized, an overarching conclusion of this study is that predestination and the external call were inseparably connected in Genevan theology from Calvin to Pictet, but the doctrine of predestination neither dominated the content nor restricted the address of the external call.

Bibliography

General

Asselt, Willem J. van. "Infra- and Supralapsarianism." In K. Pollmann (et al.), *The Oxford Guide to the Historical Reception of Augustine from 430 to 2000, Part III*. Oxford: Oxford University Press, 2013.

--- *Introduction to Reformed Scholasticism*. Grand Rapids: Reformation Heritage Books, 2011.

--- and Eef Dekker (eds.). *Reformation and Scholasticism: An Ecumenical Enterprise*. Grand Rapids: Baker Academic, 2001.

--- et al. (eds.), *Reformed Thought on Freedom: The Concept of Free Choice in Early Modern Reformed Theology*. Grand Rapids: Baker Academic, 2010.

Ballor, J. *Covenant, Causality and Law: A Study in the Theology of Wolfgang Musculus*. Göttingen: Vandenhoeck & Ruprecht, 2012.

--- David S. Sytsma and Jason Zuidema (eds.). *Church and School in Early Modern Protestantism: Studies in Honor of Richard A. Muller on the Maturation of a Theological Tradition*. Leiden: Brill, 2013.

Baskwell, P.J. *Herman Hoeksema: A Theological Biography*, (unpublished dissertation, 2006)

Beeke, Joel R. "The Order of the Divine Decrees at the Genevan Academy: From Bezan Supralapsarianism to Turretinian Infralapsarianism." In Roney and Klauber. *The Identity of Geneva*: 57-75

--- *The Quest for Full Assurance: The Legacy of Calvin and his Successors*. Edinburgh: Banner of Truth, 1999.

--- *Debated Issues in Sovereign Predestination: Early Lutheran Predestination, Calvinian Reprobation, and Variations in Genevan Lapsarism*. Göttingen: Vandenhoeck & Ruprecht, 2017.

Graafland, C. *Van Calvijn tot Barth: Oorsprong en ontwikkeling van de leer der verkiezing in het Gereformeerd Protestantisme*. Zoetermeer: Boekencentrum 1987.

--- *Van Calvijn tot Comrie: Oorsprong en ontwikkeling van de leer van het verbond in het Gereformeerd Protestantisme*, vol. III, part 5 & 6. Zoetermeer: Boekencentrum, 1996.

Graham, W.Fred (ed.) *Later Calvinism: International Perspectives*. Sixteenth Century Essays & Studies vol. XXII. Missouri: Missouri State University, 1994.

Hall, Basil. "Calvin Against the Calvinists." In *John Calvin*, ed. Gervase Duffield. Grand Rapids: Eerdmans, 1966. p. 19-37

Haykin, Michael A.G. *The Life and Thought of John Gill (1697-1771): A Tercentennial Appreciation*. Studies in the History of Christian Thought. Leiden: Brill, 1997.

Maag, Karin. *Seminary or University? The Genevan Academy and Reformed Higher Education, 1560-1620*. Aldershot: Scolar Press, 1995.

Manetsch, Scott M. *Calvin's Company of Pastors: Pastoral Care and the Emerging Reformed Church, 1536-1609*. Oxford: OUP, 2013.

Muller, Richard.A. *Christ and the Decree: Christology and Predestination in Reformed Theology from Calvin to Perkins*. Durham: Labyrinth Press, 1986.

--- *Post Reformation Reformed Dogmatics*, 4 vols. Grand Rapids: Baker Book House, 1987-2003.

Nettles, Thomas J. *By His Grace and for His Glory: A Historical, Theological, and Practical Study of the Doctrines of Grace in Baptist Life*. Grand Rapids: Baker, 1986.

Rouwendal, Pieter L. *Het aanbod van genade: Twee studies*. Apeldoorn: De Rots, 2002.

--- " In Selderhuis, *Companion*.

Roney, John B., and Martin I. Klauber (eds.). *The Identity of Geneva: The Christian Commonwealth, 1564-1864*. Westport, Connecticut/London: Greenwood Press, 1998.

Schelven, A.A. van. *Het Calvinisme gedurende zijn bloeitijd. Genève – Frankrijk*. Amsterdam: Ten Have, 1943.

Selderhuis, Herman J. (ed.). *A Companion to Reformed Orthodoxy*. Leiden: Brill, 2013.

Thomas, G.M. *The Extent of the Atonement: A Dilemma for Reformed Theology from Calvin to the Consensus (1536-1675)*. Carlisle UK: Paternoster 1997.

Toon, Peter. *The Emergence of Hyper-Calvinism in English Nonconformity, 1689-1765*. London: The Olive Tree, 1967; reprint: Weston Rhyn: Quinta Press, 2003.

Trueman, Carl.R., and R.Scott. Clark (eds.). *Protestant Scholasticism: Essays in Reassessment*. Carlisle: Paternoster Press, 1999.

VanDoodewaard, William. *The Marrow Controversy and Seceder Tradition. Reformed Historical-Theological Studies*. Grand Rapids: Reformation Heritage Books, 2011.

Veenhof, C. *Prediking en uitverkiezing: Kort overzicht van de strijd, gevoerd in de Christelijk Afgescheidene Gereformeerde Kerk tussen 1850 en 1870, over de plaats van de leer der uitverkiezing in de prediking.* Kampen: J.H. Kok 1959.

Vos, A. "Scholasticism and Reformation" in: W.J. van Asselt and Eef Dekker, *Reformation and Scholasticism*: 99-120.

Wisse, Maarten, Marcel Sarot, and Willemien Otten (eds.). *Scholasticism Reformed: Essays in Honour of Willem J. van Asselt.* Leiden: Brill, 2010.

Woolsey, Andrew A. *Unity and Continuity in Covenantal Thought: A Study in the Reformed Tradition to the Westminster Assembly.* Grand Rapids: Reformation Heritage Books, 2012.

CALVIN

Primary Literature

Calvin, John. *Ioannis Calvini Opera quae supersunt omnia ad fidem editionum principum et authenticarum ex parte etiam codicum manu scriptorum; additis prolegomenis literariis, annotationibus criticis, annalibus Calvinianis indicibusque novis et copiosissimis.* Eds. Guilielmus Baum, Eduardus Cunitz, and Eduardus Reuss. Braunschweig: Schwetschke, 1863.

--- *Joannis Calvini Opera omnia: Denuo recognita et adnotatione critica instructa notisque illustrata : auspiciis praesidii conventus internationalis studiis calvinianis fovendis.* Geneva: Droz, 1992 –

--- *Joannis Calvini Opera Selecta.* Eds. Petrus Barth and Guilelmus Niesel. 5 vols. Munchen: Christian Kaiser Verlag 1926-1936.

--- *Bondage and Liberation of the Will: A Defense of the Orthodox Doctrine of Human Choice against Pighius* Ed. A.N.S. Lane. Transl. G.I. Davies. Grand Rapids: Baker, 1996.

--- *Calvin's Calvinism* [*De Aeterna Dei Predestinatione*]. Transl. H. Cole. Grand Rapids: RFPA, n.d.

--- *Commentaries.* Transl. by the Calvin Translation Society. Grand Rapids: Baker, 1999 [reprint].

--- *Institutes of the Christian Religion* (1536). Transl. by F.L. Battles. Atlanta: John Knox Press, 1975.

--- *Institutes of the Christian Religion*, ed. John T. McNeil. Transl. Ford Lewis Battles. Philadelphia: Westminster Press, 1960.

--- *Institutes of the Christian Religion.* Transl. Henry Beveridge. Edinburgh: T&T Clark, 1863; reprint: Grand Rapids: Eerdmans, 1989 [1995]..

--- *Institution de la religion chrestienne, nouvellement mise en quatre livres, et distinguée par chapitres, en ordre et methode bien propre. Augmentée aussi de tel accroissement, qu'on la peut presque estimer un livre nouveau.* Geneva : Jacques Bourgeois, 1561.
--- *Letters of John Calvin,* Vol. II. Transl. Jules Bonnet. Philadelphia: Presbyterian Board of Publication, n.d.
--- *Sermons of M. John Calvin on the Epistles of S. Paule to Timothie and Titus.* Transl. L.T. London: G. Bishop and T. Woodcoke, 1579; facsimile Edinburgh 1983.
--- *Sermons on the Book of Micah.* Transl. Benjamin W. Farley. Phillipsburg, New-Jersey: P&R Publishing, 2003.
--- *Sermons on Election and Reprobation.* Transl. John Field. Audubon: Old Paths Publications, 1996, reprint of a translation of 1579.
--- *Sermons on Genesis: Chapters 11-20.* Transl. Rob Roy McGregor. Edinburgh: The Banner of Truth, 2012.
--- *Sermons sur le Livre de Michée,* publiés par Jean Daniel Benoit, Vol. V of the *Supplementa Calviniana.* Neukirchen-Vluyn: Neukirchener Verlag des Erziehungsvereins, 1964.
--- *Sermons on Melchizedek & Abraham, Justification, Faith & Obedience.* Willow Street USA: Old Paths Publications 2000.
--- *Tracts and Letters* Ed. Henry Beveridge and Jules Bonnet. Grand Rapids: Baker, 1983 [reprint]
Pighius, Albertus. *De libero hominis arbitrio et divina gratia, Libri decem.* Cologne: Melchior Novesianus 1542.
--- *Sermons sur la Genèse,* Supplementa Calviniana Vol XI/1. Neukirchen-Vluyn: Neukirchener Verlag, 2000.

Secondary Literature
Allen, David L. "The Atonement: Limited or Universal." In David L. Allen and Steve W. Lemke. (eds.). *Whosoever Will: A Biblical-Theological Critique of Five-Point Calvinism.* Nashville: B&H, 2010.
Armstrong, Brian G. *Calvinism and the Amyraut Heresy: Protestant Scholasticism and Humanism in Seventeenth-Century France.* Madison: University of Wisconsin Press, 1969.
Boer, E.A. de. *The Genevan School of the Prophets: The Congregations of the Company of Pastors and their Influence in 16th Century Europe.* Geneva: Librairie Droz S.A., 2012.
--- "John Calvin's 'Disputatio de Praedestinatione': The Relevance of a Manuscript on his Doctrine of Providence and Predestination." *Dutch Reformed Theological Journal/Nederduitse Gereformeerde Teologiese Tydskrif* Vol. 50. No. 3&4, 2009: 580-94.

Boersma, Hans. "Calvin and the Extent of the Atonement," *Evangelical Quarterly,* 64/4 (1992).

Clifford, Allan C. *Calvinus: Authentic Calvinism. A Clarification.* Norwich: Charenton Reformed Publishing, 1996.

Cottret, Bernard. *Calvin. Biographie.* Lattès: S.I. 1995.

Graafland, C. *Van Calvijn tot Barth: Oorsprong en ontwikkeling van de leer der verkiezing in het Gereformeerd Protestantisme.* Zoetermeer: Boekencentrum 1987.

--- *Van Calvijn tot Comrie: Oorsprong en ontwikkeling van de leer van het verbond in het Gereformeerd Protestantisme.* Vol. I, Parts 1 & 2. Zoetermeer: Boekencentrum, 1992.

Helm, Paul. *Calvin and the Calvinists.* Edinburgh: The Banner of Truth Trust, 1982 [1998].

--- "Calvin, Indefinite Language, and Definite Atonement." In David Gibson and Jonathan Gibson (eds.), *From Heaven He Came and Sought Her: Definite Atonement in Historical, Biblical, Theological, and Pastoral Perspective.* Wheaton: Crossway, 2013: 97-120.

Hesselink, I. John. *Calvin's First Catechism: A Commentary,* Columbia Series in Reformed Theology. Louisville: Westminster John Knox Press, 1997.

Holtrop, P. *The Bolsec Controversy on Predestination from 1551 to 1555.* Lewiston, N.Y.: Edwin Mellen, 1993.

Jacobs, Paul. *Prädestination und Verantwortlichkeit bei Calvin.* Neukirchen: Kreis Moers 1937.

Janse, Wim. "The Controversy between Westphal and Calvin on Infant Baptism (1555-1556)." *Perichoresis* 6.1. 2008): 3-43.

Kendall, R.T. *Calvin and English Calvinism to 1649.* Oxford: Oxford University Press, 1979.

--- "The Puritan Modification of Calvin's Theology." In W. Stanford Reid (ed.). *John Calvin: His Influence in the Western World.* Grand Rapids: Zondervan, 1982.

Lillback, Peter A. *The Binding of God: Calvin's Role in the Development of Covenant Theology.* Grand Rapids: Baker Academic, 2001.

Melles, G. *Albertus Pighius en zijn strijd met Calvijn over het liberum arbitrium.* Kampen: Kok, 1973.

Moehn, W.H.T. *God roept ons tot Zijn dienst: Een homiletisch onderzoek naar de verhouding tussen God en de hoorder in Calvijns preken over Handelingen 4.1-6:7.* Kampen: Kok, 1996: 277-290. English translation: *God Calls Us to His Service: The Relation Between God and his Audience in Calvin's Sermons on Acts.* Geneva: Droz, 2001.

Muller, Richard A. *Calvin and the Reformed Tradition: On the Work of Christ and the Order of Salvation.* Grand Rapids: Baker Academic, 2012.

--- *The Unaccomodated Calvin: Studies in the Foundation of a Theological Tradition.* New York/Oxford: Oxford University Press, 2000.

Neuser, Wilhelm H. "Calvin als Prediger. Seine Erklährung der Prädestination in der Predigt von 1551 und in der Institutio von 1559." In Michael Beintker (ed.) *Gottes freie Gnade. Studien zur Lehre von der Erwählung.* Wuppertal: Foedus, 2004.

Nicole, Roger. "John Calvin's view of the Extent of the Atonement." In: *Standing Forth. Collected Writings of Roger Nicole.* Geanies House, Fearn, Ross-shire: Christian Focus Publications 2002. Originally published in *Westminster Theological Journal,* Vol. XLVII, No. 2, Fall 1985.

Parker, T.H.L. *Calvin's Preaching.* Edinburgh: T&T Clarck 1992.

Parsons, Michael, *Calvin's Preaching on the Prophet Micah. The 1550-1551 Sermons in Geneva.* Lewiston: The Edwin Mellen Press, 2006.

Ponter, David W. "Review Essay: John Calvin on the Death of Christ and The Reformation's Forgotten Doctrine of Universal Vicarious Satisfaction: A Review and Critique of Tom Nettles' Chapter in Whomever He Wills" in *Southwestern Journal of Theology,* Volume 55, Number 1, Fall 2012, 139-159 (Part one), and Number 2, Spring 2013, 253-271 (Part two).

Prosperi, A. *L'eresia del Libro Grande. Storia di Giorgio Siculo e della sua setta.* Milano: Feltrinelli, 2001.

Rimbach, Harald. *Gnade und Erkenntnis in Calvins Prädestinationslehre. Calvin im Vergleich mit Pighius, Beza und Melanchthon.* Frankfurt am Main: Peter Lang, 1996.

Rouwendal, Pieter L. "Calvin's Forgotten Position on the Extent of the Atonement." *Westminster Theological Journal,* Vol. LXX, No. 2, Fall 2008.

Schulze, L.F. *Calvin's Reply to Pighius.* Potchefstroom, S-Africa: Pro Rege-Press, 1971.

Selderhuis, Herman J. (ed.). *The Calvin Handbook.* Grand Rapids: Eerdmans, 2009.

Shepherd, V.A. *The Nature and Function of Faith in the Theology of John Calvin.* Macon, Georgia: Mercer University Press, 1983.

Spijker, W. van't. *'Die Fransman...' Calvijn in 1536.* Kampen: De Groot Goudriaan 1986.

Wallace, Ronald S. *Calvin's Doctrine of the Word and the Sacrament.* Edinburgh/London: Oliver and Boyd, 1953.

BEZA

Primary Literature

Beza, Theodore. *A Little Book of Christian Questions and Responses.* Transl. by Kirk M. Summers. Allison Park: Pickwick Publications, 1986.

--- *Ad Acta Colloquii Montisbelgardensis Tubingae edita Theodori Bezae responsionis.* Geneva: Joannes Le Preux, 1588

--- *Ad sycophantarum quorandam calumnias quib vnicum salutis nostræ fundamentum, id est aeternam Dei praedestinationem evertere nituntur, responsio Theodori Bezae Vezelii.* Geneva: Conrad Badius, 1558.

--- *Brefve exposition de la table ou figure contenant les principaus poincts de la religion Chrestienne.* n.p.[Geneva]: Jean Rivery, 1560.

--- *Correspondance de Théodore de Bèze,* tome I (1539-1555). Geneva: Librarie Droz, 1960.

--- *Cours sur les épîtres aux Romains et aux Hébreux 1564–66 d'après les notes de Marcus Widler. Thèses disputées à l'Académie de Genève, 1564–67.* Ed. Pierre Fraenkel and Luc Perrotet. Travaux d'Humanisme et Renaissance, CCXXVI. Geneva: Librairie Droz, 1988.

--- *De praedestinationis doctrina et vero usu tractatio absolutissima, editio secunda.* n.p. [Geneva]: Eustathius Vignon, 1583.

--- *Propositions and principles of divinitie (…).* Transl. anonymus. Edinburgh: Robert Waldegrave 1591.

--- *Quaestionum & Responsionum christianarum libellvs. In qvo praecipva christianae Religionis capita kat' epitomhn proponuntur.* n.p. [Geneva] I. Crispinus, 1570.

--- *Sermons sur l'histoire de la passion et Sepulture de nostre Seigneur Iesus Christ.* Geneva 1592.

--- *Sermons svr l'histoire de la resurrection de nostre Signeur Iesus Christ.* Geneva: Ian le Prevx, 1593.

--- *Sermons sur les trois premier chapitres du Cantique, de Salomo.* Geneva 1586.

--- *Tractationum Theologicarum, in quibus pleraque Christianae Religionis dogmata aduersus haereses nostris temporibus renouatas solidè ex Verbo Dei defenduntur* (3 vols.). Geneva: Io. Cripspinum 1570 [1582].

--- and Anthony Fayus, *Theses theologicae in schola Genevensi ab aliquot sacrarum literarum studiosus sub DD, Theod. Beza & Anthonio Fayo ss. Theologiae professoribus propositae & disputatae.* Geneva: Eustathius Vignon, 1586.

--- and Anthony Fayus, *Theses theologicae in schola Genevensi ab aliquot sacrarum literarum studiosus sub DD, Theod. Beza & Anthonio Fayo S.S. Theologiae professoribus propositae & disputatae. In quibus methodica locorum communium S.S. Theologiae epitome continetur. Altera editio emendatior & auctior priore.* Geneva: Eustathius Vignor., 1591.

Secondary Literature

Backus, Irena (ed.). *Théodore de Bèze, 1519-1605: actes du colloque de Genève, septembre 2005.* Geneva: Droz, 2007.

Baird, Henry Martyn. *Theodore Beza, the Counselor of the French Reformation 1519-1605.* New York: G.P. Putnam's Sons, 1899.

Baschera, Luca. "Aristotle and Scholasticism." In: Kirkby Torrance et al. (eds.) *A Companion to Peter Martyr Vermigli.* Leiden: Brill, 2009: 133-160

Baumann, Michael. *Petrus Martyr Vermigli in Zürich (1556–1562). Dieser Kylchen in der heiligen gschrifft professor und laeser.* Göttingen: Vandenhoeck&Ruprecht, 2016.

Beeke, Joel R. "Theodore Beza's Supralapsarian Predestination," in *Reformation and Revival Journal,* vol. 12 nr. 2, 2003.

Blacketer, Raymond. "Blaming Beza. The development of definite atonement in the reformed tradition" in David Gibson and Jonathan Gibson (eds.). *From Heaven He Came and Sought Her: Definite Atonement in Historical, Biblical, Theological, and Pastoral Perspective.* Wheaton: Crossway, 2013: 121-141.

--- "The Man in the Black Hat: Theodore Beza and the Reorientation of Early Reformed Historiography" in Jordan J. Ballor, David Sytsma and Jason Zuidema (eds.). *Church and School:* 225-241.

Bray, John S. *Theodore Beza's Doctrine of Predestination.* Nieuwkoop: B. de Graaf, 1975.

Buisson, F.E. and M. Engammare. *Sébastien Castellion. Sa vie, son oeuvre: 1515-1563.* Genève: Droz, 2010.

Campi, Emidio. *Shifting Patterns of Reformed Tradition.* Göttingen: Vandenhoeck & Ruprecht, 2014.

--- and Peter Opitz (eds.). *Heinrich Bullinger. Life-Thought-Influence. Zurich, Aug. 25-29, 2004. International Congress Heinrich Bullinger (1504-1575),* Vol. 1. Zurich: TVZ, 2007.

--- and Rüdi Reich. *Consensus Tigurinus. Die Einigung zwischen Heinrich Bullinger und Johannes Calvin über das Abendmahl.* Zurich: TVZ, 2009.

Clavier, H. *Theodore de Beze. Un apercu de sa vie aventureuse, des ses travaux, de sa personnalité.* Cahors: Coueslant, 1960.

Dufour, Alain. *Théodore de Bèze: poète et théclogien*. Geneva: Droz, 2006.
Geisendorf, Paul F. *Théodore de Bèze*. Geneva: Alexandre Jullien, 1949; reprint 1967.
Groot, D.J. de. "Melchior Wolmar. Ses relations avec les réformateurs français et suisses." *Bulletin de l'Histoire du Protestantisme français*, 83. 1934.
Guggisberg, Hans Rudolf and Bruce Gordon, *Sebastian Castellio, 1515-1563. Humanist and Defender of Religious Toleration in a Confessional Age*. Aldershot: Ashgate, 2003.
Heppe, H. "Theodor Beza, Leben und ausgewählte Schriften." *Leben und ausgewählte Schriften der Väter und Begründer der reformierten Kirche*, III. Elberfeld: Friderichs, 1861.
Holtrop, P. *The Bolsec Controversy on Predestination from 1551 to 1555*. Lewiston, N.Y.: Edwin Mellen, 1993.
Hotson, Howard. *Johann Heinrich Alsted 1588-1638: Between Renaissance, Reformation and Universal Reform*. Oxford: OUP, 2000.
James III, Frank A. *Peter Martyr Vermigli and Predestination. The Augustinian Inheritance of an Italian Reformer*. Oxford: Clarendon Press, 1998.
Kickel, Walter. *Vernunft un Offenbarung bei Theodor Beza. Zum Problem des Verhältnisses von Theologie, Philosophie und Staat*. Neukirchen-Vluyn: Neukirchener Verlag, 1967.
Lee, Brian J. *Johannes Cocceius and the Exegetical Roots of Federal Theology. Reformation Developments in the Interpretation of Hebrews 7-10*. Göttingen: Vandenhoeck & Ruprecht, 2009.
Mallinson, Jeffrey. *Faith, Reason and Revelation in Theodore Beza*. Oxford: OUP, 2003.
Maruyama, Tadakta. *The Ecclesiology of Theodore Beza. The Reform of the True Church*. Geneva: Droz, 1978.
McPhee, Ian. *Conserver or Transformer of Calvin's Theology? A Study of the Origins and Development of Theodore Beza's Thought (1550-1570)*. (Unpublished Ph.D. dissertation, Cambridge, 1979).
Moran, Bruce T. "Alchemy, Prophecy, and the Rosicrucians: Raphael Eglinus and Mystical Currents of the Early Seventeenth Century," in Piyo Rattansi and Antonio Clericuzio (eds.) *Alchemy and Chemistry in the 16th and 17th Centuries*. Dordrecht: Kluwer, 1994.
Muller, R.A. "The Use and Abuse of a Document: Beza's *Tabula Praedestinationis*, The Bolsec Controversy, and the Origins of Reformed Orthodoxy." In: Carl R. Trueman and R. Scott Clark, *Protestant Scholasticim*: 33-61.

Rait, Jill. *The Colloquy of Montbéliard. Religion and Politics in the Sixteenth Century*. Oxford: OUP 1993.
--- *Shapers of Religious Traditions in Germany, Switzerland, and Poland, 1560-1600*. New Haven: Yale University Press, 1981.
Sallmann, Martin. "La Faye, Antoine" in Hans Dieter Betz, Don S. Browning, Bernd Janowski and Eberhard Jüngel (eds.) *Religion Past and Present*. Leiden: Brill Online, 2012.
Schlosser, Friedrich Christoph, *Leben des Theodor de Beza und des Peter Martyr Vermigli. Ein Beytrag zur Geschichte der Zeiten der Kirchen-Reformation*. Heidelberg: Wohr und Zimmer, 1809.
Sliedrecht, C. van. *Calvijns opvolger Theodorus Beza. Zijn verkiezingsleer en zijn belijdenis van de drieënige God*. Leiden: J.J. Groen en Zoon, 1996.
Steinmetz, David. *Reformers in the Wings*. Philadelphia: Fortress Press, 1971.
Torrance, Kirkby e.a. (eds.). *A Companion to Peter Martyr Vermigli*. Leiden: Brill, 2009.
Veen, M.K. van. *De kunst van het twijfelen. Sebastian Castellio (1515-1563): humanist, calvinist, vrijdenker*. Zoetermeer: Meinema, 2012.
Venema, Cornelis P. *Heinrich Bullinger and the Doctrine of Predestination: Author of "the Other Reformed Tradition"?* Grand Rapids: Baker, 2002.
Wright, Shawn D. *Our Sovereign Refuge. The Pastoral Theology of Theodore Beza*. Bletchley, Milton Keynes: Paternoster 2004.

DORT

Primary Literature
Acta et Documenta Synodi Nationalis Dordechtanae (1618-1619). Vol. I. Acta of the Synod of Dort. Eds. Donald Sinnema, Christian Moser and Herman J. Selderhuis. Göttingen: Vandenhoeck&Ruprecht, 2015
Acta Synodi Nationalis (…) Dordrechti habitae Anno 1618 et 1619. Accedunt Plenissima, de Quinque Articulis, Theologorum Judicia. Lugduni Batavorum [Leiden]: Isaac Elzevir, 1620.
Canons of Dort. In: Ph. Schaff (ed.). *Creeds of Christendom*, III, 1877.
Spanheim, F. *Disputationum Theologicarum Syntgama*, I. Geneva: Petrus Chouët, 1652.
Registres de la Compagny des Pasteurs de Genève, Tome XIV et dernier (1618-1619). Ed. Nicolas Fornerod. Geneva: Droz, 2012.

Secondary Literature
Bavinck, Herman. *Gereformeerde Dogmatiek* II. Kampen: J.H. Bos, 1908.

Campi, Emidio. "John Diodati (1576-1649), Translator of the Bible into Italian." In idem, *Shifting Patterns of Reformed Tradition*. Göttingen: Vandenhoeck & Ruprecht, 2014.

Comrie, Alexander and Nicolaus Holtius. *Examen van het ontwerp van tolerantie [...]*, VII. Amsterdam: Nicolaas Byl, 1756.

Ferrari, Andrea. *John Diodati's Doctrine of Holy Scripture*. Grand Rapids: Reformation Heritage Books, 2006.

Glasius, B. *Geschiedenis der Nationale Synode in 1618 en 1619 gehouden te Dordrecht in hare voorgeschiedenis, handelingen en gevolgen*. Leiden: P. Engels, 1860.

Goudriaan, A. and F. van Lieburg (eds.). *Revisiting the Synod of Dort (1618-1619)*. Leiden: Brill, 2011.

Maag, Karin. "From Professors to Pastors: The Convoluted Careers of Jean Diodati and Théodore Tronchin" in Jordan J. Ballor et al. (eds.). *Church and School*, 243-254.

McComish, William A. *The Epigones. A Study of the Theology of the Genevan Academy at the Time of the Synod of Dort, with Special Reference to Giovani Diodati*. Allinson Park, PA: Pickwick Publications, 1989.

Nauta, D. "Spanheim, Fri(e)dericus" in D. Nauta et al. (eds.) *Biografisch Lexicon voor de geschiedenis van het Nederlandse protestantisme*, vol. II. Kampen: Kok, 1983, 410-411.

--- "Spanheim, Fri(e)dericus, filius" in: D. Nauta et al. (ed.) *Biografisch Lexicon voor de geschiedenis van het Nederlandse protestantisme*, vol. II. Kampen: Kok, 1983, 411-413.

Sinnema, Donald. *The issue of reprobation at the Synod of Dort (1618-19) in light of the history of this doctrine*. (Unpublished PhD. thesis, Toronto, 1985).

TURRETIN

Primary literature

Amyraut, Moyse. *Brief traité de la predestination et de ses principales dependances*. Saumur: Lesnier & Desbordes, 1634.

--- *Brief Treatise on Predestination and its Dependent Principles*. Transl. Richard Lum. n.p. [Dallas?], 1985.

Turretin Benedict. *Profit des chastimens, ou, Sept sermons sur l'exhortation contenue en l'Epist. Aux Hebrieux chap. XII. v. 5. 6. 7. 8. 9. 10. 11*. Geneva: Pierre Aubert, 1630.

--- *Sei homilie sopra le parole di Iesu Christo, Luc. XII. v. 5.6. etc*. Geneva: Pietro Alberto, 1623.

Turretin, Francis. *Institutio Theologiae Elencticae, in qua status controversiae perspicue exponitur, praecipua orthodoxorum argumenta proponuntur et vindicantur et fontes solutionem aperiuntur*. Geneva, 1679-1685.
--- *Institutes of Elenctic Theology*. Transl. G.M. Giger, ed. J.T. Dennison Jr.. Phillipsburg, NJ: P&R Publishing, 1992-1997.
--- *De satisfactione Christi Disputationes cum indicibus necessariis. Adjectae sunt ejusdem duae disputationes I. De circulo pontificio. II De concordia Jacobi & Pauli in articulo justificationis*. Leiden: Frederic Haring / Utrecht: Ernest Voskuil, 1696.
--- *Recueil de sermons sur divers passages de l'ecriteure sainte*. Geneva: Samuel de Tournes, 1686.
--- *Sermons sur divers passages de l'ecriteure sainte*. Geneva: Samuel de Tournes, 1676.
---, Johann Heinrich Heidegger and Lucas Gernler *Formula Consensus Ecclesiarum Helveticarum Reformatarum circa Doctrinam de Gratia Universali & Connexa, aliáque nonnulla capita*. n.p., n.d..

Secondary Literature

Armstrong, Brian G. *Calvinism and the Amyraut Heresy: Protestant Scholasticism and Humanism in Seventeenth Century France*. Madison: University of Wisconsin Press, 1969.

Beach, J. Mark. *Christ and the Covenant. Francis Turretin's Federal Theology as a Defense of the Doctrine of Grace*. Göttingen: Vandenhoeck & Ruprecht, 2007.

Beardslee III, John W. *Theological Development at Geneva under Francis and Jean-Alphonse Turretin (1648-1737)*. Ph.D. diss. Yale University, 1956.

Bruce, James E. *Rights in the Law. The importance of God's Free Choices in the Thought of Francis Turretin*. Göttingen: Vandenhoeck & Ruprecht, 2013.

Budé Eugène de. *Vie de François Turrettini, théologien Genevois (1623-1687)*. Lausanne, 1871.

Burnett, Amy Nelson. "How to Preach a Protestant Sermon: A Comparison of Lutheran and Reformed Homiletics," in *Theologische Zeitschrift*, Jahrgang 63, Heft 2. Basel: 2007.

Dennison, Jr., James T. "The Twilight of Scholasticism: Francis Turretin at the Dawn of the Enlightenment," in Carl R. Trueman and R. Scott Clark, *Protestant Scholasticism*: 244-255

Heyd, Michael. *Between Orthodoxy and the Enlightenment: Jean-Robert Chouet and the Introduction of Cartesian Science in the Academy of Geneva.* The Hague: Martinus Nijhof, 1982.
--- "Orthodoxy, Non-Conformity and Modern Science." In M. Yardeni (ed.), *Modernité et non-conformisme en France à travers les ages.* Leiden: Brill, 1983.
Hunter, William B. (ed.), *A Milton Encyclopedia,* vol. V. Bucknell: BUP, 1979.
Jensen, Paul Timothy. *Calvin and Turretin. A Comparison of their Soteriologies.* (Ph.D. diss. University of Virginia. 1988).
Jorio, Marco (ed.). *Historisches Lexikon der Schweiz.* Basel: Schwabe, 2002-2014.
Kaiser, Christopher B. *Creational Theology and the History of Physical Science. The Creationist Tradition from Basil to Bohr.* Leiden: Brill, 1997.
Keizer, Gerrit. *François Turrettini. Sa vie et ses œuvres et le consensus.* (PhD. diss. Lausanne, 1900).
Klauber, Martin I. "The Helvetic Formula Consensus (1675): An Introduction and Translation." *Trinity Journal 11:1.* Spring 1990.
Philips, Timothy R. "The Dissolution of Francis Turretin's Vision of *Theologia*: Geneva at the End of the Seventeenth Century." In Roney and Klauber, *The Identity of Geneva*: 77-92.
Stam, F.P. van. *The Controversy over the Theology of Saumur, 1635-1650. Disrupting Debates Among the Huguenots in Complicated Circumstances.* Amsterdam/Maarssen: APA-Holland University Press, 1988.
Wenneker, Erich. "TURRETTINI, François." In *Biographish-Bibliographisches Kirchenlexicon,* Band XII. Herzberg 1997, 735-738.

PICTET

Primary Literature
Pictet, Benedict. *Brevis Syllabus Controversiarum.* Geneva: Societatis, 1711.
--- *Cinq Catechismes pour Instruire les jeunes gens dans la Religion Reformée.* Geneva: Jean Antoine Querel, 1715
--- *De consensu ac dissensu inter Reformatos et Augustanae Confessionis Fratres dissertatio.* Amsterdam: Gallet, 1697.
--- *Christian Theology.* Transl. F. Reyroux. London: Seeley and Burnside, 1834.
--- *L'Examen des Chretiens. Ou Sermon sur Apoc. III. v. 1. 2. 3.* Geneva: Querel, 1716.

--- *Huit Sermons sur L'Examen des Religions*. Geneva: Societe des Libraires, 1701.
--- *Medulla Theologiae Christianae Didacticae et Elencticae*. Geneva: Societatis, 1711.
--- *Quatorze Sermons sur Divers Textes de L'Ecriture Sainte*. Geneva: les Frères de Tournes, 1719.
--- *La Morale Chrêtienne ou l'Art de Bien Vivre*. 2 vols. Geneva: pour la Compagnie des Libraires, 1695.
--- *La Théologie Chretienne et la Science du Salut ...* 2 vols. Amsterdam: G. Gallet, 1702.
--- *La Théologie Chretienne et la Science du Salut ...* 3 vols. Geneva: Cramer, 1721.
--- *Theologia Christiana (...) Ex Puris S.S. Literarum Fontibus Hausta*. Geneva: Cramer et Perachon, 1696 [1716].
--- *Traite Contre L'Indifférence des Religions Ou L'On Établit les Fondemens de la vraye Religion, & l'on répond aux principales Objections des Athées, des Déistes, & autres Libertins*. Geneva: Cramer & Perachon, 1716; first edition 1692.
Johannes Alphonsus Turrettinus. *In Pauli Apostoli ad Romanos Epistolae Capita XI Praelectiones Criticae, Theologicae et Concionatoriae*. Lausanne & Geneva: M.M. Bouchet & Socior, 1741.
--- *Cogitationes et dissertationes theologicae (...) volumen alterum*. Geneva: Barrilot, 1737.

Secondary Literature
[anonymous], *The Confessional: or a Full and Free Inquiry into the Right, Utility, Edification and Success of Establishing Systematical Confessions of Faith and Doctrine in Protestant Churches*. London: S. Bladon, 1767.
Budé, Eugène de. *Vie de Bénédict Pictet, théologien genevois (1655-1724)*. Lausanne: Georges Bridel, 1874.
Fatio O. *Louis Tronchin: une transition calvinienne*. Paris: Garnier, 2015.
Gootjes, Albert. *Claude Pajon (1626-1685) and the Academy of Saumur: The First Controversy over Grace*. Leiden: Brill, 2014.
Klauber, M.I. *Between Reformed Scholasticism and Pan-Protestantism: Jean-Alphonse Turretin (1671-1737) and Enlightened Orthodoxy at the Academy of Geneva*. Selingsgrove: Susquehanna University Press, 1994.
--- "Family Loyalty and Theological Transition in Post-Reformation Geneva: The Case of Bénédict Pictet (1655-1724)," *Fides et Historia*. Winter/Spring, 1992.

--- "Reformed Orthodoxy in Transition: Bénedict Pictet (1655-1724) and Enlightened Orthodoxy in Post-Reformation Geneva." In W. Fred Graham (ed.). *Later Calvinism. International Perspectives.* Kirksville, Missouri: Sixteenth Century Journal Publishers, 1994.

--- "The Uniqueness of Christ in Post-Reformation Reformed Theology: From Francis Turretin to Jean-Alphonse Turretin." In Jordan J. Ballor et al. (eds.) *Church and School.*

Pitassi, Maria-Cristina. "From Exemplarity to Suspicion. The Genevan Church between the Late Seventeenth and Early Eighteenth Centuries." *History of European Ideas* Volume 37, Issue 1, 2011, pages 16-22.

--- "Arminius Redivivus? The Arminian Influence in French Switzerland, and at the Beginning of the Eighteenth Century." In Leeuwen, Marius van and Keith D. Stanglin (eds.). *Arminius, Arminianism, and Europe.* Leiden: Brill, 2009.

Rex, Walter E. "Bayle, Jurieu, and the Politics of Philosophy: A Reply to Professor Popkin." In Thomas M. Lennon et al. *Problems of Cartesianism.* Kingston, [Ont.]: McGill-Queen's University Press, 1982.

Selles, O.H. "A Case of Hidden Identity." In Roney and Klauber (eds.), *The Identity of Geneva*: 93-109

Appendix

Diderot and D'Alembert. *Encyclopédie, ou Dictionnaire raisonné des sciences, des arts et des métiers,* vol. 7. Paris: Briasson, David, Le Breton & Durand, 1757.

Goltz, Hermann Freiherr von der. *Die reformirte Kirche Genfs im neunzehnten Jahrhundert oder der Individualismus der Erweckung in seinem Verhältnis zum christlichen Staat der Reformation.* Basel/Geneva, 1862

McNutt, Jennifer Powel. *Calvin Meets Voltaire. The Clergy of Geneva in the Age of Enlightnment, 1685-1798.* Farnham, UK: Ashgate, 2013.

Zwaag, W. van der. *César Malan (1784-1864). Prediker van het Frans-Zwitsers Réveil.* Utrecht: De Banier, 1997.

Index of names and subjects

Abra(ha)m	27, 33, 34n, 35n, 39, 41, 70-72, 75, 121, 127-128, 130, 146, 152, 227n, 289
Academy of Geneva	9-10, 70, 79, 86-88, 157n, 159, 162, 172-173, 188, 190, 192, 245-246, 249, 253, 261, 265, 280, 299
Adam	22, 37, 89 99-100, 106-107, 112, 115n, 138, 168, 171, 187n, 194-195
Alembert, Jean le Rond d'	296-297
Allen, David L.	29n
Alsted, Johann Heinrich	81n
Ames, Joseph	104n
amyraldians, amyraldists, amyraldism	186n, 187n, 189n, 190, 197n, 198n, 199, 219, 246, 253-254, 257, 264-265, 298, 304, 320
Amyraut, Moyse	185-191, 196, 199, 246, 253, 257, 268n, 270n, 302
Andreae, Jacob	82, 123, 145, 219
antecendent	194, 222n, 258, 311
Aquinas, Thomas	1, 7, 104
arbitrium, liberum, see: choice, free	
Aristotle, aristotelism	3, 90n
arminians, see: remonstrants	
Arminius, Jacob	3, 157
Armstrong, Brian	83n, 86n, 172, 186n
Asselt, Willem J. van	1, 3n, 7n, 8n, 11n, 26n, 83n, 87n, 118n, 140n, 194n, 213n
assurance	23, 36, 37, 55-57, 72, 85, 96, 134, 141-142, 144n, 146, 149 161-164, 177-178, 214-215. 221, 225-228, 232, 235-236, 261, 274-282, 288, 290, 312-313, 317

Atonement
- classic formula on –   28-30, 57, 61, 122-123, 151, 164, 166-167, 180-181, 183, 185n, 200-201, 220
- extent of –   12, 28-31, 57, 61, 82, 122-125, 145, 147-148, 151-151, 155, 164-167, 179-181, 183, 191, 200-202, 219-221, 231-232, 262, 262-266, 281-282, 288, 290, 301, 304-305, 316-317
- hypothetic universal –   28-29, 183n, 185, 186n, 187n, 199, 200
- non-Anselmian doctrine of –   160
- particular (definite, limited) –   28-29, 31n, 122-125, 145, 151-152, 166, 179-181, 183, 200-202, 204n, 220, 231-232, 262-263, 277, 282, 290, 304
- universal (general, indefinite)–   5-6, 28-29, 31n, 247, 262, 290, 304
Augsburg Confession   263-266
Augustine   43, 54, 58-59, 80, 101, 113, 133n, 140n, 142-143, 218, 309, 313

Backus, Irena   85n, 88n
Baird, Henry Martyn   79n
Balcanquall   166n
Ballor, Jordan J.   3n, 36n, 81n, 157n, 247n, 261n
baptism   38, 66, 125, 127n, 203n, 207, 247, 265-266, 279, 292
baptist(s)   5-6
Bartholomew's night, st.   159
Baschera, Luca   140n
Basel   13, 16n, 79, 93n, 191
Baskwell, P.J.   6n
Battles, Ford Lewis   13n, 14n, 23n, 25
Baum, J.W.   79n
Baumann, Michael   102n
Bavinck, Herman   174
Bayle, Pierre   246, 250n
Beach, J. Mark   189n, 192-193, 202n, 204n
Beardslee III, John W.   192
Beeke, Joel R.   9n, 57n, 118n, 119, 142n, 160, 171-173, 192-193, 255
Benoit, Jean Daniel   64n
Bergh, W. van den   31n
Bern   16n, 79, 88, 90n, 93n, 96n, 97, 102
Betz, Hans Dieter   81n

Beveridge, Henry	25, 26n, 27n, 49
Beza, Theodore	3, 8-11, 29, 57n, 79-183, 195-198, 200-202, 205n, 211, 214, 217-224, 231, 233-236, 243-244, 256-257, 259, 261, 266, 268, 278, 282, 285, 288, 290, 294, 296, 298, 302-306, 308, 311-320
Bibliander, Theodore	101n, 102
Bierma, Lyle	31n
Blacketer, Raymond A.	29n, 81n, 148n, 166n
Boer, Erik A. de	15n, 16n, 18, 24n
Boersma, Hans	28n
Bogerman, Johannes	171
Bolsec, Jerome	15-17, 20-22, 38, 42, 54, 61, 63-64, 71, 76, 79-80, 83-84, 87-91, 93-98, 103, 111, 144-145, 219, 301-303, 320
Bonnet, Jules	16n, 49n
Boston, Thomas	5, 189n
Bourges	79
Bray, John S.	83-84, 103-104
Bremen	88n
Bremen, delegates of – to the synod of Dort from	166n-168, 170, 182n, 183
British delegation to the synod of Dort	166-167, 181n
Browning, Don S.	81n
Budé, Eugene de	188n, 192, 254-255, 280
Buisson, F.E.	81n
Bullinger, Heinrich	13, 54, 79-80, 85n, 88-97, 101-103, 111-114, 117n, 118, 123, 134n, 137, 142, 144-145, 147, 185n, 302-303
Burnett, Amy Nelson	222n
call	
- effectual or internal –	4, 43n, 54, 60, 78, 94, 107, 133, 135-136, 142, 168, 176, 178, 195, 199, 203, 205-206, 208-209, 213, 217, 223, 225-226, 230, 236, 240, 243, 269-270, 273-274, 288, 309-310, 318
- external or outward –	*passim*

Calvin, John	1-103, 111-114, 116-118, 121-158, 164, 166, 172, 174-177, 182-186, 192-193, 196, 198, 200, 203, 205n-208, 210-212, 214, 217-224, 231, 233-236, 243-245, 250, 255, 261, 266, 282, 285, 288-290, 294-299, 301-322
calvinism	1, 3, 10
Cameron, John	187n
Campbell, George	189n
Campi, Emidio	85n, 88n, 89n, 90n, 102n, 159n, 160, 161n, 171
Cappel, Louis	187n, 197n
cartesianism	190n, 191n, 245
Cartesius (Descartes), René	190n
Castellio, Sebastian	80, 86, 100n, 125, 126n, 131-132, 136-140, 143-144, 317
catholic, roman	1, 4n, 87n, 189, 234n, 245n, 246, 250, 254, 257, 286-287, 297n, 299, 302
cause(s)	
- deficient -	139
- efficient -	96, 139
- final -	100, 167, 169-170
- first and secondary /middle -	54, 97, 99-100, 120, 138, 197
- impulsive -	206, 238n
- instrumental -	55, 131n, 138-139, 206, 238n
- material -	100
- of God's hatred	100n, 119-120, 145, 147
- of sin and unbelief	18, 23, 26, 27, 52-54, 85, 91-95, 97, 111, 115-117, 118, 137-141, 145, 147, 162-163, 178n, 194, 199n, 213, 219, 257, 261, 273, 311, 320
- privative -	96-97
- proximate and remote -	27, 54, 95, 96n, 116, 140n
Chamier, Daniel	246n
charitable judgment	39, 77, 130-131, 146, 315, 317
choice, free *(liberum arbitrium)*	14, 91n, 186n, 239
Chouet, Jean-Robert	190n, 191, 245
Christ	
- as cause and foundation of the calling and salvation	164-165, 176, 180, 228

- as (not) the foundation of election	169n, 227
- as Head of the elect	72, 164, 170, 176, 201, 203, 208, 262, 266
- as Mediator	45n, 85, 121-123, 126, 131n, 135, 163-164, 176 177, 195-197, 199-201, 203, 214, 262, 264, 266, 272
- as the mirror of election	55, 76-77, 142, 146
- as the object of faith	28, 55-56, 71, 76-77, 141, 214-215, 220, 243, 274-275, 282, 294-296, 312, 316
-'s death, see: atonement	
church	
- marks of the –	39, 270
- members of –	39, 41, 44, 57, 65-67, 72, 75, 128, 130, 146, 152-153, 208-209, 220, 233-235, 244, 257, 261, 270, 281, 288, 291, 308, 315
- visible or invisible	39-41, 59-60, 129-131, 146, 204-205, 207-209, 220, 225, 269-270, 306-308, 319
circumcision	33-34, 37, 75, 130
Clarck, R. Scott	3n, 4n, 80n, 190n, 207n, 245n
Clericuzio, Antonio	81n
Clifford, Allan C.	28n
Cole, H.	16n, 53n
company of pastors	86, 245, 253
Comrie, Alexander	174, 186n
condition(s)	
- *a priori and a posteriori* –	206, 238n
- faith and/or repentance as –	41, 45, 47, 57, 128, 131, 135-136, 146, 153, 155. 164-165, 178, 180-182, 185, 201, 205-207, 210-212, 214, 221-222, 239, 248, 259, 268-270, 272, 274-275, 284, 306, 308, 310
- in the external call	42, 44-52, 57, 61-62, 66, 68-69, 132, 135, 146 147, 153-154, 182, 206-207, 210-211, 221, 238-239, 242, 269-273, 294, 307-312, 319
- (non-)meritorious –	46-48, 135, 221
- knowledge of sin and misery a –	48-49, 74, 135, 211-212, 221, 223, 240, 273, 311

344 - Index of names and subjects

- of the covenant of grace	19, 31, 33-38, 44, 46-47, 52, 62, 69, 127-128, 146, 153, 180, 186, 193, 202, 204, 206, 208, 212, 219-220, 228, 233, 239, 261, 268-269, 275, 310
Confessio Belgica	87
Confessio Gallicana (French Confession)	87-88, 175
congregation, zie: church	
Consensus Tigurinis	90n, 101n
consequence	79, 84, 120, 139, 194, 197, 212-213, 216, 222n, 258, 274, 311
contingency	121, 194, 206
continuity and discontinuity	4, 12, 129, 147-148, 183, 192-193, 219, 222, 301, 304-305, 308-309, 311-313, 317, 320
Contra-remonstrants	158, 172, 302
corruption	48n, 52, 99-101, 106-107, 119, 122, 133, 137n, 139n, 140n, 162, 171-172, 175, 195, 199, 249, 258n, 259, 271, 273, 277, 286, 289, 292-293
Cottret, Bernard	13n
covenant	
- administration / dispensation of the -	69, 127-128n, 164, 201-206, 218, 231, 233, 267, 303-304, 307, 313
- condition(s) of the -	see: condition
- (un)breakable	33, 36, 41, 59, 128
- community	36-39, 44, 51-52, 57, 61, 65-69, 71, 75, 77, 303, 309, 315
- essence of the -	203, 205, 208, 220, 235, 269, 306-310
- partakers or members of the -	36-37, 44, 52, 66, 69, 126-127, 146, 151-152, 192, 202-204, 205, 217-219, 221, 230-231, 233, 235, 244, 265-267, 279, 303-304, 307, 314, 316-317
- parties in the -	202-203, 208, 266
- creation	5, 26, 99-101, 104n, 106-107, 112, 122, 149, 163, 171, 173, 175, 178n, 195, 198, 199, 251n, 255-256, 286
Cunningham, William	189

damnation	23, 37, 48n, 53n, 70, 76, 85, 91-92, 95-97, 104, 112-116, 119, 126, 132, 137-138, 143, 147, 163, 167, 171n, 172, 175n, 178n, 196-198, 248, 260, 263-264, 279, 284, 287, 315
Daneau, Lambert	222n, 234n
Davies, G.I.	14n
decrees of God in general	193n, 227, 251n, 255-256, 286
- (un)conditional	153n, 193, 227, 256-257
- does (not) necessitate events	120-121, 139-140, 194, 227, 256
Dekker, Eef	3n, 8n
Dennison, James T.	188n-190n, 192, 245n, 246n
Descartes, see Cartseius	
Diderot, D.	296-297
Diodati, John	8, 10-11, 157-183, 188, 219, 221, 236, 302-304, 320
discontinuity: see continuity	
doctor, office of	9, 142
Dort, synod and canons of	3, 7, 9, 11, 157-160, 166-168, 170, 173-183, 185-186, 190, 196, 198, 201n, 202, 217, 219, 221, 245, 248, 250, 256-258, 264n, 265, 271, 280, 282, 294, 296, 302, 305-306, 308, 319
Dufour, Allain	79n
ecclesiology: see church	
Edinburgh	189n
effect	80, 93n, 114n, 139n, 141-142, 161, 164, 180, 194, 197, 213, 216, 227, 229, 258-259, 274-276, 279, 311, 313, 318
efficiency of Christ's death, see: atonement, classic formula of	
Egli(nus) Raphael	81n
election *passim*	
- assurance of –, see faith, assurance of	
- general –	27, 32n, 33, 37, 41, 44, 59-60, 68, 78, 127, 286, 303, 306-307
- *gradus* in –	27, 37, 39, 121
Emerson, Everett	31n
Engammare, Max	70n, 81n
Erskine, Ralph and Ebenezer	5

Esau	33, 34n, 71-72, 75-77, 119, 127, 171, 197n, 225, 248, 315-316
euarestia	see, will in God
eudokia	see, will in God
execution of the decree	78, 85-86, 89, 99-101, 112-113, 115-117n, 120-122, 132, 134, 145, 150, 155-156, 163, 193, 198, 200, 202-203, 213, 225, 244, 255, 257, 259, 262, 266, 268, 272, 282, 303, 318
Ezekiel	34, 45, 46n, 81, 127n, 132, 211
faith	
- acts of -	212, 214-217, 221, 240, 243, 274-277, 282, 312-313
- as a condition, see: condition - faith as a -	
- assurance of -	23, 36-37, 55-57, 72, 85, 96, 134, 141-144, 146, 149, 161-164, 177-178, 214-215, 221, 225-228, 232, 235-236, 261, 274-279, 281-282, 288, 290, 312-313, 317
- definition of -	56-57, 141, 214-215, 277, 312-313
- object of - see: Christ	
Fall (of Adam)	18, 23n, 26-27, 89, 99-101, 104n, 112-113n, 118, 120-122, 130, 137-138, 141, 144, 149, 195, 198-197, 203, 210, 248, 251n, 255-259, 286n
Farel, William	7, 13, 102, 298
Farley, Benjamin W.	64n, 65n, 67n
Fatio, Oliver	85n, 245n
Faye, Antoine la (Fayus, Anthonius)	79n, 81, 114n, 117-118, 120, 123-124, 128, 130, 141, 144-145, 157n, 161-162, 169n
Ferrari, Andrea	159n, 160
Field, John	37n, 75n
Forbes of Corse, John (Forbesius)	268
foreknowledge (prescience) of God	24, 89, 94, 106-107, 112-113, 178, 195, 199, 258

Formula Consensus	187n-188, 191-205, 210n, 214n, 220-221, 245-247, 249-250, 253-255, 263-267, 280, 290n, 296, 304
Fornerod, Nicolas	158n, 160, 167, 171n-173, 181n
Fraenkel, Pierre	81
France	10, 13, 79, 88n, 90n, 159, 185-188, 190n, 298
Francillon	297
Franeker	88n
Frankfurt	14
freedom, see: choice, free	
Fuller, Andrew	5, 7n
Gallatin	297
Geisendorf, Paul F.	79n
Geneva	*passim*
Georgius of Sicily (Georgio Riolo Siculo)	15-17, 21, 42
Germany	79, 173n
Gernler, Lucas	191
Gibson, David and Jonathan	28n, 29n
Giger, G.M	189
Gill, John	5, 7n
Glasius, B.	158n
God	
- as (not) being the author or cause of sin	53-54, 89, 93-95, 111, 113, 116, 137-141, 145, 147, 162-163, 178, 194, 199n, 218-219, 257-258, 261, 264, 283, 311-313, 314, 320
Goltz, Hermann Freiherr von der	296-297
gomarists, see: Contra-remonstrants	
Gomarus, Francis	157, 171n, 172, 183
Gootjes, Albert	274n
Gordon, Bruce	81n
Goudriaan, A.	158n
Graafland, C.	3, 9n, 10, 17, 22n, 31, 62, 113n, 306
Graham, W. Fred	10, 255n
Grenoble	249n
Groningen	88n
Groot, D.J. de	79n
Guggisberg, Hans Rudolf	81n

Haldane, Robert	299
Hall, Basil	83n, 86n
Haller, B.	96, 97
Haykin, Michael A.G.	5n
Heidegger, Johann Heinrich	191
Heidelberg	10, 88n, 173n, 174n
Heidelberg Catechism	87
Helm, Paul	28n, 29n, 31n
Heppe, Heinrich	31n, 79n
Herborn	88n, 159
Hesselink, I. John,	14n
Heyd, Michael	190n, 191n
high (hyper) calvinism	5
Hodge, Charles	189
Hoekema, Anthony	31n
Hoeksema, Herman	6, 7n
Holt, Mark P.	86
Holtius, Nicolaus	174, 186n
Holtrop, P.N.	15n, 20, 83, 89n, 95n, 145
Hotson, Howard	81n
Huguenots	187, 246n, 298
Hunter, William B.	190n
Hussey, Joseph	5
hypocrites	40, 41n, 51, 66, 130, 146, 152, 206n, 208, 225, 227, 229, 234-235, 243-244, 270, 295, 314-315
hypothetic universalism	28-29, 166, 183-185, 199
infralapsarism	26-27, 118-120, 145, 171-175, 182-185, 192, 196-200, 219, 221, 256-257, 281, 303-304, 320
Isaac	33-34, 72, 75, 127, 130
Ishmael	33, 37, 51, 71, 75, 77, 121, 127, 130
Islam, see: Mohammedanism	
Italy	15n, 159, 187n
Jacob	33, 71-72, 75-77, 127, 171, 225, 315-316
Jacobs, Paul	17
James III, Frank A.	102n
Janowski, Bernd	81n
Janse, W.	2, 38n
Jensen, Paul T.	192-193
Jerusalem	133, 223, 229, 236-238, 316

Jesuits	193, 200
Jesus: see Christ	
Jorio, Marco	190n
Judaism	250n, 254, 280, 284
Jüngel, Eberhard	81n
justification	41n, 47-48, 70-74, 104n, 107, 110, 116n, 142, 147, 149, 154n, 161, 168-169, 176, 177, 198, 201, 243, 248, 268, 286n, 314
Kampen	14
Keizer, Gerrit	188n, 189n, 191n, 192
Kendall, R.T.	9n, 28n, 83n,
Kickel, Walter	85, 93n, 118
Klauber, Martin I.	10n, 118n, 160n, 190n, 191n, 195n, 201n, 205n, 246n, 247n, 249n, 250n, 255, 263n, 264n, 265, 266n, 280
La Rochelle	175
Lane, Anthony N.S.	14n, 15n,
latitudinarianism	291
Lausanne	79-80, 85, 90, 95-97, 111
Lee, Brian J.	125n
Leeuwen, Marius van	249n
Leiden	88, 157, 159, 173n, 174n, 187n, 188, 189n, 249
Lemke, W.	29n
Lennon, Thomas M.	245n
Lieburg, F. van	158n
Lillback, Peter A.	19, 31n, 33n, 35n, 36n
Lismanin	102
Lombard, Peter	7
Louis XIV	190n, 246
Lucca	159, 187n
Lum, Richard	185n
Luther, Martin	7, 13
Lutherans	79n, 82, 87n, 90, 159, 167, 200, 202, 219, 222n, 247, 249, 252-254, 263-266, 280-281, 298, 302, 304, 320
Lyon	188, 234n, 245
Maag, Karin	10, 157n
Malan, César	299
Mallinson, Jeffrey	85
Manetsch, Scott M.	4, 9n, 10, 13n, 65n, 86

Marrow Controversy	5
Maruyama, Tadaktada	83, 85n, 129-130, 142n, 153n
Maurice of Nassau	158
Maurice, Charles	190
McComish, William A.	159, 160n, 167-171, 173, 180, 188
McNeil, John T.	25n
McNutt, Jennifer Powel	297-298
McPhee, Ian 101n	
Melanchthon, Philip	13, 22n, 87
Melchizedek	70-71
Melles, G.	14n, 15n, 20
Mestrezat, Jean	190n
Mestrezat, Philippe	190, 246
Moehn, W.H.Th.	19, 68
Mohammedanism	254, 280, 284
Montauban	88n, 188
Montbeliard	82, 122-126, 146, 151, 164, 302, 304
Montpelier	88n, 246n
Moran, Bruce T.	81n
Morus, Alexander	190
Moulin, Pierre du	161, 166
Muller, Richard A.	3n, 4, 11n, 15n, 20n, 22n, 28n, 29, 64n, 80n, 84, 88n, 89n, 95n, 101n, 103n, 104, 111, 148, 261
Mümpelgarten: zie Montbeliard	
Musculus, Wolfgang	36, 87
Nantes, Edict of	190n, 191, 246, 252, 298
Nassau, delegates of –	
to the synod of Dordrecht	168
Nauta, D.	173n, 174n
necessity	113, 120, 140, 148, 194, 219, 227, 256
- absolute –	120, 192, 194
- of compulsion or coercion	89, 112, 120, 133, 194
- of concupiscence or corruption	113
- conditional –	120
- of the consequence (*necessitas consequentiae*)	120, 139
- of the consequent (*necessitas consequentis*)	120, 139
- of dependence	194, 206
- of the Fall	112-112, 120, 194

- hypothethical -	139, 194, 206
- natural -	120
- physical or internal -	194
- voluntary -	120
Netherlands, the	6, 88n, 157, 187-188, 251n, 320
Nettles, Thomas J.	5n, 29n
Neuchatel	102, 249n
Neuser, Wilhelm H.	14n, 15n, 16n, 18, 22n, 23n, 77, 95n
Nicole, Roger	28n
Nimes	188
Opitz, Peter	85n, 89n, 102n
Orange	88n
order of salvation	72, 104, 197, 255
Orleans	79
Osterwald, J.F.	296
Otten, Willemien	3n
Pajon, Claude	274n
Pareus, David	166
Paris	79, 187-188
Parker, T.H.L.	18, 64n
Parsons, Michael	19, 65, 70n
Paul	24, 32n, 33-34, 45n, 48n, 52, 54-55, 63-64, 71, 81, 99, 119, 143, 227, 230, 240-241, 247-248, 253, 279, 283-284, 286, 288, 293-294
Pelagius, (semi-)pelagianism	165, 198-200, 225, 239-240
perdition, see: damnation	
Perkins, William	10
Perrotet, Luc	81n
perseverance	32n, 35-37, 52, 80, 143n, 149, 160-165n, 168-167, 171, 179, 183, 219, 229, 241, 264, 273, 279, 291n
Peter	33, 132, 224-225, 227, 259, 288-289, 294
Philips, Timothy R.	190n, 246n
Pictet, Benedict	7-11, 157, 189, 245-320
Pighius, Albert	14-18, 20-21, 38, 41-47, 54-55, 61, 64, 69, 76, 80-81, 95-96, 111, 132, 219, 300, 308, 320
Piscator, John	172, 183
Pitassi, Maria-Christina	249n
Place, Josué de la	187n

Plasger, Georg	38n
Poland	102
Ponter, David W.	29n
postredemptionism	186, 198n, 219
praedamnatio	260, 264
praeteritio	99n, 171n, 260, 264
preaching	*passim*
predestination	*passim*
Prescience, see foreknowledge	
promises	1, 11, 17, 19, 29-30, 33-35, 37-38, 41-47, 50-52, 55-57, 61-62, 66, 68, 72, 74, 76-77, 114, 127-128, 135-136, 141, 153, 164, 179, 181-183, 202-207, 210-215, 217, 219-222, 228-230, 232-233, 235n, 236-237, 239, 241-244, 257, 260, 266, 268n, 271-275, 277, 287, 290, 294-295, 306, 308-312, 315, 317, 319-320
propositum	99, 101, 116, 132n, 144, 147, 163, 177n, 195n, 258n
Prosperi, A.	15n
Prussia	252, 266
Puritans, Puritanism	9, 298
Pyrrhonism, see: cartesianism	
Raitt, Jill	79n, 82n, 126n, 128n
Rattansi, Piyo	81n
Rebecca	75
Reformation	4, 7, 9-11, 13, 29, 86-88, 90, 111, 149, 303
Reich, Rüdi	90n
Reid, J.K.S.	16n
Remonstrants (arminians)	11, 157-161, 163-164, 166n, 168-170, 172-173, 175-176, 180-181, 185-186, 193, 198, 200, 203, 219, 239, 247, 249n, 250, 252, 258, 262-265, 281, 297, 302, 304
reprobation *passim;* see also 'election,' 'predestination' and 'cause of sin and unbelief'	
responsibility	17, 19, 76, 91n, 92n, 112-113, 145, 148, 157n, 194, 224n, 284-285
Reveil	299
Rex, Walter E.	245n

Index of names and subjects - 353

Reyroux, F.	251n, 255n, 258n, 259n, 267n, 269n, 270n
Rimbach, Harald	18
Roney, John B.	10n, 118n, 160n, 190n, 246n, 249n
Rousseau, Jean-Jacques	296, 297n
Rouwendal, Pieter L.	11n, 28n, 118n, 124n
Ryssen, Leonard	189
sacraments	37-39, 41, 75, 130-131, 134, 136n, 205, 229, 234, 267-270, 272, 286n, 291
Sadolet, Jacob	49, 72
Sallmann, Martin	81n
Sampaulier (Sampaulinus), F.	97
sanctification	17, 22-24, 107, 110, 123, 127n, 142, 146, 149, 165n, 168, 176, 177n, 197-198, 203, 224-229, 232, 234-236, 238-239, 241, 257, 260-261, 268n, 275, 278, 284-286, 295, 314
Santen, Leo van	103n
Sarot, Marcel	3n
Sarx, Tobias	185n
Saumur	7, 88n, 184-190, 193n, 197n, 219, 221, 245, 253, 265, 280, 302, see also: amraldism
Schaff, Philip	158n, 168n, 175n, 177n, 181n, 191n
Schelven, A.A. van	10, 296
Schlosser, F. Ch.	79n, 111
Schmalkaldic League	90n
scholasticism	1, 3, 4, 82-83, 85, 119-120, 123, 138, 139n, 143, 147, 189n, 192, 200, 219, 253n-255, 280, 296, 298, 320
Scotland	5, 189, 299
Scotus, John Duns	7
seceders, Dutch	6
Sedan	88n,
Selderhuis, Herman J.	3n, 10n, 11n, 13n, 18n, 26n, 83n, 158n, 160n, 185n, 207n
Shepherd, V.A.	19, 46n, 52
sin,	
- cause of -, see: cause of sin	
- original -	52, 96n, 119, 172, 249, 268n, 299
Sinnema, Donald	85-86, 89n, 117n-119, 142n, 158n, 160n, 161n

Sliedrecht, C. van — 79n-80n, 83-87n, 95n, 101n, 117n
Socinus, socinians, — 189n, 193, 219, 258, 296, 302
Spanheim, Friedrich (or Frederic), elder and younger — 173-175n, 187n, 188, 221, 249
Spiera, Francesco — 15
Spijker, W. van 't — 13n
Spinoza, Baruch de — 250n
Stam, Frans Pieter van — 13n, 187n
Stanglin, Keith D. — 249n
Steenblok, Cornelis — 1, 6, 7n
Steinmetz, David C. — 79n, 84, 86, 87n, 113n, 117n
Stephens, W. Peter — 89
Strasbourg — 13-14, 87
sufficiency of Christ's death, see: atonement, classic formula of
Summers, Kirk M. — 115n
supralapsarism — 26-27, 85, 90n, 101, 118-119, 144, 147, 160, 171-175, 181n, 182-183, 185, 196, 198-200, 248, 257, 303-304, 320

Swiss Cities, Swiss Confederation, Switzerland — 10, 90n, 111, 187-188, 191, 249n-250, 265-266, 303

Swiss delegates to the synod of Dordrecht — 167
syllogism — 84, 93, 95, 142
Sytsma, David S. — 3n, 81n, 157n, 247n
Testard, Paul — 197n, 270n
Thomas, G. Michael — 9n, 28n, 82n, 90n, 113, 124n, 125, 136
Toon, Peter — 5
Tronchin, Louis — 190-191, 245-246, 250n
Tronchin, Theodore — 8, 10-11, 157-183, 188, 190, 219, 221, 236, 245, 302-304, 320
truce, twelve years – — 157
Trueman, Carl R. — 3n, 4n, 80n, 190n, 245n, 261n
Turretin, Barbe — 249
Turretin, Benedict (Benoit) — 173, 187, 222
Turretin, Francis — 8, 10-11, 157, 160, 173, 175, 185-246, 249-259, 261, 265-272, 274-282, 285, 288-290, 294-296, 298, 302-320
Turretin, Jean-Alphonse — 192, 246-249, 251-253, 265, 297, 303

Index of names and subjects - 355

Utrecht	1, 188, 189n
VanDoodewaard, William	6n
Veen, M.K. van (Mirjam)	18, 81
Veenhof, C.	6n
Venema, Cornelis P.	89n
Vermigli, Peter Martyr	87, 98, 101-102, 139-140, 144, 320
Vernes, Jacob	296
Vernet, Jacob	297
Vezelay	79
Vial de Beaumont, Jacques	249
Viret, Pierre	15n, 79
vocation, see calling	
Voetius, G.	7n, 29n
Voltaire	296
Vos, A.	8
Wallace, Ronald S.	18-19, 61
Wenneker, Erich	188n
Westphal, Joachim	38
Widler, Marcus	81n
will in God	
- approving will, *euarestia*	210, 237n, 238, 271, 308, 316
- commanding or revealed will	69, 210, 236-237, 308, 316
- decreeing or secret will, *eudokia*	114, 122, 196n, 197, 210, 236-238, 271, 308, 316
- no two opposite wills	42, 63-64, 308
will, free, see: choice, free	
Wisse, Maarten	3n
Wolmar, Melchior	79, 86
Woolsey, Andrew A.	31n, 86, 125, 129, 136n
Wright, Shawn D.	83-85
Zeeland, delegates of – to the synod of Dordrecht	170
Zuidema, Jason	3n, 81n, 157n, 247n
Zurich	16n, 79-80, 88, 90, 93n, 96, 102, 191
Zwaag, W. van der	299n
Zwingli, Huldrych	7, 13

CPSIA information can be obtained
at www.ICGtesting.com
Printed in the USA
BVHW04*0826290818
R9004400001B/R90044PG525134BVX8B/1/P